DATE		

GALEN'S PROPHECY

GALEN'S PROPHECY

TEMPERAMENT IN HUMAN NATURE

by Jerome Kagan

with the collaboration of

Nancy Snidman
Doreen Arcus
J. Steven Reznick

BasicBooks
A Division of HarperCollins*Publishers*

Designed by Barbara DuPree Knowles

LIBRARY OF CONGRESS CATALOGING-IN-PUBLICATION DATA
Kagan, Jerome.
  Galen's prophecy : temperament in human nature / by Jerome Kagan with the collaboration of Nancy Snidman, Doreen Arcus, J. Steven Reznick.
    p. cm.
  Includes bibliographical references and index.
  ISBN 0–465–08405–2
  1. Temperament in children. 2. Inhibition in children. 3. Temperament in children—Physiological aspects. 4. Inhibition in children—Physiological aspects. 5. Environment and children. 6. Nature and nurture. I. Title
BF723.T53K34 1994
155.2'6—dc20   93–42664
                                                                              CIP

94 95 96 97 ❖/RRD 9 8 7 6 5 4 3 2 1

For Leah

What makes a subject hard to understand . . . is not that before you can understand it you need to be specially trained in abstruse matters, but the contrast between understanding the subject and what most people want to see. Because of this the very things which are most obvious may become the hardest of all to understand.
—LUDWIG WITTGENSTEIN, *CULTURE AND VALUE*

CONTENTS

PREFACE

It has proved profitable in young, emerging sciences to base inquiry on reliable facts rather than on historically popular abstract ideas. The trusted reality that served as the origin of the research to be summarized is the mundane observation that some people are excessively restrained when they meet a stranger, wary when they confront an unexpected event, or cautious when they must act with a risk of possible failure. Fiction is full of examples that contrast this personality with its complement—the sociable, fearless, bold agent who is unaffected by these everyday events. Walter Matthau and Jack Lemmon in *The Odd Couple* are a well-known movie example.

These two categories of people are represented, albeit by different words, in every current theory of personality, as well as in the essays of ancient Greek philosophers and physicians who believed they understood the basic forms that human character assumed. The melancholic and sanguine types described first by Hippocrates and later by Galen became the introvert and extrovert in Carl Jung's vocabulary. These distinctive styles are present in similar, and remarkably undisguised, form in school-age children. The quiet, shy, tense child who sits in back of the classroom usually migrates to the edge of the playground to watch, sometimes with envy, the sociable, seemingly confident peer who easily organizes classmates for a game.

Although folk theory is often at odds with evidence from psychological research, in this case the community belief that these two traits emerge early and are stable over time matches the scientific record. These psychological qualities are among the best preserved aspects of human nature. Assured of a robust fact that would not vanish tomorrow or be shown to be an artifact in next month's journals, one naturally asks why. Now gentle consensus is replaced with strident controversy. Although few would quarrel with the truism that a person's biology and experience unite in an enigmatic but, surely, seamless way to produce each of these two profiles, it is meaningful to wonder about both the nature and the magnitude of the biological contribution. Of course, the magnitude can never be a fixed quantity and will vary with historical, contextual, and personal conditions. Nonetheless, it is useful to determine whether the influence of a person's distinctive biology is minimal, modest, or major with respect to a specific quality. The contribution of a child's biology to the frequency of bruised knees is tiny compared with its influence on juvenile obesity or, to pick a more extreme example, the intellectual profile of a child with Down's syndrome.

Opinion regarding the force of temperament in the creation of introverts and extroverts has cycled ever since a physician named Galen of Pergamon suggested, seventeen hundred years ago, that inherited constitution, in concert with diet and climate, constitutes the basis for melancholic and sanguine individuals—hence the title, *Galen's Prophecy*. The first chapter describes the change in Western thought from the explicit acknowledgment of the influence of biology by the ancients, which lasted until the end of the nineteenth century, to a rejection of hereditary forces, during the first half of this century, and a maximization of the shaping hand of social experience.

When I was a graduate student in the early 1950s, few questioned the assumption, which had become dogma, that biology was superfluous in explanations of human variation in skill, motivation, habit, and mood. The most important reason for this unquestioned faith was the political necessity of maintaining that the many thousands of European immigrants who began to settle in America soon after the Civil War, and in increasing numbers after 1900, possessed the same natural ability and humaneness as those born to the immigrants who had arrived in the seventeenth century. The premise that the proper arrangement of experience, in family, school, and neighborhood, can make everyone roughly equal in competence, contentment, and civility was held, along with the beatitude of personal liberty, with such conviction that few stopped to brood about its truth value, lest they lose the rational foundation of each day's plans and the passion needed to support liberal legislation. This ethical imperative was sustained by the broad dissemination of Pavlov's discovery of animal conditioning in a St. Petersburg laboratory. If a dog can learn to salivate to the sound of a metronome, surely the average child could be taught anything.

It would take more than fifty years before a number of psychologists would challenge that progressive idea. As the new cohort of scientists was discovering some of the limitations in Pavlov's grand dream, events in the society as well as in the academy were undermining the attractiveness of the assumption that experience can build or repair any psychic component in any sane person. The ethology movement, associated in most minds with Konrad Lorenz and Nikolaus Tinbergen, reminded twentieth-century investigators that each animal species inherits a preparedness to learn and execute particular behaviors that serve adaptation. It is difficult to prevent a newly hatched duckling from following its mother or to teach a rat to approach a brightly lit, noisy object moving up and down at an erratic speed. Today, neuroscientists are unraveling the brain circuits that mediate the duck's approach and the rat's avoidance.

Research on cognitive functions along with a secular change in values led to the collapse of an uncritical loyalty to the extreme view that environmental events could explain all forms of psychological variation—thought and emotion as well as habit. Studies of the child's acquisition of intellectual talents revealed that reward and punishment were unable, alone, to account for either the time of emergence or the substantial variation in language, memory, and thought. Chomsky's acerbic critique of B. F. Skinner's account of how children acquire language catapulted him to fame, while administering a near-lethal blow to the behaviorists' traditional arguments. At the same time, history was revealing the fault lines in the psychoanalytic proposition that conflicts over sexuality, acquired in the family over the first decade of life, were the foundation of neurotic symptoms. The youth who became young adults in the 1960s had been freed of considerable guilt over erotic motives, yet the same proportion of adults remained burdened with anxiety, phobias, depression, suicidal ideas, and psychosomatic ills. It was clear that something was wrong with the notion that childhood encounters could explain the differences between a chronically frightened adult and a jovial, relaxed one. Thus, by the 1970s, a small band of scholars had become receptive to the suggestion that some children begin life with a temperamental bias that made it easy or difficult to acquire an anxious profile.

Alexander Thomas and Stella Chess took advantage of these first doubts and suggested, almost forty years ago, that infants differ in a number of temperamental dimensions. The family, acting on the behavioral consequences of these inherited qualities, produces a character type that combines in a seamless tapestry the child's biology and experience, as Galen had anticipated two millennia earlier. Although Thomas and Chess's position is not controversial today, it was not received with applause by most professionals during the first years following its publication. It took almost a decade for psychologists and psychiatrists to begin systematic examination of their concepts.

Chapter 2, which summarizes the fruits of these investigations, revolves around two philosophical questions that penetrate the logic of most of the arguments in this text. The first is epistemological. What kind of evidence should be gathered to discover significant facts about human temperaments? The choice made by Thomas and Chess, as well as by others, was to rely on verbal answers to questions. Thomas and Chess used the parents' descriptions of their infants and children as the primary bases for the nine temperamental dimensions they invented. Psychologists in university departments had also become committed to questionnaires as the method of choice to measure variation in human moods, motives, and behavior. Hence, when developmental psychologists became curious about children's temperaments, they also devised questionnaires that asked parents to describe their infants and toddlers.

The sole defense of this strategy was the assumption that even a mother who worked full-time had over a thousand hours of close contact with her one-year-old. Thus, her statements had to be more accurate than a one-hour observation of a child by an unfamiliar psychologist in an equally unfamiliar laboratory. That argument is only reasonable, however, if we suppress the fact that some parents are exceptionally biased observers and that some temperamental qualities are not easily detected by parents. Although we now know that many parents do not provide accurate descriptions of their children, this knowledge did not become irrepressible until recently. Hence, most of the current facts about children's temperaments have the particular meaning that is derived from answers to questions constructed in the language of backyard conversation. In order to appreciate this problem, imagine a group of biologists who are seeking the causes of an exotic illness but are restricted to the words patients use to describe their ailments—headache, sour stomach, chills, muscle tightness, and fatigue.

A second philosophical question asks whether a behavioral quality like shyness lies on a continuum with sociability or whether extreme shyness and sociability represent discrete categories with different origins. This issue is not simply a narrow, academic quarrel. If patients who have a phobia of elevators possess a brain physiology that is qualitatively different from that of others, rather than one that is just a little more excitable, scientists should look for the unique origins of this fear, as well as for a special cure. Although biologists could treat snakes and lizards on a continuum with respect to speed of locomotion, they believe it is more useful to emphasize the fact that these two species move in qualitatively different ways. I defend the decision to treat extremely fearful and fearless children as belonging to qualitatively different categories, while recognizing that this view remains controversial.

The concept of temperament refers to any moderately stable, differentiating emotional or behavioral quality whose appearance in childhood is influenced by an inherited biology, including differences in brain neurochemistry. That definition implies that future scientists will discover a large number of temperaments. Some may occur at prevalence rates so low they will not be present in the typical volunteer samples social scientists recruit. The detection and documentation of these qualities will occupy a large number of scientists for, hopefully, a smaller number of decades. Our research group has been interested in only two members of this large set—the cautious compared with the bold child—whom we have named *inhibited* and *uninhibited*. I resisted an initial temptation to call them high and low anxious because, as I indicate in chapter 3, there are at least four different emotional states that belong to a family of affects currently named fear or anxiety. We are interested in one very particular state that is provoked when a child confronts an unfamiliar person, place, or event. The inhibited child reacts initially with restraint, avoidance, or distress because his limbic system is easily aroused by unfamiliarity. The uninhibited child typically approaches the same events because of a different profile of limbic arousal. The heart of this book, chapters 4 through 7, summarizes our attempts over the last fifteen years to persuade ourselves and others that inhibited and uninhibited children inherit unique neurochemistries that affect their thresholds of reactivity to novelty, leading them to react in opposite ways to experiences that are transformations of the familiar and require a brief period of adjustment.

Most people hold a misconception about research. They regard the activity of scientists as similar to tourists planning a holiday to a foreign country. One first decides where to visit; then finds books with vital information about the new place; purchases plane, boat, or rail tickets; and finally sets out to enjoy the products of the carefully planned effort. Most scientists, however, and especially psychologists, are vagabonds, wandering from place to place, and stopping occasionally at an especially pleasing location stumbled upon by accident. Two chance discoveries, separated by almost twenty years, motivated me to change from a hunter-gatherer to a settled pastoralist, content for a while to plow the field of temperament because the yield was plentiful.

After discharge from the armed forces in 1957, I joined the staff at the Fels Research Institute in Yellow Springs, Ohio. The profit in that choice could not have been anticipated; hence, I deserve no credit for foresight. The Institute—which, sadly, does not exist today—was founded in the late 1920s in the hope that gathering detailed observations on typical middle-class Ohio children, from infancy to adolescence, would reveal some of the secrets of human development. Many scientists spent part or, in some cases, most of their careers at Fels, collecting information on the families who were members of this ambitious longitudinal study. I went to Fels hoping to integrate the extensive corpus of historical data with a contemporary assessment of those who had grown to adulthood. One of the discoveries, made with Howard Moss, was that a small group of extremely fearful toddlers retained in their adult personality, in subtle and transformed ways, aspects of their early temperament. I should have pursued that discovery in 1962 but did not, although I thought about it often. The next relevant event occurred over fifteen years later in Boston, when Richard Kearsley, Philip Zelazo, and I were studying the effects of day care on young infants who were born to Chinese-American or Caucasian-American families. The former children were more inhibited than the latter, even though both groups of infants attended the same day care center we administered in South Boston. This observation recalled the fearful Fels children and motivated a more intense brooding over the new discussions of temperament provoked by Thomas and Chess.

Therefore, it seemed productive in 1979 to initiate, first with Cynthia Garcia-Coll and later with Nancy Snidman and J. Steven Reznick, systematic longitudinal studies of inhibited and uninhibited children. The results of those investigations, described in chapters 4 and 5, persuaded me that these were temperamental categories with inherited physiological foundations. However, many respected colleagues were not convinced. They pointed out that our first study began with children who were twenty-one months—old enough for their families to have sculpted a fearful or fearless profile. That criticism has merit, and because I was convinced there would be prophetic signs of the inhibited and uninhibited styles in the opening weeks of life, Nancy Snidman, Doreen Arcus, and I studied over six hundred four-month-olds, with the explicit aim of detecting the psychological features that would predict the two profiles in the second year. Fortunately, nature was generous and we found those signs in displays of thrashing of limbs and crying in response to unfamiliar visual, auditory, and olfactory events.

About one in five healthy Caucasian infants reacts to stimulation with vigorous motor activity and distress, and about two-thirds of these highly reactive four-month-olds become inhibited children. About two of every five infants inherit a bias that favors a relaxed, minimally distressed reaction to stimulation, and two-thirds of these become uninhibited in the second year. The initial temperamental biases are not deterministic, however; some inhibited two-year-old children changed their behavioral demeanor before they entered kindergarten. These discoveries, which remain the peak intellectual experience in this long journey, are summarized in chapters 6 and 7.

A word about the biology that is part of the theoretical definition of temperament is in order. The contrasting descriptions of the psychological and physiological processes that affect behavior are like the alternative perceptions of the drawing of the vase-faces illustrated in most psychology textbooks. As the viewer shifts his focus from one part of the drawing to another, the perception of a vase reverses suddenly into two facial profiles. An equally dramatic change in conception occurs when a scientist moves her focus of attention from the psychological processes of perception, interpretation, and coping to the physiological processes that are derived from the chemistry and physiology of brain circuits. Both the psychological and the physiological processes are partially autonomous. If a person does not interpret a sharp criticism, task failure, or loss of a friend as a threat, there may be minimal changes in physiological targets such as heart rate and blood pressure, whereas these targets will respond with much greater magnitude in a person who psychologically treats the same events as a stressor. Only some children react with a rise in heart rate to what an observer views as a threatening event; only some medical students become physiologically aroused when they give their first grand rounds presentation. Social scientists usually attend to the person's interpretations of a stress, awarding the mind an executive privilege that makes physiology a slave of the subjective conceptualization.

On some occasions, however, the biology gains a position of dominance. A person vulnerable to panic attacks sometimes can do little to prevent his physiology from defeating an extreme effort of will directed at repelling the imminent feeling of terror. Thus, scientists interested in the influence of physiology on behavior typically see only the biological mechanisms—like one view of the vase-faces—and do not accommodate to the psychological processes. These investigators expect a simple, direct relation between an imposed stress and a physiological response.

These single-minded perspectives have frustrated efforts to appreciate the complexity of the interdependent relations between these two systems. Consider an analogy from linguistics. One group of scholars probes the separate semantic and syntactic features of an utterance, indifferent to the context of the sentence. The pragmatist, on the other hand, analyzes the mutual understandings of speaker and listener, minimally interested in the meaning and arrangement of the individual words. But the request "Knock it off" is ambiguous if we do not understand both the envelope of privileged meanings associated with the trio of words and the immediately prior extralinguistic events. Both are necessary if we are to know what was intended and understood.

A temperamental category is defined, theoretically, by a combination of psychological and biological features. Unfortunately, the psychological characteristics are much clearer at the present time. However, when the central physiology that contributes to the behavioral displays is known with greater certainty and can be measured in most laboratories, the classifications of inhibited and uninhibited will require physiological evidence. Because these measurements are not possible now, the current temperamental classifications rest primarily with behavior. Similar transitions have existed in other domains in the past. The diagnosis of epilepsy in the nineteenth century, for example, was based on observed convulsions alone. When EEG, MRI, and PET methods became available, the new brain data were added as features of the diagnostic category, even though no one would be called epileptic if they did not have convulsions in addition to a distinct EEG profile. Thus, one might ask, "What is the current value of the physiological evidence, if the classification of a child's temperament rests primarily with behavior?" I explain in chapter 7 that the value of the biology lies in the persuasive power of the interpretations of the behavioral profile. An inhibited temperament is presumed to rest on an excitable limbic physiology. Any biological data in accord with that assumption increase our faith in that idea. Temperamental concepts are as psychological as they are physiological. If a young child displayed no behavioral evidence of fear to unfamiliarity, he would not be classified as inhibited no matter what his physiological pattern.

A temperamental profile is an emergent phenomenon that requires both biological and experiential conditions acting together over time. This suggestion is no different from the accepted view that the precocious ability to speak well-articulated, four-word sentences early in the second year requires both a special biology and a set of supporting experiences; neither process alone can bear the weight of explanation.

Some psychologists resist acknowledging the contribution of physiology because of a worry that if they let the camel's nose under the tent, he will soon be inside forcing all the residents to leave. I do not believe that the phenomenon of a shy or bold child will ever be understood with, or predicted from, physiological knowledge alone. Temperamental phenomena cannot be reduced to biology. Biological sentences cannot replace psychological ones, for the same reason that the language that describes the history of a hurricane will never be replaced with propositions descriptive of the single molecules of air and water in the storm because the former sentences refer to processes applicable to very large numbers of molecules. The camel will never become the only resident in the tent.

I am not completely happy with the influence of these two early temperamental biases. It is difficult for an aging, politically liberal social scientist, trained to believe in the extraordinary power of the social environment, to take unreserved satisfaction from the implications of these last fifteen years of research. I confess to an occasional sadness over the recognition that some healthy, attractive infants born to affectionate, economically secure families begin life with a physiology that will make it a bit difficult for them to be as relaxed, spontaneous, and capable of hearty laughter as they would like. Some of these children will have to fight a natural urge to be dour and to worry about tomorrow's tasks. Many will be successful in coping with their dysphoria, but others, like Sylvia Plath, will not. That seems unfair. More troubling is the possibility that, for a very small group of children, neither family love nor personal effort will be able to tame every bout of acute, intense anxiety. I used to hold, with fervor, the nineteenth-century assumption that will was omnipotent; everyone should be able to suppress actions that disrupt the community or hurt others, and everyone should be able—of course, with effort—to gain control over tense, worried moods. Wittgenstein's melancholy was probably exacerbated when he confessed in a diary entry that he was not sufficiently intelligent to expel his moments of despair. I wish that will were stronger.

There is, however, one benevolent consequence of my new perspective. I have become more forgiving of the few friends and family members who see danger too easily, rise to anger too quickly, or sink to despair too often. I no longer blame them privately and have become more accepting and less critical of their moods and idiosyncracies. Obviously, this attitude has helped my relationships with them, for I no longer demand, with a hint of moral arrogance, that they simply gain control of themselves. I recognize the danger in carrying this permissiveness too far, but I, too, have no choice.

Accuracy and beauty are expected to travel as close together in science as the blend of lyric and melody in the arias of *La Bohème*. And they often do. Newton's equations of motion are in such good correspondence with everyday observations that they provoke, in those who understand them, the unique feeling of being in the presence of beauty. But the aesthetic emotion generated by an idea, unlike the more strictly cognitive appreciation of its accuracy, is dependent on the beholder. Our discoveries on temperament might have been regarded as beautiful by Galen, but I fear that many Americans and Europeans will not be so moved because the facts are not plumb with the current conception of what most would like to believe is true. Their mood might resemble that of Einstein, who considered the equations of quantum mechanics ugly because chance, not a well-ordered set of fixed relations among nature's elements, was the director of matter in motion. However, contemporary physicists like Steven Weinberg, trained a half century later, regard the same equations as sublimely beautiful. I trust that when society recognizes that temperamental variation does not pose a threat to democratic and egalitarian ideals, understanding the origins and developmental progressions of these traits will engender the same delight that most feel when they reflect on Mendel's explanations of wrinkling in peas or the recent discovery that the genetic anomaly that produces Huntington's disease is an abnormal repetition of a DNA sequence—a genetic stutter—at the tip of one of the human chromosomes.

When I look at my earlier beliefs from the other side, I notice serious aesthetic flaws in the assumption that any child can become schizophrenic and that all cases of depression or panic are psychologically traceable to parental failures twenty years earlier. This matrogenic hypothesis reached its peak in the years before and right after the Second World War, when maternal behaviors became the origins of all mental flaws. Karl Menninger, in a 1933 issue of *Atlantic Monthly*, traced the hatred of the world to the failures of mothers to tend their children properly. These flawed, simplistic social explanations generate in the suffering agents and their families an undeserved guilt and sporadic anger that are anything but beautiful.

As each child begins life's journey, she is given a dozen or so pigments, a few brushes, a canvas, and instructions to paint as lovely a scene as she is able. There is no need to feel a blue mood of failure if a carefully painted sunrise is a little less than perfect because a needed pigment was not originally put in the kit. It is the effort that deserves the dignity we award one another as each of us works, sometimes painstakingly, on our mural.

Finally, I should explain the form of the presentation. I decided early to try to speak not only to my colleagues in psychology, biology, and psychiatry, but also to educated readers interested in these ideas who are not specially trained in the niceties of behavioral science. Some of the evidence is presented here for the first time; therefore, my colleagues will want to have the details that interested readers are willing to accept on faith. In order to accommodate both audiences, while permitting the reading to remain as smooth as possible, I have provided extensive descriptions of procedures and the results of statistical analyses, as well as bibliographic information, in the extensive notes associated with each chapter. I have also included descriptions of the procedures used for selected studies so that readers can judge their relevance to the main arguments. The meaning and truth of every conclusion in science are dependent on the source of the evidence. Stimulation of a brain area often has different consequences in varied species or when different behavioral assessments are used. If the data on the children in our studies had come only from parental descriptions rather than direct observations, I am certain that the story told here would be palpably different. For that reason, I have tried to be explicit about subjects and methods in the investigations I regard as providing supporting evidence.

I am indebted to a great many students and colleagues who have contributed in major ways to this research. The three most continuing relationships are acknowledged on the title page: Nancy Snidman, Doreen Arcus, and J. Steven Reznick. But many others must be thanked, including Cynthia Garcia-Coll, Jane Gibbons, Jill Kalen, Michelle Gersten, Maureen Rezendes, Anna Costes, Hilary Sokolowski, Katherine Baak, Ruth Bell, Allison Rosenberg, Gail Agronick, Jennifer Davis, Susan Brandzel, Annie McQuilken, Sherry Gardner, Philip Campbell, Carl Schwartz, Joseph Biederman, Jerrold Rosenbaum, Peter Ellison, John Hendler, Sarah Schenck, Cele Kagan, Ann Densmore, Robert Klein, Sergio Lavarreda Anléu, mayor of Panajachel, Guatemala, and Tomasa Martinez Barrera. I thank my loyal, efficient secretary, Paula Mabee, who patiently retyped each chapter more times than she wishes to remember. Anne Harrington and Milton Heifetz read parts of the manuscript and helped me clarify issues that had been obscure. Nina Gunzenhauser's careful editing has forced me to make many arcane sentences more comprehensible, and I am in her debt.

The research has been supported primarily by grants from the John D. and Catherine T. MacArthur Foundation, and I am deeply indebted to their staff and board. Supplementary funds came from the Leon Lowenstein Foundation, William T. Grant Foundation, National Institute of Mental Health, Foundation for Child Development, and Spencer Foundation. Tom James was president of the Spencer Foundation in 1979, when it awarded us the first grant that permitted the initial investigation to proceed. Finally, a sabbatical award from the James McKeen Cattell Fund for 1992–93 permitted me to finish this book free of academic responsibilities. Without these many generosities, this section of my imperfect mural would have remained untouched.

CHAPTER ONE

The Idea of Temperament: The Past

Genio y hechura hasta sepultura.
("Natures and features last to the grave.")
—SPANISH SAYING

Every age has a preferred explanation of the obvious differences among people that are always a focus of curiosity and a topic for gossip. The most persuasive accounts attribute most of the human variation to one causal mechanism, for the mind likes single-process explanations over those that involve multiple forces; the latter are difficult to grasp and therefore less pleasing.

The most fundamental division among the diverse explanations contrasts inherent qualities, present at birth and operating throughout life, with a history of experiences. The arguments that emphasize inherent processes assume that humans are basically different and usually attribute the differences to physiology—in ancient times to bodily fluids and, since the turn of the century, to genes. The arguments for experience, which assume that humans begin life fundamentally similar, award potency to air, water, diet, and—over the past three hundred years—to social encounters. This division between internal and external influences is linked to the ancient split in Western thought between material and mental processes—body versus soul.

It is not surprising that the reigning philosophy of a society favors one or the other of these views, for a preference for one of these frames has political implications. In societies that practice slavery—ancient Rome, for example—citizens are tempted to believe that they are fundamentally dissimilar to those they command. If one's position as citizen or slave could have been the result of the vicissitudes of life, exploiting another person could become ethically uncomfortable. A belief in inherent differences mutes the occasional guilt that might rise in the slave holder. Therefore, one might expect that the interpretation of psychological variation held by these societies would favor endogenous differences.

The Ancient View in the West

The Greeks and Romans believed that a balance among the four humors of yellow and black bile, blood, and phlegm, present in all persons, created an opposition within each of two pairs of bodily qualities: warm versus cool and dry versus moist (see figure 1.1). These four qualities were related to the four fundamental substances in the world: fire, air, earth, and water. The Greeks assumed, without a detailed appreciation of genetics or physiology, that the balance among these qualities produced an invisible inner state that was responsible for the observed variation in rationality, emotionality, and behavior. Children and women, for example, could not help being impulsive and irrational, for they were born with an excess of the moist quality.

Galen, an extraordinarily perceptive second-century physician born in Asia Minor, elaborated these Hippocratic ideas by positing nine temperamental types that were derived from the four humors. (The word *temperament* comes from the Latin verb *temperare,* "to mix.") In the ideal personality, the complementary characteristics of warm-cool and dry-moist were exquisitely balanced. In four less ideal types, one of the four qualities was dominant. In the remaining four types, one pair of qualities dominated the complementary pair; for example, warm and moist dominated cool and dry. These latter four were the temperamental categories Galen called melancholic, sanguine, choleric, and phlegmatic. Each was the result of an excess of one of the bodily humors that produced, in turn, the imbalance in paired qualities. The melancholic was cool and dry because of an excess of black bile; the sanguine was warm and moist because of an excess of blood; the choleric was warm and dry because of an excess of yellow bile, and the phlegmatic was cool and moist because of an excess of phlegm.

Although the concentrations of the four humors and the relative dominance of the derived qualities were inherent in each individual's physiology, nonetheless they were somewhat susceptible to the influence of external events, especially climate and diet. The body naturally became warmer and more moist in the spring; hence, people became more sanguine. When the body became cooler and drier in the fall, a melancholic mood became more prevalent. Differences in climate and the resulting differences in foods also contributed to differences in personal qualities. Hippocrates—born about 460 B.C.—believed that Asians (he probably meant those living on the Indian subcontinent) were gentler than Mediterranean groups because of the more stable, gentler climate in the former area.

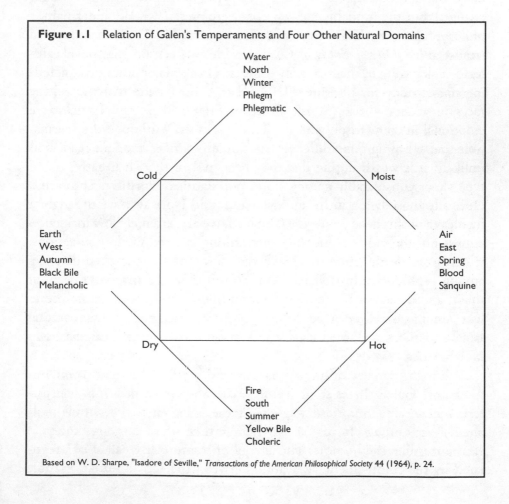

Figure 1.1 Relation of Galen's Temperaments and Four Other Natural Domains

Water
North
Winter
Phlegm
Phlegmatic

Cold

Moist

Earth
West
Autumn
Black Bile
Melancholic

Air
East
Spring
Blood
Sanquine

Dry

Hot

Fire
South
Summer
Yellow Bile
Choleric

Based on W. D. Sharpe, "Isadore of Seville," *Transactions of the American Philosophical Society* 44 (1964), p. 24.

When the Arabs began to dominate North Africa and the Middle East in the seventh century, they translated Galen's books and adopted his precepts with little change. Ibn Ridwan, an eleventh-century Islamic physician, attributed the presumed impulsivity, inconstancy, and timidity among Egyptians to an unhealthy balance among the body humors traceable, in part, to the extremely humid and hot climate of the region of the Nile.

Galen's ideas remained popular until the end of the nineteenth century. Alexander Stewart called the four types sanguine, bilious (instead of choleric), lymphatic (instead of phlegmatic), and nervous (instead of melancholic). The blood and liver remained the organs of influence in the first two types, but the watery lymph replaced phlegm, and the brain replaced black bile as the basis for the nervous type. Thus the tissues of origin changed, but the fundamental concepts were preserved. Alexander Bain, a philosopher at the University of Aberdeen, wrote in 1861 an influential treatise titled *On the Study of Character*. He was certain that people differed biologically in their capacity for each of the major emotions, including the capacity for pleasure. He noted in a brief aside that the "Celtic races in general—Irish, Welsh, Scottish, Highlanders, and French—are emotional in comparison with the Teutonic races." Although the speculation that ethnic groups differ in emotionality strikes modern readers as unlikely, it is worth noting that the prevalence of the Rh negative blood type varies considerably among world populations. Northern Europeans, especially those living in Ireland, Scotland, and Norway, have the highest incidence of this gene, while the Chinese have an extremely low incidence. This is not the only genetic difference among isolated world populations; it is reasonable therefore to suggest that some of the genetic differences among reproductively isolated human groups might involve aspects of mood and behavior. Interestingly, schizophrenia seems to be more prevalent among Israeli-born adults of European background than among Israelis of the same social class whose genetic background originated in North Africa.

Although the view of human nature held by the Chinese two millennia before Galen shares some features with the Greek position, it is different in several important ways (see table 1.1). First, the seminal balance was among forces of energy, rather than among concrete substances like the humors. The energy of the universe called *ch'i*, regulated by the complementary relation between the active, initiating force

Table 1.1	*Chinese Categories of Nature*				
			Elements		
	Wood	*Fire*	*Earth*	*Metal*	*Water*
Seasons	Spring	Summer	Late Summer	Autumn	Winter
Emotions	Anger	Joy	Compassion	Sadness	Fear
Tastes	Sour	Bitter	Sweet	Salt	Acrid
Organs	Liver	Heart	Spleen	Lung	Kidney

After M. Yosida, "The Chinese Concept of Nature," in *Chinese Science*, ed. S. Nakayama and N. Sivin (Cambridge: Harvard University Press, 1973).

of *yang* and the passive, completing force of *yin*, must be in balance for optimal physiological and psychological functioning. The more concrete processes derived from the *ch'i* and related to the seasons and human emotions overlap with Western views. The five, rather than four, basic elements were wood, fire, earth, metal, and water; each had a dynamic relation to at least one other element (for example, wood enters into and becomes fire, and the ash of the fire becomes earth). Because there were five elements, there had to be five seasons, so summer became two seasons instead of one. Not surprisingly, fear was linked with winter, but the Greeks would be surprised that anger was associated with spring, for this was the season of their sanguine temperament. For our purposes, however, the most important fact is that the Chinese were far less interested in temperamental types. The energy of *ch'i* is always changing; hence, a person's moods and behavioral style could not be too permanent. The idea of inheriting a fixed emotional bias was inconsistent with the premise of continual transformation. A person might be melancholic temporarily, but not because he was a melancholic type.

Apparently, the Western mind has a special attraction to stable elements forming the foundation of the world. For the ancient Greeks, humans had to possess material vehicles for the oppositions of cool-warm and moist-dry that had the same degree of reality, stability, unity, and seamlessness characteristic of air, water, fire, and earth. Blood, phlegm, and yellow bile fit these criteria well. Black bile, however, was more hypothetical and a trifle magical. Hippocrates believed it was secreted by the liver; Galen thought it was a toxic discharge in blood. Although black bile had beneficial effects on digestion, it was the most dangerous humor, for an excess could cause serious ailments and melancholia. Christian scholars in the Middle Ages argued that God gave humans the melancholic humor as punishment for Adam's eating the apple.

Remnants of Galen's ideas exist today in rural Malay communities. The Malay combined Western and Eastern ideas by substituting inherited "inner winds"—called *angins*—for the humors. Most of the time one does not know the mixture of angins one possesses, nor does an observer, for it is revealed only during trance states. The Malay prefer slightly different temperamental types, however. The melancholic (*dewa penchil*) and the choleric (*dewa somaduru*) were retained, but the phlegmatic and sanguine were replaced with two different categories. The lazy, impulsive, mildly antisocial gambler (*dewa laleng*) has no obvious analogue in Galen's theory. Nor does the person who combines hedonism, exhibitionism, and a concern with cleanliness (*dewa muda*). The latter category is most foreign to Western minds, but apparently not to the Malay. The fact that the Malay did not invent analogues to the sanguine and phlegmatic types is curious. The absence of the former might be related to the generally restrained interpersonal style favored by Malay mores; an excessively sociable posture violates community values. Hence, this temperament would be linked with gambling and asocial behavior. The absence of the phlegmatic is more puzzling. If a temperament with a low energy level is as basic as Galen thought—and is supported by observations of infants—why did the Malay overlook it? Perhaps scholars better acquainted with the Malay will be able to explain this paradox. But we should not lose sight of the fact that the melancholic is present in Malay folk theory, suggesting its universal appeal to human intuition.

A salient difference between the ancient Greek and Chinese views, on the one hand, and modern interpretations of variation, on the other, is that the former regarded the underlying force as permeating the entire body, while the latter assumes that a particulate essence is the foundation for the surface profile. The Greek qualities of moist, dry, warm, and cold, as well as the Chinese *ch'i*, infuse the entire person. By contrast, a chemical neurotransmitter operates in specific places. The contemporary view is a bit counterintuitive, for it is somewhat less credible to attribute a holistic quality, such as a depressed mood, to a bit of chemical acting in a place far removed from the surface manifestation of the psychological characteristic than to attribute the mood to a fluid force permeating the body. But such is the character of science; it corrects eminently reasonable but, unfortunately, false ideas.

It is not exactly clear why, in positing the melancholic type, Galen muted the difference between a fearful, phobic adult and a depressed one, rather than awarding each mood separate status, as the Chinese did. Although contemporary psychiatry makes a clear and valid distinction between phobia, panic, and generalized anxiety, on the one hand, and depression, on the other, this distinction was absent from writings on mental illness from Hippocrates to the late nineteenth century, when Freud awarded special status to phobic symptoms as distinct from depression. For two thousand years the melancholic profile consisted of a blend of depression and fear, with the former given slightly greater emphasis than the latter. Perhaps the real but modest association between anxiety and depression made it easy for most observers to assume that the correlation was greater than it actually was.

Although Robert Burton's seventeenth-century treatise *Anatomy of Melancholy* argued that the moods of sorrow and fear can occur separately, he minimized the differences between the two states. Both moods could be brought on by a variety of causes, including the stars, old age, improper diet, or the air. Burton was convinced, however, that melancholia was inherited: "I need not therefore make any doubt of melancholy but that it is a hereditary disease, mediated by the individual's body temperature which one receives from our parents." Surprisingly, Burton noted that people with dark skin and hair are protected against melancholy. We shall see later that blonde, blue-eyed, fair-skinned children are more prone to fearful behavior than Caucasian children with darker hair, eyes, and skin.

Perhaps one reason why the ancients did not distinguish between fear and depression was that doing so would have created a need for a fifth personality type and marred the perfect symmetry of a system that had one major personality type for each pair of qualities. The Greeks assumed that the universe was symmetrical; hence, nature would not have constructed human personality asymmetrically. Dirac, the gifted twentieth-century mathematician who saw the relation between the equations of Heisenberg and Schrödinger, followed Keats in insisting that beauty was the first criterion to apply in choosing among alternative mathematical proofs.

Premodern Conceptions

Galen's bold inferences were not seriously different from contemporary speculations that schizophrenics have an excess of dopamine and that depressives have insufficient norepinephrine. The idea that bodily substances influence thought, mood, and behavior, like the notions of space and time, is easy to believe. Kant accepted Galen's four types with only minor changes. He made blood the only important humor and, anticipating Freud, assumed that individual variation in energy was critical. He added the gloss that the sanguine and the melancholic were emotional types, whereas the choleric and phlegmatic were action types. Kant distinguished between affect and action because he recognized the imperfect relation between invisible internal processes and manifest behavior and believed that humans possessed a will that could control the behavioral consequences of strong desires and feelings.

The same contrast was captured in the nineteenth century in the comparison between temperament and character. The former referred to inherited emotional biases, the latter to the expression of these biases in behaviors everyone could see. The observed behavior was a function of both life experiences and temperament. The pragmatist, for example, was a character type who might possess either a sanguine or a melancholic temperament. One psychologist translated the Kantian ideas into a psychological hypothesis. After a rich description of the history of inquiry into temperament and character, especially the views of nineteenth- and twentieth-century Europeans, Abraham Roback offered his insights into the essence of character. He agreed with the majority view—ancient and modern—that individuals inherit, to different degrees, dispositions for certain passions, desires, and emotions. Accepting Freud's view that ego tamed id, however, he noted that humans, unlike animals, had the ability to inhibit their desires if the relevant actions violated ethical standards. A person's character is "an enduring psychological disposition to inhibit instinctive impulses in accordance with a regulative principle." The sanguine type must occasionally inhibit the tendency to act impulsively because of strong feelings; the melancholic must inhibit the urge to become anxious and withdrawn. Thus, a temperamentally sanguine person who has made too many ill-advised decisions can become overly cautious, while a melancholic who has learned to control anxiety may appear spontaneously sociable. The idea that the character type does not provide a reliable insight into temperament is the essence of Jung's distinction between a person's hidden anima and public persona.

A major change in nineteenth-century essays on temperament was a focus on the biology of brain tissue and a search for visible signs of that biology somewhere on the surface of the body. The German physician Franz Gall was influential during the first half of the century, but he incurred the enmity of a large segment of the scientific community by suggesting that variations in human intentions and emotions were based on differences in brain tissue that could be detected with measurements of the skull. Gall's crass materialism angered colleagues with opposing philosophical views, who refused to believe that a person's character was determined by brain tissue and, therefore, lay outside the will. Further, many scholars did not believe that the anatomy of the brain had any implications for human behavior, which was seen as separable from the domains of natural science. Gall and his student Joseph Spurzheim, however, using everyday terms to name primary human characteristics like hunger, sex, and greed, assigned to each of these qualities a location in the brain, hoping that the psychological function would reveal brain structure. That is, they reversed the modern strategy of using knowledge of the brain to explain behavior by using knowledge of behavior to infer brain structure.

Spurzheim went on to consolidate Gall's ideas, retaining the essential premise of a location for each primary human characteristic and, reflecting nineteenth-century prejudice, assigning more space in the cranial cavity to emotional than to intellectual processes. Love was located in the cerebellum, aggression in the temporal lobe, and timidity in the upper lateral and posterior part of the head near the parietal area. The vigorous positivism in Spurzheim's arguments was motivated by the need to expunge metaphysical and religious ideas from scientific explanations of human nature. With George Combe, a Scottish lawyer who proselytized these ideas, Gall and Spurzheim believed it was time to place human behavior in its proper place as a part of natural law.

Toward the end of the nineteenth century, these ideas were elaborated with an expansion of the number of supposedly revealing physical features. More important, the external features were seen not as directly influential but only as indirect signs of the real, but invisible, inherited causes. Many believed that the shape of the body and face and the color of the eyes, hair, and skin—the products of deep, unknown biological factors—were associated with particular human qualities. Until the mysterious factors were discovered, it was reasonable to use the visible marks as diagnostic of temperament. Skin, hair, bones, eyes, skull, and eyebrows contained the most sensitive clues to an individual's personality. We shall see later that at least one of these beliefs was not bizarre.

In a book that enjoyed eight editions, Joseph Simms awarded the face more diagnostic power than the contemporary psychologists Paul Ekman and Carroll Izard would dare. Simms described five ideal types—two variations on what William Sheldon later called the mesomorph, two of the ectomorph, and one endomorphic type—and assigned the expected psychological traits to each. Even American schoolteachers were indoctrinated with these ideas. In 1897 Jessica Fowler wrote a manual to help teachers diagnose their young pupils' psychological qualities. A "veneration for elders" was predictable from excessively drooping eyes.

Constitutional traits were also associated with susceptibility to specific illnesses. George Draper, a physician at Columbia University, motivated by the observation that some body types were especially vulnerable to contracting polio during the 1916 epidemic, suggested an association between selected constitutions and particular diseases. People with brown eyes were more likely to have ulcers and gall bladder problems, while blue-eyed adults were at risk for tuberculosis. It is of interest that Hippocrates believed that tall, thin adults were especially vulnerable to diseases of the lungs.

Cesare Lombroso and Ernst Kretschmer, in classic treatises, suggested an association between body type, on the one hand, and crime or mental disease, on the other. Lombroso acknowledged that crime had social and climatic correlates, but he claimed that adults who fell at one of the extremes of a normal body type were most often represented among criminals and that dark-haired men were more likely than blondes to be criminals. Kretschmer invented new names—asthenic, pyknic, and athletic—for the three classical body physiques and considered the first two body types more vulnerable to major mental illness. Schizophrenics were often tall, thin, narrow-faced asthenics; manic depressives were likely to be chubby, broad-faced pyknic types. But these two psychiatric categories represented extremes of two basic, inherited temperaments that were relevant to all people: cyclothymes were relaxed, affectively spontaneous extroverts, and schizothymes were timid, emotionally subdued introverts.

Kretschmer enjoyed greater acceptance than Gall because he offered plausible, although unverified, biological mechanisms that made his arguments more palatable. These speculations formed the basis for Sheldon's famous book on personality and physique. Sheldon measured a large number of morphological dimensions from the photographs of four thousand college men and collapsed the resulting seventy-six categories into three basic body types, each rated on a seven-point scale and each having a corresponding set of psychological qualities. The ectomorph was tall and thin and an introvert; the endomorph was round and fat and an extrovert; and the mesomorph was broad and athletic and energetically assertive. Sheldon argued, as Simms had forty years earlier, that these personality features were not simply the direct result of the person's biology but the product of environmental pressures that acted upon a person who inherited a particular physique.

Sheldon's work began when the eugenics movement in America had reached a crest and was published as the Nazis were threatening Europe. The idea that inherited physical qualities characteristic of specific ethnic groups were associated with behavior was too close to Hitler's version of Aryan types, and this research, as well as the eugenics movement, stopped suddenly. Promotion of the formerly popular idea that the physical differences among Scandinavians, Italians, Jews, and blacks were linked to intelligence and morality had become a sign of both irrationality and amoral prejudice. The abrupt end to broad discussion of these hypotheses is not surprising, for tucked away in Sheldon's book was the provocative suggestion that Negroes are more often aggressive mesomorphs, while Jews are more often intellectual ectomorphs. When the Harvard anthropologist Ernest Hooton wrote in 1939 that some bodily constitutions were naturally inferior and linked to criminal behavior, his essay had a defensive tone, because Hooton was aware that this view had become unpopular to many Americans. All temperamental ideas, which had enjoyed the support of professors, presidents, and corporation executives during the early part of the century, were forced underground for several decades.

The Primacy of Experience

Signs of erosion in the Galenic view had already begun during the Enlightenment, especially in England and its revolutionary colony, with the claim that childhood experience was the most powerful sculptor of personality and character. John Locke proposed that the contents of all children's minds were essentially alike and that later differences in knowledge were due to what the child heard and saw and which habits were praised and punished. This was a revolutionary idea, even though today it seems transparently true. To understand this change in premise, it is important to note that a growing segment of the populace in eighteenth-century England wanted a democratic, egalitarian society in which neither religion nor pedigree was the basis for special status. That may be one reason why essays on temperament were less common in England than in France or Germany. The members of the new middle class wished to believe in their legitimate access to power through their efforts. It would be to their advantage, therefore, if princes and priests were found to be inherently neither more virtuous nor more intelligent than paupers.

A theory that bolstered the ethical idea of meritocracy was implicit in the associationism of Alexander Bain and David Hartley, which two hundred years later became the movement called behaviorism. Behaviorism rose rapidly in America in the second decade of this century, in part because of John Watson's promotion of Pavlov's discoveries and an increasingly liberal political climate among educated people who wanted scientific evidence to quiet the stridency of a eugenics movement that was pressing for sterilization of retarded and mentally ill adults as well as restriction of immigration. The urgent political imperative required adoption of the extreme position that human behavior was completely free of biology. The chant among social scientists in the 1920s was that humans had no instincts. Zing Yang Kuo, one of the most dogmatic of the behaviorists, even denied that human sexual behavior had any basis in biology. The concept of heredity was superfluous in psychology. The acts of love were simply learned by imitation and sustained by habit. A sixteen-year-old's infatuation with another was no different from excitement over a baseball game or a new pair of shoes.

A basic premise of behaviorism is present in contemporary computer programs that attempt to describe how a person learns new facts and rules. Stated simply, if two ideas occur close together in time, and especially if the occurrence of one predicts the occurrence of the other, the ideas become associated. What is remarkable is that this simple idea, which has its sphere of validity, rooted out all other formative mechanisms, even though reflection on everyday experience reveals some of its flaws. Each of us is bombarded constantly by a large number of events that occur close in time, with an earlier one predicting a later one. Yet we do not associate all of these linked events. We associate some names and faces easily, some poorly. Some students learn arithmetic with ease, some with difficulty. Moreover, if learned associations were the basis of all human behavior, why would adults living in different places and cultures and encountering such varied experiences be so similar in their motives, reactions to threat, and loyalty to family? The proponents of associationism brushed these objections aside because of the political attractiveness and logical simplicity of the argument.

Locke's claim remains strong today, 250 years later, for the same reasons. The contemporary world is composed of different groups of interdependent people with different politics, religions, and economies. We recognize that the survival of each depends upon the survival of all. In such an atmosphere it is useful to believe that all people are basically alike in their talents, motives, and moods. Competition for property and status must be among equals in a free-market democracy. It would be unsettling if one segment of the population were inherently more impulsive, anxious, timid, or intelligent than another. If persistent effort and carefully acquired skills are not the main reason for the disparity in wealth and privilege, a charitable society would have to care for those whose biology was not well adapted to their community, and a rational society would train for responsible positions only those with the appropriate biology. This tiered system of rank, which resembles both Plato's vision of the republic and the feudal hierarchy of the Middle Ages, is regarded by modern Western societies as evil.

The idea that all humans are basically similar in their psychological qualities became especially important in America following the Civil War and the arrival of the first wave of European immigrants. Politically liberal Americans wished to believe that if the foreigners attained a proper education they could command a fair measure of security and dignity. The suspicion that a large number of the immigrants were biologically tainted, an idea disseminated by some respected scholars and magazines during the opening decades of this century, challenged that democratic hope. The commitment to political egalitarianism, historically stronger in the United States than in continental Europe until the 1950s, holds that members of all ethnic groups can attain the political dignity enjoyed by the majority. The number and diversity of these minority groups have swelled over the past decade, and the community is responding to the legitimacy of these claims for fairer treatment in institutions, as well as in informal social relationships. Progress may be slow, but it is continuous and real.

Temperament and Politics

The desire for an egalitarian society generates resistance to the suggestion that some of the sources of human variation are inherent, even when that variation has no implications for the political ideal. Obviously the motivation behind a stubborn defense of the idea that all humans begin life with essentially similar emotional and behavioral biases is the wish to support the political imperative. If all individuals are, indeed, basically alike in their potential for cognitive talent, emotional exuberance, and behavioral skill, and if science remains the arbiter of ethics, then all should be safe from prejudicial action by those with more power acting against those with less. With Francis Bacon, however, I believe it is possible to separate one's moral convictions from the study of nature and to let the natural phenomena guide one's inferences.

The history of science has on occasion been marked by direct conflict between a popular belief with moral implications and a new scientific idea supported, but not yet completely proved, by empirical evidence. The two most famous examples in Western science involve conflicts with the premises of Christian philosophy. The first was the Copernican-Galilean claim that the earth revolved around the sun; the second was Darwin's argument for the mutability of species and the evolution of humans from animals. Both hypotheses challenged the religious view that earth and humanity were God's special creations.

Although science had won these contests with the Church by the end of the nineteenth century—even though the Vatican did not concede until 1992 that Galileo was correct—the contemporary community holds other morally tinged convictions to be irrevocably true. The popular assumption that the differences in children's moods, skills, and behaviors are primarily the result of early family experiences is one example. This premise has moral overtones because it places the responsibility for asocial and fearful children directly on parents. Excessive aggressiveness or timidity in a child is a sign that the family has done something wrong. This prejudice resembles the early Greek supposition that hallucinations, depression, and delusions were signs that the patient had violated a moral standard. During the last decade, the parents of schizophrenic adults have organized into a group to protest the assumption that family experience is the main culprit in the onset of this psychosis.

Darwin knew that the idea of evolution, which he consolidated during and after the voyage of the *Beagle* in the 1830s, would be criticized by many, including his wife, Emma Wedgewood, because it contradicted the biblical explanation of life. Society's resistance to evolution was both politically and morally motivated, for many people were afraid that anarchy would result if a majority came to believe that humans were the kin of animals. People might stop believing they were creatures of God born with a special imperative to be moral. This fear was exaggerated, and the dire predictions proved false. Europeans today are more concerned with starvation in a distant African village than their predecessors were in 1860.

One seeming danger in questioning the potency of family experience is the possibility that parents will become negligent if they learn that their daily behaviors are not the only, or the most critical, influence on their children. Perhaps they will stop caring for them. This apprehension, too, is ill founded. Most parents care for their children because, like chimpanzee mothers, they cannot do otherwise. Jean-Paul Sartre kept writing long after he decided that his sentences had little effect on the world, noting in his memoir, *The Words*, "I write because I have to write." Parents who minister to a crying infant, play peek-a-boo with their one-year-old, and tell stories to their five-year-old do not do so because they have decided, rationally, that these acts of caring will have a major effect on their child's future. It is difficult, although possible, to be unloving toward one's children. Parents will not stop nurturing children simply because scientists might discover that many forces, including temperament, share formative power with their actions toward and affection for their children.

The suppression of temperamental forces is made a bit easier by a new trend that celebrates surprising scientific discoveries before their validity has been established. The publicity given to cold fusion is one example. There are several reasons for this uncritical attitude. First, science has become an important source of entertainment on prime-time television. To entertain a broad audience at the end of a working day, producers must use surprise to command attention. The impulse to shock is rationalized by the fact that some valid discoveries in physics and molecular biology are counterintuitive; "absurd yet true" is how Richard Feynman described quantum mechanics. The ideas behind black holes, receding galaxies, gene therapy, and insertion of fetal tissue into the brain are fantastic and prepare the community to believe any news report originating in a laboratory, no matter how strange. In the fall of 1992, many newspapers around the nation gave first-page coverage to a study published in *Nature* claiming that infants under one year could add and subtract. The December 1992 issue of *Science News* listed this result as one of the significant discoveries of the year. Because surprise value occasionally replaces the probability of truth in the dissemination of science to the public, and the media more often report evidence claiming that early experiences, rather than temperament, have long-lasting consequences, people are willing to believe that exceedingly irritable or fearful children are the products of unfortunate encounters that occurred before the babies understood their first word.

The willingness to believe these extraordinary claims is strengthened by increasing scientific specialization. Darwin, an amateur naturalist, felt free to observe plants, mussels, turtles, worms, primates, and human facial expressions, and Ivan Pavlov, trained as a physiologist, did not hesitate to study conditioning in animals. But many younger scientists today feel constrained to study only the phenomena that their discipline has defined as its territory and to avoid intruding into another's space. In the field of psychology, this strict partitioning of inquiry has motivated many child psychologists to defend the power of environmental experiences for all human behavior, because learning has been the central theme of psychology ever since the popularization of Pavlov's experiments. Unfortunately, because ideas of temperament involve biological processes, some psychologists regard these concepts as lying outside psychology and as a threat to the importance of learning.

Public awareness of many unwelcome facts has made it harder to defend the beauty of empirical truth. If chemical pollution of air and water, AIDS, incompetent physicians, and scientific fraud are true, then knowing the truth is somewhat less attractive than it was one hundred years ago. These historical changes permit many to escape from an ambivalent acceptance of unpleasant facts to an uncritical acceptance of weaker but more satisfying claims. At present, it is less disruptive to society—and therefore more pleasing—to assume that all infants are basically similar than to posit temperamental types. Many parents are more willing to believe that an infant must be on the mother's body during the first twenty-four hours to develop normally than to consider the suggestion that some infants are inherently irritable from birth.

Finally, remnants of the Greek partition of soul and body contribute to an unspoken indifference to temperament. Some commentators predict that when a majority believe that molecules in the brain have a major influence on the experiences of love, joy, and sadness, these emotions will become less beautiful. I doubt that. These experiences have an immediacy and power that cannot be muted simply because one knows that opioids might be contributing to a conscious perception of serene relaxation. People will not stop mourning, laughing, or falling in love because they know that some have inherited a physiology that makes these feelings a bit more probable or a bit more intense.

Most social scientists, as well as government and foundation officials, argue forcefully for the basic similarity of all human groups and the capacity of all humans to change their personal qualities through experience. Some believe that to acknowledge temperamental differences is equivalent to promoting prejudice against the poor, especially against people of color. A popular, but incorrect, interpretation of the brief for temperament is that it is inconsistent with civil rights legislation; hence, scientists who argue for temperament court criticism because of its politically dangerous implications. But fears of radical social consequences have proved exaggerated in the past. Darwin did publish the *Origin of Species*, evolution became acceptable, and British society did not become anarchic. Acceptance of the idea of temperament will not lead to repeal of civil rights laws or increased discrimination. Temperamental differences do not imply differential access to freedom or power; acceptance of inherent variation is perfectly compatible with democracy and egalitarianism.

Introverts are no less entitled to society's gifts than extroverts. If it turns out that introverts are less frequently represented in the United States Senate, as is likely, it is partly because of their choice of life style, not because of a community prejudice against shy people. If hyperactive boys have a higher than average arrest rate, that fact does not imply that the police preferentially seek out youth with this characteristic. Next year's scores on the Scholastic Aptitude Test will have a broad distribution, and those with high scores will be more likely to be admitted to college than those with low scores. Some unbalanced social profiles are not the result of prejudice.

But, unfortunately, it is politically divisive at present to talk about Galen's temperamental types. America's racial tensions are not helped by claims that Asians, Blacks, and Caucasians might have different affective profiles, or that some adolescents find it easy to mug an old woman. What is not appreciated, however, is that temperamental differences are malleable by experience. There is no rigid determinism between the inheritance of a particular temperament and a later behavioral profile.

If scientists prove that Asian infants are more placid than European babies, an idea we explore in chapter 8, no obvious political implications for vocation, education, or political power follow. Neither the ethics nor the laws of a society need to accommodate to the facts of science. If our informal mores and formal laws always took into account what was true in nature, adultery would not be a crime, for most primates, including chimpanzees, are promiscuous. And schizophrenics and bipolar depressives would be sterilized because genes contribute to a susceptibility to those psychoses.

Suppose, as we will see in chapter 5, that on average tall, thin adults with blue eyes become anxious in response to challenge a little more easily than others. I doubt if a November referendum would approve the proposition that the former should not have access to positions of high responsibility. American voters would reject such a notion because they appreciate, intuitively, that a temperamental quality is only one aspect of the whole person. Adolescents who are over six feet tall perform better on basketball courts than those who are shorter, yet no one suggests that youth shorter than six feet not be allowed to participate in this sport. When the psychological health of a society demands that most have the ability to perform its varied tasks, it is perfectly responsible for the society not to accommodate to every biologically based difference that might affect, in a subtle way, a person's everyday functioning. The idea of temperament is not socially dangerous, even though the concept of inherent temperamental differences, like a speck of dirt on a fresh snow field, mars the democratic ideal by implying that some children are lightly burdened before the race of life begins, while others start with a tiny unfair advantage.

Freud's Influence

Freud was a critical figure in this story because, trained in medicine rather than philosophy, he was as interested in differences among people as in universal human characteristics. Freud was especially curious about the biological and experiential factors that made some persons vulnerable to extreme emotional states. A woman's fear of drinking from a glass—a symptom in one of Freud's first cases—could not be traced to any physical quality of the object; hence, Freud had to leap over sensation and invoke complex mental processes. The popularity of the theoretical ideas he invented in the opening years of this century was aided by an enthusiasm for Darwinian principles and a local European community trying to cope with anxiety over sexuality.

Freud made four important changes in the remnants of Galen's views. First, he supported Locke by awarding extraordinary power to early experience and minimizing, although not denying, the relevance of temperament. Second, he substituted one bodily substance—the energy of the libido—for the four humors and assumed a balance among the motives, thoughts, actions, and feelings assigned to id, ego, and superego. The idea of a biologically based psychological energy, the meaning of libido, was not completely novel. Nineteenth-century physicians had elaborated the ancient belief that the amount of energy, called *vis nervosa*, was an inherited personal quality that was less abundant in those unfortunate persons who developed fears, depression, and neurasthenia.

Pavlov exploited this idea to explain why some dogs became conditioned easily while others resisted the laboratory procedures. Pavlov thought that the former group of animals had a strong nervous system that permitted them to adjust to the stimulation and unfamiliarity of the conditioning procedures. Pavlov intended that description to be flattering, for adaptive themes, muted in Galen, began to color temperamental concepts after Darwin's seminal work. Galen had written as if each psychological type sought an adaptation to fit his or her bodily humor. Pavlov and his followers inserted an evaluative frame of adaptation and implied that some temperaments functioned better than others. The sanguine was the best type; the melancholic, with a weaker brain, was the least desirable.

The idea that individuals vary in psychological energy and therefore in strength of brain activity may seem odd to modern readers. Current psychiatric theory, however, holds that depressives have low levels of central norepinephrine, the primary neurotransmitter of the sympathetic nervous system, which maintains body temperature by producing energy. One of the therapeutic drugs for depression acts by increasing the concentration of norepinephrine in the synaptic cleft. Moreover, infants differ in the vigor of their motor activity and the loudness of their vocalizations. Some four-month-olds thrash their limbs and squeal with delight; others lie passive and quiet. A high energy level leaps to mind as the best description of the active infants. In the classic monograph on hysteria written with Breuer, Freud wrote, "Differences which make up a man's natural temperament are based on profound differences in his nervous system—on the degree to which the functionally quiescent cerebral elements liberate energy."

The creative element in Freud's thinking was to locate the free-floating energy in sexuality, while accepting the popular view that heredity influenced the amount of libido a person possessed. Jung recognized the error in Freud's decision to make repression of sexuality the sole cause of symptoms. He accepted the concepts of repression and the unconscious, but his experiences as a psychiatrist to severely disturbed patients at the Burghölzli Hospital in Zurich, and no doubt his introspections, were discordant with Freud's claim. Jung's understanding of his own shy childhood, introverted adult style, and sensitivity to body tone, revealed in *Memories, Dreams, Reflections*, did not correspond with Freud's explanation of the profile of the introvert. Freud made the psychological system more dynamic, however, by suggesting that the distribution of libido changed during the oral, anal, phallic, and genital stages of development. Perhaps his most original hypothesis was that different personality types were a function of the child's experiences during each of these four stages. Whether this idea is valid or not, few question its novelty.

Although Freud's early writings awarded influence both to temperamental differences in amount of libido and excitability of the nervous system, as well as the experiences that created the public character, his later writings gave greater importance to childhood experiences, and, accordingly, the contribution of temperament faded. The current popularity of the premise that childhood experiences are part of the causal web in adult anxiety and depression prevents a proper appreciation of the revolutionary character of Freud's ideas. Although the ancients were open to the suggestion that psychological variation within the normal range could be influenced by childhood experience—even Plato accepted that argument—they regarded the serious mental afflictions of depression, mania, and schizophrenia as physiological in origin. The ancients believed that some environmental factors were potent, including air, diet, exercise, rest, and excretion and retention of fluid, but none was social in nature. Islamic physicians in the tenth century, following Galen, never thought of attributing the distinctive behavioral traits of Egyptians to their social experiences. Freud undermined the sharp boundary between an anxious, somewhat shy introvert not yet ready for a psychiatrist's office and the delusional melancholic by arguing that both syndromes were influenced by early social encounters.

The Freudian revolution also challenged the traditional assumption that, because will controls actions, everyone is continually responsible. Freud argued that the unconscious can sneak behind will to do mischief. The hysteric is not feigning a paralysis or a fear of leaving the safety of the home and therefore cannot be held responsible for these behaviors. In 1924, Clarence Darrow defended two middle-class adolescents—Nathan Leopold and Richard Loeb—who had killed a thirteen-year-old boy. Relying on Freudian ideas, Darrow argued that childhood experiences had produced an emotional immaturity in the murderers and that therefore they were not totally responsible for their crime. Two respected psychiatrists supported that claim, and the judge, finding these views persuasive, sentenced the two young men to life imprisonment instead of death.

The suggestion that insight into one's unconscious wishes frees the shackled will remains appealing in democratic societies because it implies that freedom is the key to psychological health. The Freudian metaphor equates individual political liberty with psychic freedom and the removal of despotic coercion with the lifting of repression. I suspect this is one reason why Freud's ideas were so attractive to Americans and to the English but had a less enthusiastic reception on the continent. Before World War I, France and Germany were less favorable to egalitarian ideas than were the two more liberal nations.

Freud's ideas were a watershed because for centuries medical commentaries on human mental illness had focused primarily on the minority of adults with serious pathology, not on the majority who were apprehensive about money, friends, illness, and death. Galen, Hippocrates, Robert Burton, and Henry Maudsley were concerned with the small number who had extremely irrational fears, presumably because of an inherited vulnerability. When philosophers, rather than physicians, wrote about the uncertainties to which all humans were susceptible they used different terms. Benjamin Franklin, who claimed that uneasiness was the salient human motive, recognized that this state was endemic to human nature because of a natural tendency to worry about loss of status, love, or wealth. But he did not place these everyday apprehensions on a continuum with the fear that one might choke to death on a piece of food or be possessed by the devil. The small proportion with such irrational phobias were assigned to a different category, separate from the large majority who simply brooded about fame, food, friendships, and fortune.

Freud softened that division and persuaded many that a terror of leaving one's home and worry about one's debts could be derivatives of the same conflict. By providing an experiential basis for fears that was appropriate for all—everyone felt guilt over sex and hostility—he implied that anyone could develop a phobia. Freud let his readers believe that "little Hans," the patient in one of Freud's most famous cases, was no different temperamentally from any other child; his extreme fear of horses was the result of unusual experiences in the family.

The recent trend toward describing clinical cases as if they were physiological diseases to be treated with drugs, with little discussion of conflict, trauma, or early family experience, represents a dramatic break with a tradition that lasted for most of this century. Freud made it possible for the British psychiatrist John Bowlby to suggest that adult anxiety and dependency could derive from loss of a mother forty years earlier, and for Alan Fogel, of the University of Utah, to write that "an attempt to comprehend the human mind and self that is not grounded in a theory of personal relationships . . . is unlikely to yield edible fruit and attractive flowers. Human cognition and the sense of self are fundamentally and originally relational." The hypothesis that serious anxiety, depression, or a chronic phobia of heights could be due to a history of early social encounters did not occur to the wisest commentators on human nature for over two millennia. Only in this century did family conflict and maternal rejection become the mysterious black bile.

Psychoanalytic theory slowly turned minds away from a category of person who was especially vulnerable to acquiring a phobia to a category of environments that produced fear. The adjective *fearful* became a continuous dimension, varying in intensity, on which anyone could be placed. Because everyone experienced conflict anyone could become phobic, and the idea of a vulnerable temperament was replaced with the notion of unusually stressful experiences. A metaphor that captures this contrast is a rope bridge that collapses under a load. The traditional assumption was that all bridges must carry loads of varying weight;

hence, a bridge that collapsed under a load within the normal weight range must have been structurally weak. This is the temperamental premise. Freud, and especially his followers, argued that in most cases the collapse was caused by an unusually heavy load. The psychological burdens included childhood seduction, harsh socialization of hostility and sexuality, loss of a love object, and fear of the anger of an authoritarian parent. Even though there are many more children who are socialized harshly by autocratic parents—or rejected by indifferent ones—than there are hysterical patients, this theoretical stance won admirers quickly because of political factors.

History was midwife to the substitution of stressful encounters for constitutional biases. Many Americans were threatened when, after the First World War, a number of prominent scientists, joined by influential journalists, suggested that some immigrants were less fit genetically than Americans whose forebears had arrived earlier. An opposing group of politically more liberal scientists and journalists quieted this provocative claim by suggesting that Pavlov's discoveries meant that all children were essentially similar at birth and that conditioned experience supplied the only shaping hand. William McDougall's acerbic critique of this position in his social psychology textbook was drowned out by the rising voice of Watsonian behaviorism. As we have seen, the ideological struggle between those who argued for the power of experience and those who favored biological types of children was decided in favor of the former when Hitler's philosophy of genetically flawed and superior populations rendered biological typing morally indefensible.

By the late 1930s psychoanalytic explanations of fearful symptoms had replaced those based on temperament, and the barrier between normal and abnormal dissolved. Every adult was potentially vulnerable to suicidal depression, schizophrenia, and phobia if environmental conditions became adverse. Thomas Szasz even persuaded some that serious mental disease was a social construction, a morally tinged evaluation (by a majority) of symptoms that anyone could acquire.

The ideological competition between biological forces and social experiences favored the latter during the first two-thirds of this century. At present the two perspectives are at approximately equal strength—as they should be. There is a danger, however, that the biological argument will gain an unwarranted ascendancy because scientific progress is more rapid in the neurosciences than in psychology. It would be unfortunate if the contributions of experience were dismissed in the new enthusiasm for biology.

The Return of Ideas of Temperament

The independent products of science and history forced the return of temperament concepts. One set of persuasive facts was provided by the discovery that closely related strains of animals raised under identical laboratory conditions behaved differently in response to the same intrusions. In the 1960s John Paul Scott and John Fuller studied over 250 puppies from five different breeds—basenji, beagle, cocker spaniel, Shetland sheepdog, and fox terrier—at the secluded Jackson Laboratories in Bar Harbor, Maine. In one assessment of an animal's timidity, a handler took a puppy from its cage to a common room, placed the puppy a few feet away, stood still, and observed the animal's behavior. The handler then slowly turned and walked toward the puppy, squatted down, held out his hand, stroked the puppy, and finally picked it up. The puppies who ran to the corner of the room, crouched, and issued a high-pitched yelp early in the sequence were classified as timid. The five breeds of dogs differed dramatically in their degree of timidity. The basenjis, terriers, and shelties were more timid than the beagles and cocker spaniels. But the rearing environment was important; all animals were less timid if they had been raised in a home rather than in the laboratory. Twenty years later other scientists discovered that Labradors, Australian kelpies, boxers, and German shepherds differ in the avoidance of unfamiliar objects. The German shepherds are the most timid; the Labradors are the least fearful.

House cats, too, differ in timidity. The small proportion of pet cats who consistently withdraw from novelty and who fail to attack rats have a lower threshold of excitability in specific areas of the amygdala than the majority of cats who do not withdraw and who generally attack rats. Similar stories can be told for a great many species. Mice, rats, wolves, cows, monkeys, birds, and even paradise fish differ, within species or among closely related strains, in the tendency to approach or to avoid novelty. Goats of the Nubian strain are more fearful than animals from the Alpine strain when isolated from other animals for a short period. The chestnut-sided warbler hesitates before feeding in a novel area, whereas the bay-breasted warbler is much less timid. The environment can affect the genetic bias, however. When song sparrows and swamp sparrows are raised under identical laboratory conditions, the juveniles of the former species are more avoidant in unfamiliar contexts. But when both species are reared in a natural habitat, the song sparrow is no longer more cautious. Because the song sparrow is a generalist who feeds in many different sites, it is useful to this animal to overcome an initial avoidant bias. Apparently it does just that.

It is not surprising that fearful behavior can be bred in animals, but it is surprising that doing so requires only a small number of generations. Some quail chicks become chronically immobile when they are placed on their backs in a cradle and restricted by a human hand; remaining immobile is one measure of fear in birds. If chicks who display the fearful trait are bred with other fearful animals, it takes only eight generations to produce a relatively uniform line of birds that show immobility for as long as two minutes, whereas most chicks display immobile periods of thirty to fifty seconds. It is equally easy to establish a line of birds that show very brief periods of immobility.

The reasonable expectation that strain differences in behavior should be associated with differences in physiology is confirmed by other studies. Quail chicks that have been bred to be highly social—they seek other chicks when they are isolated—react differently from chicks bred to be minimally social. When the former animals are isolated and given an injection of corticotropin releasing hormone (CRH), they show an enhanced secretion of corticosteroids, while the minimally social chicks do not. Thus, the physiological consequences of CRH depend, in part, on the temperament of the animal.

White rats from the Sprague Dawley strain who are unusually emotional in a novel environment have significantly higher concentrations of brain norepinephrine than minimally emotional rats from the same strain. In another rat strain, some animals display exaggerated neural activity—called potentiation—in the hippocampus following high-frequency stimulation of the lateral amygdala; others do not. The former animals do not show ulceration of the stomach following immobilization, while the latter develop ulcers following similar restraint. Because all the animals come from the same highly inbred strain, it is likely that the tendency to show or fail to show the potentiation represents a genetic quality.

The Maudsley Reactive strain of rats has been bred over generations to be fearful in unfamiliar situations. The amount of defecation in a brightly lit open field, which is aversive for a rat, is used as the index of fear. A nonreactive strain has been bred to be minimally fearful. The differences between the two strains emerge early, by thirty days, and are not due to postnatal experiences. Compared with the nonreactive animals, the reactive animals have a higher density of beta adrenergic receptors on the heart. As a result, they display both higher heart rates and higher blood pressure.

These results may seem to have little relevance to humans because they involve birds and rats, but similar strain differences also exist in primate groups. South American squirrel monkeys of two different strains, reproductively isolated by only a thousand miles of jungle, vary in their morphology, physiology, and behavior. Chimpanzees form male alliances and are sexually promiscuous; gorillas do not form such alliances and are less promiscuous, usually maintaining lasting bonds to female consorts. About 20 percent of rhesus monkeys are extremely fearful and timid in unfamiliar environments, have tense muscle tone as infants, and show physiological reactivity in targets that are linked to fearfulness.

There are even sanguine, melancholic, and choleric monkeys. When the behaviors of three closely related species of macaques were compared in their tendency to approach or to withdraw from an unfamiliar human, bonnets were most likely to approach, while crabeaters, the smallest of the three species, were the most fearful. The largest animals, the rhesus monkeys, were the most aggressive. When these three species were observed under different conditions of novelty and restraint, the aggressive rhesus were the least disturbed and showed the smallest increases in heart rate. The fearful crabeaters were the most disturbed and showed the largest increases in both heart rate and glucocorticoids. The bonnets, who tend to be passive and avoidant, showed modest increases in both heart rate and glucocorticoids. When crabeater, rhesus, and pigtail monkey infants were reared in isolation for six months, however, the rhesus displayed the most disturbed social behavior, whereas crabeater monkeys showed almost normal social behavior. Thus, the influence of temperament on development varies with experience and the nature of the stressful intrusion.

Temperamental factors are even linked to immune function in monkeys. One group of crabeater males lived in a stable group of four or five monkeys for the twenty-six months of the experiment. A second, stressed group of animals also lived in groups of four or five monkeys, but the composition of the group changed each month; the frequent changes generate uncertainty in the crabeater monkey. The scientists also observed the animals twice a week for about a half hour to determine which were social and affiliative—they groomed and stayed close to other monkeys—and which were social isolates. After the two years of either stressful or minimally stressful social experience, the integrity of each animal's immune system was measured by drawing blood for three weeks and evaluating the ability of the T lymphocytes to respond appropriately to an antigen. Lower levels of cell proliferation to the antigen indicate a compromised immune system. Only the animals who lived under social stress and in addition were temperamentally prone to be social isolates showed a severely compromised immune system. The affiliative animals who had experienced the same level of social stress showed a healthier immune response. This finding illustrates the important principle that a disease state requires both a stress and a potentially vulnerable target system.

The fact that very small variations in the genetic composition of closely related animals are associated with distinct profiles of behavior and physiology requires accommodation. If an animal's temperament influences not only its reaction to total isolation but also its immune competence, it is likely that similar factors are operative in humans. The combined effect of these studies has been to place the idea of temperament in a more favored position in interpretations of human behavior.

The Contribution of Psychology

The questions that dominate each new cycle of a discipline are influenced, in a dialectic fashion, by those of the prior cycle. The three obvious eras in psychology's short history are easy to detect. Psychology was carved out of philosophy, and therefore it is not surprising that the nature of conscious experience was the focus of the first empirical studies. But the limitations of introspective descriptions of a person's perceptual experiences became apparent by the turn of the century, and younger scholars, admiring the experimental success of colleagues in physiology, abandoned their philosophical parents to seek a closer identification with experimental physiologists. The historical accident of Pavlov's discovery of conditioning supplied the theme of the new laboratory research. Conditioning of animals was a perfect target for experimental manipulation of behavior and was in sympathy with the pragmatic attitudes of American society. But after a reign of fifty years, this movement, too, revealed its vulnerable side and yielded to a third cycle, which was a compromise between those who wished to study the more complex intellectual and emotional qualities of humans and those who remained loyal to experimental manipulations and more certain knowledge. Once again, history selected the specific interest that would satisfy both goals. Piaget's writings, linguistic theory, the ease of performing experiments on memory and perception, and the introduction of computers together channeled academic energy to the study of cognitive functions.

Research on human temperament has until now been peripheral to all three cycles because the phenomena of temperament are not amenable to experiments and involve differences among people, not universal qualities. But I suspect that this position will change in the future, for psychology has remained close to study of the brain. Neuroscience is a biological discipline and biology is the science of exceptions. Each species differs from the next in small details of physiology, anatomy, and behavior. That fact will motivate psychologists interested in human behavior to recognize that, on many occasions, they should expect that only some individuals will react to an event in a particular way and that uniform consequences will not always occur. The acceptance of that principle will force confrontation with the question *why*. When that time comes, the study of temperament may become a major focus of psychological inquiry. Signs of this change emerged in the 1960s. New discoveries in biology and psychology were inconsistent with the behaviorist principles that all responses could be taught and all stable behaviors were the result of patterns of rewards and punishments. Although parents knew that some children found learning to play the piano difficult, psychologists had to discover that rats found it easy to learn to avoid eating food that was followed by nausea if the food had a distinctive taste but would not learn to avoid the same food if a distinctive light, kept on while the rat was eating, was used as the signal. Birds, however, acquired the avoidant habit to the food more easily when a light rather than a distinctive taste accompanied it. This surprising fact suggested that animals differ inherently in their preparedness to learn particular habits in response to events in the environment.

Male swamp and song sparrows, raised under identical laboratory conditions, are biologically prepared to sing different songs. If both species of birds hear taped recordings of a particular bird song, they will, as adults, sing nonidentical songs. If the birds are prevented from hearing any songs;

they will sing songs that are simpler than those heard in nature but still different from each other. These discoveries led scientists to replace the concept of learning with the concept of privileged acquisition. The adjective *privileged* is intended to imply that each species is born with a central nervous system that biases the animal to find some habits easy to acquire, some difficult, and some impossible. Children belonging to different temperamental categories, like closely related species, also differ in the ease with which particular emotions and accompanying behaviors become habitual.

While laboratory experiments were demonstrating the influence of temperamental differences, psychiatrists and clinical psychologists were beginning to treat the working poor in large numbers. It was becoming apparent that in comparison with the economic security of college-educated professionals, the poor lived with economic and social stresses that were not the product of childhood conflicts and fantasies. A young woman in the inner city who was afraid to leave her apartment because of drug dealers in the neighborhood could not be diagnosed as a hysteric, fixated at the phallic stage, because she was afraid that if she left her home she would be unable to control her sexual impulse to seduce a man—the psychoanalytic interpretation of agoraphobia in the 1940s. Nor did it seem reasonable to interpret the reading failure of a child living with an illiterate unwed mother as due to the child's guilt over hostility toward his mother. Ludicrous as it now seems, a popular psychoanalytic interpretation of reading failure in the 1950s was that some children regarded reading as an aggressive act and, therefore, guilt over hostility toward a parent could impede the learning of this skill.

Another concept that died was the idea of sublimation. A half century earlier, many scholars believed that many important goal-related actions were symbolic attempts to attain sexual pleasure; the star athlete, the creative poet, and the skilled surgeon were all sublimating their libidos in practicing their talents. Today the claim that Michael Jordan was sublimating frustrated sexuality would be treated as a bad joke. A 1968 review of children's phobias insisted that all fears derived from conflict; temperament was irrelevant. Only nineteen years later, a review of phobias published in the same journal contained no mention of Freud's ideas. There was not even a reference to Freud in the long bibliography; the fall from grace of psychoanalytic theory was that fast.

Hans Eysenck, one of the important early voices after the long period of silence on temperament, returned to old concepts with new words. He rejected the distinction between temperament and character and returned to Galenic ideas by positing two independent axes. One axis represented Jung's distinction between extroverts and introverts, similar to the contrast between the sanguine and the melancholic. The introvert is biased to withdraw from social interaction, to be cautious in situations with risk, to avoid conflict, and to take pleasure in solitary behavior. The extrovert seeks excitement, enjoys sociability, and exhibits a carefree, spontaneous, and more impulsive style. At right angles to this axis is a second axis, with the emotionally excitable person at one end and the subdued, restrained person at the other. This opposition resembles Galen's contrast of the choleric with the phlegmatic. Both extroverts and introverts can be either excitable or restrained.

Thomas and Chess

The change in Zeitgeist permitted Alexander Thomas and Stella Chess, two psychiatrists working in New York, to introduce the idea of infant temperament in the late 1950s. Solomon Diamond had also suggested earlier that fearful, aggressive, impulsive, and apathetic children were temperamental types whose behaviors were influenced in part by heredity and in part by experience. But the psychological community was not ready for this message, and the extensive study of children's temperament had to wait for the important Thomas and Chess monograph that appeared about twenty years later.

In defining a temperamental quality, Thomas and Chess emphasized the distinctive style of a behavior, rather than the goal sought or the competence with which the behavior was displayed. They inferred nine temperamental dimensions from lengthy interviews with eighty-five middle- and upper-middle-class parents. Unfortunately, the parents were not representative of American society; most were Jewish and faculty members of a university. Although Thomas and Chess made some direct observations of the older children, the nine temperamental dimensions were based primarily on the parents' answers to direct questions about their infants. The nine categories were: (1) general activity level, (2) regularity and predictability of basic functions, like hunger, sleep, and elimination, (3) initial reaction to unfamiliarity, especially approach and withdrawal, (4) ease of adaptation to new situations (obviously correlated with the third category), (5) responsiveness to subtle stimulus events, (6) amount of energy associated with activity, (7) dominant mood, primarily whether happy or irritable, (8) distractibility, and (9) attention span and persistence.

The lack of independence of the nine dimensions—the child who approaches unfamiliar people is typically more adaptive and a bit happier—motivated Thomas and Chess to create three abstract categories, each based on a profile of several of the dimensions. The most common was the *easy child*, about 40 percent of their sample, who, as we shall see, resembles the child we call *uninhibited*. These children were regular and approached unfamiliar objects with a happy and engaging mood.

The second category, called *slow to warm up* and comprising about 15 percent of their sample, resembles the child we call *inhibited*. These children reacted to unfamiliarity with withdrawal and mild emotional distress. The third category, called the *difficult child* and comprising about 10 percent of the sample, was characterized by minimal regularity, frequent irritability, withdrawal from unfamiliarity, and very poor adaptation. The children in this small group were the most likely to develop psychiatric symptoms; two-thirds had developed such symptoms by age ten. These three categories made up about two-thirds of the Thomas-Chess sample; the remaining third were difficult to classify and did not fit any of the three more obvious types.

Regular evaluation of the children through the fifth year revealed minimal preservation of most of the dimensions. The largest correlations—about 0.3—reflected stability across ages two to four years, but not from infancy to four years of age. In a follow-up when the subjects were between eighteen and twenty-two years of age, Thomas and Chess used clinical interviews and questionnaires to evaluate adjustment. Although there was no relation between an easy or a difficult temperament in the first two years and quality of adult adjustment, the children who had been classified as difficult in the third and fourth years were less able to cope with life's stress than those who had had an easy temperament.

Thomas and Chess acknowledged that their nine dimensions and three categories were influenced by the nature of their evidence, namely, interviews with parents. It is not surprising that when middle-class mothers are asked to describe their infants they talk about characteristics that make caregiving easy or difficult and either conform to or violate the ideal traits they and the community value. Does an infant approach or avoid new people? Is the infant easy to feed and bathe? Does the infant soothe easily? Does the infant sleep through the night or wake fitfully?

Suppose that seventeenth-century naturalists had asked experienced African hunters to classify animals. The informants might have placed tigers and pythons in the same category because they share the quality of being potentially dangerous to humans and put mice and lizards in a different category, even though pythons and lizards are phylogenetically closer than tigers and pythons. Folk theory is not always an accurate source of information about nature.

Thomas and Chess are not to be faulted for the categories they invented. The absence of a deep understanding of the physiological patterns that form the foundation for temperamental types leaves most investigators little choice but to focus on the most obvious behavioral profiles. Ptolemy and Copernicus also chose the obvious when they studied the moon and the near planets. As astronomers now know, the moon and Mars are not very important objects in the sky; they tell us little about the origins of the solar system, have little effect on our weather, and are of minimal consequence for current theory in astrophysics. But five centuries ago, both objects represented interesting, lawful phenomena that could be observed and described. Steven Weinberg comments that understanding is advanced when scientists are not overly cautious and are willing to entertain an idea that is not yet proved beyond doubt. The proper attitude is to ask whether an idea is worthy of being taken seriously.

The Rise of Neuroscience

Progress in neuroscience has contributed to the scientific community's receptivity to the ideas of Thomas and Chess. Biologists across the world have entered a phase of discovery reminiscent of the developments in physics during the first two decades of this century, when the components of the atom were becoming realities instead of hypothetical possibilities.

The brain contains over 150 different chemicals—monoamines, amino acids, hormones, and peptides—which, along with their receptors, influence the excitability of specific sites in the central nervous system. The number of combinations of these molecules exceeds ten million. Individuals inherit different concentrations of most of these chemicals (and their associated receptors); hence, one can at least imagine how a child or an adult might be especially vulnerable to sadness, depression, or anxiety.

Scientists are conservative and resist explanations that do not rest on a rationale built of robust facts arranged in a logical argument. The environmental explanation of why a child was excessively fearful was so familiar and reasonable that most psychologists were reluctant to relinquish it until another, equally commanding one was provided. Neuroscientists were supplying these new explanations with fresh facts and arguments that assumed inherited variation in neurochemistry and neurophysiology. Alvin Weinberg, a former director of the Oak Ridge Laboratory in Tennessee, has noted that any scientific domain that illuminates a neighboring one has proved to be of great value in science. Study of temperament requires the understanding of behavior, affect, and physiology; hence, it should contribute to each of these related fields of scholarship.

But when we shift from either a parent's verbal description or direct observations of an infant to the data from a physiologist's laboratory, we must invent a different set of categories; desires, feelings, and conflict are awkward ideas in biology. A description of the circuits—involving thalamus, visual cortex, temporal lobe, hippocampus, and association areas—that are activated when I meet someone I have not seen in twenty years does not require any words for intention, desire, or reward. And nerve cells do not seek satisfaction or avoid disappointment.

Concepts of temperament include, as part of their theoretical definition, an inherited neurochemical and physiological profile that is linked to emotion and behavior. But the relations between the physiology and emotion or behavior are complex and not yet understood. There is generally a poor correlation between how tense, anxious, or fearful a person feels and the amount of increase in heart rate, blood pressure, or level of cortisol in response to a stressful event. A person's subjective feelings do not map well on presumably relevant physiological indexes. When subjects are asked to engage in a psychologically stressful task—for example, difficult arithmetic problems—the physiological signs rise in some persons, but not in all. The physiology and psychology of affect states are not closely yoked.

When scientists cannot understand a phenomenon they often search for one better understood that shares qualities with the puzzling event. The ancients thought the source of the body's heat could be likened to the operation of a furnace; the action of the heart heated the body cavity, while breathing cooled it. Some of the qualities of heated and cooled liquids were known and provided a useful model to explain how the heart and blood influenced the body and human emotions. Because an animal or human who is excited feels warm to the touch, whereas the skin of someone who has suffered shock is cold, it was reasonable to guess that a person with warm blood would be quick to anger and that one with cold blood would be slow to become irritable.

On occasion, scientists make the bolder move from recognizing an analogy between two phenomena to the stronger assumption that the mechanisms of the well-understood event are identical to those of the less well-comprehended one. Such a leap often fails in fine detail because it is extremely rare for two systems to share most of their primary characteristics and functions. There is no mechanical system that is exactly like the brain, heart, kidney, or stomach. There is no other event in nature exactly like the sensations humans feel in a Vermont forest in early October or while laughing at a joke. Extrapolations from animal physiology to human psychology have to proceed with caution. It is sometimes argued that the relation between biological and psychological phenomena should be similar across a variety of species. In a somewhat caricatured scenario, a scientist develops an assay for a new chemical that is supposed to influence the brain—serotonin is an example. That important discovery is followed by a host of investigations that compare levels of that chemical with signs of aggressive or fearful behavior in mice, rats, cats, monkeys, panic patients, and air traffic controllers. The results are usually different in some of the samples, and controversy arises. This attitude became extreme at the height of behaviorism, when explanations of learning referred to a few fundamental mechanisms that applied to all animals and all habits. But a biological process exists in a particular class of organism of a particular age in a particular context; all must be specified. The concentration of serotonin has very little psychological meaning without adding the constraint of species, age, and situation.

There is a dangerous trend to idealize and therefore to overgeneralize a process and to award it universal significance that covers all species and contexts. Nine-month-olds show a decrease, but four-year-olds an increase, in heart rate when they see a stranger. High cortisol levels characterize not only fearful five-year-olds but also active, enthusiastic one-year-olds. The list of examples can be expanded. Although contemporary science is empirical, as Aristotle would have wished, it is, oddly enough, also Platonic in its desire to award to every basic process a mystical essence that transcends local conditions.

One obstacle to a better theory of temperament is the absence of appropriate words or images to describe the phenomena. Although the idea of bodily substances influencing behavior is ancient, descriptions of the relevant mechanisms continue to evade us, first, because the relation is always probabilistic and, second, because it changes with age and experience. When a functional relation is neither deterministic nor stable indefinitely, it is neither comprehended nor communicated easily.

An Initial Definition

Temperamental constructs are defined, ideally, by inherited coherences of physiological and psychological processes that emerge early in development. The defining behaviors are not always present at birth; some may require maturation before they appear. For example, an excitable amygdala makes it more likely that an infant will show vigorous motor activity, defensive postures, and irritability to unfamiliar stimulation. But the connections between the central nucleus of the amygdala and the ventromedial hypothalamus (VMH) are immature at birth; therefore, the defensive postures mediated by the VMH are not provoked by an excitable amygdala in a newborn.

Further, environmental conditions can modulate the behavioral profile; levels of motor tension and crying are not constant from day to day. And daily experiences permit some children to learn to control their irritability and, later, their fear. It is even possible that experiences that reduce levels of uncertainty can alter the excitability of the limbic systems or change the density of receptors on neurons. Handling a newborn rat for fifteen minutes a day for twenty-one days alters permanently the density of receptors for glucocorticoids in cells of the hippocampus. Thus, temperamentally driven behaviors are not immutable; on the contrary, they can be unusually malleable.

Moreover, membership in a temperamental category simply implies a slight initial bias that favors certain affects and actions. We choose the word *bias* rather than *determination*, for the physiology merely affects the probabilities that certain states and behaviors will occur in particular rearing environments. An analogy in a familiar domain is the relationship between temperatures under 32 degrees and the likelihood of a blizzard. Most of the time when the temperature falls under 32 degrees there is no blizzard; but there is never a blizzard at 50 degrees. Having a particular biological profile increases the probability that a child will be fearful, but it does not guarantee that fact. If the child is not born with the temperamental bias she is unlikely to show the blend of physiology, behavior, and mood that characterizes those who have the special vulnerability to fear. This child may show one of the components—she might be fearful in some situations—but she will not show the combination of features that defines the temperamental type.

Like a zygote only one hour old, temperament is a potential. There is no guarantee of an indefinitely stable profile because environmental factors are always potent. Every temperamental concept implies an actualizing environment that permits the defining behaviors to appear. The one-day-old infant born with the genes and physiology that represent a potential for fearful behavior does not yet belong to the category we called *inhibited*. Only if and when she becomes fearful in the second year will the child be called *inhibited*. Thus, we borrow from biology the fruitful pair of concepts called *genotype*—the inherited genetic profile—and *phenotype*—the visible results of the interaction between that profile and the environment.

Further, a fearful child can learn to control the urge to withdraw from a stranger or a large dog. Lions can be trained to sit quietly on a chair even though that posture is not typical for their species. The role of the environment is more substantial in helping a child overcome the tendency to withdraw than in making that child timid in the first place. Thus, we are setting aside the earlier distinction between innate temperament and acquired character because it treated the former as a separable, autonomous Platonic essence. Instead, we emphasize the character type that combines biology and experience in the empirical measurements until the time when scientists better understand and can evaluate the central physiology that contributes to the behavioral profile. The child is always in a context, and the behaviors and moods observed are the product of a particular temperament reacting to specific events, as Whitehead insisted. Ice, water, and steam are different forms of the same molecule exposed to different conditions. There is no molecule of H_2O anywhere in the world that is not in some environmental context. Similarly, there is no pure temperament that transcends all rearing environments.

The power of genes is real but limited—a principle that operates even during the growth of the embryo. Although the human genome ensures in most cases that the newborn's brain will have a cerebellum, frontal lobe, and hippocampus, with particular types of neurons in each site, the exact number and location of those neurons varies as a function of local chemical events in the vicinity of the migrating cells. If a mother drinks too much alcohol during her pregnancy, the brain of the newborn can be very different from that of most infants. No human quality, physical or psychological, is free of the contribution of events within and outside the organism. Development is a cooperative mission and no behavior is a first-order, direct product of genes. To rephrase Quine, every psychological quality is like a pale gray fabric woven tightly of thin black threads representing biology and white ones representing experience, but it is impossible to detect any quite black or white threads in the gray cloth.

CHAPTER TWO

What Is Temperament?

Two seemingly incompatible conceptions can each represent an aspect of the truth. . . .
They may serve in turn to represent the facts without ever entering into direct conflict.
—LEWIS VICTOR DE BROGLIE, *DIALECTICA I*

The ancient, intuitively reasonable partition of the human psyche into thought, feeling, and action requires some additional terms to describe the striking individual variation in these three highly abstract functions. *Intelligence* remains the favorite way to describe differences in reasoning. During the last century, *character* named the distinctive behavioral styles, while *temperament* referred to the variation in emotional reactivity. But the positivism of twentieth-century psychology, exploiting defensible arguments, insists on a marriage of character and temperament so that measurement is less ambiguous. It is not yet possible to evaluate with precision the ease with which a child experiences an emotion, independent of some behavioral display, be it a change in crying, smiling, or other motor reaction. These responses necessarily combine character and temperament. Perhaps future methodological advances will permit separate evaluations of the behavioral and affective qualities, affirming the nineteenth-century separation of public demeanor from its more private foundations.

Although separating the semantic territories of cognition, emotion, and behavior permits scientists interested in one domain to ignore the other two, there are, of course, few thoughts that are bleached of feeling and even fewer emotions that are untouched by evaluation because the reflective frontal lobes and the emotional limbic areas are locked together in circuits that carry information to and from each site. Indeed, it is likely that without the continuing influence of sensations originating in heart, gut, skin, and muscles and transmitted to the frontal lobes by limbic structures, many decisions would appear impulsive or irrational. Antonio Damasio has described a middle-aged man who through surgery lost that part of the ventral frontal cortex that receives neural traffic from the limbic area. Although his IQ remained high and his conversations sophisticated, he began either to make impulsive decisions or to be unable to decide at all. The rationalists who are convinced that feelings interfere with the most adaptive choices have the matter completely backwards. A reliance on logic alone, without the capacity to feel the anticipatory states of joy, guilt, sadness, or anxiety that might follow a particular judgment, would lead most people to do many, many more foolish things. Wise commentators on human nature in our own as well as other cultures have nominated emotion, not logic, as the basis for human civility and prudent selection of alternatives. Even Charles Sanders Peirce, the nineteenth-century philosopher who devoted much of his scholarly life to an analysis of logic and reasoning, understood that emotion, not rationality, guided most human decisions. Listen to Peirce in his Cambridge, Massachusetts, lectures on *Reasoning and the Logic of Things:*

> Men many times fancy that they act from reason when in point of fact, the reasons they attribute to themselves are nothing but excuses which unconscious instinct invents to satisfy the teasing whys of the ego. The extent of this self-delusion is such as to render philosophical rationalism a farce. . . . Reason then appeals to sentiment in the last resort. . . . Reason, for all the frills it customarily wears in vital crises, comes down upon its marrow bones to beg the succour of instinct.

Many economists prefer to assume that selection of a strategy is based only on a rational calculation of the acts that are in the agent's best interest. A few go further to suggest that any other calculus is maladaptive. This extraordinary claim is motivated in part by the fact that it is easier to describe and to analyze irrational decisions, ignoring emotion, than to explain how emotions impact reason. It is in the theorists' interest to deny the relevance of processes they cannot describe rigorously. The human mind likes clearly defined, mutually exclusive categories that are free of inconsistency and can be inserted into calculable algorithms. But that may not be nature's way. It is possible to estimate the economic cost of marrying, having a first child, or submitting an honest tax return, but I doubt that these calculations, even if performed unconsciously, play a major role in those decisions for most people.

The Referents for Temperament

Temperament conventionally refers to stable behavioral and emotional reactions that appear early and are influenced in part by genetic constitution. The focus on the genetic contribution invites both an appreciation of pleiotropism—the fact that one set of genes can have different consequences—and a search for characteristics that, on the surface, seem to have no relation to behavior or emotion—for example, physique, skin color, eye color, or susceptibility to selected illnesses. The behavioral profile associated with high blood pressure or asthma might be as valid a temperamental category as Jung's extrovert. This open attitude invites a broad definition of temperament as any inherited profile that is marked by a distinct behavioral-affective style. One advantage of this permissive attitude is that it mutes worry over whether the most critical feature of an introverted temperament, for example, is a vulnerability to fear, a reactive sympathetic nervous system, or a reserved social manner.

The disadvantage of stressing only one feature that is part of a larger, coherent pattern—a common habit during early stages of inquiry—is that a single feature can belong to a number of different categories. The ability to fly, for example, is characteristic of both birds and bats; both fish and mammals have the ability to swim. It is rare for one characteristic, like a guarded manner, an ectomorphic build, or a mood of depression, to define a single homogeneous group of individuals. I shall adopt the contrasting strategy, which has been generative in biology, of searching for sets of correlated qualities that might have a common origin. The study of temperament is likely to result in faster progress through use of this style of inquiry.

It will also be useful to relinquish, or at least hold in abeyance, the twin ideas that there are only a small number of temperaments and that each is displayed across a broad range of situations. Cognitive scientists are beginning to appreciate the mistake of overgeneralization and are now specifying the context in which a mental process takes place. A similar analytic plan should be implemented with the profile of emotional-behavioral displays that define each temperament.

A third, more subtle error that permeates current theory, as well as nineteenth-century thought, is the imposition of the dimension of strong-weak, and by implication good-bad, on the physiology that mediates varied temperaments. These antonyms are easy to generate and to understand, but they are mischievous. Neurons, axons, and dendrites do not vary in strength. A circuit from the ear to the cortex to the limbic lobe that is easily aroused by an unexpected sound is neither stronger nor weaker than one that is minimally responsive. Further, the easy semantic association between *strong* and *adaptive* has led some scholars to replace the former adjective with the latter. The mind bolts at the possibility of an adaptive but weak system; hence, strong, good, and adaptive become fused into one idea. But there is no a priori reason to assume that a responsive amygdala is more or less adaptive than one that requires more stimulation before it discharges.

The imposition of an evaluative frame on temperamental categories is more obvious now than it was in Galen's era because of the pressure from both pragmatic philosophers and evolutionary biologists to make adaptation the premier criterion to apply to every living form. It will be useful to accommodate to the evidence with less prejudice and to infer the temperaments, no matter how large the final number, from the facts, refraining as far as possible from judging the adaptiveness of the trait. Most Americans would, if asked, probably reply that an introverted temperament is less adaptive than an extroverted one. But after being told that a large number of eminent writers, composers, computer programmers, mathematicians, and scientists were introverts, and that more incarcerated criminals were extroverts, they might wish to change their earlier judgment.

Views of Temperament

The definitions of a temperamental type proposed by the creative scientists most often cited—Buss, Plomin, Rothbart, Bates, Eysenck, Carey, Strelau, Goldsmith, Campos, Cloninger, and Chess and Thomas—agree on four criteria. A temperamental category refers to a quality that (1) varies among individuals, (2) is moderately stable over time and situation, (3) is under some genetic influence, and (4) appears early in life. The disagreements center on the qualities nominated as primary, which are due, in part, to differences in the developmental stage studied and, more important, to the source of evidence.

Almost all of the contemporary work on adult temperament, in Europe as well as America, is based primarily on replies to questionnaires, even though there are serious differences between an adult's self-evaluation and direct observations of that person. For example, when adults fill out a questionnaire, 40 percent state that they are shy, but only 15–20 percent inherit a temperamental bias to be unusually shy. Most adults who say they are shy do not belong to the temperamental category favoring this quality.

Moreover, the questionnaires typically reveal only a small number of temperaments, in part because the items are restrictive. Robert Cloninger believes that the avoidance of danger, seeking of novelty, and dependence on social rewards constitute the primary temperamental types. Buss and Plomin, on the other hand, posit emotionality, activity, and sociability as the three major temperaments. The particular questions with the highest loadings on the three Buss-Plomin temperamental factors ground the abstract words in concrete images. The four affirmative answers that define emotionality, for both men and women, are (1) I am somewhat emotional, (2) I am easily frightened, (3) I cry easily, and (4) I get upset easily. These statements refer primarily to the emotions of anxiety, fear, and depression, not anger, guilt, shame, or disgust. Although subjects were asked about anger, their answers did not correlate highly with the answers to the four questions noted above. Thus, emotionality is probably indexing a combination of conscious fear and depression (inferred from the admission of frequent crying), which is reminiscent of Galen's melancholia. The two answers that define sociability best, for both sexes, are (1) I like to be with others, and (2) I make friends easily. This factor, which is similar to Jung's extroversion and Galen's sanguine type, confounds a desire to be with people—sociability—with a feeling of uncertainty when with unfamiliar people, which is more definitive of shyness. Several investigators have noted the relative independence of feelings of discomfort when with strangers and the motivation to be with friends. A person can be high (or low) on both qualities.

The activity factor has a misleading name, for it seems to refer primarily to psychological energy. The three answers that define it best are (1) I am very energetic, (2) I am always on the go, and (3) I like to keep busy all the time. Adults answering yes to these questions may not necessarily be athletic or walk with a fast tempo; rather, they invest a great deal of psychic energy in goal-related tasks—the opposite of Galen's phlegmatic type.

An appreciation of the origins of most questionnaires and their statistical analyses reveals three serious problems with this method of discovery. Francis Galton, a nineteenth-century scholar interested in the genetics of personality as well as of intelligence, selected from an English dictionary a list of words in common parlance used to describe different kinds of people. This list was sharpened fifty years later by Gordon Allport and a colleague, who also relied on a dictionary. L. L. Thurstone then analyzed the ratings of thirteen hundred people who were asked to use sixty of these adjectives to describe a large number of their acquaintances. Thurstone decided that the sixty adjectives could be reduced to five relatively independent factors. That conclusion was the origin of the current belief that personality consists of five continuous traits: extroversion, agreeableness, conscientiousness, emotional stability, and imaginative curiosity. An important reason why these five emerged as salient traits is that they are among the qualities most Americans and Europeans would first inquire about if a friend said that a new tenant had just moved into her apartment house. These traits help one to decide if one wants to get to know the stranger better.

Scientists interested in temperament conclude that introversion, extroversion, emotionality, psychic involvement in work, and, arguably, responsibility-impulsivity are the five major temperamental types. It is easy to see the similarity between these latter five concepts and the personality factors of extroversion, emotional stability, imaginative curiosity, and conscientiousness. It is important to note, however, that empathy, cynicism, a sense of humor, preference for a gay lifestyle, moral outrage, sensuality, fatalism, and a host of other stable and significant human qualities are missing from both lists.

The fallacy in relying on this form of discovery is obvious. No other natural science decided on its major concepts by going to the dictionary. Imagine what the basic animal species would be if a nineteenth-century biologist had made a list of all the animals named in a dictionary of the time and asked a large number of adults to describe them. Those who lived away from the ocean would never have seen mussels, those who lived on the coast would be unfamiliar with rattlesnakes, and few would have an acquaintance with the platypus. Further, animals that might not be in the dictionary—the coelocanth, for example—would fail to get on the list.

Roger Davis and Theodore Millon offer a second analogy. Suppose an investigator asked a large number of informants from different cultures to describe the physical characteristics of the people they knew. A factor analysis of the terms generated would probably yield factors for sex, race, age, height, weight, and attractiveness. These factors are of some interest, but such an analysis would omit many theoretically significant qualities, would fail to include features not visible to observers—like vulnerability to diseases—and, more seriously, would treat unusually tall and short individuals who had a pituitary disorder as simply extreme values on a continuum of height.

Thus, a serious problem with the current set of personality and temperament traits is their origin. Most questionnaires are limited to qualities described with words taken from everyday conversations. The questions do not violate most people's ethical sensitivities—they do not inquire about preferences for types of erotic play—or ask about deep beliefs, in part because psychologists do not consider attitudes a part of personality. Further, people are not questioned about loyalty to ancestors or a preference for hot or cold foods (as Chinese psychologists might do), or, as Freud would have insisted, about slips of the tongue and dreams. If Nepalese psychologists constructed personality questionnaires, they would ask different questions and, I suspect, infer different personality factors. It is reasonable, therefore, to be a bit skeptical of the claim that the replies to current questionnaires capture most of the significant variation in human personality or temperament.

A second problem stems from the way the answers are analyzed. Typically, psychologists apply factor analysis to the replies of a large number of people, expecting a small number of personality factors. Factor analysis is a mathematical technique that detects the responses that are correlated and presents each of the correlated clusters as a factor. A personality factor can emerge, however, only if the original questionnaire contains several items that reflect the same quality; the more questions dealing with that quality, the more central the factor will be. If, for example, there is only one question that measures a significant but rare characteristic, and the answer to that question is not correlated with others, it will not emerge as a factor. For example, if only 1 percent of a large sample of subjects answer yes to the question "Do you believe the world will be destroyed before the year 2000?" the psychological processes behind that answer would not emerge as a factor because too few subjects answered in the affirmative and their answer would probably not correlate with others on the questionnaire. A factor analysis of the symptoms of the serious adult diseases would yield factors for respiratory problems, cancer, and cardiovascular illness because each has a large number of correlated symptoms. Osteoporosis and glaucoma would probably not emerge as separate factors, even though they are distinct disease states, because they have a small number of symptoms and are less frequent. The omission of less frequent types is a flaw in current questionnaire studies of personality and temperament.

Moreover, the use of factor analysis to discover the basic personality types is based on the controversial premise that the variation among individuals in a particular factor is the result of varying combinations of the same set of fundamental processes. A person who reports that he likes people, parties, action, and jokes would be classified as an extrovert. The factor analysis assumes that the underlying processes that produce a mildly extroverted person are the same as those that produce an extreme extrovert. In some cases, this assumption has to be incorrect. A person with a thyroid disorder or one in the middle of a manic episode may be an extraordinary extrovert but for reasons that are not at all applicable to the mild extrovert.

A third problem is that the current list of presumed basic personality categories is too broad. Emotional stability is presumed to cover all undesirable emotions; there is no differentiation among anxiety, moral outrage, or sexual frustration, even though there is no good reason to assume that adults who become intensely anxious are also prone to anger, disgust, or moral outrage. If the neural bases for specific emotions are different, as they probably are, we should not posit a general factor of emotionality. Similarly, the factor of conformity, or agreeableness, does not distinguish between those who conform to authority and those who conform to peers. In short, the five factors omit too much and are insufficiently differentiated. They represent culturally salient, abstract ideas on which large numbers of American adults seem to vary. That fact is important, but it is an insufficient basis for the claim that these five traits exhaust the significant personality types—case closed. Nonetheless, the five factors do tell us something of interest, even though they do not exhaust the domain of adult temperament or personality.

Temperament in Infants

When infants are the targets of study, it is easier to invent temperamental concepts that appear close to central nervous system processes. Mary Rothbart, an influential investigator, makes ease of arousal to stimulation, which she calls *reactivity*, and the ability to modulate that arousal, called *self-regulation*, the two fundamental temperaments of this first developmental stage. Reactivity refers to the ease with which motor activity, crying, vocalization, smiling, and autonomic and endocrine responses are provoked by stimulation, as measured by response time, intensity, and time to peak magnitude. Self-regulation refers to the processes that modulate reactivity, like attention, approach, withdrawal, attack, and self-soothing. Rothbart acknowledges that reactivity and self-regulation are related, giving the example of a reactive child who first cries at seeing a stranger and, moments later, regulates the distress by withdrawing.

There are, however, some problems with these bold, imaginative claims. First, Rothbart assumes that reactivity can be reflected in any one of the many response systems available to the infant. Thus, both infants who vocalize frequently and those who smile would be classified as reactive. As we shall see in chapters 6 and 7, however, infants who are vocally reactive differ in significant ways from those who display their reactivity through smiling or crying. Rothbart also assumes that autonomic responses—such as a large change in heart rate—as well as vigorous limb movements represent reactivity. Infants who show a large heart rate change to challenge but are not motorically reactive, however, are very different at age two from children who as infants moved their limbs vigorously but were autonomically unresponsive.

Rothbart also fails to specify the context in which the signs of reactivity are displayed. Most four-month-old infants are more reactive motorically to visual than to auditory events, but some are minimally reactive motorically to visual stimuli and smile at human speech. Infants who cry at forced restraint of their hands are different, as two-year-olds, from those who cry at seeing an unfamiliar person, and these two types of children are different from those who smile and babble at the same intrusions. I have not seen an infant who was aroused by every type of event; some were excited by moving sights but not by sounds, and others showed the reverse profile. Thus, reactivity may be too general a construct and should be parsed into different types based on the specific reactions to particular situations. I suspect that when this is done the contextual specificity will be so obvious that the superordinate category will lose some of its theoretical attractiveness.

An example may help. We will describe in chapter 6 a scoring scheme for infant reactions to varied stimuli that kept motor activity, vocalization, smiling, crying, and heart rate separate. We did not create an overall index of reactivity because the correlations among the five responses were low. Further, when we assessed cortisol levels in these infants at five and seven months, those with high cortisol values showed frequent motor activity, smiling, and vocalization but rarely cried. This fact, which was replicated with a group of Guatemalan Indian infants, suggests that high levels of cortisol during early infancy may index the ease of nondistressed reactivity to stimuli. Had we combined crying with vocalization and smiling in order to create an overall index of reactivity, we would not have made this discovery.

But we should not discard the baby with the bath water. Infants do vary in motor activity, vocalization, smiling, and crying, and those who react in one or more of these domains are different in the second year from those who show no reactivity in any of these modalities. Rothbart's notion of reactivity does have merit.

Self-regulation is also too broad an idea. Both withdrawal and approach are self-regulating responses, but these two distinct profiles have different consequences. Every infant does something following an intrusion; hence, all infants self-regulate. The more important issue is the preferred form of self-regulation, whether crying, freezing, turning away, or moving toward the new event. We shall see in chapter 7 that the idea of self-regulation is better conceptualized as quality of arousal. Some infants who react easily assume a joyful state, reflected in vocalizing and smiling. Others who are equally reactive cry when they become aroused. These two types of highly reactive infants become different children.

Jan Strelau places Rothbart's two temperamental categories in the brain by positing two central nervous system processes—excitability and inhibition—an idea that originated in Pavlov's writings. A reactive infant is presumed to have an excitable brain. The infant who regulates arousal well and does not move into a distressed or an excessively excited state presumably has a strong inhibitory system. Although Jeffrey Gray is concerned primarily with the state of anxiety, rather than with temperaments, the two brain systems he describes—the behavioral approach system and the behavioral inhibition system—are related to Strelau's categories. Children with a strong behavioral inhibition system are sensitive to punishment and show behavioral restraint to novelty and anticipated danger.

One problem with all these approaches is that they are top down. Their creators begin with a theoretical ambition to keep the number of constructs at a minimum, without a persuasive rationale for that choice, because the mind prefers a small number of ideal types. Early-nineteenth-century biologists divided the entire animal kingdom into only four types—radiata, molluscs, insects, and vertebrates, not unlike the Greek belief that air, water, fire, and earth were the four basic elements in all of nature. It is true that the animals in each of these four categories are different in form and physiology. But surely it is an error to regard the differences in physiology, morphology, and behavior between salmon and chimpanzees as relatively trivial.

To posit a small number of basic temperaments—or personality types—is analogous to stating that the only two basic childhood illnesses are disorders of the gastrointestinal and respiratory tracts. Diarrhea and colds are, indeed, frequent infant illnesses, but the same virus can cause both diarrhea and a cold. More important, otitis, cleft palate, asthma, and food allergies belong to neither of these two illness categories. It is much too early to decide on the primary temperaments of children by brute force; we need a great deal more information. I believe that future inquiry will reveal a large number of temperamental constructs. Biologists tell us that the human body has 250 different types of cells; even physicists, who strive passionately for unity, acknowledge six different quarks.

It will be useful, given our lack of knowledge, to adopt an inductive frame and remain open to new evidence. Like the late afternoon stroller in a popular Robert Graves poem, we should notice each bird as we walk casually in the forest, but if we spot a particularly beautiful cardinal hidden in a bush, we should stop to capture its loveliness. The first cohort of dedicated scientists has made a significant contribution by slashing an initial path into the forest. It is now time to open up the current abstract concepts in order to detect the larger number that will more closely correspond with observations and, further, to entertain the possibility that types of individuals, not continuous psychological processes, are in closer accord with nature's plan.

What Is a Temperamental Category?

A temperamental category is a changing but coherent profile of behavior, affect, and physiology, under some genetic control, that emerges in early childhood. At the moment, however, it is necessary to rely primarily on the behavioral and affective profile because no one has discovered the specific physiology that forms the partial foundation for any of the types. For example, the temperamental category we call *uninhibited* is defined by very low motor activity and minimal crying in response to unfamiliar stimuli at four months and sociable, fearless behavior in response to discrepant events at one and two years of age. But only about one-third of these uninhibited children, unfortunately not all, show low sympathetic tone (as revealed, for example, in minimal increases in heart rate to challenge). Hence, it is not clear if we should add this biological marker to the definition and require all children classified as uninhibited to possess this characteristic, too. Scientists will one day discover the physiological profile that characterizes most uninhibited children; for now, the behavioral evidence must remain primary.

This is a common historical sequence in medicine. All the infectious diseases were defined initially by their surface symptoms because their pathophysiology was not known. Before we learned that Down's syndrome was due to an extra chromosome, membership in the category was defined only by physical appearance; these children were called *Mongoloid.* Today the chromosomal anomaly, which can be seen under the microscope, is a vital part of the definition. The symptoms of hay fever or eczema provide another useful analogy. A half century ago, before biologists could measure immunoglobulin levels in the blood, the different allergies were defined by the symptoms patients reported. Because skin rashes in the winter and sneezing during the fall appeared to be different, eczema and hay fever were classified as different allergies. But when scientists were able to measure the blood level of an immunoglobulin called IgE, they found that the apparently dissimilar allergic symptoms were both associated with high IgE levels, while the eating of a lobster was not. When the blood level of IgE is used to index the class of allergy called *atopy*, it behaves in some families as if it were due to a single dominant gene. By contrast, the prevalence of hay fever symptoms in a family pedigree suggests a more complex form of inheritance. The use of the biological marker IgE changed the classification of allergic symptoms. Similar changes will occur when the proper physiological evidence is included in the classification of temperament.

Because scientists must rely primarily on behavior in defining temperamental types, it is conservative but rational to group behaviors that appear similar, either in form or in inferred aim. Infants vary in frequency and intensity of crying in response to stimulation or frustration; hence, many psychologists posit a category of irritability. When the biological foundations of irritability are better understood, however, we may learn that infants who cry easily at loud noises have a physiology different from those who cry when their hands are restrained. Nathan Fox, of the University of Maryland, has evidence to support this claim. Further, some profiles that appear different will be placed in the same category because of a shared physiology—as hay fever and eczema share membership in the category of atopic allergy. But we will have to wait for these discoveries. All we can do at present is to form initial groupings by similarity in behavior, recognizing that current classifications will be reshuffled in the future.

The definition of a temperamental category as a coherent profile of behaviors linked probabilistically to an inherited physiology implies a large number of categories. During the next century we may learn that the hyperactive-distractible child and the child with inexhaustible energy belong to separate temperamental categories. The potentially large variety is one reason why I like the metaphor of breeds of puppies to represent the temperaments of children. I hope that the final number will be smaller than the 810 different types Charles Fourier posited in a deductive argument that began with 12 basic feelings and emotions.

The Biological Origins of Temperament

If inherited differences in brain function contribute to temperamental types, there are two places to look for the variations—anatomy and physiology. Although I suspect that most temperaments will be traceable to physiological differences derived from neurochemistry, a few studies implicate anatomy. Domesticated strains of horses and pigs, which are usually less fearful than the wild forms of the same species, have smaller brains than the wild varieties. Some strains of inbred mice explore a novel open field; other strains explore very little. The animals who are reluctant to explore novel environments have larger projections in a specific area of the hippocampus called the mossy fiber terminals. Another example of a relation between anatomy and behavior comes from rats. The density of afferent neural traffic from the body to limbic sites can influence fear states. Two closely related strains of white rats differ in spinal cord inner- vation by axons that originate in the locus ceruleus. This anatomical vari- ation could produce differences in visceral arousal to and behavioral avoidance of novelty.

Nonetheless, it appears likely at the present time that much of the tem- peramentally based variation—it is always foolish to universalize—will rest on differences in neurochemistry and associated physiology rather than anatomy. The large number of chemicals that monitor excitation and inhi- bition in the central nervous system, including at least twelve neurotrans- mitters and thirty neuropeptides, affect their target neurons by adhering to complex molecules, called *receptors*, located on the outside of the cell. The concentration of each of the molecules and the density of receptors are both under partial genetic control. Thus, it is easy to imagine that a person born with a higher than normal concentration of a chemical that affected the excitability of the amygdala or hypothalamus might be especially prone to certain emotional states.

Opioids are one important class of chemical that modulates excitation. The rostral ventrolateral medulla (RVLM), which contains receptors for opioids, is the origin of important projections to the sympathetic nervous system. If some children possessed an unusually high density of such receptors, or a higher concentration of opioids near this structure, excita- tion arriving at the RVLM would be muted and less sympathetic activity would be provoked. This suggestion finds support in studies of monkeys. Adult female monkeys (*Macaca fasicularis*) with very effective, opioid- mediated inhibitory processes display, as expected, lower increases in heart rate in response to stress than animals with less effective opioid processes.

Some children, too, have a low heart rate and show small increases in heart rate and diastolic blood pressure when physically challenged or psy- chologically stressed. This profile of low sympathetic activity could be due to the inheritance of a special opioid chemistry. It is not obvious what word best describes individuals who have a high (or a low) concentration of opioids in that part of the medulla. It does not follow that they necessarily have higher or lower concentrations in all parts of the brain.

Corticotropin releasing hormone (CRH), produced primarily in the paraventricular nucleus of the hypothalamus, is a second molecule relevant to temperament, for it has diverse influences, most of them excitatory. One target of CRH is the anterior pituitary, which secretes the ACTH that stimulates the adrenal cortex to produce cortisol. Another target is the locus ceruleus, which produces norepinephrine, one of the most extensive molecules in the brain and the primary neurotransmitter of the sympathetic nervous system. The norepinephrine synthesized in the locus ceruleus is transported by a large number of branching axons to many parts of the brain, especially the cortex. Surprisingly, these connections are more extensive on the right than on the left side. The neurons that synthesize norepinephrine in the lateral tegmentum send a richer set of axons to limbic sites.

One important function of norepinephrine is to inhibit background neural activity in sensory areas of the cortex so that if an important stimulus occurs, the signal-to-noise ratio will be enhanced and the sensory neurons will be more likely to respond to the signal. A nice example is found in the mitral cells of the olfactory bulb. These cells are inhibited by granule cells whose resting activity is mediated by the amino acid GABA. Norepinephrine inhibits the action of GABA, thus releasing the mitral cells from the restraint imposed by the granule cells. As a result, the sensitivity of the mitral neurons to an incoming odor is increased. If norepinephrine acts in a similar way in other sensory areas, it is reasonable to infer that a person with higher than normal levels of brain norepinephrine would be more reactive to subtle or extremely low levels of stimulation. It may not be a coincidence that newborns with high plasma levels of dopamine-beta-hydroxylase (DBH), an enzyme that catalyzes the conversion of dopamine to norepinephrine, are unusually sensitive to lights, sounds, and new foods at five months of age; at one year they have an intense dislike of unfamiliar foods. It is not clear what term best describes this type of infant; should we call them "overly responsive to stimulation"?

We shall see later that among four-month-old infants who display high degrees of motor activity and frequent crying to visual, auditory, and olfactory stimulation, about one-half are highly fearful when they are one and two years old. Because norepinephrine also increases the excitability of the amygdala and its projections to the corpus striatum, cortex, and sympathetic nervous system, infants born with high levels of central nor-epinephrine may be prepared to be both more reactive and irritable to stimulation during the early months of life and highly fearful later in the first year.

This hypothesis implies that a contrasting group of children with very low levels of central norepinephrine, and therefore lower sympathetic reac-tivity, might be exceptionally fearless. Over half of a group of child psychi-atric patients who also had very low concentrations of DBH, needed for the synthesis of norepinephrine, were boys with severe conduct disorder. This discovery implies that children with very low norepinephrine levels might experience minimal fear over violating parental and community standards, in part because of lower sympathetic reactivity. Because DBH level is under genetic control, it is reasonable to speculate that some extremely aggressive boys with low anxiety over asocial behavior have inherited a chemistry that makes it easier for them, given an environment that permits aggression, to become aggressive and antisocial.

A small proportion of the adolescents and adults, in both the United States and Europe, who commit violent crimes or are chronic crimi-nals—who in turn are no more than one-fifth of all who are convicted of a crime—have lower heart rates than other, less violent criminals or non-criminals. When preadolescent boys from an urban neighborhood that produces more adolescent delinquents than most areas of the city were divided into two groups, one characterized by frequent fighting with peers and another by minimal aggression, the former had significantly lower heart rates while sitting quietly in a chair. One investigator wrote, "From age 11 onward there is significant evidence to suggest a relation between low heart rate and aspects of antisocial behavior. . . . Psy-chopaths are less capable of experiencing fear."

Although the lower sympathetic tone among chronic delinquents or criminals could be due either to medullary or to central processes, there is some basis for favoring the latter mechanism, for persistently antisocial adults also show low levels of activation in the electroencephalogram (EEG). There is a reciprocal loop between the limbic area and the cortex; the more traffic in that loop, the greater the cortical activation. Limbic sites, including the amygdala, make a major contribution to fear, sympathetic reactivity, and cortical activation. Thus, it is possible that the lower heart rate and lower level of cortical arousal of some recidivist criminals might be due in part to a less reactive amygdala, which in turn could be the consequence of a neurochemistry that mutes the activity of the neurons in this and related structures.

The plot thickens. As we noted earlier, the right cerebral hemisphere receives more norepinephrine-secreting axons from the locus ceruleus than does the left hemisphere. As a result, a lesion to the right hemisphere, produced by ligating the cerebral artery on the right side, leads to a greater reduction in norepinephrine than ligation of the artery serving the left hemisphere. Anxious children and adults have greater EEG activation in the right frontal pole, while low-anxious children and adults have greater activation of the left frontal area. Further, if adults smile while viewing film clips provocative of a pleasant feeling, they often show greater EEG activation on the left than on the right side. If they display facial expressions of disgust in response to a repugnant film clip, they are likely to show greater activation on the right side.

It is possible, therefore, that some temperamental qualities are linked to asymmetries in the activity of the left and right hemispheres. One scientist has speculated that differential activation in the two frontal areas of the brain mediates the quality of emotional experience—joy, on the one hand, or fear and sadness, on the other. When activity in the left frontal area dominates the right, a person describes a predominant feeling of calmness, happiness, or satisfaction. When activity in the right frontal area dominates the left, a person reports a mood of sadness, anxiety, tension, worry, depression, or guilt.

The more posterior areas of the brain—the parietal and temporal lobes—are assumed to mediate the intensity of the emotional experience. The emotion is more intense if the right side is more active; the emotion is muted if the left side is more active. We shall see in chapter 7 that ease of becoming aroused is independent of whether the person becomes distressed or joyful.

Thus, there are, theoretically, four types of affective experiences, each linked to a different pattern of neural activity. When the right frontal and the right parietal areas are dominant, the mood is intense anxiety or fear, but when the right frontal and left parietal dominate, the mood is sadness; sadness is a less intense emotion than fear. When the left frontal and left parietal are dominant, a calm mood predominates. But when the pattern of dominance is left frontal and right parietal, the happy mood becomes intense joy. If these profiles of frontal and parietal activation are due, in part, to inherited differences in neurochemistry, the dominant mood of some persons could be influenced, at least in part, by genetic factors.

Adults who acquire brain lesions in the left hemisphere (hence, the right hemisphere is probably more dominant) experience a sudden change in mood characterized by increased worry, anxiety, or depression. When the right hemisphere is compromised by a lesion, the resulting change in affect is more likely to be indifference or euphoria, sometimes associated with sudden, unexpected laughter. The more substantial role of the right hemisphere in mediating the intensity of emotion was revealed when subjects awaiting surgery were injected with a drug (sodium amytal) that inactivated either the right or the left hemisphere. Before and after the injection the subjects were shown photographs of faces displaying either a broad smile, disgust, or a neutral expression and were asked to judge the intensity of the emotion. The adults judged the facial expression as less emotional when their right rather than their left hemisphere was inactivated. Suppression of the right hemisphere led to a greater muting of the perceived intensity of the affect. When normal adults—through use of an ingenious apparatus—processed emotional or neutral films with either the right or the left hemisphere, they judged the films as more unpleasant when they were processing the information with the right hemisphere than when they were processing it with the left. Further, adults with right hemisphere damage were poorer in judging the emotions of faces than those who had suffered left hemisphere damage.

Infants under two years of age who had suffered focal brain damage either in the posterior region of the right hemisphere or the frontal region of the left hemisphere smiled less often than normal children when the mother tried to elicit smiles from them. Although these observations are based on a small number of infants, the evidence is in accord with the idea that the left frontal area is more involved in the mediation of a happy emotional state. Hence, when the left hemisphere is released from control by a damaged right hemisphere, smiling should increase. If the right posterior area mediates intensity of emotion, infants with lesions in this area should show shallower emotion. At the least, this evidence implies an asymmetric monitoring of the quality and intensity of different affect states.

The greater involvement of the right hemisphere in fearful states is even present in rhesus monkeys. Marc Hauser, who filmed monkeys in their natural habitat on a small island off the coast of Puerto Rico, performed a frame-by-frame analysis of their faces when they were displaying expressions of fear or threat to another animal. The most frequent expression was a fear grimace characterized by a retraction of the lips. As with humans, the left side of the mouth began to move slightly before the right side over 90 percent of the time. Because the right hemisphere controls the muscles on the left side of the body, this fact suggests greater involvement of the right hemisphere in the fear grimace.

Although these new facts would not have surprised Galen, they pose a direct challenge to contemporary discussions of chronic moods. Many psychiatrists and psychologists assume that human moods are epiphenomenal to successes, failures, disappointments, conflicts, and defenses, which in turn are products of past experiences. Were we loved? Were we securely attached to our parents? Were we popular in school? Do we have high self-esteem? A person's usual mood is presumed to be a psychological construction built from a history of past encounters. Given a particular childhood, anyone could be sublimely happy or chronically anxious. But this explanation ignores the fact that some people living in abject poverty have lighter moods than those who have had repeated successes. It is difficult to understand T. S. Eliot's chronic dysphoria, given his worldly victories, or the joviality of a homeless man who sleeps most nights on a park bench.

The Measurement of Temperament

We have repeated, perhaps too often, that the meaning of every scientific construct depends on its source of evidence. The most popular source of information on children's temperaments comes from asking parents, most often mothers, to describe or to rate their children on a variety of observable behaviors. The work summarized in later chapters used direct observations of children's behaviors in standard situations. Unfortunately, the correlation between parents' ratings of a particular quality and behavioral observations is modest at best, and under some conditions it is minimal. Thus, statements based on these two different sources of evidence are not synonymous in meaning.

We are not the first to criticize parental reports. Almost sixty years ago, psychologists noted the poor relation between what actually happened during the first year of an infant's life and the mother's descriptions of those events when their children were twenty-one months old. Similarly, Gordon Allport, in his 1937 text *Personality*, acknowledged two serious limitations on adult verbal reports: they may be falsified, and they are less valid if respondents have inadequate intelligence or limited insight.

One reason for the poor agreement between what a parent says and what a camera records is that each parent holds an abstract symbolic construction of the child that removes inconsistent facts. The words we use to describe our experiences, on the one hand, and the perceptual schemata created by the same events, on the other, appear to be stored in different places in the brain. A person with damage in the temporal lobe may be unable to retrieve the name of an attribute of an animal—for example, the tail of a monkey—but can recognize the same attribute when it is illustrated in a picture.

A parent's verbal description of a child competes with a nonverbal representation composed of all prior perceptual and affective experiences with the child. Further, the verbal categories demand a consistency to which the perceptual schemata are indifferent. The mind does not like the categorical awkwardness of an infant who both cries and smiles frequently. Even though such infants exist, most parents will amplify one characteristic and minimize the other. As a result, the infant will be described as frequently fretful or frequently happy, but not both. This deep-seated mental disposition is the basis for one of the most serious flaws in parental report.

Reliance on adult descriptions of children has a hermeneutic quality, for the semantic descriptions are loyal to the special biases inherent in words. Over twenty-five years ago, Charles Osgood and his colleagues demonstrated that people speaking different languages use the evaluative contrast of good versus bad as a first dividing principle in categorizing people, objects, and events. Knives are bad, stoves are good, and descriptions of knives and stoves are guided by that evaluative frame. So, too, with parental report. Mothers distort their children's behavior to fit their scheme of the ideal. The parent who wants an outgoing, happy child and is threatened by a quiet, serious one may deny the child's shyness and exaggerate her sociability. The evaluative frame parents impose on the descriptions of their children colors their answers to all questions. Indeed, the inclination to give socially desirable answers on questionnaires can be more heritable than the personality traits measured by the questionnaire.

A second problem is that parents are not equally discerning in their observations or consistent in their interpretations of their children's behavior. Some parents cannot discriminate accurately among infant cries that are occasioned by restraint, hunger, or overarousal; some fail to detect the difference between smiles of assimilation and smiles of excitement. Thus, scientists who rely on questionnaires must limit their questions to behaviors that are not too specific, such as "Does your child smile a great deal?" Further, the parents' accuracy of description varies with their background and personality. Mothers who never attended college perceive their infants as less adaptive and less sociable than do college-educated parents. Mothers experiencing any kind of stress have a lower frustration tolerance and are prone to exaggerate their infants' irritability. Depressed Irish mothers with their first child were more likely to describe their six-week-old infants as irritable than were experienced mothers or mothers free of depression.

Third, parents use different referents in their evaluations; as a result, they are vulnerable to contrast effects. A young mother who has not had extensive experience with infants has a less accurate base for judging her first child than one with three children. The former is more likely to describe her infant as irritable and demanding than is the mother of three or four children. If the first child was extremely irritable and the second only a little less irritable, but still more irritable than most, the mother will rate the second child as far less irritable than observations reveal because she is contrasting the second with the first child. This phenomenon is also seen clearly in mothers of fraternal twins, who usually rate the two children as much less similar than observers do because the mother exaggerates the differences between the two siblings. The estimate of the heritability of a quality like language skill is therefore higher when the data come from parental report than from observation.

Fourth, scientists can ask the parent to rate only psychological qualities that she understands, in words that are part of a common vocabulary. Hence, most psychologists must restrict their set of temperamental categories to a small number of easily understood ideas—for example, activity level, smiling, fear of novelty or strangers, crying in response to limitations, soothability, and duration of attention to events. But scientists synthesize a temperamental construct from disparate sources of information, some of which are not available to the mother. For example, there is a small group of infants who, in addition to low irritability and frequent smiling, have a low heart rate, low muscle tension, and greater activation of the EEG in the left frontal area. The psychologist may give a novel temperamental name to this combination of qualities, but a mother cannot be asked to rate her child on this abstract category, for she does not have access to the child's heart rate, muscle tension, or EEG readings. Put plainly, because the parental reports describe only the child's observed behaviors they cannot differentiate between fearful dispositions that derive from a temperamental bias and those that were acquired without any biological contribution. If a person trips coming down the stairs, we cannot know if the accident was due to a defect in the person's vestibular apparatus or the result of a misperception of the visual cues. Additional information is necessary to make that distinction. The same is true of temperamental categories.

Fifth, as we shall see in chapter 7, a small proportion of young infants (fewer than 10 percent) display very rare reactions to specific events in the laboratory. One infant may scream following a large drop in heart rate at hearing an unexpected human voice; another will display extreme levels of motor excitability on seeing a colorful mobile. These statistically rare responses are unlikely to be observed at home. But even if a vigilant mother happened to note these reactions when they occurred, they would be forgotten if they were inconsistent with the infant's more typical behavior. The parent's prototype of the child would tempt her to dismiss these rare reactions. The small number of infants who show these less common behaviors, however, often become atypically fearful in the second year.

Sixth, mothers often impose different meanings on the same behavior. One mother will regard shy behavior as an index of her child's sensitivity, another will interpret it as caution, and still another will regard it as an index of fearfulness. Thus, if a questionnaire asks, "Is your child afraid of other children?" the first two mothers will answer negatively, while the third will answer in the affirmative, even though the children behave similarly with peers. The answer to the apparently simple question "Is your child afraid of strangers?" is valid only if the investigator can be certain that all respondents share a similar understanding of the question and, more important, that the phrase "afraid of strangers" refers to a set of observable events that most people would agree reflect that feeling.

The ambiguity regarding the meaning of a subject's answers to questionnaires is seen clearly in a study of identical and fraternal adult male twins who were asked to fill out a popular personality questionnaire. An affirmative reply to the following two statements was heritable:

It is hard for me to find anything to talk about when I meet a new person.

It is hard for me to start a conversation with strangers.

But an affirmative reply to the following two statements showed minimal heritability.

I feel nervous if I have to meet a lot of people.

I doubt whether I would make a good leader.

The two pairs of statements seem to refer to the same psychological trait, namely, a feeling of uncertainty or anxiety with others. Yet the use of slightly different language in the second pair of statements led to an entirely different conclusion regarding the genetic contribution to introversion and its emotional features. Richard Shweder has written forcefully on the difficulty of translating Hindi words for emotions into English. Less extreme, but nonetheless real, differences exist among parents within our own society who have grown up in different class or ethnic groups. The words *afraid* and *anxious* do not have the same meanings to all informants.

Most concepts rest on more than one feature. Because the concepts that describe behaviors, acute emotions, and chronic moods usually have a great many features, respondents vary in the feature they select as primary when they answer a question about a child's behavior. The question "Is your child fretful?" requires the respondent to think of a context that represents the best example of that characteristic. If one mother regards the feeding situation as most typical, while another treats separation from the mother at the day care center as the best representative, the two parents may give different replies, for there need not be a high correlation in fretfulness across the two different contexts.

When the question asks about an emotion, like cheerfulness or fear, the opportunity to emphasize different features is enhanced. If scientist and parent focus on different features of the concept, they will impose different meanings on the question and the scientist will misunderstand the parent. Wittgenstein suggested in *Philosophical Transactions* that every sentence, written or spoken, assumes a comparison sentence. The sentence "She likes the mountains" has one meaning if the implied comparison is the seaside but a somewhat different meaning if the silent comparison is the desert. Thus, when a parent answers a query about her child's fear of strangers, she is unconsciously comparing the idea of fear with other related concepts that could refer, for example, to anger, sensitivity, or developmental maturity. We cannot expect uniformity among parents in the outcome of those private comparisons, and as a result the parental replies can have different meanings.

Gottlob Frege also argued that language does not always capture a thought accurately. Each parent has an ensemble of perceptions, feelings, and ideas about her infant, and there is no word or phrase that captures the complex combination of a word's direct referents and connotations. Consider the inadequacy of language to describe the bond of love in a marriage of thirty years or the beauty of a winter sunset over the Golden Gate Bridge. George Trumbull Ladd appreciated that "the conception of any feeling differs *toto coelo* from the feeling itself."

When adults answer questions about past emotional reactions in their children or in themselves, they cannot help evaluating what they thought happened or should have happened. The answer to the question "Are you afraid of crowds?" is guided by an interpretation of the person's usual reactions in crowds. The answer might not be a sensitive index of how anxious the subject actually was, in part because the relevant vocabulary is sparse. Adults who admit to feeling anxious when speaking in public show a sharp rise in heart rate when they anticipate that challenge. But they continue to report feeling anxious even after they have been given a drug that decreases the rise in heart rate and blood pressure that often accompanies the feeling of fear. Thus the statement that one feels fearful need not be accompanied by much physiological change.

Most of the time questions about past emotions measure a person's inferences about his past behavior, rather than the actual feelings that occurred. Words name categories well and are sometimes accurate in describing dynamic events, but they are imperfect for describing feelings and sensations. Languages were invented to communicate ideas. The mind assigns experiences to relevant categories and is maximally efficient in communicating information packaged in those categories. The complaint "I feel sick" provides the physician with some useful information, but it does not specify the patient's feeling tone. There is no word to describe the experience of a crimson leaf falling in an October wind, the fragrance of a spring forest, or the feeling after standing for an hour in a crowded bus on a humid August afternoon. The passenger on the bus might say she felt tired, tense, or annoyed, but these words fail to capture the envelope of sensations in consciousness. The words *angry, tired,* or *afraid* may tell another person what class of event probably occurred to provoke a change in feeling, but they do not describe the quality or intensity of what was consciously experienced.

Everyone learns that the words *fear, afraid, tense,* and *anxious* apply to feelings associated with times of danger, failure, rejection, or criticism, and people use these words when the appropriate situation arises. The correct application of any of these words throughout the language community does not, however, mean that everyone experiences the same intensity or quality of feeling in consciousness. Color-blind children learn to call ketchup red and grass green, even though they experience color very differently from those with normal color vision. Because the dramatic range of intensity and quality of fear is not captured accurately by available language, it is necessary to gather other information and to be a bit critical of indexes of this family of emotions that rely only on words.

We celebrate poets because they come close to capturing the world as it is sensed, even though they often accomplish this with metaphors. Our admiration reflects an appreciation of how difficult it is to find the right words to capture feelings and sensory patterns. Landscape painters do better; no poet approaches Monet in capturing the Seine at dawn. George Trumbull Ladd may have been right. Parental descriptions of the emotions of children are interpretations of the child's behavior; they are far from veridical descriptions of what the child experienced.

There are, therefore, many unique influences on parental descriptions of young children's emotionally based behaviors that are absent when behavior is coded by disinterested observers in specific contexts. That is why the agreement between parents and observers is low; the correlations between the two are rarely above 0.4 and usually much lower. One mother who described her child as sociable wrote to our staff a few days after she had watched her daughter interact with two other unfamiliar girls in a laboratory playroom: "This was a real eye-opener for me. I always thought my child was outgoing and social. I now realize after watching her and reading the articles that she is actually uncomfortable with new people."

In one highly relevant investigation, fifty infants were observed at home weekly between the ages of four and six months. Both parents and observers were consistent over time in their evaluations of the babies' dominant mood, approach to unfamiliarity, activity, and intensity of response. But the correlations between the parents' ratings of these qualities and the observers' evaluations of the same qualities in the same children were low (about 0.2). The authors concluded, "The most important implication of these findings is that the large published literature on parent reports of their infant's behavioral style may be severely flawed." In a similar study, observers visited the homes of five-month-old infants on two occasions and noted the frequency of smiling, vocalizing, fretting, crying, banging, and kicking. The observers also asked the mothers to make ratings of these same behaviors in their infants. Once again, the two sources of data were in poor accord; the correlations averaged only about 0.2. One investigation relevant to the work described in this book compared the laboratory behavior of 135 one-year-olds in response to four discrepant events that often elicit fear—for example, a toy spider or masks—with the mothers' ratings of their children's fearfulness. Again, the correlations were low, and the mothers were remarkably inaccurate in predicting how their children would behave in response to each of the unfamiliar events presented in the laboratory.

Agreement between parents and observers remains poor even when the children are older and can describe their fears; parents and ten-year-olds do not agree when interviewed separately about the children's moods or problems. Neither do parents and teachers agree on the presence of behavior problems in preschool children. One team of investigators noted, "Our results question the assumption that these checklists measure stable traits or characteristics of young children." An exhaustive review of the degree of agreement among parents, teachers, and peers with respect to the occurrence of children's behavioral and emotional problems, in over 269 samples, revealed poor agreement on whether a child was excessively fearful, aggressive, or impulsive. The average correlation between two different informants was less than 0.3. After a review of the relevant literature, one psychologist wrote, "Good agreement between parents and child is almost never the rule."

The primary basis for diagnosing a child or adult as belonging to a particular psychological category is the clinician's evaluation of the patient's report of her mood, symptoms, and behavior. The professional debate among psychiatrists is not about the validity of this source of evidence but about the criteria that should be used to diagnose pathology, given this information. If a patient denied all feelings of anxiety, he probably would not be classified as anxious, even though observations over the course of a month revealed extreme caution and restraint or, to pull the string tighter, his blood levels of norepinephrine and cortisol were three times the normal value. By contrast, internists do not rely on a patient's report of symptoms alone but utilize X rays and laboratory tests of blood, cerebrospinal fluid, and urine. Husbands and wives know that understanding the true state of the spouse requires accommodating to more than the other's complaints. It is surprising, therefore, that psychiatrists continue to rely, sometimes completely, on patients' descriptions of their behavior and mood as the only basis for a diagnostic classification.

Arthur Kleinman, a psychiatrist sensitive to the cultural influences on diagnosis, provides a telling example. He asks readers to suppose that ten American psychiatrists are each asked to interview ten Native Americans who are in the early weeks of bereavement following the death of a spouse. The psychiatrists agree that seven of the Indians report hearing the voice of a dead spouse calling to them as the spirit travels to the afterworld. Thus their diagnosis is reliable. But deciding whether the report of hearing voices is a sign of an abnormal mental state is an interpretation that requires knowledge of the behavioral norms for bereavement in this cultural group. In many Native American tribes, hearing the voices of the spirits of the dead calling to the living is an expected and commonly experienced part of the feeling of loss that accompanies bereavement; it does not portend a protracted depression. In this case, we have a reliable judgment of what was said, but questionable validity of the diagnosis of mental disorder.

Parental descriptions of children's emotions and behaviors are simply not close enough to the events that the investigator wishes to know. I borrow from Paul Meehl an idea that conveys the nature of the problem. Suppose botanists wished to know the relation between the amount of rainfall and the magnitude of grass growth in a community over a two-year period, but they could not get direct access to the actual measurements of the amount of rainfall or grass growth. The only sources of evidence they had were the number of telephone calls to plumbers regarding flooded basements, as an index of rainfall, and the number of telephone calls to repairmen who fixed lawn mowers, as an index of the growth of grass. The correlation between the two measured variables is likely to be much lower than the magnitude of the relation between the phenomena of primary concern. For many questions in psychology, the indexes used are as indirect as the two in the above analogy.

At a deeper level, it may be that the verbal categories parents use to describe their children's behavior are incommensurable with the categories derived from frame-by-frame analyses of films of the children's behavior. One cannot substitute one set of concepts for the other, because some of the words used to describe the film analyses do not exist in the vocabulary of the parental informants. For example, the language used by Carroll Izard to describe the changes in an infant's facial muscles that accompany the brief pain of pricked skin awards a special meaning to the word *anger* that is different from the meaning understood by many parents. Thus, scientists cannot treat the parents' use of the word *anger* as if it had the same meaning Izard intended.

In a sense, the current reliance on what people say about themselves, or about others, is a return to the hermeneutic tradition of the Renaissance and away from the behavioral and experiential phenomena that must also be understood. Parental reports and direct observations of children have unique qualities, and the best we can say is that the two sources of evidence have related meanings. Progress in the study of children's temperament will remain slow if scientists continue to rely exclusively on the statements of parents, without any other evidence. If Thomas and Chess had filmed the infants in their study for twenty hours, in both home and laboratory, in addition to interviewing their parents, I suspect they would have invented a different set of temperamental categories.

Wise people have been observing children and constructing theories of human nature for a very long time. If talking to parents about children's behavior and moods were such an accurate source of information, the field of personality would be one of the most advanced domains in the social sciences rather than one in disarray. I interpret the failure of our progress to mean that verbal statements describing the behaviors of others, by parents or friends, have some, but limited, value.

Social anthropologists have reacted to the recognition that verbal descriptions of beliefs and feelings are a special form of evidence with the surprising claim that scholarly study of human behavior, culture, and social systems is qualitatively different from the epistemology of biology, chemistry, and physics. This radical suggestion confuses differences in the bases of valid knowledge with differences in sources of information. The concepts of cultural anthropology—including conflict, status, anxiety, religion, power, transcendence, witchcraft, guilt, and solidarity—are most often inferred from conversations with informants. When ten village elders tell a scientist that most members of their community are afraid of witches, the anthropologist accepts those statements and usually does not gather other kinds of evidence to verify the presence of that emotional state, arguing that the only important meaning of *fear of witches* is the statement of several informants. Anthropologists usually do not measure other reactions, such as sleep disturbance or physiology.

Biologists are less dogmatic and more skeptical of a single basis for inference. For example, biologists who use similarity in bones to trace genetic relations among species often arrive at conclusions different from those who rely on similarity in proteins. But the latter do not claim that their science of evolutionary biology is qualitatively different from that of the biologists who measure bones. Both groups of investigators recognize that the sources of information may vary, but the strategy of using objective evidence to make inferences is the same for both groups.

Whether the informants are parents describing children or elders in a New Guinea village reporting their beliefs, verbal statements represent a special and useful form of evidence. Because of the variety of semantic and syntactic forms in human languages, it is often difficult to translate statements about feelings and beliefs originating in one culture into the language of another. But neither can the language of protein chemistry be translated easily into the language that describes hundred-thousand-year-old bones. Thus, the anthropologists' argument that the study of human societies and personality rests on principles fundamentally different from those of the natural sciences is not persuasive, given the rationale that has so far been marshaled for it. If this claim is correct, it will have to be based on very different considerations.

The replacement of questionnaires with direct observations of children will bring an advance in understanding as dramatic as the one following E. H. Weber's decision, in the 1830s, to study the human perception of relative weight directly, rather than relying only on a person's verbal introspections. Although modern scholars treat Weber's experiments as simple and even obvious, it was creative in the early part of the nineteenth century to ask people to lift two objects in succession and to say if the second was heavier than the first. This simple manipulation led to the insight that the heavier the initial object, the more weight had to be added to the second in order for the person to perceive that the second was heavier. These data led to the concept of a just-noticeable difference. It is unlikely that this fact, and the exact functional relation discovered later by Fechner, would have been discovered by talking to people about their perceptual experience when they lifted plates and rocks.

The direct measurements of behavior and physiology—not necessarily in laboratories—have revealed principles that simply could not be discovered by talking with people or asking them to fill out questionnaires, no matter how many questions are asked or how carefully each is composed, because the psychological principles are not available to the subject's consciousness. Moreover, if the scientist is unaware of the principle to be discovered she will not ask about it. Let us suppose that the discovery that adults who have greater activation of the right frontal area are often dour of mood is valid. No interview or questionnaire, no matter how sophisticated, could discover that relation. Each way of gathering information is limited and can inform us about only a part of the phenomenon we wish to understand. That flaw is as applicable to the EEG and to positron emission tomography (PET) as it is to questionnaires. Therefore, the more varied the sources of evidence, the clearer the vision of the secret that nature is holding in her closed hand. The validity of this point, so obvious in the history of science, has been noted by almost every creative investigator who has written on how to do science. It is time for students of human personality to acknowledge, and better yet put into practice, that bit of wisdom.

Continua versus Categories

A final issue requiring attention is the choice between continuous behavioral dimensions and qualitative categories in describing temperaments. Thomas and Chess viewed the three major types of children—easy, difficult, and slow-to-warm-up—as temperamental categories, while treating the variation within each of the nine dimensions as continuous. For example, they described the approach-withdrawal dimension as if all infants could be placed on a continuum with respect to the tendency to withdraw or to approach unfamiliarity. By failing to say otherwise, they rejected the possibility that infants who usually approach unfamiliar people might be qualitatively, not just quantitatively, different from those who usually avoid strangers. The difference in connotation between the continuous, quantitative trait and a qualitative type is captured by comparing "Mary has unusual opinions" with "Jane is paranoid." These two women are qualitatively different.

Although temperamental categories have become more acceptable the idea of qualitative types has not, and most essays on temperament retain the notion that each characteristic is continuous. Scientists prefer this strategy because most of the characteristics that are called temperamental refer to behaviors—like crying, smiling, or avoidance—for which measured values usually form a continuous distribution. Every child can be placed somewhere on each distribution of scores.

The disciplines that study behavior, thought, and emotion during this century have favored continua over categories and linear over nonlinear relations. These presuppositions, fundamental to Newtonian physics and the philosophical writings of Kant and Leibniz, dominate the modern psychological laboratory, partly as a consequence of the dissemination of statistical procedures in the interval between the two World Wars. By the Second World War the use of inferential statistics became the mark of the sophisticated social scientist; investigators who ignored statistical analysis were treated as less competent. The correlation coefficient, t-test, and analysis of variance should be computed on continuous variables. Hence, psychologists found it useful to assume that there were no qualitative types of people; all humans could be treated as substantially similar in their sensations, perceptions, and memories. Statistical analyses were performed on continuous scores produced by different experimental conditions, not by different kinds of people. The only common exceptions were gender, age, and occasionally social class.

But entities like rocks and flowers, as well as bacteria and viruses, are patterned structures that are qualitatively different from each other and from other classes, even though scientists can invent a quantitative dimension common to several classes. The temperature and volume of a pot of water are continuously measured values, but ice, liquid, and steam are qualitatively different phenomena that emerge from particular values on these variables. The molecules of epinephrine and norepinephrine are very similar in size, weight, and atomic composition, but the functions and sites of production of the two molecules are qualitatively different.

Similarly, the reactivity of the autonomic nervous system, which contributes to temperament, cannot be placed on a continuum of arousal.

Patients with the profiles called panic, obsessive-compulsive, and social phobia showed qualitatively different patterns of autonomic response in heart, muscle, arterial vessels, and skin. The scientists wrote: "Anxiety cannot be viewed as a psychologic or physiologic continuum ranging from normal to severe pathologic anxiety. Each anxiety disorder has not only distinct subjective symptoms but distinct physiologic response patterns as well." Although the EEG spectra produced by the human brain can be described in terms of the continua of frequency and amplitude, no physiologist claims that the state of sleep, with its unique EEG signature, differs only quantitatively from the state of alertness in a performing cellist. The two states are considered qualitatively different. The small proportion of neurons in the temporal cortex of monkeys that respond specifically to objects like faces are qualitatively, not just quantitatively, different from the other cells in the vicinity.

Each scientific domain, during some period of its development, is vulnerable to believing in the existence of an invisible phenomenon that the future proves to be a fiction. Those who hold the false belief are distracted by it and invent schemes to explain or accommodate to the fiction. Descartes and Kant assumed an immaterial soul; hence, their philosophical analyses were directed at trying to understand how the body and the soul separately affected thought. Newton assumed an ether in the cosmos—an idea that lasted until Michelson and Morley's experiment on the speed of light led to a questioning of this concept. Physicists hope that the current concept of dark matter is not a replacement of Newton's ether.

In modern discussions of differences among children and adults, the assumption that most of the variation in a quality is continuous and rests on the same processes is, I suggest, analogous to Newton's ether. But the statistical analyses that psychologists want to apply require that assumption. When the evidence violates this premise, as it does in bipolar depression, the scientists may make the phenomenon a qualitative category but insist that the remaining profiles are continuous and are probably acquired through experience.

One rebuttal to the argument for qualitative distinctions points to the fruitfulness of the physical concept of energy. Fire, friction, and light are qualitatively different, but each can be placed on a single, continuous measure of energy. But this argument mutes the fact that it makes a difference whether the source of energy is, for example, sunlight or friction. A growing plant requires the energy contained in photons; a spring rose will not blossom if it is warmed by rubbing. Although the theoretical concept of energy refers to a continuous quantity, the functional relations in which energy is a mediating process often depend upon qualitative features of the energy—in this case, its source. The discovery of radiation and a quantum mechanical view of atoms motivated Bohr, Heisenberg, and others to invent mathematics that would explain the new experimental evidence. The mathematics that was created assumed qualitative, not continuous, energy bands; radiation behaved as if it came in different types.

The physicist Pierre Duhem, in a 1954 essay titled "Quantity and Quality," noted that most scientists try to describe their data in mathematical statements. Because mathematics assumes continuous magnitudes as a primary axiom—the most popular statistical procedures make a similar assumption—most psychologists classify all phenomena in terms of continuous dimensions. This premise is linked to the belief that every psychological phenomenon will be understood eventually as a result of the addition of these magnitudes. But Duhem adds that nature also consists of qualities that cannot be formed simply by adding quantities. Duhem recalled Diderot asking jokingly, "How many snow balls would be required to heat an oven?"

The modern concept of species, so fundamental in evolutionary biology, is a qualitative category defined by reproductive isolation and by clusters of correlated features or dimensions. The many graded dimensions that characterize an animal species—weight, length, metabolic rate, life span—are not of equal importance. Two species that share ten out of eleven features are not always more similar in their evolutionary history than those that share seven of eleven qualities. Mice and dogs have two eyes, two ears, and four limbs; rely on internal fertilization; and nurse their young, but only the latter animal bonds to humans. That single feature is a vital component of the cluster of characteristics that defines dogs, and it cannot be removed without changing the category in a serious way. That is why it is not possible to arrange the varied strains of macaque monkeys on a continuum of either fear or arousal to unfamiliarity. They must be viewed as qualitatively different types of animals.

The same conclusion holds for temperamental types. A large number of healthy adults and patients were studied extensively with both psychological and physiological procedures. An analysis that treated the sample as composed of smaller groups of qualitative types led to more coherent understanding than an analysis that treated the data as constituting continuous dimensions of personality or autonomic arousal. For example, a small group of adults was characterized by an ectomorphic body build, reactions to challenge with large increases in diastolic blood pressure and heart rate, and subjective reports of high anxiety. A second group was characterized by a mesomorphic body build, low sympathetic reactivity, and a subjective mood of satisfaction. These two groups could not be placed on any theoretically reasonable continuum. As David Magnusson has argued, types of people, not continuous variables, are stable over time.

David Lykken and his colleagues at the University of Minnesota use genetic evidence to argue for the usefulness of categories. Some psychological types are the result of combinations of genes in different locations that form a special configuration. When only one genetic component is missing, a totally different phenotype is produced, not just a less extreme version of the one that defines the original pattern. The mammalian eye provides an example; if the animal is to be born with a normal eye, it is necessary for a number of genes on different chromosomes to act together. If one of the genes is missing, the result is not a smaller eye but a very abnormal eye or no eye at all. This fact is one reason why siblings in the same family can be very different on some psychological qualities, even though siblings share about one-half of their genes. The Minnesota scientists call these configural traits *emergenic*; some are temperamental categories.

Extroversion in adults behaves as if it were an emergenic quality because fraternal twins are much less similar in this characteristic than they should be, given their shared genes. Perhaps unusual talents in mathematics, music, and athletics are also emergenic, for it is rare for genius to run in families. Lykken notes that Karl Gauss and a Hindu mathematician, Srinivasa Ramanujan, had extraordinary mathematical gifts, although each man grew up with uneducated parents who were not distinguished intellectually in any way.

In a hypothetical illustration, assume a psychological trait that requires inheriting two recessive genes, each with a frequency of .20, in each of five different locations. The prevalence of people with this configuration is less than one in a trillion—a rare occurrence. The expected concordance in a pair of fraternal twins would be less than 1 percent. Lykken and his colleagues suggest that the most interesting emergenic traits will be qualitative, not continuous. If this argument is valid, then the current

practice among psychologists of studying samples of thirty to fifty individuals is almost guaranteed not to detect these rare types, for there may
be no subject with the relevant profile in the sample. We shall see support for this claim in chapter 7.

Perspectives in Describing People

People rely on two different perspectives in describing others. They name
particular behaviors, emotions, and talents, either in an ipsative, intraper-
sonal frame (*Margaret is better at tennis than she is at golf*) or a comparative interindividual frame (*Margaret is better at golf than Mary*). Both
frames imply a quantitative difference in a characteristic. There are exceptions, of course; most comparisons of Mozart with other composers imply
that Mozart's talent was extraordinary and did not lie on a continuum
with that of other composers.

The perspective changes, however, when a person is described as a
member of a category and the comparison is with someone belonging to
another category. Consider the following two descriptions:

1. Mary is happier than Joan.
2. Mary is sanguine but Joan is melancholic.

The use of the category terms *sanguine* and *melancholic* in (2) implies
that the two women differ in a set of correlated characteristics, rather
than in only one dimension, and therefore are qualitatively different.

A category is a profile of characteristics and features, some of which can
be continuous, some discrete. The category vertebrate, compared with
invertebrate, rests on the discrete vertebral column as the defining feature.
A trout does not have more of something that an oyster possesses; the fish
inherited a qualitatively novel feature. Some psychologists—Paul Meehl,
for example—have suggested that when categories refer to real types in
nature they should be called *taxa*. All taxa are classes, but not all classes are
natural taxa (large red octagons are not natural kinds).

The concept of categories can lead to a more valid understanding of
some phenomena. If three children with fevers of 100, 101, and 102
degrees are infected with three different viruses, it may be useful to use
three different treatments for the infectious agents rather than view the
patients as differing only in the magnitude of their fever symptom. Measures of intelligence in infants under eighteen months do not predict IQ

scores in later childhood if the investigator treats the IQ scores as a continuum. But if one treats intelligence scores under 80, between 81 and 110, and over 110 as three discrete categories, prediction of childhood ability is much improved.

Discovery is a second advantage of categories. If a large population contains a small group—say 10 percent—who possess very high (or low) values on three qualities, but the relation among the three variables is low for the rest of the population, statistical analysis will reveal no significant association among the three variables for the entire group, and the investigator will conclude that these variables are independent. For example, in a sample of one thousand adults, there is no relation among fatigue, difficulty in breathing, and high levels of IgE. But the 10 percent who are high on all three characteristics belong to a diagnostic category called asthmatic. Similarly, there is no correlation in a large population of children among large increases in heart rate and blood pressure to stress, high levels of muscle tension, and fearful behavior. But the 10 percent who show all four characteristics belong to a category we call inhibited.

This principle can be stated more formally: If each of many dependent variables has more than one origin and these origins are independent, but one origin is common to all the dependent variables for a small proportion of the sample, then the correlations among the dependent variables will be low, even though there is a category of individuals that is high (or low) on all of the variables.

Scientific constructions of nature permit both categorical types and continuous dimensions. A prejudicial dismissal of the former because it complicates research is inimical to progress. Historically, the preference for describing an object as a member of a distinct category or as the sum of a number of dimensions has cycled. Prior to the rise of empirical science, the Platonic premise that each object had a unique essence invited a categorical view of nature. But the successful application of mathematics, especially the calculus and its assumptions of continuous qualities, to predict physical phenomena led to the overthrow of the ancient idea.

The apparent victory of continua over categories in seventeenth-century mathematics was frustrated by the ascendance of biology, for Linnaeus could not place the fauna on continua like size, weight, longevity, or size of litter. Linnaeus was forced to accommodate to the obvious categorical nature of animal species. Thus biology opted for categories, as Ernst Mayr has described:

The physical world is a world of quantification and of mass actions. By contrast, the world of life can be designated as a world of qualities. Individual differences, communication systems, stored information, properties of the macromolecules, interactions in ecosystems and many other aspects of living organisms are prevailingly qualitative in nature. One can translate these qualitative aspects into quantitative ones, but one loses thereby the real significance of the respective biological phenomena, exactly as if one would describe a painting of Rembrandt in terms of wave lengths of the prevailing color reflected by each square millimeter of the painting. . . . Many times in the history of biology brave efforts to translate qualitative biological phenomena into mathematical terms have ultimately proved complete failures because they lost touch with reality. . . . Quantification is important in many fields of biology, but not to the exclusion of all qualitative aspects. . . . Species, classification, ecosystems, communicatory behavior, regulation, and just about every other biological process deals with relational properties. These can be expressed, in most cases, only qualitatively, not quantitatively.

The origins of psychology in pathology and perception were closer in spirit to biology than to physics; Freud, Jung, Wundt, and Titchener preferred categories. As we saw earlier, however, a revolution occurred when the statistics of Fisher, Galton, and Pearson were taught to graduate students in psychology after the Second World War. These statistics were intended to analyze continuous dimensions, like speed of response and IQ scores. Soon the tail was wagging the dog, and categories were treated as if they were messages of the devil. The prejudice was aided by a frustrated cohort of clinical psychologists who felt exploited by psychiatrists in medical settings. Because psychiatrists used qualitative diagnostic categories, it was good for the morale of the psychologist to denigrate the backward medical model and to favor the more statistically sophisticated continuous dimensions of the psychologists in the academy.

Thus, most psychologists who study human behavior prefer to compare individuals on one or more continuous dimensions. The constructs of achievement motivation, introversion, anxiety, sensation-seeking, and impulsivity are a few examples. Many investigators study a single dimension that is only one component of a temperamental type. For example, parents and teachers compare children on the dimension of sociability, with the tacit assumption that it is continuous and that all highly sociable children belong to a homogeneous group. Yet this quality is only one component of a correlated cluster present in about one-third of highly sociable children who also show low sympathetic tone, low levels of cortisol, a mesomorphic body build, dark eyes, dark hair, and high positive affect. This diverse but correlated set of characteristics defines the category of uninhibited children, who are qualitatively different from most highly sociable children. Thus, the two sentences "Mary is more sociable than her peers" and "Mary is an uninhibited child" have different meanings. More important, shy, minimally sociable children are not the complement of highly sociable ones. The shy child is defined by a different set of features.

The relative usefulness of continua or categories depends on our purpose. If we wish to explain a single particular event—for example, why Mary was elected class president—we usually choose the continuous dimension of sociability. If, however, we wish to explain a large number of different behaviors over an extended period of time, it is wiser to select a categorical description.

The two descriptions are related to the distinction between situational and personal explanations. We recognize a distinction between behaviors limited to and created by a temporary, local condition (impatience while sitting in a car on a crowded highway) and behaviors that are part of a stable, coherent personality. Compare these sentences:

1. Mary was happy at her birthday party.
2. Mary is a happy person.

In (1) we imply a temporary state, whereas in (2) we imply a more permanent cluster of features.

Most psychologists are more interested in the variance attributable to contexts than that attributable to persons because of the assumption that behavior is influenced by settings. This tension is present in the construction of the two sentences above. The following two propositions seem to have the same connotations, although they begin with different ideas.

1. Frequent eating is a characteristic of obese people.
2. Obese people eat frequently.

The topic of sentence (1), which is an act, does not occur continuously; hence, the mind focuses on the situations that might motivate the act of eating. In sentence (2), however, the focus is on a stable characteristic of some people. Similarly, sentence (1) below, which begins with an action in a setting, implies a context that can be changed easily, while sentence (2) implies a set of permanent characteristics that belong to some children.

1. Becoming quiet with unfamiliar adults is a characteristic of inhibited children.
2. Inhibited children become quiet with unfamiliar adults.

The first sentence tempts the reader to compare becoming quiet with talking and to minimize any special characteristics of the child. Sentence (2) leads the reader to compare inhibited with uninhibited children and to minimize the influence of the social situation. Sentences attributing the causes of action to the permanent qualities of individuals, rather than to characteristics of situations, tempt readers to assume that biological processes rather than contextual events are causal. The mind-body duality reflects, in part, a complementarity between the more transient and the more permanent qualities of organisms.

Psychology has cycled from a preference for stable categories of people, characteristic of nineteenth-century writers (hysteria was a category, as was savage and introvert), to more malleable dimensions invented after the First World War because of a politically motivated desire to believe that all human qualities were acquired in social interaction and were amenable to change through education and altered social conditions. That is one reason why Watson's behaviorism and the learning theories it spawned were celebrated during most of this century.

The assumption of a continuously strengthened habit or talent, established gradually through practice and repeated conditioning experiences, works well as an explanation for a great many human behaviors, like playing chess, typing, and hitting a backhand down the line. But this assumption fares less well in explaining reactions that originate in the emotional arousal generated by unfamiliarity, attack, or loss. These emotional states are qualitatively different from each other in their pattern of neural activity, phenomenology, and consequent behaviors. A child's scream of fear to a masked adult is not to be treated as more or less intense than a cry of hunger or sobbing to the loss of a toy. Each is a qualitatively distinct cry. Emotional states are biologically prepared responses released by particular events, and we believe that temperamental types differ in their susceptibility to these emotional states.

A Caveat

Although it will seem obvious, it is wise to state explicitly that many differences among children may have little to do with temperament. Temperamental differences affect mainly variation in emotional mood and type of reactivity to intrusions and have far less relevance to acquired knowledge, opinions, beliefs, and the skills that children learn in school. Our current knowledge indicates that the motivation to perform well in school, the willingness to help a friend, loyalty to family, tolerance toward others, and a host of other motives and beliefs are minimally influenced by temperament. Put simply, the contents of the mind are determined primarily by exposure; the initial emotional reactions to new knowledge are influenced by temperamental processes. The prejudice between Croatians and Serbs was learned; the fear of being hurt as a result of that ethnic antagonism and the courage to court danger to oppose ethnic cleansing are partly temperamental. A great many psychological phenomena will not require an understanding of temperament, even though understanding variation in emotional states will benefit from an acknowledgement of these ideas.

Temperamental qualities have been missing from explanations of development during most of this century, as genetic factors were absent from essays on evolution during the brief period between the publication of the *Origin of Species* and the positing of genes at the turn of the century. Darwin and his immediate successors believed that environmental factors—in the form of natural selection—were the main source of the variation among animal forms. If the climate changed in the Amazon basin, new species would emerge. Darwin's critics accepted the idea of evolution but disagreed with his claim that natural selection alone could account for the formation of new forms. Something else was needed. Modern biologists appreciate that the formation of a new species also requires new DNA patterns. The organism makes a contribution to its evolution, and every new environment, no matter how enduring, will not have the same effect on all animals. This idea, called the modern synthesis in evolutionary biology, is also essential to our understanding of the extraordinary variation in human behavior.

CHAPTER THREE

The Family of Fears

The outcome of any serious research can only be to make two questions grow where only one grew before.

—THORSTEIN VEBLEN

Although most feelings are experienced more keenly than perceptions or inferences, there is, oddly enough, less cultural accord on the basic human emotions than on the essential cognitive processes. The ancient Greeks and Chinese agreed with modern scholars that perception, memory, and reasoning were fundamental intellectual activities, but their views on the fundamental emotions diverged. Tung Chung-shu, a Confucian scholar writing about 150 B.C., omitted surprise and disgust from his list of the primary human feelings but treated anger and hate, which to modern minds seem to be variations of the same state, as separate, equally fundamental emotions. A third-century Sanskrit text nominated sexual passion, anger, perseverance, and disgust as primary emotions because their acceptance or rejection defined a morally praiseworthy life, whereas fear, amusement, sorrow, wonder, and serenity were secondary feelings. The implication of this hierarchical division is that shame, guilt, anxiety, pride, and empathy are glosses on one or more of the primary affects.

The lack of consensus on the classification of the human emotions stems, in part, from a deep division of opinion on the bases for civility and morality. The ancient Greeks and Romans, as well as medieval Christian philosophers, were concerned with the disruptive affects of anger, jealousy, envy, and sexual passion; hence, these states assumed special status. David Hume, one of the brightest stars of the Enlightenment, celebrated the perceptually less salient, but benevolent, emotion of sympathy to transform feelings from a dangerous alien to an ally. Although Kant disagreed with Hume's friendly posture toward emotions, he contributed to the evolution of the modern conception of emotion as a benign, even healthy, component of our humanity, in part because human pleasure began to compete with civic order as a criterion for evaluating human feelings.

A concern with temperament requires an analysis of human emotions, for a vulnerability to some acute feeling states, as well as chronic moods, is a central feature of most temperamental types. The seminal controversy is the significance awarded to the logically separate, but psychologically entwined, features of each emotional state. Most commentators agree that acute emotions are patterns composed of some (or all) of the following components: (1) a precipitating or incentive event, in a context, is accompanied by (2) changes in motor behavior, especially face and posture, as well as in central and peripheral physiology; (3) an evaluation of both (1) and (2) may, but does not always, lead to (4) a change in a consciously experienced feeling that might be named.

Theorists with different biases vary in the emphasis they place on each of these last three features. When Walter Cannon criticized William James's suggestion that feedback from the periphery was the origin of an emotion, he assumed that a change in an animal's motor behavior was as valid an index of an emotional state as the statement "I am afraid" from a person deprived surgically of feedback from the autonomic nervous system. The problem, of course, is that one component of a complex pattern is not equivalent to the complete pattern. Every cough does not signal tuberculosis; every furrowed brow does not reveal worry.

But despite the disagreement on the profile that defines each human emotion, there is consensus that fear (the word derives from the Old English term for danger) and anxiety (the word derived from the Greek word meaning "to press tight" or "to strangle") warrant distinctive status because they vary in incentive, behavioral response, evaluation, and subjective feeling. It is likely, but not proven, that they also differ in physiology.

Our interest in inhibited and uninhibited children invites a deep analysis of both fear and anxiety. Encounter with a potentially dangerous external event is the prototypic origin of fear. In contrast, the state of anxiety, which is less reliably accompanied by facial and bodily reactions, is defined by increased tension, distractibility, and dysphoria associated with the anticipation of an event one would like to avoid. Although most cultures treat both states as inherent to the human condition, anxiety assumed a special significance after Freud made it the basis of neurotic symptoms. Some current technical reports use fear and anxiety interchangeably; for example, a patient who is phobic of spiders may be called fearful and anxious in the same paragraph because the psychiatrist's motivation is to find a drug that will reduce the unpleasant state, rather than to locate the basis for or the exact nature of the state.

The Meanings of Fear States

There continues to be debate over the distinctiveness of the physiological profiles that characterize fear and anxiety, the genetic and environmental contributions to vulnerability to each state, and the primacy of each as a source of psychopathology. The ancient Greeks were not so much interested in fear or anxiety as in the emotional states that accompanied the seriously deviant profiles of mania, depression, and delusions. The Greeks believed that external events provoked dangerous emotions through alterations of the body, but that the soul determined the particular emotion that would be experienced consciously—whether fear, anger, jealousy, or sadness. This view is remarkably similar to the modern constructivist position that assumes an emotional state to be a cognitive judgment of the combined perception of visceral information in an environmental context.

The Greeks, like the modern Balinese and Nepalese, thought envy, jealousy, and anger were more significant causes of mental illness than fear or anxiety because the former disrupted social harmony. The soul of one who had led a moral life was protected from the perturbations set off by the strong emotions and, therefore, from mania or melancholy. The soul that permitted jealousy and anger to rise lost this valuable amulet. Thus, psychopathology had ethical implications in Plato's century; it signified a failed morality.

Aristotle naturalized the emotions. By removing their moral connotations he set the stage for almost a millennium of ethically neutral, materialistic explanations of feelings. The *pneuma* was the material substance that permitted an emotion to occur. The specific emotion experienced owed its existence to a particular organization of the *pneuma* (a hypothesis not unlike Freud's arguments about the different patterns of libido in the oral, anal, and phallic stages). Although fear was one of the states, it did not enjoy a special place in human nature.

Fear assumed greater prominence during the medieval centuries when worry over God's wrath became a preoccupying concern. St. Augustine, who nominated fear as a fundamental emotion, distinguished between two states of fear. Both could be provoked by violations of moral standards, but they differed in the undesirable event anticipated. One state is best described as a fear of being punished for a sin, by God in this life or the devil in the next. The second state falls midway between the modern understanding of guilt and anxiety over rejection because of the contemplation or commission of an amoral act. This latter state, the product of temptation, leads the agent to anticipate being forsaken by a beloved or by God and, as a result, to feel uneasy. Because Augustine made no reference to the fear states created by novelty or conditioning, it is fair to conclude that he did not recognize them or, more likely, believed they were very different feelings. Most significant is the fact that Augustine saw fear as adaptive because it helped humans behave morally. John Bunyan, almost a thousand years later, reasserted that fear of God was a blessing, for it permitted one to love the Deity. Reflect on the dramatic change in premise from this seventeenth-century claim that fear is a requisite for love to the contemporary view that fear restricts the ability to love.

Existentialist views provide a stark contrast to medieval thought. The fall of traditional religious standards, combined with the social estrangement and geographic mobility that followed the Industrial Revolution, generated uncertainty as to which ethical standards deserved fierce loyalty. Kierkegaard's community was losing its moral imperatives and the capacity for intense moral emotion and vigorous moral outrage. Further, identification with community and family had become less urgent than it had been two centuries earlier. Many adults felt they could not always rely on family or friends for support because individual freedom and self-actualization had become more pressing missions. Each adult confronted the fact that he was free to decide which goals to pursue, whether or not they were in accord with the desires of family or the community.

Kierkegaard and later Heidegger and Sartre detected, before most in their society, the significant changes in psychic life that history had created. Rollo May's popular and influential summary of existentialist thought in *The Meaning of Anxiety* described the release from traditional standards felt by many middle-class Americans and Europeans. May recognized the flaw in Freud's claim that conflict was a primary source of human anxiety and realized that Kierkegaard had diagnosed correctly the first signs of affective detachment from community and family that was feeding a novel basis for worry. Kierkegaard described this dysphoria, which he called *despair*, as growing out of the uncertainty of not knowing which standards to use as guides for choice. His prescription was a leap of faith that constituted the highest human passion. The early-twentieth-century novelist Per Lagerquist understood this mood. In his short story "The Eternal Smile," God answers a dead soul, who has inquired what God intended for humans, "I only intended humans would never be satisfied with nothing."

Liberated from earlier directives and without a strong identification with institutions or community, people felt free to act as they wished. But because many were not sure what goals they should seek, W. H. Auden named our era "The Age of Anxiety." Although Kierkegaard was prescient in sensing, as early as the 1840s, the mood that would explode in Europe over the next century, Auden's diagnosis required special historical conditions, especially a working class demanding more autonomy, fragmentation of village life as a result of industrialization, and a middle class pushing to be free of the last restraints of medieval Christian ethics. These forces came together to make it possible for many individuals to realize that they had a choice in their daily decisions. The uncertainty created by that recognition, like Hamlet's vacillation, was promoted to the position of the most significant determinant of anxiety and, by inference, the most fundamental human emotion.

The mind is always prepared for uncertainty; local conditions determine its target. May's error was to assume that the major source of uncertainty in his historical time was also the primary source of anxiety in all historical periods. The existentialist diagnosis was correct; the assumption that the contemporary mood in Europe reflected a universal truth about all human nature was not. John Calvin had made a similar error four centuries earlier when he wrote that fear of God's wrath was the quintessential human concern. May failed to appreciate that the separateness and burden of choice characteristic of his time and place would not be understandable to an elder in a Malay tribe or a Tibetan village. Even if such informants were helped to understand May's message, I suspect they would not agree with him. Humans are capable of worrying about a great many things; a particular culture can promote one idea to a dominant position, but only for a while and only in some places.

Freud's Influence

If the Greek celebration of sexuality had persisted until the nineteenth century and Christian philosophy had not treated sexual passion as dangerous, sexual conflict would not have been widespread when Freud entered medical practice and he would have composed a different theory of personality. Although Freud's premises were formed just a few decades before those of Sartre and Heidegger, he seemed indifferent to existentialist ideas. In *Inhibitions, Symptoms, and Anxiety*, published in 1926, Freud shared his most mature ideas on the nature of anxiety and the reasons for the variation in this state, making anxiety more psychological and much less physiological. The important change was the decision to define anxiety as a conscious feeling provoked by a perception of the dangers of physical harm and loss of a source of love. Anxiety did not refer to processes beyond awareness and did not, as he had thought earlier, derive from the repression of libidinally rich ideas. Further, it was the excessive anxiety, and not the observable inhibition of behavior that anxiety often produced, that was the neurotic symptom.

Although Freud acknowledged that all infants were born with a preparedness to experience anxiety, his original—and controversial—suggestion was that the later development of anxiety required a conflict over sexuality. The primary danger for males was castration. Anxiety over this possibility led to a repression and transformation of the original, true source of danger to a symbolic substitute. Freud used the case of little Hans as an illustration. The anxiety-arousing idea of castration by the father was repressed and transformed into a fear of being bitten by horses, which in turn led to inhibition of activity and a reluctance to leave the house. Freud did not suggest explicitly that Hans was temperamentally vulnerable to becoming phobic. In a single paragraph at the end of the slim monograph, however, he rejected the environmental explanations of variation in fearfulness proposed by Adler and Rank and sided with the more popular view that children differed inherently in their vulnerability to fear. By stating that the cause of the variation "is an organic factor which operates in an accidental fashion in relation to the constitution," Freud argued for the relevance of temperament. It is surprising, therefore, that in the exchange of letters with Jung Freud rejected the suggestion that constitutional factors rendered some people especially vulnerable to anxiety and insisted that conflict was the only important basis for an anxious, introverted, or phobic profile.

It is also puzzling that Freud was reluctant to acknowledge the obvious fact that novelty made children fearful; this idea was popular with a majority of his colleagues and prevalent in the literature with which he was intimately familiar. Surely Freud saw children display fear in new places or when confronted by a stranger. Why did he deny those every-day observations? Freud confronts this puzzle in chapter 8 of the mono-graph. After noting that infants and young children become fearful when they are alone, in the dark, or with someone they do not know, he antici-pated Bowlby by arguing simply that "these three instances can be reduced to a single condition; namely, that of missing someone who is loved and longed for." And then, by exploiting a linguistic trick, he argued that fear of loss of a loved one resembled castration anxiety, for both represented the loss of something valuable. Apparently, Freud hoped the reader would regard the two states as identical simply because the word *loss* occurred in both statements.

Freud may have ignored unfamiliarity as a source of fear because of his concern with chronic anxiety, not the temporary fear of a new place that vanishes after several minutes. Moreover, the fact that adults, unlike chil-dren, do not display an obvious reaction to a stranger or an unfamiliar room made it easier to assume that fear of unfamiliarity was a temporary feature of childhood. Finally, Freud had a powerful drive for parsimony and consistency. He wanted only one source of anxiety. The power and aesthetic appeal of his ideas would have been diluted if he had posited several different origins. He did not heed Francis Bacon's warning, "Let every student of nature take this as his rule that whatever the mind seizes upon with particular satisfaction is to be held in suspicion."

As many have noted, Freud's ideas were not accepted by his commu-nity. The suggestion that a woman might be afraid to leave her home because she feared she might attempt a sexual attack on a stranger was surely counterintuitive and, as it turned out, incorrect. Freud's arguments would be most reasonable to that portion of the population who were experiencing tension, uncertainty, and guilt over sexuality and were try-ing to cope with these feelings. The theory would be less credible to those who were not experiencing much sexual conflict or to those who had repressed sexual motives so profoundly that they were not aware of this source of tension. Freudian scholars have argued that his ideas were more popular in England and the United States than on the European continent because more members of the two former societies were in a transitional state in which sexual ideas had become salient, but were still uncomfortable, concerns. It is also likely that the notion of mental health as a feeling of freedom from arbitrary societal restrictions would have greater appeal to members of egalitarian societies like the United States.

Freud's genius was to realize that an unusual fear could be a disguised derivative of conflict. His error was to insist that sexual conflict was the dominant cause of anxiety. Although he wrote that real, neurotic, and moral anxiety were different states, he paid no more than lip service to those distinctions and, most of the time, claimed that the neurotic anxiety derived from sexual conflict was the only important cause of symptoms.

Freud's view of anxiety was seriously different from Sartre's philosophical reflections. Freud always seemed to have a goal for each day and may never have experienced the existential angst of waking on a bright morning with no responsibility so burning it could not wait for another cup of coffee. Had Freud been born half a century later, he might have written May's *The Meaning of Anxiety* instead of *Inhibitions, Symptoms, and Anxiety*.

Fear states ascended in theoretical importance in Western societies because they came to be regarded as promoters of pathology, rather than as restraints on impulses that disrupt the community. Prior to Freud, fear was treated in the West as an inherent quality that mediated civility; the twentieth-century observer regards fear as hampering an adjustment to daily demands. Hence, psychoanalytic theory charged that fear was the culprit mood to be excised. If life's assignment is to perform tasks requiring control of hedonistic motives, fear is an ally, not an alien force. If, however, the assignment is to gain friends, fall in love, and take risks for material gain, fear is an enemy. When history altered the script people were to follow, fear displaced desire as the emotion to subdue. If humans must restrain greed, lust, and aggression, then control from above—in the form of will—is a prerequisite. But an agent's will is less potent when fear is the demon to tame, for it is more difficult to banish fear than to restrain actions aimed at attaining a desired goal. Thus history relegated the will to the ash heap of ideas where phlogiston and the ether lay gathering dust. The belief that humans can and should be free of fear and anxiety is one of the distinguishing illusions in Western thought in this century.

The Neuroscientist's Conception

Neuroscientists are imposing Aristotle's materialistic frame on human emotions. From Darwin's careful descriptions of the changes in facial muscles that signal an affect in animals to pictures of cerebral blood flow in phobic patients, the hope is to find the circuit in the brain responsible for an emotion. Not only is there no soul in these descriptions, a fact that would have disquieted Descartes, but there is little room for the thoughts that Stanley Schacter and George Mandler believe are necessary components of every emotion. In the neuroscientist's laboratory, thoughts are epiphenomenal, contributing to—but not at all necessary for—an emotional state. A rat with an intact amygdala shows enhanced body startle when a flash of light that had signaled shock in the past occurs a few seconds before a brief, unexpected blast of loud noise. The same rat without an amygdala does not show the enhanced startle. These facts are interpreted to mean that the amygdala, and especially the central nucleus, is a necessary participant in, and perhaps the origin of, fear. These conclusions imply a faith in a single, essential state with a set of variations.

Philosophers, as well as many social scientists who would have chosen philosophy had they been born two hundred years earlier, are attracted to ideas that describe abstract states, unconstrained by the context in which they are realized and the historical sequence that preceded them. Compare a typical psychological statement—"Anxiety has a curvilinear relation to performance"—with a typical biological one—"Heat loss is a function of the ratio of body surface to body mass." Although these two statements may appear similar in a formal sense, closer examination reveals their profound differences.

First, the biological sentence has a set of consensual measurement operations and metrics. All biologists understand that heat loss is measured in calories and mass in kilograms. Because the psychological sentence lacks similar agreement, its meaning and validity are ambiguous, for truth value depends on the specific indexes of anxiety and task performance used.

Second, biologists understand that the exact form of the function relating heat loss to body size depends upon the specific context of measurement—whether the person is at rest or jogging, sunbathing or swimming in a cold pool. The physiological mechanisms provoked when a person is immersed in 45-degree water are somewhat different from those activated when the person is lying on a beach in 90-degree weather. Because the physiologies are different under the two conditions, the exact relation between heat loss and size in the two contexts is different, too. The psychological sentence is silent on how the context influences the relation, even though the biological and psychological processes activated when a person is alone brooding about an ill spouse are different from the person's state after being bitten by a venomous snake. To write about anxiety without stipulating a specific context is to write half a sentence and therefore an incomplete thought. The practice of generalizing terms for psychological processes across contexts leads many to assume that the nature of an emotional state does not change when everything else does.

Gottlob Frege recognized this problem and attributed it to the human tendency to treat the separate elements of a sentence as the basic units, as linguists often do, rather than treat the entire sentence as a unit. Frege believed that the basic unit in scientific description was the entire proposition, not the noun phrase representing a topic or the predicate that described it.

Propositions assume the form of a function or an argument. A function states a general abstract relation among variables—for example, "Anxiety affects quality of performance." But arguments contain the concrete referents that award particular meanings to the function.

The statement "Anxiety bears a curvilinear relation to performance" is a function. But consider the following two arguments:

1. Magnitude of rise in heart rate bears a curvilinear relation to the speed with which small pegs can be placed in small holes.
2. Self-reports of anxiety bear a curvilinear relation to the number of words answered correctly on a vocabulary test.

Empirical research suggests that the first statement is often true; the second is not. Too many psychiatrists and psychologists write as if there were only one argument for a function that contains the word *fear* or *anxiety*, as if these were autonomous essences that transcended time and location and could be applied to any person in any situation. Use of the terms *fear* and *anxiety* must include a specification of the context in which that state is being generated and the nature of the measurements. The feelings produced by a rattlesnake in one's path, a friend's cool greeting, identification with a psychotic parent, criticism, and, yes, choice are different in their physiology, phenomenology, and envelope of anticipated actions. Future research will illuminate this issue, but given the current ambiguity it seems wiser to opt for specificity and posit different states of fear and anxiety, each defined by a profile that combines an incentive, a pattern of physiological reactivity, a set of thoughts, an envelope of behaviors, and a subjective feeling state.

The family of human fears can be likened to the families in animal phylogeny. Although the varied primate species share more features with one another than they do with rodents, nonetheless, monkeys, gorillas, baboons, and chimpanzees remain distinctive classes that react differently to challenge. One basis for this claim comes from the animal laboratory. We noted in an earlier chapter that scientists have bred, over many generations, a strain of rats called Maudsley reactive that show fear when placed in an unfamiliar environment; the signs of fear are defecation and failure to explore the unfamiliar place. A complementary, less fearful strain, called nonreactive, defecates very little and explores the same environment actively. It is tempting to assume that the reactive strain is biologically vulnerable to a variety of fear states, not just fear in a novel place. But the evidence frustrates a leap to that universal. Although reactive rats do not enter the dark arm of a maze and become immobile when placed in water—two signs of fear of novelty—they are not different from other rats in the ease with which they learn to avoid a compartment in which they were shocked when a tone, which had signaled electric shock in the past, occurs. The reactive rats do not learn to run from the compartment to a safe area any more quickly or efficiently than other animals. This fact indicates that a vulnerability to fear of novelty does not imply an equal vulnerability to the acquisition of a conditioned fear of pain and implies that the two fears are acquired through different physiologies.

The modern neuroscientist interested in emotion brings a second bias to research that was also prominent in eighteenth-century essays. Although Enlightenment writers returned to Aristotle's naturalization of the emotions, they imposed the abstract opposition of pleasure-displeasure on each emotion. The opposition of pleasure and displeasure was a materialistic translation of good versus bad, which retained the Platonic imperative to seek the good and the Christian declaration to love God and avoid evil. Fear, sadness, envy, and anger were unpleasant; joy, interest, and sexuality were pleasant. This evaluative categorization led to a muting of the differences among the emotions within each of the two opposed classes and to an exaggeration of the differences between states assigned to contrasting evaluative categories. It is likely that the words *anxiety, anger,* and *anguish* are all derived from the Indo-European root *Angh*.

Enlightenment scholars wanted to explain behavior, will, and intention in a parsimonious, logically coherent fashion. Introspection invites the conviction that each of us acts in order to achieve a pleasant feeling. It is a simple leap from that intuition to the grand extrapolation that all human emotions revolve around this dichotomy. Human consciousness misled Enlightenment philosophers, for the recognition that one is feeling pleasure involves more evaluation than does the feeling of fear. The Greek cynics regarded pleasure as a product of reflection, requiring a cognitive comparison with a prior feeling of pain and thus not primary. The state of fatigue following coerced labor is judged to be unpleasant; the fatigue following completion of a task one wished to finish is not. Aristotle came close to this insight when he suggested that pleasure accompanied the normal exercise of one's faculties and the actualization of a potentiality. Because people vary in their talents, they must also vary in the performances that give pleasure—whether a forehand slam, a well-crafted sentence, or wise advice to a friend. No single bodily state defines a human judgment of pleasure because it is, finally, an evaluation added at the end. We will make faster progress in our understanding of human emotions—and of fear in particular—if we set aside the idea of pleasure-displeasure and proceed directly to the conditions that generate each of the human emotions.

Origins of Fear States

At least three classes of events evoke fear states that, I believe, are physiologically and psychologically distinctive from one another and from anxiety. The class called *innate releasers,* larger in animals than in humans, refers to events with special physical characteristics that have a high probability, although always less than 1.0, of producing a fear state that is relatively independent of prior experiences. A single exposure to a cat can produce in a laboratory rat a fear state that will last for a while and generalize to other novel situations. Some scientists believe that this class of fear has a long evolutionary history and award this state to invertebrates. Every vertebrate species is biologically prepared to withdraw, to attack, to become immobile, or to issue a distress call to a small class of events that might signal potential harm. Among chickens, a head containing eyes with a ratio of pupil to eye that is a little over one-half has the maximal power to produce immobility. Indeed, in many animals, any pattern that resembles two staring eyes usually produces a fear state. Biologists regard the eyespot patterns on the wings of many moth species as an adaptive marking that deters birds from attacking them. In human infants and young children, a looming object, a sudden loud noise, or an unexpected change in posture elicits immobility, a fearful facial expression, a sharp cry, or all three in succession.

Certain calls produce a fear reaction in birds and primates, but sounds seem to be less potent innate releasers of fear in humans. A sudden touch or a fast movement toward or intrusion into a person's body space is more likely to produce freezing or reflex retreat. Many children will play happily with an unfamiliar toy, but if it suddenly starts to move toward them, they will retreat and cry. The power of snakes to produce a fear state without prior exposure is controversial, but most scientists agree that very little experience is needed to create a fear of snakes because of their unusual shape and form of movement. Isaac Marks, a British psychiatrist who has written an informative book on fears, recalls an incident with his two-and-a-half-year-old son:

He had never seen snakes nor did he know the word for them. I carried him over rocky terrain from a car to a beach at low tide. On the dry sand were exposed thousands of dried skeins of brown, black seaweed about a foot long looking like myriad dead eels or tiny snakes. . . . As soon as the boy saw the dried seaweed on the sand, he screamed in terror and clutched me tightly trying to stop me from sitting on the sand. When I touched the seaweed he shrieked and refused to do the same. . . . The next day he touched the seaweed a bit more readily but was still obviously afraid. A week later he was able to throw the fronds away but was still unhappy to leave them in his hand. He gradually lost his terror with continuing exposure to the frightening situation.

George Trumbull Ladd's 1895 text in psychology devoted fewer than two pages to fear—none to anxiety—and he limited the discussion to the biologically prepared reaction of fear to thunder, dark, and strangers. Ladd treated fear as a unitary state and argued, without the advantage of facts, that an adult's fear of God was on a continuum with the child's fear of snakes. John Locke rejected this idea, arguing that a child's fear of the dark was learned.

The second, more frequent basis for fear in humans is the result of conditioning, in which a distinctive stimulus has become associated with a physiological state and/or behavioral reaction. Less than seventy years after Ladd's text, some scientists wrote with certainty that most childhood fears were learned through conditioning or imitation and were not due to innate processes.

A child can acquire an avoidant response, but not necessarily a fear state, by observing another. Even a monkey will avoid a snake—real or toy—if it watches another monkey display behavioral signs of fear of the object. If the sight of someone displaying avoidance of a snake elicited a fear state in the observer, the subsequent avoidance by the latter could be regarded as a conditioned fear, with the snake as the conditioned stimulus. But it is not certain that the passive observer always experiences a fear state. For that reason, I do not include observation as a primary basis for acquiring a fear state, even though children are likely to develop a fear of animals or lightning storms if their parents become distressed at these events.

The unexpected pain of an inoculation in a doctor's office generates a special physiological profile and psychological state. The pattern of visual, visceral, and olfactory cues at the time of the inoculation very quickly becomes capable of eliciting the fear state on a later date. Watson was overzealous when he claimed that any stimulus could easily become a conditioned signal for fear. It is difficult to condition fear to the sight and smell of flowers but easy to do so to the mask of a witch. Thus, the conditioning of fear is relatively easy when the conditioned stimulus is one that has the power to elicit a special aroused state. Snakes and spiders have this power; flowers and puppies do not. Most phobias are to objects and situations that have this biologically prepared power to create uncertainty: heights, closed places, bridges, large animals, and airplanes. Few have reported a phobia to roses or down comforters. Some patients who suffer from panic attacks develop a fear of leaving the safety of their home—called *agoraphobia*—because of an acquired fear of having a panic attack while alone in a store or on the street. In this case, the thought of being alone on a street can be a conditioned stimulus for the very unpleasant state produced by the prior panic attack, and a conditioned fear of leaving the home becomes established. Morton Prince, founder of the psychological clinic at Harvard University, anticipated this modern interpretation of agoraphobia in 1912. His insight was rejected, however, both by those loyal to psychoanalytic theory, who were certain that the fear was sexual in origin, and by the more materialistic physicians who believed that the symptom was due to a brain disturbance.

A third source of fear is unfamiliarity—events that are slightly different from the cognitive representation of those experienced in the past. Technically, these events are called *discrepant*, meaning that they share some, but not all, critical features with an existing schema that was acquired in the past. One of the most fundamental truths psychology has managed to extract from nature is that new associations are formed between two external stimulus events or between events and ideas or feelings. Experiments in twentieth-century laboratories affirmed that, in this case, earlier philosophical intuitions were correct. But a related principle, no less significant, is that the more discrepant, or unexpected, the stimulus event, the more likely a new association will be formed. This fact is robust because discrepant events provoke the limbic system and, like punctuation marks in a text, signal the beginning of an important message.

In some Far Eastern cultures, the fear created by an unexpected or discrepant event—for example, news of a tragedy—is viewed as dangerous. Tibetan villagers believe that states of sudden fright cause the soul to leave the body, resulting in malaise, lethargy, and a loss of energy. This belief was shared by many nineteenth-century European physicians. A Glasgow physician sent a short communication to the *Glasgow Medical Journal* describing a woman who was looking out the window when a man passing on the street "thrusted a singed sheep's head close to the window pane. She screamed and her screams brought her mother, who found, after she got her quieted, that her mind was completely deranged and has remained in that state up till this time."

A transformation of the human face or body is the quintessential feature of the objects we call monsters (see figure 3.1). Seventeenth-century Europeans regarded monsters as they did other unexpected, undesirable

Figure 3.1 Monstrous Races (1493)

Hartmann Schedel, *Liber chronicarum* (Nuremberg, 1493), fo. 1080. Taken from K. Park and L. J. Daston, "Unnatural Conceptions," *Past and Present* 92 (1981), p. 38.

events, like earthquakes, floods, and volcanic eruptions. A century or so earlier, these events were signs of God's wrath.

Fear of the unfamiliar is not present at birth because the newborn animal has no acquired knowledge, and therefore no event can be discrepant from an acquired representation. Further, the brain must have matured to a state that permits the animal or child to compare the event in the perceptual field with his acquired knowledge by first retrieving the latter and then detecting the discrepancy between past and present. This state of brain maturation appears in humans at six to nine months of age; that is why fear of strangers does not appear before this time. Rhesus monkeys mature more quickly than human infants, and fear of the unfamiliar emerges at two-and-a-half to four months. Rhesus monkeys being raised in isolation in laboratories were exposed regularly to slides of various scenes on a screen in their cage. Some scenes depicted monkeys in a variety of poses, including threat. The monkeys showed no signs of fear until they were two-and-a-half to three months of age, when they suddenly became fearful of pictures of monkeys exhibiting threat postures. Three months in the monkey is analogous to about nine months in the human infant, the time when, universally, infants show obvious fear reactions to unfamiliar people and to unexpected separation from a caregiver. By the first birthday, infants display fear in response to a variety of unfamiliar events. One-year-olds are so sensitive to discrepancy that they even show more intense fear when an experimental cymbal-clapping toy is programmed to have unpredictable durations of silence than when the periods of silence are of equal duration and therefore predictable.

Fear of the unfamiliar is responsible for the phenomenon of imprinting in birds. A newly hatched bird will approach and follow a moving object, typically its mother. A few days later, when the brain is more mature, the bird recognizes that another adult bird is unfamiliar and avoids that animal. As a consequent, the young bird remains imprinted on the mother. Similarly, the fear reaction to unfamiliarity appears in puppies at five to seven weeks, and the critical period of bonding a puppy to its owner is between three and twelve weeks; That is why new dog owners try to become familiar with their pets in the first three months. Fear of the unfamiliar is also responsible for the observation that an animal's physiological reaction to cold, heat, or shock is much greater on the first than on all subsequent exposures. The novelty of an event is always a critical determinant of the body's reaction.

James Sully, the Grote Professor of Philosophy of Mind at University College, London, was a frequent and respected contributor to the popular literature on children's development at the end of the nineteenth century. In an 1895 essay on children's fears in *The Popular Science Monthly*, Sully focused exclusively on unfamiliarity as the major basis for fear, offering everyday examples observed in his own child:

It seems plain, it is the ugly transformation of something familiar and agreeable which excites the feeling of nervous apprehension. Making grimaces—that is, the spoiling of the typical familiar face—may disturb a child even at the early age of two months. Such transformations are, moreover, not only ugly but bewildering, and where all is mysterious and uncanny the child is apt to fear.

Sully supported the popular view, also held by Pierre Janet, that a weak nervous system rendered a person especially vulnerable to fear. That is why children were more fearful than adults and why loud sounds, which imposed a greater shock to the brain than visual events, often produced fear. Sully reflected local prejudices when he suggested that lack of knowledge renders a person unusually susceptible to fear. Fear was frequent in children because "they are naturally timid as all that is weak and ignorant in nature is apt to be timid."

One Fear State or Many?

We believe it is useful, given the evidence and our incomplete level of understanding, to treat the fear states produced by innate releasers, conditioning, and unfamiliarity as related but different from each other and from the state of anxiety. A detailed examination of the biological foundations of anxiety reveals that many different neurochemicals can influence fear-anxiety states; hence, it is likely that each chemical profile mediates a different, albeit related, state. It is significant that physiological patterns vary among patients who have different kinds of anxiety disorders.

Eighteenth-century Chinese scholars, as well as Eskimo and Yoruba informants, would agree with this declaration. The latter two societies do not have a single word for fear or anxiety but rather use different words to indicate the cause or the target of a particular state; for example, there is a term for fear of being with people, another for the state of mind that prevents sleep, and still another for a fear of leaving home. The fact that each context is uniquely labeled implies a specific affective feature to each of the states. Most non-Western societies did not invent a term for an abstract fear state that was indifferent to the precipitating situation. Their terms for fear or anxiety specify a place, a person, or an event that provokes the feeling, whether a stranger, an odd noise in a forest, or a frown from a friend. European languages are unusual in ignoring the provocative context and implying that there is only one basic emotion that varies in intensity.

It is likely that different brain circuits are associated with each of the fear states. A child's startle or scream produced by a sudden loud sound does not require the colliculus or thalamus, while the fear state created by a sound that has become a conditioned stimulus for pain requires those two structures. Fear of the unfamiliar involves, in addition, the hippocampus.

The three sources of fear also differ in the behaviors they most often generate. Three common fear reactions in children are crying, flight/avoidance, and immobility or freezing. In animals the proximity of an unfamiliar animal from the same species is the most potent basis for aggression, but in children biting, hitting, or threat displays to strangers are rare. I have seen hundreds of two-year-olds encounter an unfamiliar child, but I have never observed a child strike out as an initial reaction to that discrepancy. Crying is the most frequent reaction to innate releasers and conditioned signals, whereas freezing and avoidance are more common reactions to unfamiliarity. A child playing happily with toys hears a door open, turns, and sees an unfamiliar woman enter and sit on the floor. Over 90 percent of two-year-old children stop playing and stare quietly at the stranger—a form of freezing. It is rare for a two-year-old to cry or to flee to the mother sitting a few feet away. But if the same adult enters the room wearing a clown costume and mask, 20 percent of two-year-olds will immediately issue a sharp cry and run to the parent, suggesting that the state that produced the piercing cry is different from the one that produced only immobility.

One argument against the suggestion that releasers, conditioned signals, and unfamiliarity generate slightly different fear states is the strong likelihood that the amygdala participates in all three states. This small structure is derived embryologically from two different sources. Figure 3.2 is a schematic drawing of the major areas of the amygdala. The dorsal central area, proportionately larger in rats than in primates, is more involved in defensive aggressive reactions to novelty. The ventrally located basolateral area, proportionately larger in primates, is more involved in withdrawal. Wild rats were exposed to a variety of unfamiliar events—including unfamiliar people, placement in an open barrel, hands clapping, light taps on the back, stroking of the vibrissae, and the sight of an anesthetized rat—before and after lesions were made in the amygdala. The rats with lesions in the basolateral area showed less avoidant behavior to these discrepant events, but no decrease in defensive-aggressive behavior.

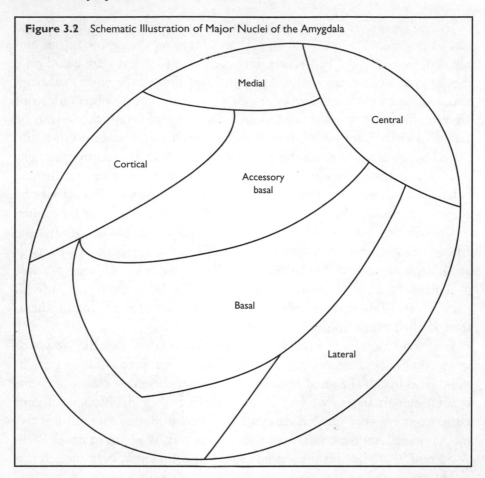

Figure 3.2   Schematic Illustration of Major Nuclei of the Amygdala

The replacement of a defensive-aggressive reaction to novelty with withdrawal, which accompanied the evolution of primates, is probably due to the increased importance of the basolateral area and, correspondingly, decreased influence of the central nucleus. Among species with both a wild and a domesticated form—for example, horses, pigs, and dogs—the domesticated strain has a smaller limbic area than the wild one. It is possible that one contribution to the decreased limbic volume is a smaller central area. Although the amygdala and its projections to motor and autonomic targets participate in the states of fear produced by innate releasers, conditioned signals, and unfamiliarity, we still believe it is likely that the complete states created by these three incentives are not identical and deserve distinct status.

Jeffrey Gray's influential monograph on anxiety over a decade ago placed less emphasis on the amygdala and more on the hippocampus and septum. Gray warned his readers, however, that his ideas were based on a special class of evidence—the extensive literature on the effects of drugs that reduce conditioned fear in animals—rather than on observations of an animal's usual reactions to novelty. The heart of Gray's theory can be stated succinctly, for he was especially clear in his basic claims. Gray suggested that the septum and the hippocampus, which are reciprocally connected, and the circuits in which these structures participate constitute a behavioral inhibition system (BIS). The BIS is provoked into activity by events that violate the animal's expectancy, predict future aversive events, or are innate releasers of fear. When any of those incentives occurs, the BIS is aroused, and ongoing activity is inhibited. Gray defined anxiety as an increase in activity in the BIS. Like Freud, he acknowledged the role of temperament, stating briefly at the end of his monograph that individuals differed in their susceptibility to the reactivity of the BIS and, therefore, in their vulnerability to anxiety.

One objection to Gray's views is his claim that the BIS responds in exactly the same way to novelty and to events that predict future punishment. It is likely, as animal research reveals, that these two classes of events create different states. When a mother warns her child, "Wait until your father comes home," the feeling created is likely to provoke a tantrum, crying, or denial, not the cessation of activity that usually occurs to novelty.

Second, Gray ignores the amygdala almost completely, even though it is richly connected to the hippocampus and is an origin of the motor and autonomic reactions to unfamiliarity that are characteristic of fear states. Gray's omission is surprising, given the evidence summarized. Every major structure that involves the septohippocampal system involves the amygdala as well. The temperamental differences in proneness to fear may involve the septum and hippocampus, but they are equally likely to involve the amygdala and its projections to the striatum, cingulate cortex, hypothalamus, and sympathetic nervous system.

When the natural sciences were young, the first questions studied concerned observable phenomena that seemed to be stable and fundamental, like light, heat, water, friction, the phases of the moon, and the annual cycle of the seasons. Progress was made in clarifying each of these puzzles, but it turned out that the investigations of light had the more profound implications for current explanations of matter. When nineteenth-century physicists discovered the relations among light, heat, frequency, and energy, the stage was set for Planck's postulate of the energy quantum, Einstein's positing of the photon, and, soon after, with the help of creative mathematics, Thomson's discovery of the electron and Rutherford's discovery of the nucleus. It is unlikely that such rapid progress would have occurred if the same cohort of talented scientists had devoted their energies to the study of water. Only some rainbows lead to a pot of gold.

The fundamental phenomena in psychology include conditioning, perception, reasoning, memory, emotion, language, and behavior to novelty; this list is not exhaustive. There is active inquiry in all these areas, and much has been learned. But these domains are not equally likely to lead to profound insights into human psychological functioning. At the moment, most scientists are betting on conditioning and memory. But it is just possible that because an organism's reactions to the unfamiliar involve a coordination of all the major brain systems—sensory, limbic, cortical, skeletal, and autonomic—understanding this class of phenomenon will provide unusually deep insights into the relations between brain and behavior.

Our primary concern is with the reasons for variation in children's reactions to unfamiliarity. Some children are consistently timid, quiet, or distressed by unfamiliar but mundane events that evoke little or no fear in most children. A three-year-old child clenches his mother's hand as they enter a large department store. When the mother asks the child to sit on a chair within her sight, his face becomes tense, he refuses to relinquish his grip, and he begins to cry. How can we understand why this child becomes frightened in this unfamiliar setting, while the vast majority adjust to the same new setting easily? The popular explanation during most of this century, offered with unwarranted assurance, was that the parents created this disposition to fear through indifference, neglect, active rejection, harsh punishment, or severe restriction of exploration that prevented the child from learning how to cope with unfamiliar challenge. These environmental explanations exploited the intuitively attractive premise that a person's profile was a product of experiences that strengthened some habits and weakened others. Put simply, and therefore with some exaggeration, an exceedingly fearful child failed to receive the proper growth experiences.

A skeptical stance toward this explanation was not possible until longitudinal studies of children followed from infancy through late childhood revealed that some extremely shy, timid children were different from others from the first weeks of life. We shall see in chapters 6 and 7 that some infants are born with a physiology that biases them to react to the unfamiliar with avoidance and crying.

Reactions to the Unfamiliar

It is not inaccurate to view the human brain as mediating four fundamental functions, each associated initially with an anatomical area. First, information from the outside world is received by parts of the cortex specialized for each sensory modality. This information is funneled down to the temporal pole and limbic area, especially the hippocampus and amygdala, for an evaluation of its emotional significance. With feelings added to the original information, the more complex product is returned to the cortex, but this time to motor areas that can mediate action and to the frontal lobes for control and evaluation.

Everyone possesses a very large number of stable representations of past experiences—the appearance and behavior of friends, the arrangement of furniture in the home, the taste of lemon, the sound of rain on the window. Deviations from these representations that cannot be understood immediately produce alert attention, but only after two or three months. During the first weeks of life, when the brain is less mature, the physical features of events possess the greatest power to recruit attention. A moving hand, a dark circle on a white background, and an intermittent sound capture attention immediately and maintain it for a few seconds. These stimuli are almost as effective ten minutes later as they were originally. But by three months the power of discrepancy to provoke attentiveness emerges. By six months of age, the physical characteristics have lost much of their potency, in favor of events that are moderate variations on past experience. Now a quiet human face with an eye patch has far more power than an animated normal face to alert the child and to produce a vigilant stare at the violation of expectation.

If the infant did not treat the face with the eye patch as discrepant but as a completely novel event, the reaction would be different. An infant does not become vigilant to El Greco's *View of Toledo* because the painting is not a transformation on what the child knows. The state of alert attention requires, first, the unconscious assignment of an event to a class that has been experienced previously and, second, detection of deviation from that class. One-year-old infants will study discrepant events far longer than totally novel events that do not share any features with their past representations. Discrepancy and novelty, therefore, refer to qualitatively different events, even though these words are often used interchangeably. Of course, the child is storing experiences continually, and with each passing year it becomes less likely that he will encounter an event that does not bear some relation to a prior percept. It is difficult to imagine an event that one cannot relate to some past idea or image.

The sequence of reactions to unfamiliarity involves related, but slightly different, circuits. The first circuit activated by encounter with an unfamiliar event creates a brief psychological state most would call *surprise*. A solitary woman reading a book in a quiet room hears an unfamiliar sound—perhaps a loose shutter rattling against the window. The auditory information travels to the inferior colliculus in the brain stem and then to the medial geniculate of the thalamus, from which two paths emerge (see figure 3.3). One path projects to the hippocampus and amygdala, a second to the auditory cortex in the temporal lobe. The hippocampus, a large structure lying under the cortical mantle with rich connections to the cortex and access to the stored cortical representations of prior sounds and their contexts, mediates an appreciation of the sound of the shutter as discrepant by comparing the stored schema with what is being heard. The task of the hippocampus, which is reciprocally linked to the amygdala, is to determine quickly if this event is unfamiliar. The auditory cortex performs a more detailed analysis of the sound to determine its origin more precisely and transmits that information back to the hippocampus and amygdala.

If a surprising event is not understood in the first second or two—that is, the person cannot classify its nature or source—a second set of circuits, involving reciprocal connections among frontal cortex, hippocampus, and amygdala, is activated and participates in the further evaluation of the information. The corresponding psychological state, which can be brief, might be called *uncertainty*. If the uncertainty is not resolved, a third state, characterized by increased activation of the amygdala, especially of the central area, produces heightened activity in the lateral and ventromedial hypothalamus, the brain stem, and the autonomic nervous system. Table 3.1 lists the primary targets of the central area of the amygdala. I call the state produced by activation of one or more of these targets *fear*, although there is no assumption that a conscious perception of a feeling of fear must accompany the changes in physiology.

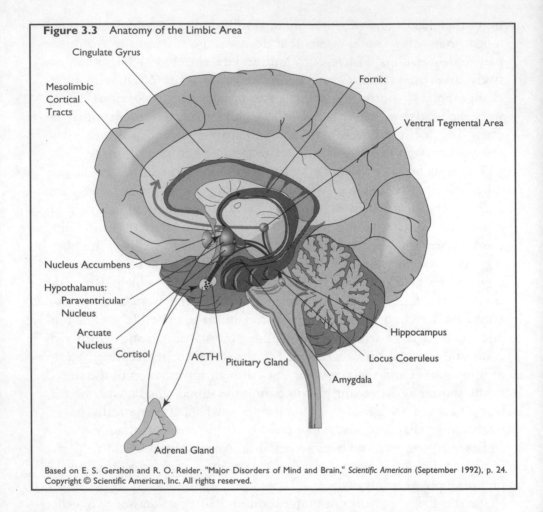

Figure 3.3 Anatomy of the Limbic Area

Cingulate Gyrus

Mesolimbic Cortical Tracts

Fornix

Ventral Tegmental Area

Nucleus Accumbens

Hypothalamus: Paraventricular Nucleus

Arcuate Nucleus

Cortisol

ACTH

Pituitary Gland

Hippocampus

Locus Coeruleus

Amygdala

Adrenal Gland

Based on E. S. Gershon and R. O. Reider, "Major Disorders of Mind and Brain," *Scientific American* (September 1992), p. 24.

The amygdala contains different collections of neurons, each with a distinct set of projections and a distinct profile of receptors for the large variety of chemicals that influence its functions. Visual, auditory, and tactile information from the thalamus and sensory cortices synapse on the lateral nucleus. Olfactory stimulation synapse on the corticomedial area, and taste and visceral information synapse on the central and perhaps the corticomedial area as well.

Projections arising in the central and medial areas of the amygdala synapse on those parts of the hypothalamus that secrete corticotropin releasing hormone (CRH), and these parts in turn stimulate the pituitary gland, a pear-shaped structure lying beneath the hypothalamus, to secrete adrenocorticotropic hormone (ACTH). The ACTH enters the blood stream and, upon reaching the adrenal cortex, leads to increased production of cortisol, a molecule with diverse and profound effects on the body's physiology.

As noted earlier, visual and auditory information arrives at the amygdala in two successive waves, the less detailed from the thalamus and the more detailed from the cortex. The lateral area sends its information to the adjacent basal area, which in turn projects to parts of the corpus striatum that mediate motor activity, as in the avoidance of a snarling dog. Simultaneously, the basal area projects to the central nucleus, which is the origin of the many motor and autonomic reactions that accompany fear states. The central area can activate the autonomic nervous system through direct projections to the medulla, as well as indirectly through projections to the lateral hypothalamus that in turn activate the medulla, sympathetic chain, and the targets that affect heart rate, blood pressure, and muscle and stomach activity.

Table 3.1 *The Projections of the Central Nucleus of the Amygdala to Other Targets*		
Target	*The Functional Consequent*	*Measurements*
Lateral hypothalamus	sympathetic activity	changes in heart rate, galvanic skin response, pupil, blood pressure
Dorsal motor nucleus of vagus	parasympathetic activity	ulcers, urination and defecation, decrease in heart rate
Parabrachial nucleus of the pons	increased respiration	panting, respiratory distress
Locus ceruleus; ventral tegmentum	production of norepinephrine	behavioral arousal, vigilance, and EEG activation
Nucleus reticularis pontis caudalis in the medulla	increased vigor of reflexes	startle
Central gray	cessation of behavior	freezing
Trigeminal and facial motor nerve	movements of the mouth and jaw	facial expression of fear
Paraventricular nucleus of the hypothalamus	release of ACTH from the pituitary	increased cortisol

From M. Davis, "The Role of the Amygdala in Fear and Anxiety," in *Annual Review of Neuroscience*, 15, 1992: 353–75, Palo Alto: Annual Reviews, p. 356.

The amygdala, especially the basolateral area, projects to the cingulate cortex, and both project to a thick band of fibers called the central gray, which serves skeletal muscles and mediates defensive postures (for example, the erect hair and arched back of a cat who has just seen a dog), as well as the child's cry of distress. One target of the central gray is the skeletal muscles of the larynx and vocal folds. Changes in the level of tension in these muscles alter the quality of vocal utterances. It is easy to detect the rise in frequency of the voice of a frightened person. Less obvious changes in the voice due to tension in these muscles are also measurable. One consequent of the increased muscle tension is a decrease in the variability of the pitch periods of vocal output. A relaxed person usually speaks in a voice that is more variable than the voice of one who is fearful.

Another projection from the amygdala synapses on the locus ceruleus, a small structure in the brain stem that synthesizes norepinephrine and distributes it to many parts of the brain. As we noted earlier, norepinephrine lowers the thresholds of excitability in sensory areas and limbic sites. Most of the norepinephrine-secreting neurons from the locus ceruleus are distributed to the cortex, while those originating in the lateral tegmentum are distributed more widely to the brain stem and limbic area.

The reason why many investigators believe the amygdala is an important participant in states of fear is that lesions of the amygdala typically produce a dramatic reduction in freezing and retreat, as well as physiological reactions that are presumed to accompany fear. A rat with a lesioned amygdala will even nibble at the ear of a cat. Lesions of the central area reduce ulceration and eliminate not only freezing but also increases in heart rate and blood pressure to stimuli that have become conditioned signals for pain and fear. The amygdala is not necessary for the learning of all aversions, however; an animal without an amygdala can learn to avoid unpleasant tastes. Thus, there is good support for the conclusion that the amygdala is necessary for the production of some fear states.

Of course, no one brain structure causes a rise in heart rate or change in voice to a discrepant event. Each set of neurons in these circuits is subject to modulation by its particular local chemistry, which in turn is monitored by the presence or absence of relevant receptors on the neurons in those sites. If a particular site has a high density of receptors for opioids, for example, a person will be less reactive to the arriving information. If the site has a high density of receptors for CRH, it is likely to be more reactive.

The basolateral and central areas are affected by different and complex chemistries. The former is influenced to a greater degree by the amino acid GABA, the latter by opioids and, in addition, CRH. Because it is likely that the concentration of and receptors for GABA and the opioids are inherited independently, there should be some individuals with an excitable basolateral area, some with an excitable central area, some excitable in both areas, and, finally, some who are not unusually excitable in either area. As we shall see, these four hypothetical types can be observed in the behavior of four-month-olds when they encounter visual, auditory, and olfactory stimuli.

Activity in the right amygdala may play a more important role in fear than activity in the left amygdala. When monkeys are in situations normally evocative of fear, electrodes in the right amygdala record greater neural activity than those on the left. Further, if a monkey receives electric shock without warning and the animal returns to that context on the subsequent day, there is a greater increase in delta activity in the right than in the left amygdala. We shall see in chapter 5 that inhibited children show greater activation of the EEG in the right frontal area than in the left.

The presence of a fear state increases the likelihood that one will remember a discrepant event and its consequences the next time it or a similar event occurs. If a road taken once a year has a sharp 90-degree turn and on one occasion a driver almost struck a truck because he made the turn too quickly, the state generated by that close call almost guarantees that the driver will remember exactly where that turn is and, on the next occasion, will slow down to prepare for it. Humans remember best, and for the longest time, those experiences that were accompanied by fear.

The suggestion that a fear state, as we have defined it, need not be conscious finds support in the fact that adults who admit to an extreme fear of snakes or spiders show an increase in skin conductance on being shown a picture of one of these feared objects, even when the picture is presented so briefly that they have no conscious recognition of seeing anything and do not report feeling fearful or anxious. Adults who have no fear of snakes or spiders do not show this autonomic reaction. Further, even though some adults with a fear of snakes, spiders, blood, or mutilation show a rise in cortisol, skin conductance, and conscious fear on seeing pictures of these feared objects, there is no relation between the intensity of the fear (or distress) experienced consciously and the magnitude of change in the biological variables.

The fourth state in the sequence that began with hearing the loose shutter is the one most people associate with the words *fear* and *anxiety*. This state is characterized by subjective awareness of a change in bodily activity created when the targets of the amygdala and the hypothalamus—heart, muscle, skin, gut—transmit the consequences of their enhanced activity back to the medulla (especially the nucleus tractus solitarius) and the parabrachial nucleus, which in turn project to the central area of the amygdala and thence to the frontal cortex. The receipt of this derivative of visceral activity by the frontal cortex, in the context of a discrepant or surprising event that cannot be understood, provides the basis for a state most call *conscious fear*. This is the state William James called fear, Freud called anxiety, and most cultures understand to be the meaning of fear.

John Searle's essay on mind placed the subjective perceptions of consciousness in a central position. The distinction between a fear state and conscious fear awards the subjective feelings an importance that Searle believes is warranted. The ancient Hebrews, like many contemporary cultures, described this state with words and phrases that refer to the heart or the gut: "Behold, Oh Lord, for I am in distress, my bowels are troubled; my heart is overturned within me" (Lam. 2:11); "My bowels, my bowels, I am pained at the walls of my heart; my heart is raising in me" (Jer. 4:19); "Thine heart shall mediate terror" (Isa. 33:11). The Yolmo of north central Nepal conceive of a bodily force called *sems*—translated as "heartmind"—that combines the idea of a future event with the conscious feelings linked to it. *Sems* mediates both fear and desire.

Theoretically, then, there are four different states that can be produced by an unfamiliar event, each involving a different pattern of brain activity: (1) an initial state of surprise produced by perception of an unfamiliar event; (2) a state of uncertainty following the first unsuccessful attempt at assimilation; (3) a state of fear accompanied by increased activity of the amygdala and its multiple targets; and (4) a state of conscious fear accompanied by the perception of afferent information from the body arriving at the frontal cortex. Although all four states can, and often do, occur close together in time, they need not always covary. The names we apply to these states are, of course, unimportant, but I believe it is useful to differentiate among them. The distinction between fear and conscious fear is the most important because the relation between enhanced activity in the heart, gut, and muscles, on the one hand, and the conscious feeling and report of fear or anxiety, on the other, is often low. One contribution to the dissociation is the fact that some people may inherit a physiology in the medulla that mutes the sensory feedback from the periphery. Two people might react to an unfamiliar event with a similar profile of autonomic activity, but one may perceive that activity while the other, with a physiology that dampens the feedback, does not. Only the former will report feeling fearful.

Individual Variation

Individuals differ in at least three qualities, influenced by physiology, that contribute to a susceptibility to the universal capacities for surprise, uncertainty, fear, and conscious fear. These three include (1) preparedness to detect subtle discrepancies; (2) reactivity of the amygdala and its projections; and (3) degree of visceral feedback to limbic sites, which influences the intensity of a conscious fear state.

No one knows if the variation in these three qualities is correlated. Biological processes are usually so specific that it is wise to assume that, in large populations, variation among these three processes is independent. Central norepinephrine is involved in all three processes and, in addition, is enhanced by CRH, which is also activated by novelty, challenge, and uncertainty. Norepinephrine increases the signal-to-noise ratio in the sensory cortex and excites hippocampal neurons, making it likely that subtle deviations in the environment will be detected. Norepinephrine also excites the central area of the amygdala, increasing the probability of autonomic reactions to uncertainty. Finally, norepinephrine axons from the locus ceruleus to the frontal cortex may contribute to the perception of visceral feedback to the brain and therefore to the intensity of the conscious fear state. Some adults are extremely sensitive to their heartbeats—they can detect each beat with unusual accuracy. About one-third of those suffering from panic attacks are quite accurate in detection of their heartbeats. Obviously, a person prone to panic who detected every tiny increase in heart rate would become susceptible to fear that an attack was imminent; the resulting anxiety state could precipitate a full-blown profile.

It is possible, therefore, that the small number of children who inherit chronically high levels of norepinephrine, CRH, or both will more often detect subtle deviations from the familiar, have vigorous visceral reactions to uncertainty, and in addition will experience a more salient state of conscious fear. Until this question is resolved, however, our major hypothesis is more modest. The fearful children we call inhibited inherit a low threshold of excitability in the basolateral and central areas and their projections to cortical, motor, and autonomic targets, which renders them especially vulnerable to the state of fear of the unfamiliar. But they may not be especially vulnerable to the states of surprise, uncertainty, or conscious fear.

The research of Robert Adamec supports these ideas. About one in every seven house cats (*Felis catus*) shows a distinct pattern of reactions to unfamiliarity that resembles that of inhibited children. These timid cats, which Adamec calls defensive, withdraw from novelty, are slow to explore unfamiliar environments, and usually do not attack rats, although they will attack mice. The defensive profile of the temperamentally timid cat first appears at about thirty days of age and becomes a stable trait by two months. It is probably not a coincidence that the amygdala of a kitten does not gain major control of the hypothalamic substrate for avoidant behavior until the end of the first month. The level of brain maturation of a one-month-old kitten is comparable to that of a human infant eight months old. It is not surprising, therefore, that stranger and separation fear appear in most infants between eight and ten months of age.

Direct measurement of neural activity in the amygdala, hypothalamus, and hippocampus in response to unfamiliar, potentially threatening events reveals that the basolateral area is unusually excitable in timid cats, for they show greater activity in the basolateral amygdala to a sound that simulates the threat howl of a cat. But timid and nontimid cats show similar levels of activity to a purring sound or to noise. More important, the timid and nontimid cats show similar activity in the hypothalamus and hippocampus to the same threat howl that evokes heightened activity in the basolateral amygdala of timid animals. Hence, it is reasonable to conclude that timid and nontimid cats differ primarily in the excitability of the amygdala, rather than the excitability of the hypothalamus or the hippocampus.

The stria terminalis and the ventral amygdalofugal pathway (VAFP) are two major fiber bundles that leave the amygdala separately but unite downstream in the central gray. Purring sounds, which normally accompany friendly social behavior and are mediated by the stria terminalis, are eliminated when that fiber bundle is destroyed. The bed nucleus of the stria terminalis, which projects to the septum and may modulate fear, is associated with the parasympathetic reactions of decreased heart rate and blood pressure. By contrast, the alarm calls and defensive withdrawal that usually accompany fear of novelty are mediated by the VAFP. It is possible that complex chemistry within the amygdala influences whether the excitation produced by an unfamiliar event provokes enhanced activity in the circuit from the amygdala to the stria and, therefore, a muting of fear, or in the circuit to the VAFP and an enhancement of fear. Adamec has suggested that this neural choice, determined by local chemical configurations within the amygdala, affects the probability of an approach or an avoidant reaction to novelty. If the physiology that mediates the avoidant behavior of temperamentally timid cats is a valid model for the consistent fear of the unfamiliar displayed by some children, our speculation that inhibited children inherit low thresholds of responsivity in the amygdala and its projections to the VAFP gains considerable support.

Anxiety

Although we are concerned with the small proportion of children who begin life with a vulnerability to fear of the unfamiliar, some older children who show restraint at unfamiliar events are also unusually anxious about future misfortune. At ages five to seven, there is a dramatic change in children's answers to the question "What are you afraid of?" During the years from three to five, the most common fears are of the discrepant and novel. During the fourth year, masks and other transformations of the human face or body ascend in importance. After the fourth birthday, large animals and the dark become important. By six years of age, however, anticipation of harm, threat, or adult evaluation replaces direct encounter with the unfamiliar. The six-year-old says he is afraid of ghosts and kidnapping; a year later, he is afraid of failing in school, rejection by peers, and possible bodily injury. By adolescence, the usual conscious fears are all anticipatory—future relations with others, the possibility of criticism, school performance, and, for some, political disruption to society. In selected non-Western cultures, sorcerers, witches, and ghosts are feared objects. At a less conscious level, identification with a person or a group who symbolically represents qualities that violate the child's standards can also produce anxiety—for example, identification with a criminal parent. Thus, with age, anxiety over possible but infrequent events replaces fear of direct encounter with the unfamiliar. Janet argued, in the famous 1927 Wittenberg College symposium on emotions, that the anxious patient is afraid of acting, not of an unexpected event. Hence, indecision or flight are common reactions.

We argued earlier, however, that the state generated by anticipation of future events is not the same as the state provoked by discrepancy. Why, then, are there hints of a link between the two states in some older children? The assumption that the small proportion of children and adults who are extremely vulnerable to any class of fear or anxiety are also vulnerable to others is likely to be correct if two conditions are met: first, the central nucleus of the amygdala and its projections participate in all fear and anxiety states, and second, some people inherit an unusually excitable central nucleus. The excitability of the central nucleus is monitored by at least five mechanisms. One is based on the concentration of chemicals (opioids, CRH, and norepinephrine are three such molecules) and/or the density of receptors for these molecules within the central nucleus that moderate its activity. A second source is the reactivity of the basolateral and corticomedial areas of the amygdala that synapse on the central nucleus. We noted that GABA plays an especially important role in monitoring the excitability of the basolateral area; hence, variation in GABA or its receptors could indirectly influence the excitability of the central area. Third, the lateral nucleus receives sensory input from the cortex; a sensory cortex that is especially excitable, perhaps because of high levels of norepinephrine, could enhance activity in the basolateral area, which in turn would excite the central nucleus. A fourth source of excitability is afferent feedback from the body through the medulla to the amygdala. A medulla with low levels of opioids would permit more feedback and theoretically could lead to a more excitable central nucleus. Finally, the excitability of the hippocampus, which is reciprocally connected with the amygdala and monitored in part by CRH and cortisol, could add to the excitability of the central nucleus.

There are, therefore, five very different bases for variation in activity of the central nucleus: (1) the chemistry of the central nucleus itself, and excitation in the (2) basolateral area, (3) sensory cortex, (4) medulla, and (5) hippocampus. The thresholds in each of these five sites are monitored by different neurochemical profiles, implying that the correlation in level of excitability among the five sites should be low in a randomly selected group of individuals. On the other hand, there may be a small group of people for whom there is substantial covariation. This select group should have an unusually excitable central nucleus, higher levels of cortical and visceral arousal, and bodily sensations that pierce consciousness frequently to create a conscious fear state that demands interpretation and a response. These people not only would have a low threshold for fear in response to the unfamiliar but, in addition, would worry about possible failure, rejection, robbery, illness, and accidents.

Mothers of some older inhibited children report that these children are exceptionally sensitive to criticism or reprimand and become guilty more easily than their siblings or friends. Inhibited children reared by parents who impose consistent socialization demands show more intense guilt than inhibited children reared with unusually permissive parents. But children who develop intense conditioned fears because of traumatic experiences or children who are susceptible to intense guilt because of family socialization practices should not be especially prone to fear of the unfamiliar. Nor should children who have identified with an alcoholic parent or a minority group that is a target of prejudice be especially prone to fear of the unfamiliar.

Children can develop any fear or anxiety state through experience, without the help of an inherited low threshold of excitability in the amygdala and its circuits. Thus, there are at least two different types of children who are consistently afraid of unfamiliarity. A large proportion of youth admit they are anxious about public speaking and examinations, but a maximum of 20 percent are born with a temperamental vulnerability to such fears. Hence, children who are temperamentally prone to fear of the unfamiliar probably represent a minority of all adults who admit to a chronic or extreme anxiety state. There is an analogy in medicine. A small number of people inherit a tendency to become overweight and, as a result, are vulnerable to a variety of diseases, including high blood pressure and diabetes. But the majority of adults with high blood pressure or diabetes did not inherit a vulnerability to obesity.

The central point is that both the report of an anxiety state and the display of a response that reflects this state are ambiguous as to origin. It will not be obvious to a casual observer whether a fearful person was born with a temperamental bias or whether the affective and behavioral profile was created by experience alone.

Although Galen and Hippocrates were prescient, they made the error of positing abstract, emotional categories that were conceived as unitary essences. They did not distinguish clearly among fear states produced by innate releasers, unfamiliarity, and conditioned stimuli, or between these states and the multiple sources of anxiety. They could not know that scientists would discover extraordinary specificity in biological and psychological phenomena and the possibility of different routes to a particular surface profile. This insight may be the major advance in our understanding of all emotional phenomena, and fear in particular, over the last half century. Not surprisingly, these advances have been accompanied by an equally disciplined analysis of cognitive phenomena. Memory is now parsed into short- and long-term, episodic and semantic, and implicit and explicit. Aphasics cannot remember, consciously, that they saw the word *apple* on a screen twenty seconds earlier but do better than chance in guessing that *-p-le* is a fragmented form of that word.

Ernst Mayr has written forcefully that biological processes and structures change over time; by contrast, most of the oxygen in the atmosphere a hundred million years ago has remained unaltered. Biological evolution is characterized by a series of transformations on an original set of chemicals, cells, and tissues to yield an extraordinarily large number of variations. Norepinephrine is produced when a single hydroxyl group is added to dopamine in the right place. The extraordinary structural similarity of dopamine and norepinephrine is the reason why they share membership in the abstract category chemists call *catecholamines*. But the similarity in the number and arrangement of atoms disguises major differences in the functional activity of the two molecules. So, too, does use of the abstract term *fear* blind us to a number of states with different origins and behavioral consequences. It is time to adopt a more analytic attitude toward psychological phenomena and to reject the denial of complexity that has been such a debilitating defense against the recognition of nature's extraordinary stubbornness and careful attention to detail.

CHAPTER FOUR

The Beginnings

We shall not cease from exploration
And the end of all our exploring
Will be to arrive where we started
And know the place for the first time.
—T. S. ELIOT, *FOUR QUARTETS*

The origins of scientific ideas, like historical movements, resist precise specification of time and place. Popular anger over the practice of indulgences had been growing for at least a century before Martin Luther pinned his list of complaints against the Church on the heavy door of the Wittenberg Cathedral in the autumn of 1517. Without the widespread dissatisfaction in that part of Germany, the Protestant Reformation would have begun later, and perhaps in a different place.

The First Clues

The current work on inhibited and uninhibited children began in the spring of 1957 at the Fels Research Institute on the campus of Antioch College in Yellow Springs, Ohio. The Institute staff had studied longitudinally eighty-nine Caucasian children born in southwestern Ohio between 1929 and 1939. These children had been observed from the early months of life through adolescence. Howard Moss evaluated the childhood information, and I interviewed and tested these individuals as young adults. We put the two sets of information together to see whether adult person-

ality characteristics could be predicted from early childhood. The most
provocative discovery was that a small group of children who had been
extremely fearful during the first three years had retained some derivatives of that quality through adolescence and adulthood. These adults
were introverted, cautious, and psychologically dependent on their
spouses or love objects. The four most fearful three-year-old boys had
chosen careers that permitted them to avoid interaction with large
groups and to control unpredictability in their daily lives: one had
become a music teacher, two had become science professors, and one
was a psychiatrist. By contrast, the four least fearful boys had chosen
competitive or entrepreneurial professions: one was a high school athletic coach, one was a salesman, and two were self-employed engineers.

Although we emphasized the influence of early family experiences in
our interpretation of this continuity, we considered the role of temperament because no other quality in the first three years predicted a salient
aspect of adult behavior. We wrote that early fearfulness "and its potential relation to constitutional variables warrant more intensive study.
Such research may provide substance to the cliche that personality is
the result of an interaction between environment and the constitutional
characteristics of the individual."

A singularly surprising result supported the intuition that the child's
biology was relevant. In another laboratory in the Institute, John and
Beatrice Lacey had observed variation among adults in heart rate variability—called respiratory sinus arrhythmia—and had written about
the origins and significance of this variation. They measured the autonomic responsivity of the adult men in the Fels sample and found that
those who displayed unusually low heart rate variability had been the
most fearful boys. No one in either research group had a compelling
explanation of this relation or an implacable faith that it was a replica-
ble fact of nature. Many other investigators, however, had speculated
on the relation between variation in autonomic activity and personality,
especially Gellhorn and Wenger, who had proposed two broad types of
individuals: one with sympathetic dominance, who was prone to introversion and fear, and one with parasympathetic dominance, who was a
relaxed, open extrovert. (Recall Kretschmer's schizothyme and
cyclothyme, described in chapter 1.) The former was characterized by
high and minimally variable heart rates, the latter by low and highly
variable heart rates.

The Laceys' finding lay dormant for over fifteen years until Richard Kearsley, Philip Zelazo, and I were reflecting on longitudinal observations of fifty-three Chinese-American and sixty-three Caucasian infants who were participants in a study designed to assess the effects of day care. Some of the infants had attended our experimental day care center in Boston from four to twenty-nine months of age; others had been reared at home, although a few attended other day care centers in the neighborhood for brief periods. All infants were observed in the laboratory on five occasions between the ages of seven-and-a-half months and twenty-nine months.

Two results were of particular significance. The Chinese infants, whether reared at home or attending our day care center, were more fearful than the Caucasians. The Chinese children spent more time close to their mothers when in unfamiliar rooms, were more likely to cry when separated briefly from their mothers, and were wary when playing with an unfamiliar child of the same age and sex. Further, many of the Chinese mothers characterized their children as apprehensive, using phrases like "stays close to me," "frets at separation," and "dislikes the dark." The Caucasian parents, by contrast, described their children as talkative, active, and prone to laughter. And, to our surprise, the Chinese infants had less variable heart rates than the Caucasians.

The Fels and day care investigations, by hinting at the influence of temperament, provided the motivation for our first deliberative study of fearful and fearless children, whom we decided to call *inhibited* and *uninhibited.*

History of a Word

We chose the term *inhibited* because it was less evaluative than *anxious* and seemed to describe the extreme restraint and timidity some children show when they confront unfamiliar people and situations. At the time, we were not aware of its earlier meanings. We learned later from Roger Smith's historical analysis that the term *inhibition* first appeared in nineteenth-century technical summaries of physiological investigations of the nervous system. Most scientists believed that the nervous system had only excitatory capabilities. Inhibition described the discovery, surprising at the time, that reflexes and autonomic reactions could be slowed and even made to disappear. Inhibition seemed an apt term, but one with emotionally charged connotations, for nineteenth-century Europeans celebrated those who could control the passions of sexuality and anger. The Russian scientist Sechenov speculated in the 1860s that the brain, too, had a capacity for inhibition. When a person inhibits an action, Sechenov conjectured, she automatically acquires the capacity for thought. When the last link of a complex reflex is prevented from occurring, thought emerges. If inhibition of action represented the material basis for rationality, surely these physiological events must also be the basis of human morality. These early neuroscientists did not resist—indeed they promoted—the expansion of their narrow technical meaning to the broader implication that variation in human character was linked to inhibitory processes in the brain. By the end of the century, physicians in many parts of Europe were attracted to the idea that the primary cause of psychosis and criminality was a deficiency in inhibition. The higher centers in the brains of these unfortunate individuals failed to control the lower ones.

Pavlov, who was influenced by Sechenov, altered the meaning of inhibition by placing it in a complementary relation to excitation and letting it refer to any force in the brain that reduced the strength of a conditioned reflex. Pavlov argued that strength, lability, and balance were the brain's three basic dimensions. Balance represented the interaction of excitation and inhibition, and the varied human temperaments were the result of different resolutions of the competition between excitation and inhibition. Galen's balance among humors had become a balance among neural elements.

Freud changed the meaning of inhibition in a serious way by substituting the repression of motives for the disappearance of reflexes. By the turn of the century, however, the community's attitude toward sexuality had become more permissive. Sex was to be enjoyed, not controlled, and inhibition became an undesirable quality. In time, the adjective described the unfortunate person who was not sufficiently free to listen to his natural, biological needs and, as a result, became anxious, even though Freud suggested that inhibition made civilization possible. Freud pitted the well-being of society, which required inhibition, against the joy of the individual. In less than a century, the connotations of inhibition had changed from the celebration of those who could control their emotions to pity toward those who could not enjoy life. Virginia Woolf should be smiling; she understood that words can mean whatever we wish them to mean—meanings are what most contradict themselves with time.

Our use of the term *inhibited* differs from the meanings intended by

Sechenov, Pavlov, and Freud. It refers to a category of child who is initially fearful and avoidant in response to unfamiliar events because of an inherited temperamental bias. But the term carries no evaluative implication whatsoever. The term *uninhibited* was conceived originally as complementary, referring to a second temperamental type who shows minimal uncertainty to the unfamiliar. Although many readers may assume that these two behavioral profiles are on a continuum, we will argue that the two types are as qualitatively different in physiology as the classes of people with very high or very low blood pressure.

Strategies of Inquiry

Two strategies of inquiry into temperamental phenomena can be pursued during this transitional period when neuroscience and psychology have not made sufficient intellectual contact and the constructs of one domain are not closely mapped onto those of the other. One research style is captured by the solitary scholar trying to imagine the hidden structures and mechanisms that lie behind a set of phenomena, occasionally using mathematical models, more frequently inventing concepts or deducing a theoretical prediction by marrying what is known to a few basic premises. Newton's invention of the law of gravitation and Einstein's theory of relativity are two of the best-known examples of this style.

Although I respect theory, I share Percy Bridgman's suspicion of a priori ideas, especially in young sciences like psychology. Too many investigators persuade themselves of the correctness of an idea through thought alone. The behaviorists' claim that a child's first sentences are products of reward and punishment and the psychoanalysts' conviction that misers experienced harsh toilet training are two illustrations. I continue to wince privately at my credulity when I told several hundred guileless undergraduates in 1954 that maternal rejection could produce an autistic child.

I distrust purely formal arguments in psychology because, although aesthetic, they usually rest on fragile information or float almost completely free of evidence. David Magnusson, of the University of Stockholm, agrees that psychologists have given theory too much supremacy:

The important elements of observation, description, and careful systematic analysis of phenomena are degraded to an extent that they are often neglected. . . . We have to restore the supremacy of analyses of the phenomena as the basis for the development of effective, fundamental theories for individual functioning.

A few high-flying Platonic idealists are needed in every scientific discipline, but they are most helpful in more mature sciences that have an extensive corpus of robust facts. They can be terrorists in the less advanced social sciences, especially in human development and personality, where firm knowledge is so fragmented that it is difficult to build a scaffold strong enough to launch the lofty principles that offer fully satisfying understanding. I like a comment by Henry Harris, a former professor of medicine at Oxford: "Rationality helps, but it is not a prescription for making discoveries." Even some mathematicians are troubled by a recent trend that permits "theoretical" mathematicians to intuit ideas and not worry too much about their rigorous proof. Arthur Jaffe and Frank Quinn, two mathematicians critical of this style, have written, "Theoretical work, if taken too far, goes astray because it lacks the feedback and corrections provided by rigorous proof." John von Neumann, too, worried that mathematical inquiry that wandered too far from its empirical source would eventually degenerate.

The physicist Howard Georgi disagrees with those of his colleagues who believe that a priori, mathematical arguments can tell us all we need to know about the essence of matter:

> I believe there are practical limits to our scientific knowledge. These limits change as technology allows us to experiment in new ways, but there are some questions that are so far beyond the grasp of any imaginable technology that they cannot be regarded as "scientific." If experiment is unnecessary, if theorists can understand the structure of the universe by sitting at their desks and doing beautiful mathematics, then these limits do not matter much. But my personal view is that nature is much more clever than we are. We particle theorists must not get too hung up on highfalutin theoretical ideas like unification, or we may lose our sense of wonder at the infinite variety of nature.

The life sciences have found an inductive strategy to be more fruitful. Most biologists have a general idea of the phenomena they wish to explain and slowly, doggedly accumulate bits of evidence that reveal, shadow by shadow, a hidden form. When a sufficient part of the phenomenon has been revealed, the mind takes a leap and guesses at the shape of the whole.

Darwin required not only the evidence collected on the *Beagle* voyage but also centuries of observations on the breeding of domesticated animals in order to invent natural selection. Crick and Watson's insight into the structure of the DNA molecule was made possible by a large corpus of data on the chemistry and crystallography of nucleic acids. The genome project is an extraordinary effort in inductive science, with thousands of investigators exploiting new laboratory techniques to discover the location of the more than 100,000 human genes on the 23 pairs of human chromosomes.

Reflection on my first twenty years of research, rather than temperament or training, has led me to favor the biologist's inductive strategy. As a young scientist, I held the typical psychologist's faith in a priori categories. It was necessary to invent such categories in order to code the discursive information contained in the books full of descriptive sentences on each child in the Fels study. But Howard Moss and I often chose the wrong categories because we did not acknowledge temperamental factors, believing that acquired defenses to threat were the best ways to understand a child's personality development. A second important blow to my earlier faith in a priori ideas occurred during a year observing children and families in a small, isolated Indian village in northwest Guatemala, where my belief in the power of early experience to determine the future was shaken. Infants who were intellectually retarded because of their confinement to a small hut showed dramatic advances after the first year, when they left the hut and encountered the variety of the outside world. These experiences began to change the premises I brought to observations and to quiet study of the technical literature. Slowly I became more inductive and analytic.

The Advantages of Analysis

A salient feature of research in biology is the search for refinements of phenomena that have been thought to be one process. Biologists are continually discovering that what was once regarded as a single event is composed of at least two distinctive entities. The objects that were once believed to belong to a homogeneous class of viruses consist of two classes, viruses and retroviruses. The anatomical anomaly of the heart called mitrovalve prolapse has two forms, one due to bacterial infection and the other, appearing earlier, embryological in origin.

When some phobic patients show a rise in heart rate and blood pressure while reporting a subjective experience of fear but others do not, some scientists are likely to question the validity of the heart rate and blood pressure data rather than to assume that there may be two different types of phobic patients. If all patients who report a chronic fear of spiders are shown the target of their fear and report discomfort but only half react with sympathetic discharge, it is reasonable to conclude that the two groups are experiencing a different emotion, rather than to insist on a single emotional state. Among a strain of normal rats there is a positive relation between the magnitude of body startle to a sudden loud sound and the amount of increase in blood pressure, suggesting that both the startle and the blood pressure response are the consequences of a unitary state of limbic reactivity. Within a closely related strain that is prone to hypertension, however, there is no relation between these two reactions, implying that the unity is broken. These examples can be multiplied a thousandfold. Biologists make progress by analyzing what was believed to be a unitary phenomenon with a single name into two or more distinctive phenomena with different names.

Many psychologists, however, resist this strategy, insisting that there is only one form of learning, one kind of memory, one class of secure attachment, one strategy of inductive reasoning, one self-concept, and one state of fear. There are at least three reasons why psychologists and psychiatrists are so averse to analysis and addicted to synthetic ideas. First, analysis requires powerful methods—electron microscopes, cleavage of genes with enzymes, and PET and magnetic resonance imaging (MRI) scans—that can reveal unexplored aspects of a phenomenon. Psychology has not enjoyed the privilege of such extraordinary methods. Without a source of novel evidence there is less motivation for analysis. There is no need to suspect the impurity of old ideas if there are no new events to challenge them.

Second, analysis proceeds best when the existing level of understanding is firm enough to serve as a base for analysis. Biologists could not differentiate between the Purkinje neurons in the cerebellum and smaller neurons in the hippocampus until the concept of the neuron had been accepted. Chemists could not distinguish between right- and left-handed crystals until the idea of a lattice composed of the atoms of a molecule had been established. Psychologists lack a firm set of consensual ideas; hence, analysis seems premature.

Finally, complexity is a factor. The major phenomena of psychology—behaviors, cognitive processes, and emotions—are so context-bound that scientists are frustrated in their attempt to freeze-frame a broad generalization. Each time they analyze their data they are reminded that their conclusions are limited to a specific context. Human preference and decision processes, for example, are dependent on how a question is posed to a subject. A simple change in the form of the inquiry—"Would you buy a Ford or a BMW?" versus "How much money are you prepared to spend on a car?"—influences the respondent's answer in a nontrivial way. Similarly, the major sources of worry among Americans appear to change when the form of the question varies only a little. When an interviewer asked in 1987, before the end of the Cold War, "What do you think is the most important problem facing the country?" unemployment was named most often as a major concern. But when the interviewer first posed four possible sources of worry (energy, quality of public schools, legalized abortion, and pollution, none of which was mentioned by most informants answering spontaneously) and asked each person to rank these four concerns, one-third selected public schools as a serious problem, despite the fact that only 1.2 percent of the original group regarded schools as a problem when the question was open-ended. The answers to the multiple-choice question implied that public schools were a serious source of worry; the answers to the open-ended question implied that unemployment was a primary concern. Data of this kind are discouraging. One can invent dozens of different ways to ask the same question. If each distinct form of interrogation yields a different result, we confront scientific anarchy. Unfortunately, there is no theory of contexts and their number seems unlimited. The reaction to this frustrating state of affairs is to move away from the complexity of concrete phenomena to abstractions that deny, or at least repress, the extraordinary specificity of psychological evidence.

Because it is difficult to argue that one method or procedure has obvious priority—it is a bit easier to do so in biology and chemistry—psychologists retreat to abstract ideas that ignore contexts completely. Although this defense is soothing temporarily, it denies nature's preferred forms and is inimical to progress. I suspect there is no construct in contemporary psychology that cannot be parsed into two or more theoretically useful ideas, whether the construct is as vague as self or as specific as memory for sentences.

The First Study

We are interested in the profiles of behavior, emotion, and physiology that define two temperamental types of children. Had nature been kind, she would have arranged a close correspondence among these three characteristics and a unified state for each category. When we saw a two-year-old cringe and withdraw from a stranger, we should have noted simultaneously a rise in heart rate and an increase in muscle tension; if we could have entered the child's mind we would have known that he felt fear. Unfortunately, to borrow from Huxley, that beautiful idea has been slain by an ugly fact. After many years of search for those pretty unities we know that the best we can hope for is partial, often modest, correlations among the three sources of evidence. There will be some correspondence among behavior, physiology, and subjective feelings in some children on some occasions but never most of the time. Each system—behavior, physiology, consciousness—is governed by its own mechanisms. That is why there is a poor relation between an adult's description of his feelings and his heart rate and blood pressure. The physiological variables we study—heart rate, cortisol, blood pressure, muscle tension—are governed, in part, by mechanisms that can influence behavior but also by mechanisms that have little to do with behavior or mood.

Two premises guided our research. First, the development of the profile that defines each type requires the contribution of both physiology and experience. Obviously, the nature and extent of the contributions of each would be different if one were to study school achievement instead of fearful and fearless behavior. A second premise, which embryologists appreciate, is that children with similar surface profiles can belong to different groups. Stated differently, children can arrive at similar behavioral profiles as a result of different histories and in possession of different physiologies. Cross-sectional investigations of children are vulnerable to the error of regarding those with similar scores on a measure as being homogeneous. The protection against this error is to study characteristics historically. Some school-age children become shy as a result of stress at home, peer rejection, or school failure. A sociable one-year-old girl in one of our studies became shy and anxious at age four after her father committed suicide. Another sociable child became shy for a ten-month period when her professional mother had to be away from home for weeks at a time. These two children differ from most of our temperamentally inhibited children in history and physiology.

In part, we chose to study inhibited and uninhibited children because the relevant behaviors are obvious—they strike all observers between the eyes. Ptolemy, Galileo, and Kepler observed the moon, stars, and the near planets because these bodies too were obvious and changes in their location over the year appeared regular. The scientist enters the garden where nature has put a tiny break in the hedge to discover treasures on the inside that were not imaginable while standing outside the wall.

The behaviors that define the two types are so common the reader may wonder why I waited almost fifteen years to pick up the trail of the intriguing discoveries at the Fels Institute. Mahlon Hoagland imagines himself making a path in the thick jungle, slashing at the underbrush, not sure of where he is or where he is going, envious of the a priori theorist who, like a graceful bird flying above the tree tops, smiles as he sees where the empiricist is slogging at a tediously slow pace. With hindsight, history might have been different. Solomon Diamond had written, over thirty-five years ago, that withdrawal from unfamiliarity was a temperamental trait, and the technical literature contained a large number of reports suggesting that introversion and extroversion were heritable qualities. About thirty years ago a child psychologist observed thirty-eight preschool children in a school setting over a two-year period. The two most stable qualities were sociability with peers and isolation from the peer group. Why, then, did I demand more evidence? Although my caution exacted the price of fifteen years of delay in probing this phenomenon, I had no choice. I had to believe first in the validity of the idea of inhibited and uninhibited children with evidence that met my standards of acceptability. I also suspect that had I invented these categories before generating the evidence that will be summarized, those conceptual inventions would be in poorer correspondence with the facts than the concepts we inferred following an inductive strategy that relied on direct observations of children.

There is a second reason why we decided to study these two profiles. No matter what species of mammal is observed there is genetically based variation within each species in the propensity to approach or to avoid unfamiliarity. T. C. Schneirla, of the American Museum of Natural History, who devoted most of his career to the pursuit of this idea, believed that the intensity of a stimulus was the critical determinant of the response selected. Animals approached stimuli with low intensity and avoided those of high intensity. Although this broad claim has some validity, unfamiliar environments are not more or less intense; they are simply different.

Scientists have not searched as extensively for variation within or between species in a large number of characteristics, but it remains a possibility that approach to or avoidance of the unfamiliar is a fundamental source of variation in every mammalian group. As we noted in chapter 3, activity in the amygdala and its projections contributes to the behavioral reactions to unfamiliarity. The concentration of the chemicals that affect the amygdala (as well as the density of the receptors) is under genetic control; therefore, variation in approach or avoidant behavior should be present in all animals. Further, the amygdala is a relatively new structure phylogenetically—it is not present in reptiles—and its chemistry is more complex than that of most brain structures; hence, it may be unusually responsive to slight variations in its neurochemistry.

Finally, it is easy to quantify the variation among young children in their moving toward or away from unfamiliar objects, people, and situations. Some infants strain to touch a set of jingling keys or a smiling face; others turn away. Perhaps our decision to study inhibited and uninhibited children was not just a function of their salience; perhaps they are two fundamental types, as Galen prophesied.

Our first systematic inquiry, initiated in the summer of 1979, rested on the assumption that a small proportion of children began life with a propensity to be shy, fearful, and avoidant in response to unfamiliar events, while others began life with a bias to be sociable and relatively bold. Experience can also produce these two profiles, but we assumed that young children with a temperamentally based profile would be more extreme in their behavior than those who had acquired a timid demeanor. Thus, the explicit strategy was to select children who were both consistent and extreme in their reactions to unfamiliarity.

Cynthia Garcia-Coll, who undertook for her dissertation the selection of a first cohort, had to solve two problems. At what age should she begin the assessments, and what incentives should she use? Two facts provided partial answers to the first question. She knew from previous work that between the ages of eight and sixteen months all children pass through a period of heightened fear of strangers and of separation. Thus it seemed wise to wait until all children had passed through this developmental stage so that variation in fear would be a function of temperament rather than rate of maturation. Second, the day care project had revealed that timidity with unfamiliar children and fear to challenge peaked between eighteen and twenty-one months. It was reasonable, therefore, to choose this age for the initial selection of the children.

One might ask why Coll did not study young infants, three to four months old, before the period of fear emerged. The answer is that young infants do not show obvious fear to novelty, especially during the first few months, and we did not have strong intuitions as to what signs might reflect the temperamental biases that eventuate in a fearful or a fearless style. We shall see in chapter 6 that such characteristics exist, but at the time we did not consider them relevant and probably would have rejected the urging of a wiser colleague to quantify activity and irritability in response to unfamiliar stimuli in four-month-old infants. That insight had to wait almost eight years.

Selection of the best incentives to provoke fear of the unfamiliar was more complex, for it depended on what criteria for fear we adopted. A change in the behavioral signs of fear could change the meaning of the construct. If one biologist uses ancient bone fragments to measure the genetic relation between chimpanzees and baboons while another uses blood proteins, the two investigators will arrive at different estimates of the time when the two species diverged. If a biologist writes, "Chimpanzees and baboons are closely related," the meaning of "closely related" depends on whether bones or proteins supplied the relevant evidence. Thus if two different sources of evidence are used to index fear, the meaning of fear may not be the same with both sources of information.

Most psychologists are certain that they have experienced fear and reject the claim that the word *fear* does not refer to a real phenomenon. In everyday conversations, the word *fear* is understood to refer to a subjective, unpleasant feeling, often accompanied by the imminent occurrence of a harmful event, that is a universal capacity in all humans. When someone says, "I am afraid," we believe we know the subjective experience to which the person refers. But psychologists use the word *fear* to name other phenomena as well. Investigators will call rats fearful even though they are not certain—and probably do not care—whether the rat has a subjective feeling of imminent danger. Psychiatrists at the University of Michigan presented phobic patients with the target of their fear while PET scans of their brains were being recorded. Although the patients reported feeling afraid and their heart rates and breathing speeded up, their brains' metabolic activity reflected only the result of the hyperventilation that is characteristic of fearful adults. When the investigators controlled for the effect of heavy breathing on oxygenation of the brain, they could not detect any brain change that corresponded to the fear state the subjects said they were experiencing.

We use the word *fear* with the understanding described in chapter 3; it is not a single state but rather a family of related states. Each is linked to a profile of behavioral and physiological characteristics even though there is partial overlap—that is, an increase in heart rate and immobility can occur in several of the states. This pluralistic view is in accord with research on animals. Lesions of the cerebellar vermis of rats reduce the occurrence of freezing behavior to novel situations but have no influence on the behavior that follows foot shock. Shock, novelty, and the conditioned signals for these events produce slightly different states in the central nervous system, suggesting that there is no unified state of fear, as there is no single state of illness or intelligence.

Our use of the term *fear of the unfamiliar* also makes no assumptions about conscious awareness. The word *fear* is used in the technical sense described in chapter 3 to refer to a state of heightened limbic arousal that often leads to distress, freezing, or avoidance of unfamiliar events. Cognitive scientists use the word *intelligence* to describe the output of a computer program; biologists use the word *kill* to describe how a white blood cell destroys bacteria. *Intelligence* and *kill* in these technical contexts do not have the meaning intended when people talk about a high school valedictorian or a homicidal maniac. Scientists often use lay language because the connotations are helpful in communication.

We are concerned with the state of fear that is generated when the unfamiliar cannot be understood immediately. Consider the following situation. A two-year-old child is playing in a room with her mother when, without warning, an adult wearing a clown costume and a red-and-white mask enters, sits down, and begins to talk to the child. Almost every child stops what she was doing to stare at the clown, often with a tense, vigilant posture. The remarkable similarity in the reactions of most children suggests that special features of this event elicit the posture of wariness. The fact that all mammalian species become wary to unfamiliar events suggests that this reaction is biologically prepared. Monkeys are more prepared to become fearful to snakes and to the disembodied heads of other monkeys than to bananas, leaves, or flowers. This statement does not mean that some events always elicit fear; it means only that it is easy for some events to provoke a fear state.

But avoidance of an unfamiliar event can also be the result of observation of a model. A child who has seen his mother scream on seeing a mouse may learn to retreat from small animals. A fear state and an accompanying withdrawal can be conditioned through the co-occurrence of a state of fear and an unexpected event. The classic example is the unexpected clap of thunder that startles a child and creates a fear state. Sometimes a single co-occurrence of thunder and fear will lead a child to react later to the faintest rumbling in the distance.

These different mechanisms underlying fear of the unfamiliar imply that an assessment of fear that relies on only one incentive—be it a stranger, a clown, or the application of a blood pressure cuff—is ambiguous as to its cause. The avoidant behavior could be the result of imitation of a model or conditioning. To determine if the fear is temperamentally based it is necessary to present children with a variety of provocative events; a child who shows fear in response to five of twelve different discrepancies is not likely to have acquired all of them through conditioning or modeling. The psychologist is on firmer ground in concluding that a child is temperamentally fearful if the child reacts to a variety of events with distress or avoidance. This was the rationale that lay behind our assessment procedures.

One more issue must be mentioned. All our work involves only Caucasian children from relatively secure, initially intact families. The reasons for this restriction are simple to understand. First, we are interested in the contribution of temperament to behaviors that can also be affected by stressful home environments. Unfortunately, social class and color are correlated in the United States, and conditions that can produce highly fearful children, such as unpredictability, neglect, and chronic illness, are more common among economically disadvantaged families than among advantaged ones. In order to avoid the confounding of causes we restricted our samples to middle-class Caucasians. There are, of course, intact, middle-class families of color that could have participated in our studies. The possibility exists, however, that Asian-, African-, and Caucasian-American children differ in temperamental profiles. We shall see later that northern Europeans, southern Europeans, and Asians may differ in some temperamental biases. In order to avoid that possibility, we restricted the ethnicity of our samples.

Coll's strategy was straightforward. She filmed 117 twenty-one-month-old Caucasian children—first- and later-born—as they encountered unfamiliar people, objects, and situations. After being greeted, the mother and infant were taken to a playroom with toys arranged on the rug. After five minutes of play, the examiner and mother joined the child on the floor, and the examiner modeled some acts that varied in complexity (for example, a doll talking on a telephone, three animals walking together through a rainstorm and then hiding under a cloth).

The examiner then withdrew without giving any special instructions to the child. Some children cried as the examiner moved away. We interpreted the distress as occasioned by the child's uncertainty about the implied obligation to imitate the examiner. After an additional period of play, an unfamiliar woman entered the room and sat on a chair for thirty seconds. Some children retreated to the mother; most stared. The woman then called the child by name and invited him to join her in performing some simple acts taken from a popular mental development assessment. Some children withdrew to the mother and would not approach. The unfamiliar woman then left, and the examiner returned to open up a set of curtains in a corner of the room, revealing a metal robot. The examiner encouraged the child to approach and touch the robot; some children refused and stood by their mothers. Finally, the examiner left and, upon a signal, the mother left the room, leaving the child alone. Some children cried as the mother left; others became distressed as the door closed.

Coll used fretting, crying, withdrawal, absence of spontaneous interactions with the examiner, and prolonged hesitation in approaching the robot or the stranger as signs of fear. The thirty-three children who displayed these behavioral signs of fear in a majority of the situations were classified as inhibited. The thirty-eight children who approached the unfamiliar woman and the robot, did not cry after the examiner modeled the acts, and did not stay close to the mother during the play period or retreat to her when unfamiliarity occurred were classified as uninhibited. The behaviors of the remaining forty-seven children were inconsistent, and these children were not followed longitudinally.

Most of the children (80 percent) who had been classified as either inhibited or uninhibited returned to the same room several weeks later and were taken through the same unfamiliar procedures in order to guarantee that their initial behavior was stable and not a temporary reaction. Fortunately each group retained the style displayed earlier (the correlation across the two sessions was .63). Incidentally, the mothers were asked to rate their children on shyness, fearfulness, and sociability. Even though Coll had selected extreme groups of inhibited and uninhibited children, the correlation between the behavior observed in the laboratory and the parents' descriptions of their children was only 0.5, supporting the claim in chapter 2 that parents are not perfect observers of these qualities.

The children were also brought to a small laboratory room where heart rate and heart rate variability in response to a set of varied stimuli were measured. The inhibited children had a less variable heart rate than the uninhibited children, replicating the results with the Fels adults and with the Chinese children in the day care study.

Nancy Snidman, who joined the laboratory soon after the selection of this first cohort, was interested in applying the techniques of spectral analysis of heart rate to these two temperament groups, because spectral analysis is a more sensitive index of sympathetic reactivity than the simpler measures of heart rate or heart rate variability. Snidman chose to study slightly older children—thirty-one months old—because spectral analysis requires the child to remain very still and twenty-one-month-olds find it difficult to inhibit movement. An added motivation for selecting a second sample was the modest size of Coll's groups (thirty-three inhibited and thirty-eight uninhibited children), which might become even smaller through attrition. Snidman assumed that if a thirty-one-month-old was extremely inhibited or uninhibited it was likely that these behaviors were the product of temperamental biases we would have seen earlier. We have learned that this assumption is not completely warranted.

Further, Snidman had to use a different assessment because Coll's procedures were not sufficiently novel to provoke much fear in two-and-a-half-year-olds. Earlier research had revealed that encountering an unfamiliar child of the same age and sex was a powerful way to produce variation in inhibited behavior. Snidman filmed a large number of pairs of thirty-one-month-olds of the same sex as they played together in a large room with both mothers present. She coded the amount of time the child remained close to the mother, hesitation in initiating play, spontaneous speech, and social approaches to the unfamiliar peer. At the end of half an hour of play a woman dressed in an unusual costume—a plastic cover over her head and torso—entered and, after a period of silence, invited the two children to approach her. Some did approach within the first thirty seconds; others retreated to their mothers and never came close to the intruder. About 15 percent of the total sample were unusually shy and timid with both the unfamiliar child and the adult stranger; another 15 percent were sociable and bold. Thus, twenty-six children were classified as inhibited and twenty-three as uninhibited.

Both cohorts of children—Coll's as well as Snidman's—were assessed again when they were approximately four, five-and-a-half, seven-and-a-half, and thirteen years of age in order to answer three questions: (1) How many children in each of the two temperamental groups retained their characteristic behavioral style? (2) Did these styles correlate with other theoretically relevant characteristics? (3) Did the two groups differ on peripheral physiological measures of limbic excitability?

The indexes of inhibited and uninhibited behavior at four years of age were based on reactions with an unfamiliar child of the same age and sex. The primary variables were hesitation to approach the other child, time staring at the other child, and time spent near the mother.

The assessment at five-and-a-half years was made in several situations on different days. One index of inhibited behavior was based on reluctance to explore three novel objects in a small, unfamiliar room. A second index, based on observations in the child's own kindergarten classroom, was derived from the total time the child was alone, staring at another child, or not engaged in any social interaction. A third index of inhibition was based on the amount of spontaneous conversation with, as well as glances at, the examiner during a one-hour battery in which a variety of cognitive tasks were administered. A final source of evidence was behavior with an unfamiliar peer of the same age and sex in a thirty-minute play session. These four separate sources of information on each child were combined into an aggregate index of inhibited behavior.

The evaluation at seven-and-a-half years was also conducted on different days. One index was derived from behavior with seven to ten unfamiliar children of the same age and sex who played for ninety minutes in a large room. Initially the children played alone for about ten minutes. Two women then entered and told the children that the plan for the session was team competitions across a series of games. There were five- to seven-minute intervals between games during which no adult was in the room. The index of inhibition was based on the total time the child was spatially distant from all other children during the free-play intervals, as well as the lack of spontaneous conversation with the other children and the adult examiners across the entire session. The second situation, a laboratory battery with an unfamiliar female examiner, produced an index of inhibition based on the elapsed time until the child had made six spontaneous comments to the examiner as well as the total number of spontaneous comments. As at four and five-and-a-half years, an aggregate index of inhibited behavior at seven-and-a-half years was created by averaging the standard scores derived from the separate assessments.

Ideally, all the evaluations should have been equally sensitive assessments of the two temperamental styles. That is unlikely. We are relatively certain that the assessment at five-and-a-half years was not as sensitive as the others, because one source of evidence came from observation of the child with a single unfamiliar peer. We have since learned that a single unfamiliar child does not generate as much uncertainty in a five-year-old as it does in a two-, three-, or four-year-old.

Preservation of Temperament

We consider first the preservation of the two temperamental profiles from the original classification at twenty-one or thirty-one months to seven-and-a-half years. Over three-fourths (77 percent) of the children classified originally as inhibited (from both the Coll and the Snidman cohorts) had an aggregate index above the mean value, reflecting an inhibited style, while three-fourths (73 percent) of those classified as uninhibited had an aggregate score below the mean. We also applied a more rigorous criterion. To be classified as inhibited (or uninhibited), a child's aggregate index at age seven-and-a-half had to be at least 0.6 standard deviations above (or below) the mean. This analysis revealed that 25 percent of the originally inhibited children met this stiffer criterion for inhibition, while only 5 percent (two children) were uninhibited; 42 percent of the original uninhibited group were uninhibited, and only one child was inhibited (see figure 4.1). Thus, one-third of the children had preserved their original temperamental style, whereas only three children had changed from one category to the other. Because the children classi-

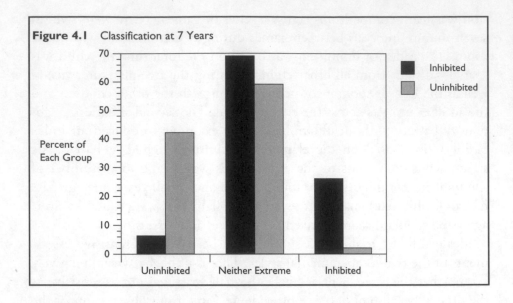

Figure 4.1 Classification at 7 Years

fied originally as inhibited made up about 20 percent of the total population sampled, we estimate that between 5 and 10 percent of a typical
population of school-age children are very inhibited in their public
behavior. This figure matches Kenneth Rubin's claim that 10 percent of
Toronto second-graders are extreme social isolates.

A typical inhibited seven-and-a-half-year-old stayed at the periphery of
the large group of peers, reading a book, painting at an easel, or standing
in a corner quietly watching another child. This vigilant staring is also
seen in timid primates. Among a small group of macaque monkeys who
were observed regularly from infancy to old age (twenty years in the
monkey), the most stable individual behavior—a "personality" trait—was
staring at another animal from a distance ($r = 0.9$). In contrast to the
inhibited child, who remained apart from others, the uninhibited child
was talkative, initiated interaction, often with smiling and laughter, and
showed a vitality that was missing from the demeanor of the inhibited
child.

Spontaneous speech with children or adults was an unusually sensitive
index of each type. Each animal species has a favored, biologically prepared reaction to novelty. Rabbits freeze, rhesus monkeys display a retraction of the muscles of the lower face called a grimace, cats arch their
back. In children, silence is a common reaction to uncertainty. The
inhibited children were very quiet with unfamiliar peers and adults at

every age, although the absence of speech distinguished the two groups most clearly at seven years. About 90 percent of the seven-year-old inhibited children either uttered less than thirty spontaneous comments with the examiner during the long individual testing session or took longer than five minutes to offer their sixth spontaneous comment. Two-thirds of the uninhibited children spoke more than thirty times, and their first six comments occurred in the first five minutes of the session.

Steven Reznick studied an independent group of one hundred children who had backgrounds similar to these inhibited and uninhibited children but were not selected originally on any behavioral criteria. These children were observed at fourteen, twenty, thirty-two, and forty-eight months in unfamiliar rooms with unfamiliar objects, people, and events. The usual criteria of hesitancy in approaching unfamiliar objects and time proximal to the mother were applied to the children's behaviors in response to these unfamiliar incentives, creating a continuous index of behavioral inhibition. There was preservation of inhibited and uninhibited behavior from fourteen or twenty months to four years of age but only for those children whose scores were in the top and bottom 20 percent of the index of inhibition in the second year. These inhibited and uninhibited children were observed at five-and-a-half years as they interacted with an unfamiliar female examiner and participated in a peer play session with seven to nine unfamiliar children of the same sex and age— the same situation described for the seven-and-a-half-year-olds. Once again, restraint on spontaneous speech with the adult examiner and the unfamiliar children provided the most sensitive differentiation of the originally inhibited or uninhibited children. This finding with an independent group supports the claim that there is a powerful link between restraint of spontaneous speech with unfamiliar people and a temperamental bias to be inhibited, as other psychologists have noted.

Terrence Deacon has suggested that the evolution of the primate brain was accompanied by a rich set of connections between the prefrontal cortex and the limbic area, which gave the primate frontal lobe increased control of the emotionally based vocalizations mediated by limbic sites. Perhaps cessation of speech is a sensitive sign of fear to novelty because of activation of an inhibitory circuit that involves the frontal cortex, anterior cingulate, central gray, and amygdala.

Inhibited and uninhibited children differ at home as well as at school. When the children in cohort one were thirty-one months old and those in

cohort two forty-three months, they were visited at home by an unfamiliar woman who coded how long it took the child to approach her and to
play with toys she had brought and the duration of time the child spent
close to the mother. The children classified earlier as inhibited took several
minutes before initiating contact with the examiner; many retreated to the
mother and remained quiet. Most of the uninhibited children approached
the stranger within several seconds and were quite vocal.

We noted earlier that when the children were five years old they were
observed in their kindergarten classrooms by Michelle Gersten. The
inhibited children were clearly more subdued and isolated. One inhibited
boy seemed to be in his own world at school. Most of the day he stared at
other children from the periphery of the room, and often he ran and hid
behind a tree. One inhibited girl, who spent most of the time alone, was
easily intimidated by the boys in the room and froze when a boy
intruded into her space. A second inhibited girl usually failed to respond
when another child spoke to her, and she spent much of the time staring
at other children. Another inhibited girl displayed an unusual response
following a quarrel with a peer. She left the scene, sat on a chair with her
arms folded, and screamed when anyone approached. After several minutes in this posture she crawled under a table and stared at the other children. These very unusual actions were never observed in any uninhibited
child. Kenneth Rubin, who studies school children in Canada, has noted
that inhibited eight-year-olds are not always unpopular with peers, but
they are often perceived as sensitive, shy, and withdrawn.

The Adolescent Profile

The children in Coll's and Snidman's samples were seen last when they
were between twelve and fourteen years old; thirty-six inhibited and
twenty-eight uninhibited youth came to the laboratory for a two-hour
assessment with an unfamiliar female examiner and, on a separate occasion, for a long interview with Carl Schwartz, a child psychiatrist, who
was responsible for the adolescent assessment. The most striking result
was that the external demeanor of most children had changed little since
their assessment at age seven. Spontaneous speech and smiling during the
lengthy session with the examiner were the most distinguishing features.
The adolescents who had been classed as inhibited eleven years earlier
were quieter and smiled much less often than the uninhibited children.

Many inhibited youth answered only the questions posed and neither elaborated nor asked any questions. The difference between the groups in spontaneous smiling was more striking. Uninhibited children smiled as they greeted the examiner, and many smiled as they failed a difficult test item, as if they were laughing at themselves. Inhibited children rarely smiled following failure, and most remained dour throughout the battery.

When ratings of spontaneous conversation and smiling were combined to create indexes of an inhibited or uninhibited style, two-thirds of the children who had remained inhibited from the second to the seventh year were quiet and serious. Only five were as lively and affectively spontaneous as the typical uninhibited child. Among the youth who had been uninhibited from the second to the seventh year, 40 percent had preserved that style from age seven to age thirteen; only two had become unusually subdued and quiet. Thus about one-half of the adolescents retained their expected behavioral demeanor, while only 15 percent had changed in a major way.

These data represent remarkable stability over an eleven-year interval. A one-hour laboratory observation of children at twenty-one or thirty-one months detected the two temperamental types with sufficient sensitivity that over one-half were still displaying some of the salient features of their category, while only seven children had seriously changed their style. This result should quiet those psychologists who claim that laboratory observations cannot be as revealing as parental report. No longitudinal study of the relation between parental descriptions of two-year-olds and the behavior of adolescents has come close to revealing this degree of preservation of two such complex psychological qualities.

Other Qualities of Inhibited Children

The two temperamental groups had similar intellectual abilities. There was no difference in mean IQ score (or variability) on the Wechsler Intelligence Scale. Further, we presented cognitive tests on every battery in order to examine differences in heart rate reaction to challenge. The cognitive performances of the two groups were never significantly different before a stress was imposed. Thus we are relatively confident that the language, memory, and reasoning talents of the two temperamental groups are similar.

When the inhibited children became anxious, however, they were more vulnerable to memory impairment. We usually measured each child's memory for information—often verbal but occasionally pictorial—early in the battery, before a series of difficult challenges had been presented. Inhibited and uninhibited children performed similarly on these tests. We then administered two or three difficult test procedures intended to generate failure on some items, assuming that the failure would raise the child's level of uncertainty. These were followed by another test of memory. The inhibited, but not the uninhibited, children usually did less well on this second test, either because the uninhibited children were not made anxious by the intervening challenge or because the anxiety generated by the challenge does not impair recall memory in uninhibited children. We favor the former interpretation because other research has shown that almost all children show a loss of memory accuracy when performance anxiety is raised experimentally. The absence of a serious impairment in memory in most of the uninhibited children suggests that the prior task failures did not engender much uncertainty in this group.

The inhibited children were also reluctant to take risks. Each five-and-a-half-year-old was asked to throw a ball into a basket and to fix the distance he wished to stand in front of the target. Inhibited children usually decided to stand just one or two feet from the basket; the uninhibited children often chose to stand four or five feet away, as if they enjoyed the greater challenge. When the four-year-olds were asked to name the source of a series of taped familiar sounds, the inhibited children were more reluctant to guess; we presume that they did not want to make a mistake. A year-and-a-half later the children were administered three tasks designed to assess a reflective or impulsive style. The correct answer on each item of the tests was not obvious immediately, and the child had to consider alternatives before answering. For example, on one test the child saw an outline picture of an object, animal, or person—the standard—and four very similar pictures, only one of which was identical to the standard. The child had to select the one picture that was identical to the standard. More inhibited children showed very slow reaction times, but a few were very fast. The reaction times of the uninhibited children fell between these extremes.

The adolescents were given a procedure called the Stroop Interference Test. Many years ago a young psychologist was intrigued by the fact that adults take a little longer to name the color in which a word is printed (for example, the word *green* is printed in red ink) than to name either a swatch of red or to read aloud the printed word *green*. Stroop devised a test that has became popular, for hundreds of investigators have explored this surprising and robust phenomenon. When subjects see a word printed in one of several familiar colors and are told to ignore the word and say aloud only the color, they show a delay of two to three hundred milliseconds in retrieving the color word, presumably because the semantic meaning of the printed word activates some of the same circuits that are involved in retrieving the correct name of the color.

These facts motivated scientists interested in pathology to see if patients with panic disorder showed delays when the words had threatening content. Such a reaction would indicate that the patients were especially vulnerable to symbols of fear and threat. The expectation was affirmed, for panic patients took longer to name the colors of words like *fear, shy,* and *anxious* than to name the colors of neutral words. Adults without symptoms took similar times to name the colors of threatening and nonthreatening words.

These findings motivated us to try the Stroop procedure with the thirteen-year-olds. The adolescent sat in front of a TV monitor and saw fifty-four single familiar words printed in one of six familiar colors. One-third of the words were neutral (*museum, boat*), one-third had a pleasant emotional connotation (*love, fond, friend*), and one-third had threatening connotations (*drown, kill, shy, poison*). More of the inhibited than uninhibited adolescents showed their longest reaction times while naming the colors of the threat words compared with the emotionally pleasant words, suggesting a stronger emotional reaction to threat and, therefore, greater interference in retrieving the color term.

Accuracy of perceptual processes is also affected when inhibited children must analyze scenes symbolic of threat or danger. The two groups were equally accurate in detecting subtle differences between two simultaneously presented pictures that were neutral in content. But inhibited children made more errors if the pictures had emotional content (for example, a woman with a bleeding finger holding a knife), suggesting that the threatening scene created a state in inhibited children that impaired perceptual analysis.

A different form of restraint appeared in motor behavior. Each four-year-old was asked to watch and then to imitate an examiner who fell backward onto a mattress. Most of the uninhibited children fell back in a free, unrestrained fall with their heads hitting the mattress. One-third of the inhibited children, however, fell cautiously to a sitting position.

The inhibited children may have acquired a conception of self, presumably unconscious, as passive and fearful. The five-year-olds heard a taped story, supported by twenty pictures, describing two children, one of whom was fearful and the other fearless. The boys saw illustrations of male figures; the girls saw female figures. The story described the children being caught in a serious storm, trespassing on a man's property, and attempting to jump across a broad ravine. Differential attentiveness to the two figures on the pictures was regarded as an index of identification. The children who had been consistently inhibited from the earliest assessments through five years looked more often at the fearful child, whereas the consistently uninhibited children looked more often at the fearless child.

In another procedure, the five-year-olds were asked to describe a series of thirteen pictures, presented one at a time on a screen. Eleven pictures illustrated an active and a passive member of a dyad—for example, an animal approaching another animal who was lying down, an adult pointing a finger at a passive adult, or an animal chasing a child; the active member was sometimes on the right and sometimes on the left side of the screen. The child's preference for attending to the active or the passive figure was based on the percent of time the child attended to that type of figure relative to the proportion of time the child looked at that side of the screen for all thirteen pictures. The children who were consistently inhibited looked longer at the passive figure, while more of the consistently uninhibited children looked longer at the active figure.

It is not surprising that, according to their mothers, more inhibited five-year-olds had strong fears of lightning storms, swimming in oceans or lakes, going to bed alone in the evening, fires, kidnapping, robbers, and large machines. Psychiatric interviews with the parents of twenty-two inhibited and nineteen uninhibited children from Coll's cohort (those seen first at twenty-one months) revealed higher rates of anxiety in the parents of the former group. These adults had higher prevalences of social phobia (18 versus 0 percent) and anxiety disorders that lasted from childhood through the adult years (22 versus 6 percent). Further, 20 percent of the children who had remained inhibited from twenty-one months through seven years had a clinically meaningful anxiety syndrome.

The mother of one seven-year-old inhibited boy captured the essential characteristics of this temperamental category:

> If something is new and different, his inclination is to be quiet and watch. He is aware of this and has compensating and coping strategies. His friends do not see him as shy. It's unfamiliarity that is the cause of his behavior, not only unfamiliar people—it has to do with newness.

Because we did not wish to prejudge the possibility of sex differences we included an equal number of boys and girls in the original selection of the inhibited and uninhibited groups. The girls who had been categorized initially as inhibited were more likely than boys to retain that style at both seven-and-a-half and thirteen years. A similar sex difference was found in a study of a large number of twins at the University of Colorado. A sample of 178 pairs of monozygotic and dizygotic same sex twins were observed in the laboratory at fourteen, twenty, and twenty-four months. Twelve of the fourteen children who were extremely inhibited across all three sessions were girls; twelve of the nineteen consistently uninhibited children were boys. We will see in chapter 6 that the same sex difference is present in the second year. But first we examine some physiological differences between the two temperamental groups to determine if each temperamental type possesses a biological profile that is in accord with our assumptions regarding differences in limbic excitability.

CHAPTER FIVE

The Physiology of Inhibited and Uninhibited Children

In your results you cannot be too concrete and in your methods you cannot be too general.
—ALFRED NORTH WHITEHEAD

While the stability of the inhibited and uninhibited behavioral profiles suggests a temperamental bias, it is an insufficient basis for assuming a heritable contribution. For that we must show meaningful links between behavior and physiology. The relation between brain physiology and behavior is a new domain of inquiry, far from even a preliminary synthesis. Scientists who study temperamental variation in children who are not psychiatric patients are usually limited to measuring peripheral processes that are distant from the central origins of primary interest. We believe that temperamentally inhibited children have a more reactive circuit from the limbic area to the sympathetic nervous system than do uninhibited children. The most convincing way to prove that claim would be to measure the origins of the sympathetic system deep in the brain by placing electrodes in the amygdala and hypothalamus, as Adamec did with his timid cats, and noting whether these sites were more aroused by unfamiliarity in inhibited children.

A technique called positron emission tomography (PET) might be better at validating this idea, for it allows scientists to determine roughly which areas of the brain are temporarily active metabolically. Although PET does not pinpoint the site of activity as precisely as electrodes placed in collections of neurons, it would be far better than studying peripheral targets like the heart or the skin. But the PET procedure is expensive; the cost of PET for our sample of children would be more than $100,000. More important, it requires the subject to take a radioactive substance into his body. Most parents would not permit an investigator to inject a radioactive chemical into a child who does not have a psychiatric problem.

Psychologists interested in temperament have a choice of strategy that is influenced partly by how they balance two complementary motives. One motive is the desire for certainty in the knowledge that may be discovered. Many investigators derive their prime satisfaction from discovering facts that seem maximally free of error and ambiguity. This motive contrasts with the hope that the knowledge gained will be maximally relevant to the central question that piques the investigator's personal curiosity. Scientists motivated by this imperative experience their greatest joy when they discover something new about a phenomenon in which they have a deep interest, even though the knowledge may be less certain.

Among scientists interested in aspects of human nature, some study human subjects, others study animals. The former recognize the problems inherent in that choice. They know that their conclusions are likely to be less certain than if they had studied analogous phenomena in rats, cats, dogs, or monkeys. But they also appreciate that if they selected an animal species that displayed a quality apparently related to their primary interest, there would be no guarantee that the analogous phenomenon was mediated by the same mechanism responsible for the phenomenon in humans.

Many years ago, Robert Tryon, a psychologist at the University of California, wanted to understand the genetic contribution to intelligence in humans. He decided to study rats trained to learn a special maze because he could control their mating. He made the critical assumption that a rat learning his maze was analogous to a human learning a new cognitive skill. That is, he assumed that a rat who learned the maze in a few trials with minimal errors was more intelligent than one who took many trials and made many errors. He tested many rats and selected those who learned his maze either quickly or slowly. He bred the smart rats with other smart rats and the dull rats with other dull ones over many generations. In time, the offspring of the two different pedigrees differed dramatically in how quickly they learned the maze. Unfortunately, it turned out that the rats who were competent on Tryon's maze were incompetent on a different type of maze. Moreover, the smart rats differed from the dull ones in characteristics that had little to do with intelligence but were related to motivation and fear. Compared with the dull rats, the smart rats were more highly motivated for food and more fearful when handled by a human or placed in an open space. Hence, Tryon's years of labor turned out to be not very relevant to a deeper understanding of human intelligence, even though he had total control over the mating and rearing of the animals and his findings should have permitted more certain conclusions about the genetics of human mental ability.

Even though there are fearful rats, cats, dogs, and monkeys, it is possible that the physiological bases for fear in these animals are not the same as those that mediate shy, timid behavior in children. Thus, one could spend as many years as Tryon studying animals and not learn much about the biological bases of an inhibited temperament. We chose to study children and accepted the serious limitations on certainty that this choice entailed.

Interest in the physiology that might contribute to the differences in fearful behavior invited measurement of two important peripheral systems. The first, the sympathetic nervous system, is activated when a person is threatened by challenge, danger, or novelty that cannot be assimilated. It controls many important bodily functions, including heart rate, blood pressure, pupillary dilation, and muscle tension. When a threat occurs, there is often a rise in heart rate and blood pressure, dilation of the pupil, and increased tension in selected muscles, including the muscles of the larynx and vocal folds. Over sixty years ago, J. A. Barré suggested that the phobias of the hysterical personality were due to an "oversensitive and overreactive sympathetic nervous system," which Freud also sensed: "The nervous apparatus of the circulation is more accessible to cerebral influences [in the hysteric] than the normal and, hence, we find nervous palpitation, tendency to syncope, excessive blushing, and paling." We measured seven sympathetically influenced reactions: heart rate, heart rate variability, heart rate acceleration, blood pressure, pupillary dilation, muscle tension in the vocal folds, and urinary norepinephrine. Heart rate and acceleration were assessed at every age. Change in pupil size and voice were measured at five years, urinary derivatives of norepinephrine at five and thirteen years, and blood pressure at seven and thirteen years of age. Other laboratories have found that heart rate and blood pressure changes to challenge are moderately stable over a year and, in addition, seem to be heritable.

A second system that can be provoked by novelty and threat is the hypothalamic-pituitary-adrenal axis. The adrenal gland attached to the top of the kidney has an inner mass called the medulla, which secretes epinephrine, and an outer cortex that secretes a hormone called cortisol. Both molecules are secreted under stressful conditions. Epinephrine has an excitatory effect on heart rate, whereas increases in cortisol contribute to an increase in available blood sugar, local muting of inflammation, and other temporary processes that help the body deal with acute stress. Sows who secrete high levels of cortisol in response to injections of ACTH (a molecule secreted by the pituitary that provokes secretion of cortisol) show more stereotyped motor movements (chewing, biting, licking, sucking, and rooting) than animals who show only a small increase in cortisol. Although the temporary consequences of an increase in cortisol are generally beneficial, chronically high cortisol levels, over a period of years, are potentially harmful. That is why Hans Selye coined the phrase "stress syndrome" to describe the consequences of high stress over a long period of time.

The central neural controls of the targets of the sympathetic system and adrenal gland lie in a set of brain structures that are not understood completely. As we noted in chapter 3, we should not conceive of these peripheral reactions as originating in specific places; rather, the peripheral reactions are derivatives of a set of circuits. The origin of daily tides is in neither the moon nor the earth but in the gravitational attraction between the two. Thus, it is misleading to assume that the amygdala is the sole origin of inhibited behavior or a rise in blood pressure. The amygdala is an important participant in a set of circuits that mediate both fearful profiles and increased blood pressure.

As we present a summary of the physiological characteristics of inhibited and uninhibited children, the extraordinary complexity of the relation between psychological and physiological phenomena should be kept in mind. For example, a person's report of how much muscle tension he is experiencing is not highly related to actual measurements of muscle activity in the face and legs. Some adults who say they feel anxious show no signs of that psychological state in their heart rate, blood pressure, or plasma levels of catecholamines, while other adults who say they feel calm show these biological signs of arousal. Three investigations make this point well.

Among the American men and women working at the United States

Embassy in Tehran in 1979 when it was taken over by Iranians, 52 were held captive for 444 days and tested immediately after their release. A large number who reported feeling relaxed and healthy, implying that they had coped well with their stressful experience, had elevated levels of cortisol and urinary catecholamines as well as signs of limbic arousal and psychological stress. A similar dissociation between conscious feelings and the body's reactions was also observed in panic patients who reported feeling anxious while taking difficult psychological tests but were not physiologically more active than normal adults. A third example comes from a study of adults asked to solve difficult mathematical problems while cardiovascular reactions, plasma catecholamines, and self-reports of emotions were obtained in two sessions ten days apart. There was a minimal relation between the person's report of anger or irritation over the frustrating tasks and the magnitude of rise in heart rate or blood pressure. Further, although the heart rate and blood pressure values were moderately stable over the interval between the two sessions, norepinephrine levels in the plasma, which rise following a change in posture from sitting to standing, were not stable. Thus there is even a dissociation between two different indexes of sympathetic activity to the same challenge.

One important reason for the relative independence of conscious feelings and physiology, as well as independence among different physiological variables, is that each target system is especially responsive to a narrow range of incentives that is related to its unique biological purpose. Most bodily systems are less responsive to mildly stressful psychological intrusions, like arithmetic questions. Physical exertion always produces a large rise in heart rate or blood pressure because the primary biological function of the heart is to deliver blood to the body. A psychological test does not always produce a strong need for oxygenated blood, and therefore there is a small rise in heart rate and blood pressure. Further, neurons in the medulla affect the level of cardiac functioning by acting as filters between brain processes and the activity of the heart. Thus when a state of uncertainty occurs, there need not always be a corresponding change in heart rate. Cooling the outside air to 45 degrees will always produce vasoconstriction of the arterioles under the surface of the skin; presentation of a feared object may not.

Nonetheless, scientists interested in the relation between a psychological state and peripheral physiology usually do not ask their subjects to run a treadmill, nor do they cool the laboratory and look for relations between physiological changes to these biological incentives and the subject's conscious state or personality. Rather, investigators prefer to create laboratory conditions that are appropriate for the psychological state and assume, perhaps gratuitously, that the physiological systems being evaluated at that time will also respond appropriately, as if the heart, arterioles, pupil, and muscles were slaves of the psychological state induced. It is possible that, on occasion, people who show behavioral signs of increased anxiety to psychological challenge will show a large rise in heart rate while running on a treadmill, but not to psychological challenge. We shall see in chapter 7 that inhibited children showed a larger rise in heart rate to a drop of dilute lemon juice than to many unfamiliar events.

Some scientists conceive of the psychological and biological reactions to a particular event as a unitary phenomenon integrated at a high level of organization in the brain. Hence, if a psychological incentive produced a distinct, appropriate behavior (for example, a wary face), it should also produce a corresponding reaction in whatever physiological system was being measured at that time. As we have hinted, this hope is simply not supported by the facts. Each biological variable provides, at best, partial information about a psychological state. Hence, it is not possible to rely on any one peripheral biological measure as an index of a psychological state or stable trait. Herbert Weiner, who has reviewed the extensive evidence on this issue, concluded that each bodily target— muscles, lungs, heart, skin, or gut—is controlled by local physiological mechanisms that are specific to that target. Heart rate, for example, is influenced by neural and hormonal factors, two different pacemakers, blood pressure, and negative feedback mechanisms in the medulla that are modulated by a half dozen different chemicals. In addition, as we have noted, a person's conscious involvement in a psychological task and interpretation of the imposed challenge are more important determinants of sympathetic reactivity than the objective difficulty as judged by a scientist. The sympathetic physiology of a subject trying to meet the challenge will be different from that of one who feels helpless. Because the investigator usually does not know the subject's private psychological state, the relation between the challenge presented and the biological response across a large group of people will be weak. Thus, there are usually low correlations between a psychological dimension and magnitude of change in most targets.

On reflection, it would be odd if the activity of any one biological target were closely yoked to a particular psychological state. The peripheral targets are activated by chemical and electrical events. A conscious feeling of anxiety is a symbolic evaluation that need not involve much change in peripheral activity. Indeed, a person with spinal damage who is not receiving any afferent information from his body will report feeling fearful or happy. Thus, the psychological states most people call fearful, anxious, and uncertain are not yoked in a simple way to changes in heart rate, skin conductance, blood pressure, or plasma levels of cortisol and norepinephrine.

It is even possible that the two domains are incommensurable, meaning that it is not possible to reduce one to the other because the underlying metrics are fundamentally different. The data produced by the first linear accelerators built thirty years ago are incommensurable with the data generated by today's experiments with more powerful accelerators. That pessimistic conclusion does not imply, however, that measuring physiological activity has no advantage in the study of temperament. If some inhibited children show unusually high sympathetic reactivity, our faith in the hypothesis that an inhibited temperament is the partial result of excitability of the amygdala and its circuits would be enhanced, even though a large rise in heart rate might have minimal implications for a subject's conscious psychological state. The concepts of economics—gross domestic product, money supply, balance of payments—are incommensurable with those of neurophysiology—receptors, neurotransmitters, neural thresholds. But changes in the economic activity of a community can influence the mood of many of its residents, and a particular resident's mood can affect her brain activity. Hence, for some people in some places under some conditions there can be a low-level association between level of unemployment and heart rate, even though there is no direct causal relation between the former and the latter and the measurements of one domain cannot be mapped onto the other.

Sympathetic Activity

The variation in absolute heart rate while sitting quietly did not consistently differentiate the two temperamental groups. We shall see in chapter 7 that resting, sitting heart rates also failed to distinguish inhibited from uninhibited children after four months of age, although prior to four months resting heart rate is more sensitive. However, magnitude of heart rate acceleration to a change in posture and selected psychological intrusions, which is a more direct measure of sympathetic activity, did differentiate the two groups. For example, the five-year-olds were asked to listen to a taped story while they watched twenty slides illustrating two children in the story. The inhibited children displayed heart rate accelerations to more of the slides than did the uninhibited children.

The heart rates of the adolescents were gathered during a variety of procedures. During the initial hour, the adolescent was asked to connect lines on a page as quickly as possible, to insert a stylus into a set of small holes, to listen to and then remember a list of words, to place a set of small pegs into holes on a wooden board, and to stand quietly for a minute. During the succeeding session, which was shorter and in a different room, the adolescent had to listen to a series of numbers and recall them and then listen to a series of randomly presented letters and arrange them into a meaningful word.

Although the average heart rate across the two laboratory situations was moderately stable, each adolescent's highest and lowest heart rate in each of the two situations was remarkably stable. The heart rate during the various episodes in the battery was averaged over phases of each episode. The highest (or lowest) rate refers to the highest (or lowest) average rate for a particular phase, not to the shortest (or longest) interval between two successive heart beats. There is a good reason for this extraordinary stability of extreme heart rate values. Each person's heart rate varies as a result of inherent fluctuations associated with temperature, blood pressure, and respiration, as well as with the specific challenge being confronted at the moment. During the initial laboratory session, over 80 percent of the subjects attained their highest heart rate when they stood up; the standing posture produces a reflex sympathetic reaction in the cardiovascular system and a subsequent rise in heart rate. The lowest heart rates were typically attained when the adolescent was trying to put the metal stylus into the small hole without hitting the metal edge of the aperture—a task that requires extreme attentiveness and control of extraneous movement. The highest heart rate during the second laboratory session was usually attained when the adolescent was trying to determine the word that could be spelled from randomly presented letters. The lowest heart rate was attained for most when they listened to the numbers they were asked to remember. Each incentive pushed the heart rate toward an extreme value; hence the highest and lowest values may reflect important characteristics of the person's sympathetic and parasympathetic system. If so, they might be more stable than the average heart rate over all the procedures, which included some minimally stressful ones.

The significance of peak values is seen in other studies, as well. The peak frequency, not the mean or the fundamental frequency, of the isolation call of monkeys separated from their familiar environment is the most sensitive discriminator of different strains of animals. Many years ago, Albert Ax found that the maximal or minimal change in physiological measures—heart rate, blood pressure, and muscle tone—differentiated states of anger from states of fear much better than mean values. Consider an analogy. The stability of the average speed of walking over the course of seven days in one hundred people will be lower than the stability of the speeds displayed when the same individuals are running to catch a bus and each is pushing his physical system toward its limit.

When the highest and lowest heart rate values were examined together, inhibited adolescents were more likely to have high values on both measures. Further, more inhibited than uninhibited youth had large rises in heart rate when their posture changed from sitting to standing during the final baseline at the end of the battery. This fact is in accord with the hypothesis that the inhibited adolescents have a more reactive sympathetic response to challenge.

There are two possible interpretations of the fact that not all inhibited youth show a large heart rate increase to challenge. One possibility is that there may be two very different types of inhibited children, those who show large heart rate accelerations to challenge and those who do not. The second possibility is that a large rise in heart rate to challenge is simply one feature of an inhibited temperament but not necessary for membership in the category. Inhibited children are also more likely to have blue eyes and an ectomorphic body build, but neither feature is a necessary criterion for the classification. We prefer this second view, because it is likely that the inhibited children who do not show large heart rate accelerations inherit, independently, central or medullary mechanisms that mute heart rate reactivity, even though they are physiologically similar in their central limbic mechanisms to the inhibited children with large heart rate accelerations.

The fundamental feature of inhibited children is a high level of excitability in the amygdala and its first-order projections to the hypothalamus, cingulate cortex, medulla, central gray, and corpus striatum. The heart is a downstream target, several synapses removed from the amygdala and monitored by medullary mechanisms that can be physiologically independent of those that render the amygdala excitable.

This conceptual solution is attractive because, as we have noted, peripheral phenomena like cardiac acceleration are poor indexes of central ones, and norepinephrine levels in the blood are not highly correlated with levels in the brain. Further, people vary in the specific target that reveals sympathetic reactivity to stress. Some inhibited children reveal sympathetic reactivity by displaying large dilations of the pupil; more inhibited than uninhibited five-year-olds had large pupillary dilations under cognitive stress. Other inhibited children showed sympathetic reactivity in higher concentrations of norepinephrine metabolites in the urine. More inhibited than uninhibited five-year-olds had higher concentrations of MHPG, a derivative of norepinephrine, following the stressful laboratory battery. The same was true for inhibited adolescent males during the test battery.

These separate indexes of sympathetic activity (heart rate acceleration, rise in diastolic blood pressure, dilation of the pupil, and norepinephrine derivatives in the urine) imply that inhibited children possess a more reactive sympathetic system. The correlations among these physiological variables are low, however, and usually less than half the inhibited children show the expected high level of responsivity on each measure.

Other Physiological Features

The inhibited adolescents showed a reaction that is related more directly to excitability of the amygdala in a procedure based on an interesting discovery made by a group of Yale University scientists. A rat who suddenly hears an unexpected, loud blast of sound jumps as part of a startle reflex. If, in addition, the animal experiences pairings of a light followed by electric shock, the light becomes a conditional signal for a fear state. The Yale researchers found that when the conditioned light signal occurs just before the blast of sound the magnitude of the animal's startle is enhanced; this phenomenon is called *potentiated startle*. Presumably the fear state created by the light, which signaled shock, enhances activity in the circuits that mediate the startle reflex.

These scientists performed a series of lesions in different parts of the brain to determine which structures mediate the potentiated startle.

Nature was kind, and the evidence permitted them to conclude that when the central nucleus of the amygdala was removed, potentiated startle vanished—even though the animal continued to startle at a loud blast of sound. Thus it is fair to conclude that the central nucleus is critical for a conditioned fear state and, further, that potentiated startle is a possible index of activity in the central nucleus.

In humans, a reflex eye blink to a sudden loud sound is a reliable component of the larger bodily startle. The amplitude of the blink can be potentiated by a state of fear or anxiety, as can the latency—the brief interval of time between the sound stimulus and the blink. If an adult anticipates being shocked, latency to the reflex blink in response to a loud sound is about thirty-two milliseconds, eight milliseconds faster than when the adult feels safe. Peter Lang has discovered that when adults see a slide with threatening content a few seconds before they hear a brief blast of loud noise, the latency to the blink is faster and the amplitude larger than when a neutral scene precedes the loud noise. This phenomenon seems to be the human analog of the potentiated startle in animals.

The adolescents participated in a procedure similar to that used by Peter Lang. The adolescents, who had electrodes on the muscle under the right eye and wore earphones, saw either a neutral, positive, or threatening slide (twelve slides of each type) two, three, or four seconds prior to hearing a loud sound. Marie Balaban measured the latency to the reflex eye blink in response to the loud sound; the average latency was about forty milliseconds. As expected, more adolescents—from both groups—showed faster latencies after the threatening pictures than after the neutral ones, suggesting a potentiation of the startle response. But the small proportion of adolescents who showed very fast latencies after the threatening scenes (less than thirty-four milliseconds) contained twice as many inhibited as uninhibited children (32 percent versus 16 percent). But once again, not all inhibited youth showed this index of limbic excitability, and there was not a high correlation between fast blink latencies and high heart rates.

Inhibited and uninhibited children also differed in muscle tension. Even casual observation reveals greater muscle tension in the trunk, but especially in the face, of inhibited children. As a result, when inhibited children become emotional their faces are less expressive. During the laboratory session at five years of age, each child was asked to simulate a facial expression appropriate to a state of happiness, sadness, anger, and fear. Inhibited children showed less movement of the upper face, eyes, and mouth.

Wendy Coster quantified the greater muscle tension in inhibited children more accurately by taking advantage of Philip Lieberman's program to quantify the increased tension in the skeletal muscles of the vocal folds and larynx. Increased tension is accompanied by a decrease in the variability of the pitch periods of spoken utterances. Variability of the pitch periods in a child's vocal utterances was measured first under minimal stress, when the child simply repeated single words like *dog, tub,* and *cake.* After repeating these words in a recall memory procedure the five-year-old child was asked a series of six questions for which one of the words was the correct answer (for example, "What is it that we have at a birthday party?"). The inhibited five-year-olds showed significantly lower variability to the questions, suggesting greater tension in the muscles of the larynx and vocal folds, presumably a result of the cognitive stress of trying to retrieve the correct answer from the set of six words.

The reduced variability is probably a consequence of greater activity in the fibers of the central gray serving the larynx and/or increased vasoconstriction of the arterioles serving these muscles. The latter process is sympathetic in origin, and both effects are potentially traceable to the central nucleus of the amygdala.

We also examined cortisol levels in the child's saliva at five and seven years of age. If inhibited children are more reactive to threatening situations, they should show greater reactivity in the axis from the hypothalamus to the pituitary to the adrenal cortex and therefore should secrete higher levels of cortisol. (Cortisol in saliva is unbound to protein, compared with the bound molecule in blood plasma.) Saliva samples were obtained at home during the early morning hours on three days on which the child was not ill. In addition, saliva was gathered after the laboratory sessions at five and seven years.

The inhibited children had significantly higher cortisol levels at five years of age, but the two groups did not differ at seven years. Although the stability of cortisol levels from five to seven years was low, more children who had cortisol values above the mean value at both five and seven years were inhibited rather than uninhibited. The nine inhibited children with high cortisol levels at both five and seven years differed from all the other children in significant ways. In a play session with the unfamiliar peers of the same sex and age at five years of age, three of the nine remained proximal to their mothers for the first five to ten minutes. A fourth child sat passively in the middle of the room doing nothing, and a fifth glanced at her mother frequently during the thirty-minute session.

Interviews with the mothers revealed that six of these nine showed signs of limbic arousal and extreme fearfulness. One child was constipated during infancy, retained urine during the first three years, and showed many contemporary fears. A second child was unusually irritable during infancy and at age four had a fear of blood, bugs, and defecation. A third had allergies, chronic constipation, and colic during infancy; at five years she was afraid of playing alone and woke up frequently during the night with nightmares. A fourth child had a spastic colon as an infant, was plagued with nightmares, and was afraid of being alone. A fifth child displayed extreme separation fear during infancy and was asthmatic. A sixth child was constipated during infancy, showed a chronic fear of leaving home to go to nursery school, and was afraid of leaving her backyard. Not one of the uninhibited children, even those with high cortisol levels, showed these unusual symptoms of fear. There was, therefore, the suggestion of a relation between cortisol level at ages five and seven years and inhibition, but it did not strike one between the eyes.

Aggregation of Physiological Measures

Although the inhibited children differed from the uninhibited youngsters in the physiological measures just described, the differences were modest for each variable, the correlations among the different measures were low, and the most discriminating variables differed for the sexes. The fact that not all inhibited subjects showed elevated reactivity on most of the variables is in complete accord with studies of patients belonging to distinct anxiety groups. It is rare for all patients to show enhanced sympathetic responses or elevated cortisol levels. Further, patients with different symptoms (such as a phobia of snakes or blood, panic, or generalized anxiety disorder) showed different profiles of physiological reactions. Variation, not consistency, is the message nature is sending. "The diagnostic subgroups [of anxiety] differ in physiological responses quantitatively as well as qualitatively. Moreover, even within a diagnostic subgroup, physiological response patterns may vary greatly because the diagnostic categories . . . are not homogeneous."

Thus, none of the biological variables we measured can be used alone to diagnose an inhibited or an uninhibited temperament. This state of affairs has an analogue in the low correlations between a person's biological fitness and each of the separate factors that contribute to the more coherent, integrated characteristic of fitness. One reason is that all the genes in a particular person are not equally active in all bodily tissues.

The low to modest correlations between the behaviors of an inhibited child under stress and the physiological systems measured at the time imply that we cannot assume an abstract state of high arousal. Rather, it is more useful to hypothesize a family of states, each linked loosely to a profile of physiological activity. The state produced by initiating conversation with an unfamiliar examiner is different from the one created by trying to solve difficult intellectual problems or the state that follows failure on those problems. Although the inhibited adolescents may be more vulnerable to all three states, each state is associated with its own biological profile. Given the specificity of biological processes it is not surprising that there is a low correlation between heart rate and pupillary dilation or blink latency to noise while viewing a threatening scene. Scientists are in the frustrating position of not having any single, unusually sensitive physiological sign of an inhibited or uninhibited temperament. Although more direct measurement of brain activity might provide such a victory, this state of affairs is not unusual. Although more schizophrenic patients than normals show subtle disturbances in eye tracking, not all schizophrenics display this response and some depressives show the same anomaly. Most investigators find low correlations among diverse sets of peripheral physiological measures presumed to index uncertainty or anxiety. As we noted earlier, each of the biological variables we measured has its own specific control mechanisms, and there is no reason to expect that these local processes will be correlated.

Some inhibited children attained high heart rates, others had high concentrations of cortisol, others showed large rises in diastolic blood pressure, suggesting that activity in each of these targets requires at least three independent factors. One is the presumed low threshold in the amygdala and its projections, which we regard as one criterion of an inhibited temperament. A low threshold in these circuits increases the likelihood of high values on all the peripheral targets served by the amygdala. But each target is also monitored by its own local chemistry and neurophysiology through mechanisms that are probably inherited independently of the amygdalar threshold. Thus, a child or adolescent who has high reactivity in a particular target has to inherit both the amygdalar excitability and the chemistry and physiology that render that target susceptible to excitation. Finally, each individual adopts a psychological stance toward a laboratory intrusion. Some subjects are able to control uncertainty through effort; others do not treat the stressor as containing any fear potential. And among those who perceive the threat, some will feel helpless, while others will attempt to control their arousal. Each of these psychological states is associated with its own peripheral physiological profile. Given these conditions, one would be suspicious if there were a high correlation among any one combination of stressor, behavioral reaction, and physiological response. That is why only some subjects display a large change in a particular physiological measurement.

It is also rare for all members of a particular category to behave in the same way in response to a given procedure. Behavioral reactions are influenced by specific contextual factors. Seymour Epstein has argued persuasively for aggregating behaviors over a variety of situations to arrive at a more sensitive estimate of an individual's basic disposition. The forces that influence a child's behavior in a particular situation are partly the result of the child's more permanent qualities and partly the product of unique elements in the measurement situation. Some children are fearful with unfamiliar adults, others with unfamiliar objects. That is why we measured behavior to both people and toys and assumed that the children who were more fearful to both incentives were more likely to be temperamentally inhibited than those who were timid in only one context. Each situation contains local constraints that influence a person's behavior; observing in different situations and aggregating the data often permit the investigator to detect the individual's inherent disposition.

Similarly, aggregating across a number of relevant physiological variables should provide a more sensitive index of the limbic state for a particular child. If the amygdalar influence is present to some degree in all the targets measured, aggregating will cumulate that influence. This is the logic used by neuroscientists who aggregate across several dozen event-related potentials to a stimulus in order to detect a wave form of interest. Scientists who gather autonomic data have not been as open to this idea. Many seek a magic bullet—the one peripheral biological response that will discriminate two patient populations or two groups with different personalities. But no one has found any peripheral biological variable that cleanly separates two psychological categories.

Robert Abelson provides a telling analogue. The probability of a base-ball player's getting a hit during a particular time at bat as a function of his athletic talent (measured by all of his past performances) is small. The actual correlation between a hitter's talent and the likelihood of a success-ful hit is only .11. Most baseball fans find this fact counterintuitive and assume the correlation is much higher. Over the seven-month baseball season, however, the effect of talent cumulates. As a result, at the end of the season the skilled athlete has a higher batting average than the less talented player. Abelson writes, "The attitude toward explained variance ought to be conditional on the degree to which the effects of the explana-tory factor cumulate in practice." The same conclusion is appropriate to the relation between single biological measurements and behavior. Mea-surement of a single physiological variable in a specific situation should not have a high correlation with most psychological qualities. But the relation of biology to behavior should be higher if the scientist cumulates behavior across diverse situations and physiology across different biologi-cal variables.

Because it is reasonable to expect more inhibited than uninhibited children to be reactive across several physiological targets, we aggregated across measures to create an average index of physiological reactivity, hoping that the difference between the two groups would be clearer. We averaged the standard scores for eight physiological variables gathered on the children in the first cohort when they were five years old: (1) average heart rate; (2) heart rate variability and (3) pupillary dilation during a set of cognitive procedures; (4) total norepinephrine activity in the labora-tory urine sample; (5) mean cortisol level at home and (6) mean cortisol level in the laboratory; (7) variability of the pitch periods of vocal utter-ances gathered under cognitive stress; and (8) the standard deviation of the fundamental frequency values of the vocal utterances. There was a better relation between this composite physiological index and the mea-sure of inhibition at every age than with any one variable in the aggre-gate. The correlation between the aggregate and the index of inhibition at twenty-one months was .70; between the aggregate and the index of inhibition at seven years the correlation was .64 (see figure 5.1). The multiple correlation predicting inhibited behavior at seven years from a combination of inhibition at twenty-one months and the aggregate phys-iological index at age five was .62 (compared with .52 when only behav-ior was the predictor).

Figure 5.1 Relation between Aggregate Physiological Index at Five and One-Half Years and Index of Inhibition from the Peer-Play Session at Seven and One-Half Years for Children Selected to be Inhibited or Uninhibited at Twenty-One Months

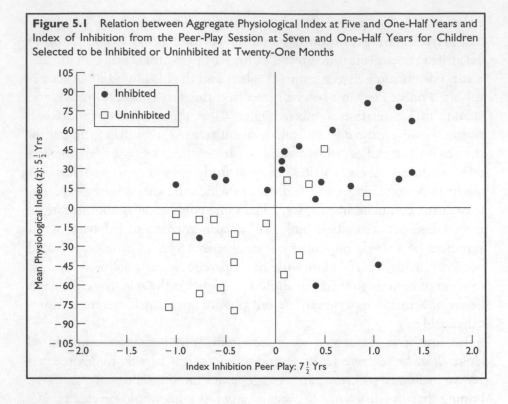

Cerebral Asymmetry

Other investigators, especially Richard Davidson and Nathan Fox, have made discoveries that contribute to an understanding of the central physiology of the two groups. A large body of clinical literature implies that lesions of the anterior left hemisphere, often due to stroke, are followed by an increase in dysphoria, while lesions of the right anterior area are followed by an indifferent mood or, occasionally, unexpected bouts of laughter. These facts suggest that the right hemisphere participates more fully in states of fear or anxiety, while the left is more active in states of joy and relaxation, as we noted in chapter 2. Asymmetry of brain function was anticipated over a century ago by Paul Broca's discovery that the left hemisphere participates more fully in speech than the right. This claim, surprising at the time, provoked speculation that the brain was specialized and did not function as a unity. By the turn of the century, some scholars were suggesting that emotionality was a more central function of the right hemisphere and rationality a more salient feature of the left. The cultural stereotypes of the sexes guaranteed that the right hemisphere would be treated metaphorically as the female half and the left as the male component of the human brain. This division probably influenced Freud's suggestion of a dichotomy between unconscious and conscious ideas and contributed to the popularity of the story of Dr. Jekyll and Mr. Hyde.

Few would quarrel with the suggestion that inhibited children are more tense, fearful, and emotionally subdued than uninhibited children. Hence, they might show evidence of greater activity in the right hemisphere than uninhibited children. One index of difference in relative activation of the anterior areas of the right or left hemisphere is the degree of desynchronization of alpha frequencies. When the eyes are closed and the subject is relaxed and not thinking about any topic, electrical recordings from the scalp reveal a dominant rhythm of six to twelve cycles per second (Hz), called alpha. When the eyes are open or the subject is engaged in thought, alpha activity vanishes—that is, it is desynchronized. That phenomenon is interpreted as signaling that the brain is more active.

If the dysphoric mood of inhibited children is due, in part, to greater activity in the frontal area of the right hemisphere than of the left, then inhibited children should show greater desynchronization on the right than on the left side. This prediction was confirmed by Richard Davidson, Nathan Fox, and their students. Rona Finman, a student working with Davidson, studied groups of extremely inhibited and uninhibited children in the third year of life, using procedures similar to the ones we have described. The inhibited children stayed close to their mothers in an unfamiliar room and retreated to her when unfamiliar events were introduced. The uninhibited children played apart from their mothers and approached the unfamiliar objects. Resting EEG activity was obtained on all children several months later.

The inhibited children showed greater activation in the right than in the left frontal area; the uninhibited children showed greater activation on the left side. These differences between inhibited and uninhibited children in asymmetry of activation are restricted to the frontal area; the relation between asymmetry and temperament is absent in posterior areas. It is important to add that adults who admit to extreme shyness, anxiety, or depression also show greater activation in the right than the left frontal area, compared with those who report being extroverted.

The asymmetric activation could be due, in part, to hemisphere differences in neural activity in the ipsilateral loop between the amygdala and frontal cortex. Because inhibited children are sympathetically reactive, afferent feedback from the heart, circulatory vessels, and other sympathetic targets to the amygdala should be greater in inhibited children. The visceral feedback ascends to nuclei in the medulla and pons and from there to the amygdala, which in turn projects to the frontal cortex. The projections to the cortex could form one basis for the desynchronization of alpha activity. The bias favoring right frontal activation in inhibited children could reflect greater reciprocal activity in the loop on the right side. Uninhibited children presumably have greater activity in the loop on the left side.

There is one more source of evidence favoring the hypothesis of greater right-hemisphere activation among inhibited children. When the children were four years old they were shown ten different pictures, each illustrating two figures, one on the left side of the scene and one on the right, and were asked to describe the scene. We coded whether the direction of the child's first glance was to the right or to the left. Most children should make their initial glance to the right because of the usual dominance of the left hemisphere. Eighty percent of the uninhibited children did look initially to the right on a majority of the pictures; however, only 50 percent of the inhibited children did so. Two-thirds of the uninhibited children looked to the right initially on eight of the ten pictures, compared with only 13 percent of the inhibited children. The fact that inhibited children were more likely to look initially to the left suggests that as early as four years of age they showed signs of an asymmetry in cerebral activity favoring greater right-side activation.

Two Case Histories

Carl Schwartz's interview with a firstborn thirteen-year-old boy who has a younger sibling illustrates a reasonable outcome of a classically inhibited child who has grown up in a middle-class family with a scientist father. Tom was not only the most inhibited child at every assessment from twenty-one months to seven years but also consistently high on most of the physiological signs measured at five and seven years. At thirteen years, he had a high heart rate and a large rise in diastolic blood pressure to standing, together with a tall, thin ectomorphic physique and narrow face, which are characteristic of about 25 percent of inhibited boys.

Tom sat stiffly, trunk tense, on the front edge of his chair for most of the interview, occasionally biting his lip or twisting his hands together. His mood was usually controlled and steady. With the exception of a brief period late in the interview when he smiled as he talked about his girlfriend, his face remained impassive and his straightforward answers were clipped rather than elaborated. His demeanor is captured by the adjectives *contained, subdued,* and *reserved.*

Tom is unusually intelligent and is performing very well in school. He is in the top 5 percent of his class in mathematics and English and is aware and proud of these academic talents. He feels especially gifted in mathematics and wants to be a scientist, because "I like thinking about problems. . . . I like learning" and, as he noted later, "I like to do things by myself."

Tom recalls always having been shy, but his memory of shyness is most vivid during the period from five to eleven years. He remembers that during this time he felt uncomfortable whenever he was with other children; he would sweat and wish that it were easier to approach peers. Tom developed during these years several fears that may have been precipitated by specific events. One night when he was sleeping at a relative's home the house caught fire and everyone had to be evacuated. Tom described the fright he felt that evening; for several years afterward he was concerned that his own house might burn down. When the same relative died a year later, he worried that his parents might be killed in an automobile accident or not return after an evening out. He was also afraid of diving into a pool in his backyard and of being alone in the dark. He had frequent nightmares—he called them weird dreams—in which monsters attacked him or a witch cooked him in a pie. As an adolescent, however, Tom has no fears of animals, closed places, heights, or water and functions well both at school and at home.

Although his timidity and shyness began to be muted at about age eleven, Tom still feels that they are problems. He becomes a bit apprehensive when his parents are not home by 11:00 P.M. or when he is not "trying [his] hardest in school." Even though Tom is close to the top of his class, his school performance is a continual source of uncertainty and the primary target of his temperamentally based uncertainty.

As he enters adolescence, Tom has accommodated well to his temperamental bias. Should the future be generous, he is likely, given his intellectual ability, academic talent, and motivation for science, to become an introverted, productive scientist and a gratified husband and father who will not need psychiatric help. Tom fits Jung's description of the introvert; he reacts to unfamiliarity with more uncertainty than most and, like two other famous introverts who were shy children—Alfred North Whitehead and T. S. Eliot—has chosen a life of the mind.

Let us contrast Tom with Ralph, another firstborn boy born to professional parents who also enjoyed a secure, upper-middle-class home. Ralph was one of the three most uninhibited boys at every age of assessment and, at five and seven years, was the most talkative child in the entire cohort. He showed very few of the physiological signs of limbic arousal as a child and, at age thirteen, showed only one sign—a relatively high heart rate.

Ralph was different from Tom in every way. He was a mesomorphic boy with a broad frame, longer hair than we see in most adolescent boys, wearing an open plaid shirt revealing a tie-dyed T-shirt and a baseball cap with the front turned around on his head. He sat back in his chair, completely relaxed throughout the interview, spoke in a confident voice, displayed no nervous movements of the hands or trunk, and engaged the interviewer almost as a peer, despite the twenty-five-year difference in age between them.

Ralph was remarkably nondefensive. He answered the interviewer's questions with appropriate elaborations and showed no reluctance to admit personal faults. Ralph is very intelligent, and until last year he received excellent grades in his academic courses. He was in the ninth grade, and last term he had received his first failing grades in English and science because he had "been goofing around." But he was minimally anxious and matter of fact in describing these current academic difficulties, which he sees as temporary. Ralph plays the drums and thinks he may want to be a professional musician.

Ralph could recall no emotionally significant events in his life except the death of his grandmother; "I've had a boring life." He has no current fears, although he was temporarily afraid of dogs for a four-year interval beginning at age three because a large dog had jumped on him. But he has a dog, and his fear is gone. He also had a temporary fear of flying in airplanes from seven to nine years. During this period he often flew with his parents, and they told him about plane crashes that were described in the newspapers. But that fear is also gone. Ralph remained calm as he described these earlier apprehensions, as he did when he talked about his temporary school problems. Ralph is sociable, has many close friends, and does not regard himself as shy in any way. The relaxed mood, absence of motor tension, and nondefensive attitude are representative of most of the uninhibited adolescents.

Other Features of the Two Temperamental Types

The association between the two temperamental styles and sympathetic reactivity was theoretically reasonable and anticipated. But the two temperamental groups differed in other qualities that were unexpected, some even surprising.

ALLERGY SUSCEPTIBILITY

The two groups differed in susceptibility to atopic allergies, especially eczema and hay fever. More inhibited than uninhibited children had one or both symptoms, and the prevalence of these symptoms was higher in the relatives of inhibited children. We interviewed, by telephone, a large number of first- and second-degree relatives of inhibited and uninhibited children and inquired about a large number of medical symptoms—sixty-four in all—including allergies. There was no difference between the relatives of the inhibited and the uninhibited types in the incidence of most of the symptoms, but the relatives of the inhibited children reported eczema and/or hay fever more often than the relatives of the uninhibited children. One possible explanation rests on the fact that chronically high levels of cortisol can compromise the white blood cells that keep levels of IgE low. When these protective white blood cells are diminished in number, IgE levels rise and attack the mast cells in the respiratory tract and skin, causing them to burst and release their contents, which produces the symptoms of eczema and hay fever. It is reassuring that college-age, as well as older, adults (aged between fifty and eighty-eight years) who admit to being extremely shy are also more prone to hay fever.

EYE COLOR AND PHYSIQUE

About 60 percent of older inhibited children are blue-eyed, while 60 percent of uninhibited children have dark eyes. Further, significantly more family members of inhibited children—parents, grandparents, aunts, uncles, and siblings—are blue-eyed, while more relatives of uninhibited children have brown eyes. Allison Rosenberg asked teachers from a large number of kindergarten and first-grade classrooms in geographically dispersed New England schools with predominantly Caucasian children to select the one child in the class who was the shyest and most timid and fearful and the one who was the most fearless and outgoing and to record the eye color of each. More shy, timid children were blue-eyed, while more sociable, fearless children were brown-eyed.

The modest association between blue eyes and a more timid, vulnerable personality is present in our unconscious stereotypes. Doreen Arcus tallied the eye colors that staff artists gave to characters in seven famous Walt Disney films. The artists were more likely to paint blue eyes on characters who were vulnerable to fear—Pinocchio, Dopey, and Cinderella—but paint darker eyes on less anxious characters like Grumpy, Peter Pan, and Cinderella's stepsisters.

Variation in the coat color of closely related animal strains, which is a result of differential melanin production, is often associated with differences in fearful behavior. For example, a strain of rats with the genes for black fur (non-agouti) is tamer than rats with gray fur (linked to the agouti gene), and foxes with a darker coat color are less fearful than those with lighter coats.

A second distinguishing feature is reminiscent of Sheldon's hypothesis, presented in chapter 1, that tall, thin ectomorphic men are more often introverted, while broad-framed mesomorphs are more often extroverted. More inhibited children in both cohorts, especially boys, had an ectomorphic body build and a relatively narrow face, while more uninhibited children were mesomorphs with broad faces. An ectomorphic physique is associated with a narrower face—compare Fred Astaire and T. S. Eliot with Clark Gable and Ernest Hemingway. Doreen Arcus has discovered that at both fourteen and twenty-one months inhibited children have narrower faces—measured at the bizygomatic or high cheek bone—than do uninhibited children.

Other scientists have reported a consistent association between a tall, thin physique and aspects of inhibited behavior. Walker found that tall, thin two- to four-year-old children were especially cautious, minimally assertive, and easily hurt by adult criticisms, while the mesomorphs were energetic, assertive, and, if they were boys, aggressive. Two-thirds of the most ectomorphic children were rated by their teachers as more fearful than the average child; two-thirds of the mesomorphs were rated as the most aggressive children. A similar relation was reported for Dutch children.

About thirty years ago I studied a group of third-grade Caucasian children and found that 60 percent of the ectomorphic boys were cautious and reflective when they had to decide which answer was correct on a test that required them to choose the correct response among similar alternatives; not one mesomorphic boy was that cautious. It is even possible that an analogous relation exists in dogs. Of twenty-four breeds listed by the American Kennel Club, those with a more ectomorphic build—the ratio of the standing height at the shoulder to the cube root of the animal's weight—were rated by accredited judges as more timid than breeds with a lower ratio.

The combination of blue eyes, ectomorphic build, and a narrow face is more common among northern Europeans; brown eyes, a mesomorphic build, and a broad face are more prevalent among southern Europeans. There is one explanation, admittedly speculative, of this association. Students of hominid evolution believe that Homo sapiens, originating in Africa, began to migrate about sixty to a hundred thousand years ago. The glaciers had not receded, and the temperature was relatively cold when Homo sapiens emerged in northern Europe about thirty to forty thousand years ago. Because the thermoregulatory mechanisms of these immigrants were set for an average temperature of seventy degrees, the new residents in the much cooler climate would have benefited from a genetically based adaptation that would help them maintain body heat. One possibility would have been a mutation that produced heavy rolls of fat; this change did not occur. Another possible mutation would have produced thick body hair; this, too, did not occur. A third possible mutation would have increased the efficiency of the sympathetic nervous system, which affects body temperature. One of the mechanisms involves an increase in the level of norepinephrine, the major neurotransmitter of the sympathetic nervous system. Another mechanism increases the level of activity of other molecules that increase norepinephrine level—for example, CRH. Because the metabolic steps in the manufacture of norepinephrine are mediated by several different enzymes, some of which are controlled by one or a few genes, it is possible that such a change in DNA occurred. There are inbred mouse strains that support this idea.

Let us suppose that one of the many possible relevant mutations occurred, permitting some people to produce more central norepinephrine. As a result, the sympathetic nervous system would be more effective, and these people would find it easier to maintain a higher internal temperature, partly through more efficient constriction of the capillary beds on the surface of the skin, preventing the loss of body heat to the outside air, and partly through an increase in basal metabolic rate, which raises internal temperature. These fortunate Europeans may have paid a price for their warmer bodies, however. Higher levels of central norepinephrine or CRH, which is enhanced by norepinephrine, could have lowered thresholds of reactivity in those limbic sites, especially the amygdala and its circuits, that mediate a propensity to fear of the unfamiliar. Evolution does not work logically, and this set of features could not have been predicted. Because developmental processes usually influence more than one cell type, altering one developmental process during evolution often has multiple consequences, not all of which are desirable.

As for the blue eyes, high levels of norepinephrine can inhibit the production of melanin in the iris; blue-eyed people have the same number of melanocytes as brown-eyed people, but these cells do not produce much melanin. In addition, high levels of norepinephrine increase levels of circulating glucocorticoids, which can inhibit both melanin production and the growth of facial bone. Some biologists have suggested that genes on human chromosome fifteen control proteins that are involved in both pigmentation and the growth of facial skeleton.

The sympathetic ganglia, adrenal medulla, melanocytes, and facial bone are all derivatives of a cluster of cells called the neural crest that appears in the young embryo at the lateral border of the neuraxis. When the neural folds fuse, at about four weeks after conception, these cells dissociate from their neighbors and migrate to become the target tissues described above. The sympathetic ganglia and adrenal medulla contribute to cardiovascular reactivity; the melanocytes control the production of melanin in the iris of the eye and skin; and the growth pattern of facial bone determines the shape of the face. It is tempting to speculate that changes in the genes monitoring the chemistry of the neural crest cells of northern Europeans thirty to forty millennia ago contributed to the profile of features that characterize the prototypic inhibited child, summarized in table 5.1.

One intriguing study links inhibited or uninhibited behavior to activity of the melanocytes. A Russian geneticist, D. K. Belyaev, selected from a large group of silver foxes living on a Siberian animal farm the 10 per-

Table 5.1 *Characteristics of Inhibited Compared with Uninhibited Children*

1. Reluctance to initiate spontaneous comments with unfamiliar children or adults
2. Absence of spontaneous smiles with unfamiliar people
3. Relatively long time needed to relax in new situations
4. Impaired recall memory following stress
5. Reluctance to take risks and cautious behavior in situations requiring decisions
6. Interference to threatening words in the Stroop Procedure
7. Unusual fears and phobias
8. Large heart rate accelerations to stress and to a standing posture
9. Large rises in diastolic blood pressure to a standing posture
10. Large pupillary dilations to stress
11. High muscle tension
12. Greater cortical activation in the right frontal area
13. Atopic allergies
14. Light-blue eyes
15. Ectomorphic body build and narrow face

cent that were minimally fearful of humans; most retreat when a human approaches them. He bred the tame, minimally fearful animals only with other tame ones, as Tryon did when he tried to breed rats for intelligence. It took only eighteen generations to produce litters in which all the offspring were tame and minimally fearful—not unlike dogs. The notable discovery, which Belyaev did not anticipate, was that dark melanin spots appeared in the animals' fur as an accompaniment to the decreased timidity over successive generations. In addition, lower corticosteroid levels (a molecule related to cortisol in humans) were also correlated with the increase in tame, fearless behavior. These surprising facts suggest that the biological processes that mediate fear of novelty, melanin production, and corticosteroid levels share some of the same genes. In the deep past, northern and southern Europeans were reproductively isolated for more than the eighteen generations that were necessary to produce the tame silver foxes, perhaps long enough for alterations to occur in genes, or in the timing of gene expression, that influenced neural crest profiles combining behavior, physiology, body build, and melanin production. Nature can work in strange ways.

Heritability

The association, albeit modest, between the physiological indexes of sympathetic and hypothalamic-pituitary-adrenal activity and either inhibited or uninhibited styles implies the influence of genetic factors. Although many reports point to the heritability of adult introversion and extroversion, there have been fewer studies of the heritability of fearful or fearless behavior in children. One popular method of assessing genetic factors is to study identical and fraternal twins. If the former are more similar than the latter in a particular behavior, when both members of each pair live in the same home, it is reasonable to assume that the greater similarity of the identical twins is due to their identical genes. One particularly persuasive investigation revealed that identical two-year-old twins were more similar than nonidentical twins in their reaction to a stranger but were not more similar in their behavior with their mother, implying that the reaction to unfamiliarity is influenced by genetic factors.

But the behavioral expressions of different genes are far from determinant. Consider a stark example. Some children who inherit a rare chromosomal abnormality called Turner syndrome—they have one X chromosome and no Y—develop anorexia. Others with apparently the same chromosomal anomaly develop mild mental deficiency—a very different syndrome. Of course, most adolescents with anorexia or mental deficiency do not have this genetic anomaly.

It is important to note that statements about heritability based on the greater similarity of identical compared with fraternal twins have a meaning that is different from statements about inheritance based on finding the genes linked to a specific behavior. Some people misinterpret heritability coefficients, which theoretically can vary from 0.00 to 1.00, as implying a fixed value for the inheritance of a particular quality, like head circumference. The heritability of a quality is a statistical estimate of the proportion of variation that is ascribable to genetic influences and is based on the degree of similarity among people who have different degrees of genetic relatedness. But an inherited quality that was also influenced in a major way by the home environment could yield a heritability coefficient that was low. Consider the size of a three-year-old child's comprehension vocabulary. Although genetic factors probably influence linguistic competence, children who hear speech a great deal at home, especially in direct conversation with parents, will have larger vocabularies than those exposed to less adult speech. Hence, fraternal twins living in the same home will be very similar in their comprehension vocabulary. Because the heritability coefficient in twins is based on the difference in degree of similarity between identical and fraternal twins, the heritability of comprehension vocabulary might be small.

The environment always plays an important role in the expression of genetically influenced characteristics. It is especially important when the behavior of interest—the phenotype—takes different forms or when children with the same genotype grow up in very different environments. For example, children with the genes favoring an uninhibited profile are less anxious over violations of standards than are inhibited children. Imagine one child with the genes for an uninhibited temperament growing up in an environment that punished aggressive behavior, while another grew up in an environment that permitted the same behavior. When these two children became adolescents, it is likely they would show different behavioral profiles; the former might be a class leader, while the latter might be a delinquent, even though the two began life with the same genetic composition. These interactions between genotype and environmental experiences are common and point to the difficulty of predicting with exactitude a psychological outcome of a particular temperament if one does not have a deep knowledge of the sustaining environment. We shall revisit this issue in chapter 7.

There are several well-known longitudinal studies of heritability of the two temperamental categories in twins. Adam Matheny, who has been studying a cohort of identical and fraternal twins at the University of Louisville, reports that identical twins are more similar in their display of inhibited behavior than fraternal pairs; the heritability coefficient was about 0.5. An analysis of approximately 350 seven-year-old twin pairs discovered a similar degree of heritability for shy, fearful behavior. The Institute for Behavioral Genetics at the University of Colorado in Boulder is conducting a longitudinal study of a large number of same-sex twin pairs who were first observed at fourteen months and are being followed through late childhood. A total of 178 twin pairs (92 identical and 86 fraternal pairs) were observed at fourteen months, and a majority were observed again at twenty months of age. The indexes of inhibited and uninhibited behavior were based on the child's behavior in unfamiliar rooms and following exposure to unfamiliar people and objects. The behaviors indexing inhibition were the usual ones: latency to (1) leave the mother upon entering an unfamiliar room, (2) play with the toys in the room, (3) approach a stranger who entered the room, and (4) approach an unfamiliar toy introduced into the room, plus (5) the total time spent close to the mother. The standard scores for each of these behaviors were averaged to form an overall aggregate index of inhibition.

Two estimates of the heritability of the two behavioral categories were computed. One was based on the entire sample of children; the second was based on the extremely inhibited and extremely uninhibited children, as in Garcia-Coll's and Snidman's research. The heritability coefficients for inhibited and uninhibited behavior in the second year, for all the twin pairs, were between 0.5 and 0.6; the heritability estimates were higher (0.7 to 0.9) when the sample was restricted to children who were extremely inhibited or uninhibited (greater than one standard deviation from the mean).

When these same children were two years old, one twin pair played with another pair of the same sex, unfamiliar to them, in a laboratory playroom for about a half hour. The behaviors measuring inhibition were a long latency to play with the toys, total time spent close to the mother, time staring at one or both of the unfamiliar children, and avoiding interaction with the unfamiliar peers. Inhibited children spent more time close to their mothers staring at the unfamiliar peers. As expected, the identical twins behaved more similarly—both were either inhibited or uninhibited—than did the nonidentical twins (the correlation for the identical twins was .82 compared with .47 for the fraternal twins, yielding a heritability of about .70). When the extremely inhibited children— the top 20 percent in the distribution of scores—were selected from the larger group of 314 children, heritability was even larger. Thus, inhibited and uninhibited behaviors are heritable and, further, the extremely inhibited child may be qualitatively different from the moderately shy child.

The complementary role that genes and environment play in shaping inhibited and uninhibited types is similar to their combined effects on physiological or physical features. For example, although a tendency to obesity is inherited in a small proportion of the population, many adults become overweight because of their dietary habits, not because of genes. Further, some who inherit the genes for obesity could have remained at normal weight if they had watched their diets. "Response to the environment is mediated by the genotype. . . . While we are all likely to increase in weight if we eat more and exercise less, only a few of us are prone to become morbidly obese."

The same conclusion holds for inhibited and uninhibited children. Many shy, quiet adolescents did not inherit that disposition; they acquired it. Only a proportion of very shy adolescents began life with an initial temperamental bias. Some children are born with a physiology that nudges them to react to unfamiliarity with restraint, avoidance, cessation of speech, and occasionally crying. Others begin life with a physiology that makes it easier to be spontaneous, relaxed, and eager to approach unfamiliar events. The physiological data implicate inherited variation in the excitability of the amygdala and its projections as one basis for these contrasting styles. If these two temperamental categories are heritable, as we have found, differences in the excitability of these circuits should be present during infancy, and we should be able to predict who will become inhibited or uninhibited long before the second birthday. The next chapter summarizes our attempts to do just that, fortunately with success.

CHAPTER SIX

Early Predictors of the Two Types

When water turns ice, does it remember one time it was water?
—CARL SANDBURG

Although the stability, heritability, and physiology of the inhibited and uninhibited profiles imply the influence of genetically monitored biological mechanisms, most of the children described in chapter 4 were not observed for the first time until the middle of the second or third year. Two years is sufficient time for environmental events to affect a child's behavior and physiology. It is easy to argue, given the Zeitgeist, that a stressful home environment could produce a fearful two-year-old who acquired a reactive sympathetic nervous system, while a benevolent family could create an uninhibited child with low sympathetic reactivity.

One forceful rebuttal to this argument would be the discovery in young infants of characteristics reflecting limbic reactivity that were unlikely to be shaped by the home environment but that predicted the profiles of fearful and fearless behavior. This evidence would add credence to the position that these qualities are inherent in the infant's physiology. Such a demonstration, however, would require the prior solution of a conceptual problem. Young infants do not display the distress to and avoidance of unfamiliarity that are characteristic of inhibited two-year-olds. A distinctive reaction to discrepant events does not become reliable until three to four months, and at this early age the typical response is increased attentiveness or reaching toward a new object, not avoidance or crying. Thus, in order to prove that inhibited and uninhibited children possess different physiologies as infants, one must find responses that are products of the same physiologies that are believed to mediate fearful and fearless behavior in the second year. We have discovered two profiles that predict these two classes of behavior and are theoretically concordant with the notion that the inhibited and uninhibited children are born with different thresholds of excitability in the amygdala and its circuits.

As we saw in chapter 3, the lateral area of the amygdala receives sensory information from visual, auditory, and tactile modalities; olfactory information synapses on the medial area, and taste on the central area. There are, of course, connections among these areas (see figure 6.1). The lateral nucleus sends its information to the adjacent basal area, and a fiber bundle from the basolateral area projects to the ventral striatum and ventral pallidum, whose projections to brain stem nuclei mediate the vigorous flexing and extending of arms and legs infants display when they are aroused. A select proportion of neurons in the basolateral and striatal areas discharge to novel, unfamiliar events. The basal area also sends information to the anterior cingulate, which is involved in distress cries. The basal and medial nuclei send information to the central nucleus in the dorsal part of the amygdala; there is much less transfer, if any, in the

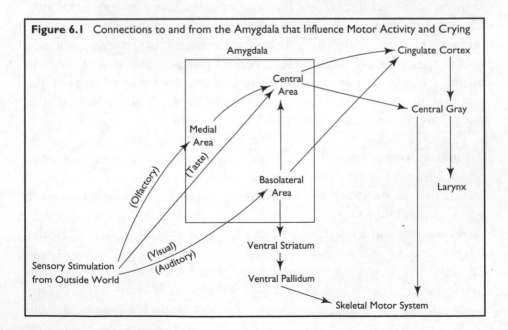

Figure 6.1 Connections to and from the Amygdala that Influence Motor Activity and Crying

reverse direction. The central nucleus is the origin of many circuits that have a profound influence on emotion and behavior. One projection is to a fiber bundle called the central gray, which mediates defensive reactions and a freezing posture to threat in animals. Activity in this circuit leads to motor spasticity and arching of the back, often seen in highly aroused infants. The central nucleus of the amygdala also projects to parts of the cingulate cortex that, as we have noted, exert an influence on distress cries in animals and humans. When the cingulate is stimulated, cries are produced; when it is lesioned, the typical cries of monkeys following separation are muted. Both the cingulate and central nucleus project to the central gray, which sends fibers to the vocal folds and larynx, permitting the expression of distress cries. Hence, heightened excitability in the amygdala should be accompanied by fretting and crying to stimulation as well as changes in motor activity.

The excitability of the basolateral and central areas is monitored by different chemistries and afferent traffic. Theoretically, the excitability of each area should be inherited independently. Thus, there should be at least four different types of infants. Infants who are highly excitable in both the basolateral and central areas should display frequent flexing and extending of the limbs, spasticity, and arching of the back, together with crying to unfamiliar stimulation. Infants who are minimally excitable in both areas should display low levels of motor activity and minimal irritability. Infants with a highly excitable central area but a minimally excitable basolateral area should show infrequent motor activity but frequent crying. Finally, infants with an excitable basolateral area but a minimally excitable central area should show frequent motor activity but minimal irritability. The first group should be the most inhibited, the second group the most uninhibited.

This expectation matches evidence from other laboratories. Two-day-old infants were permitted to suck on a nipple connected to an apparatus that measured the rate and amplitude of sucking. Most infants suck in bursts; that is, they suck five or six times, pause for a few seconds, suck again, pause, and so on. After the infants sucked water for two minutes, the liquid was suddenly changed and sugar water was delivered when the infant sucked. Two minutes later, an even sweeter sugar solution was delivered. Most infants showed briefer pauses between sucking bursts (resulting in a faster rate of sucking) following the change from plain water to sugar, reflecting a heightened level of arousal. But some infants showed a dramatic increase in arousal, while others displayed a relatively small rise in sucking rate. Because sensory information in the sweetened water eventually synapses on the central nucleus, the variation in sucking rate could reflect differential excitability in this nucleus. When the same children were observed in unfamiliar situations two years later those who had shown the largest increase in arousal were more inhibited than those who showed minimal arousal to the sweet taste, supporting the speculation that inhibited children possess an excitable amygdala.

In another study, newborns who were extremely irritable during a moderately stressful examination became the most fearful nine-month-olds. A similar predictive association was found with unusually irritable, reactive three- to four-month-olds who became fearful later in the first year. These sources of evidence suggest a relation between high or low levels of motor activity and/or extreme irritability to new events during the first weeks of life and the later emergence of an inhibited or uninhibited profile in the first or second year.

The Infant Assessments

Initially, Nancy Snidman enrolled one hundred healthy Caucasian infants born under unusually favorable circumstances. The infants were born at term to well-educated, middle-class mothers who had limited their intake of alcohol, coffee, and tobacco during the pregnancy. Although these restrictions limit the generality of our conclusions, they have the advantage of assuring us that the behavioral differences we observed were probably not due to variations in maternal health, prenatal conditions, or specific practices associated with rearing by economically disadvantaged or poorly educated parents.

When the evidence began to indicate that the infant behaviors did predict inhibited and uninhibited profiles in the second year, Doreen Arcus enrolled a second, much larger cohort of over five hundred infants with the same demographic and health profile in order to obtain a more accurate estimate of the prevalence of the various types and, more important, to discover whether the family environment in the first year influenced the development of the two types. We shall refer to the smaller group of one hundred infants as Cohort 1 and the larger group as Cohort 2. Cohort 1 was observed at two, four, nine, fourteen, and twenty-one months and finally at three-and-a-half years of age. Cohort 2 was observed at four, nine, fourteen, and twenty-one months of age. There were similar proportions of boys and girls, as well as first- and later-born children, in the two cohorts. We will consider first the predictive relation between the behavioral profile at four months and behavior in the second year.

Each four-month-old infant was assessed while rested, content, and reclining in a cushioned seat set at an angle of about 60 degrees. After the examiner placed heart rate electrodes on the infant's chest, she asked the mother to look down at her infant and smile but not talk while she gathered resting heart rate for one minute. The infant then heard some taped sentences, saw three different colorful mobiles move back and forth in front of his face, had a cotton swab dipped in dilute alcohol placed under the nostrils, heard a female voice speaking different syllables, heard a balloon popped behind his head, and, finally, saw the mother return and stand in front of him for a minute.

These episodes provoked different patterns of reactivity. The colorful, moving mobiles produced increases in limb movement; the most frequent pattern was flexing of a leg or an arm on three or four of the trials, but quiet, attentive staring on the other trials. The two auditory episodes— sentences and syllables—generated much less motor activity but more vocalization. About one-third of the infants showed a distinct fear reaction to the sentences or syllables. The typical sequence was rapt attention on the first trial or two, followed by a fearful facial expression and then a punctate cry. This sequence was rare on the other episodes because no other event provided such a clear violation of an established schema. Most four-month-olds have acquired a well-defined representation of the combination of a human face and spoken sounds. We presented the vocal element with no visual support. Hence, this event was discrepant and provoked a fear reaction in some infants.

The application of the cotton swab to the child's nostrils produced the most fretting. About one-third of the infants were motorically active and irritable, but it was not clear if the arousal was due to the olfactory stimulation per se or the presentation of the cotton swab close to the face.

Most infants showed no reaction to the sudden bursting of the balloon; about one-third showed increased motor activity, and only one-quarter of the infants cried, usually after five or six seconds. The typical reaction to the mother during the two baselines was attentiveness with occasional vocalizing and smiling. Although smiling was infrequent it occurred most often to the mothers and to the sentences and syllables, typically on the later trials, suggesting that the smile reflected a recognitory assimilation of the human voice.

We computed from the videotapes of each session a quantitative index of each child's motor activity by summing the occurrence of movements or extensions of the limbs and arching of the back. We also coded the amount of crying, fretting, and fussing as well as vocalization and smiling. There were four distinctly different profiles of reactivity.

About 20 percent of the infants in both cohorts showed vigorous motor activity on about one-third of the trials and, in addition, fretted or cried during two or more episodes. The motor activity was not the random thrashing of limbs seen often in hunger but a repetitive flexion and extension of legs and arms that ceased when the stimulus was removed. These reactive infants pumped their limbs vigorously, occasionally extending them in a spastic posture for a brief interval. On some trials, these infants arched their backs, lifting their trunks from the seat, while displaying an unhappy facial expression. Further, on some trials when their motor activity was intense, they would cry following the increase in movement, suggesting that the distress was a consequence of becoming overaroused. The infants who showed this combination of frequent, vigorous motor activity and distress were called *high reactive.*

The smallest group, about 10 percent, showed frequent, vigorous flexing of limbs, but they rarely arched their backs or cried. This group was called *aroused.*

Approximately 25 percent made up a third group, which we called *distressed.* These children showed infrequent motor activity but cried on two or more of the episodes. They were most likely to cry in fear to one or both of the auditory episodes.

The largest group, approximately 40 percent, occasionally moved an arm or a leg but showed minimal spasticity and arching and rarely fretted or cried. These infants were more likely to smile on a few trials and to vocalize on about a dozen trials. We called these infants *low reactive.* These four reactive types, summarized in table 6.1, constituted about 95 percent of the sample; the remaining 5 percent were difficult to classify, either because they were unable to complete the battery or because their profiles were ambiguous.

The infants were classified into one of the four groups by two independent judges who studied the videotape on each child and evaluated the vigor of motor activity, frequency and intensity of crying, and the

Table 6.1   *The Four Reactive Types*

Type	Percent of Sample	Motor	Fret/Cry
High Reactive	20	High	High
Low Reactive	40	Low	Low
Distressed	25	Low	High
Aroused	10	High	Low

ease with which a distressed infant was soothed. If there was disagreement between the two judges, the child was not classified. Vocalization and smiling were not used in these classifications; these responses will be considered later in the chapter. The classifications, made without any knowledge of the child's home environment or future behavior, were highly correlated with quantitative tallies of motor responses and fretting/crying made by different coders. The correlation between these two completely independent sources of information was 0.8.

The four discrete categories of infants were slightly better predictors of later fearful behavior than the continuous quantitative scores because they included judgments of the intensity and quality of activity and distress. Vigor of movement, spastic muscle tone, intensity of crying, and consolability are complex phenomena that are difficult to quantify with a discrete code defined only by frequency or duration of a response. The categorization of an EEG record as diagnostic of petit mal epilepsy, for example, requires a human judgment; no one has written a computer program that is as accurate as the experienced neurologist's evaluation of an EEG record. Similarly, the decision to classify a microwave spectrum as originating in a distant star requires a complex evaluation of the energy profile by a knowledgeable astronomer. This argument is not a defense of the mystery of human judgment but a recognition of the value of informed judgment that integrates a number of features that are components of a phenomenon.

The four reactive profiles were less obvious at two months of age— recall that Cohort 1 was seen at two months—because motor activity was less frequent and because more infants became distressed and failed to complete the battery. The difference in behavior between two and four months is not surprising. One important function of the frontal lobes is to control the reactivity of limbic and brain stem sites and to replace a stereotyped reaction with a more adaptive response. The reciprocal circuits between the limbic area and the frontal cortex are immature during the opening eight to ten weeks of life but gain some initial control over limbic function by four months. As a result, there is noticeably less distress to intrusions, such as a physician's examination or inoculation, at six months than at two months of age, and a smaller increase in cortisol following these stressful events.

Fear in the Second Year

Almost all young children become temporarily subdued on encountering an unfamiliar place or person. A brief cessation of action in response to discrepancy is universal in mammals. Jeffrey Gray attributes this inhibition to a neural system involving a circuit between the septum and hippocampus. We wanted to distinguish between the small number of children who became highly fearful easily and the majority who simply showed a brief period of restraint.

The state of fear of the unfamiliar can be likened to a color; in the band of wavelengths humans call *red*, there are shades varying from the light red of a peach to the saturated red on a Christmas card. Similarly, the state of fear varies in intensity and particular behaviors reflect different intensities. For example, cessation of play and vocalization in response to a discrepant event indexes a less intense fear than do wide eyes, an open mouth, and a frozen posture. And the latter profile may in turn reflect a less intense fear than a scream and reflex retreat to a parent. We had to select an intensity level to use as the criterion for coding fear, for the frequency and intensity of a behavior are incommensurable dimensions. No one knows whether three low-intensity fears, indexed by cessation of action, should be treated as equal to, greater than, or less than the intensity of one loud, fearful cry as an index of a child's fearfulness. This problem is not unlike that of physicians having to decide on the criteria to diagnose a person as manic. The physician usually relies on more intense symptoms before diagnosing the disease and prescribing medication.

We set rather stringent but standard criteria for classifying a child's behavior as fearful. Specifically, a child's reaction to each of the unfamiliar procedures was coded as fearful if he cried in response to the event; we did not code behavior as fearful if the child simply stopped talking, looked at the mother, or even moved closer to touch the parent, who was always nearby. These latter reactions are indicative of a mild fear state, but they were common responses to our unfamiliar intrusions, and we wished to use the signs of a more intense state. In addition, each battery contained two, three, or four situations in which the child encountered an unfamiliar adult or object—for example, a stranger, a metal robot, or a clown. If the child did not approach the stranger or the unfamiliar objects, despite a friendly invitation to do so, the reluctance was coded as fearful.

We rejected laboratory procedures that would frighten almost all children and sampled a variety of unfamiliar events, rather than relying on one or two. Children have different home experiences, and if a particular event was more familiar to one child than to another, differences in behavior could reflect the variation in experience rather than differences in temperament.

Three kinds of events are likely to elicit fear in young children. One class is an intrusion into their personal space, such as the placement of electrodes on the body or a blood pressure cuff on the arm. Unfamiliar objects and actions also generate fear, and we presented infants with robots, toy animals, papier-mâché puppets, flashing lights, and the unexpected appearance of a toy clown striking a drum. Finally, young children become apprehensive in response to unfamiliar people, especially those who behave in an atypical way, assume unfamiliar facial expressions, or wear novel costumes. By exploiting all three types of unfamiliarity we could be more certain that a child who showed fear in response to two or all three of these incentives was indeed highly fearful.

Typically, less than a third of the children cried in fear to any particular episode, and no procedure evoked a fear response in more than two-thirds of the children. This fact implies that the children who displayed at least four or five fears have a special susceptibility to becoming apprehensive. Most children played quietly with the toys during the initial five minutes of acclimation to the examination room, accepted the heart rate electrodes and blood pressure cuff, tasted sweet and sour liquids, were attentive to the puppets, and stared at the unfamiliar woman wearing a white laboratory coat. Although some children hesitated before putting a hand into the cups that contained water or red or black liquid, most did so after urging by the examiner. Most children became subdued but did not cry when the examiner frowned and spoke in a stern voice as they reached for the rotating toy. When the stranger entered the large play-room and sat quietly a few feet away, about three-quarters of the children stared at her. When she invited them to approach and play with her toys, most did so. When she rose and uncovered a robot in a cabinet, all the children stared initially, then turned away to play with a toy. When the woman invited the child to approach the robot, about half did so; the other half remained playing or stayed close to the mother.

The episodes that produced a fear score because the child cried usually occurred in the small testing room. The fear-producing procedures were the application of the electrodes and blood pressure cuff, the rotating wheel when it generated noise, the examiner's initial request to taste liquid from an eye dropper, puppets, the examiner's frown and stern voice to the rotating toy, and the approach of the stranger dressed in a white laboratory coat and gas mask. The episodes that most often generated a fear score because the child failed to approach occurred in the large play-room. These episodes were the encounters with the stranger, the robot, and the clown; although very few cried to the stranger and the robot, 18 percent cried in fear to the clown.

The highest fear score obtained by any child at any age was fourteen, and only four children—5 percent—showed as many as ten fears on any of the batteries. Table 6.2 shows the distribution of fear scores for the two cohorts at the three ages.

Table 6.2 *Distribution of Fears at Nine, Fourteen, and Twenty-One Months (Percent of Each Age Group)*

	Cohort 1 Number of Fears			
Age	0–1	2–3	≥4	Mean Fear
9 mo. (N = 100)	47%	30%	23%	1.9
14 mo. (N = 97)	36%	28%	36%	3.0
21 mo. (N = 99)	34%	35%	31%	2.7
	Cohort 2 Number of Fears			
Age	0–1	2–3	≥4	Mean Fear*
9 mo. (N = 230)	68%	20%	12%	1.4
14 mo. (N = 460)	40%	32%	28%	2.6
21 mo. (N = 369)	36%	33%	31%	2.7

*Standard error of the mean was .12 at nine months; .10 at fourteen months; and .12 at twenty-one months.

About one-third of the fourteen- and twenty-one-month-old children showed no fear or only one fear; one-third showed two or three fears; and one-third displayed four or more fears. This distribution persuaded us to divide the fear scores at each age into terciles and to assign a child to one of three fear groups at each age. A child was classified as showing low fear if she displayed zero or one fear, moderate fear if she displayed two or three fears, and high fear if she displayed four or more fears.

Fear was lowest at nine months and highest at fourteen months. The most common developmental pattern was an increase in fear from nine to fourteen months, followed by a small decrease from fourteen to twenty-one months. This profile is reasonable because of a maturational transition in brain growth between nine and fourteen months that involves connections between limbic sites and frontal cortex. Although young infants will, on occasion, assume a wary face and fret when they encounter a discrepant event, parents and scientists have noted the reliable appearance of distress or avoidance to discrepant events at about eight to nine months of age and an increase in this fearful reaction over the next six months. The two most frequent situations, often seen in the home, are crying at the appearance of a stranger and when the mother, or primary caretaker, leaves the child in an unfamiliar place. The latter reaction, called separation fear, peaks soon after the first birthday. Occasionally, the infant will cry when the mother leaves the infant at home, but crying is far less frequent in a familiar setting.

Why should there be a rise in fear to unfamiliarity as the infant approaches the first birthday? In chapter 3, we saw that the adult reading in a quiet room who suddenly hears the sound of a shutter retrieves from memory similar sounds and their probable causes and evaluates whether the sound is due to one of these familiar sources. If the person concludes that the wind is the cause for the sound, there is no fear and the mind returns to its prior occupation. If the person cannot assign the sound an origin that is understandable, a state of uncertainty is generated. If the event persists and still the person cannot comprehend it and believes there is nothing he can do to cope with that event, a state of fear emerges.

The critical basis for the fear is cognitive—the ability to compare the retrieved schemata of similar sounds with the sound being perceived at the moment, and the failure to assimilate the latter. This ability is fragile in the five- and six-month-old but robust in the twelve-month-old because the ability to retrieve a past event and compare it with the present is enhanced in a major way after eight months of age. The clearest demonstration of this claim is observed when an infant watches an adult hide a toy under one of two cloths but is prevented from reaching the toy for several seconds because of a barrier between the infant and the covered toy. When the barrier is removed the six-month-old typically does not search under any of the cloths, while the one-year-old reaches quickly and correctly. The older child was better able to remember the place where the toy was hidden; the six-month-old did not remember long enough to execute a reaching response. Research with monkeys suggests that growth of connections between the temporal lobe and limbic system, especially the hippocampus and amygdala, on the one hand, and the frontal cortex, on the other, results in firmer synaptic connections among the three sites. The density of synapses in limbic areas peaks at about four months in the monkey, comparable to twelve to fifteen months in the human child. One might regard the growth of synapses as the completion of a circuit that links sensory cortex, limbic sites, and frontal areas. Once this circuit is functioning efficiently, the infant can retrieve the past more effectively and compare the retrieved structures with events in the perceptual field. But the circuits are incomplete before six months in the human infant, and as a result infants have difficulty retrieving the immediate past and comparing it with the present. If the infant cannot retrieve the representations of the people she knows and cannot compare those retrieved schemata with the unfamiliar stranger standing in front of her, she is protected from fear. Thus, fear of strangers is absent in most four-month-old infants but is obvious by ten to twelve months.

The increase in fearful reactions to the unfamiliar episodes from nine to fourteen months can be explained by the fact that a large number of nine-month-old infants may not have passed through the critical transition to the new stage of retrieval memory, but all would have done so by fourteen months. Recall that the timid behavior of defensive cats does not appear until one month of age. The end of the first month in the cat is roughly comparable to nine months in the human infant and three to four months in the monkey. The striking parallel in the age of appearance of fear of novelty in these three species implies that fear of the unfamiliar, unlike conditioned fear, requires the maturation of reciprocal circuits that involve the temporal lobe, hippocampus, amygdala, and frontal lobes. These circuits are not functional during the opening weeks of life.

The Stability and Predictability of Fear

Many children retained their level of fear across the twelve-month interval from nine to twenty-one months (correlation was .37). High fear at nine months, which was characteristic of only 10 percent of the infants, predicted continued high fear at fourteen and twenty-one months. The stability of the continuous fear score from nine to fourteen months (correlation = .51) was similar in magnitude to the stability from fourteen to twenty-one months (correlation = .44) across all children. Only 6 percent of the children went from low to high fear from fourteen to twenty-one months, and only 5 percent changed from high to low fear across these ages. Thus, only a small proportion of children changed their level of fear in a major way during the second year.

We turn now to our primary question. Can we predict the level of fear at nine, fourteen, and twenty-one months from the behavioral profile at four months? The answer, fortunately, is yes. The high reactive four-

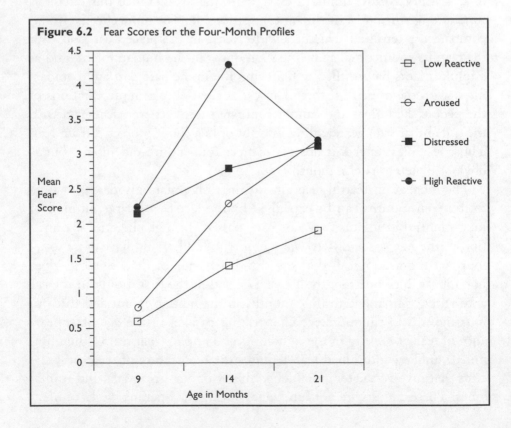

Figure 6.2 Fear Scores for the Four-Month Profiles

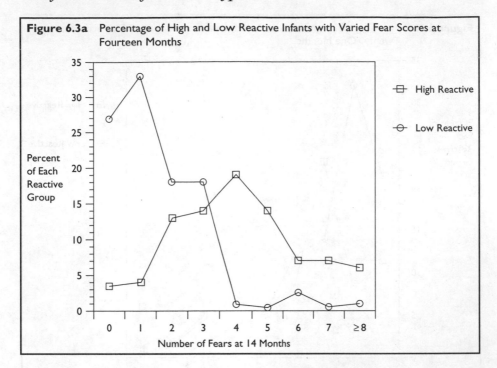

Figure 6.3a Percentage of High and Low Reactive Infants with Varied Fear Scores at Fourteen Months

month-olds were the most fearful at every age; the low reactive infants were the least fearful; the other two groups—distressed and aroused—showed intermediate levels of fear at each age (see figure 6.2).

Sixty-two percent of the high reactive infants in Cohort 2 showed high fear at fourteen months, and only 10 percent of them showed low fear; sixty-two percent of the low reactive children showed low fear at fourteen months, and only 10 percent showed high fear (see figure 6.3a). Further, 36 percent of the low reactives were low fear at both fourteen and twenty-one months, while 4 percent were high fear; 35 percent of high reactives showed high fear at both ages, and only 3 percent were low fear (see figure 6.3b). The comparable proportions for Cohort 1 were almost identical; 30 percent of low reactives were low fear at both ages, and not one child was high fear, while 36 percent of high reactives were high fear, and only one child (4 percent) was low fear in the second year.

A complementary way to summarize the results refers to the proportion of different fear profiles at fourteen and twenty-one months that contained each of the four reactive types. Seventy percent of the infants who had low fear (zero or one fear) at both fourteen and twenty-one

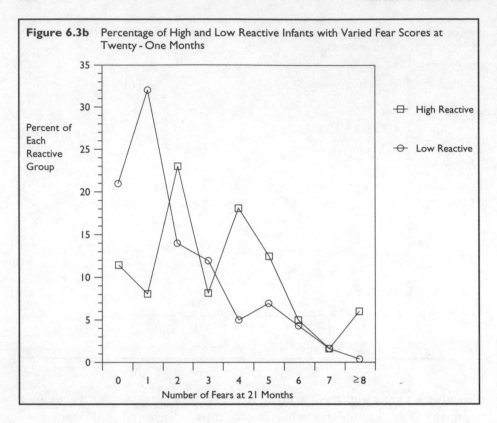

Figure 6.3b   Percentage of High and Low Reactive Infants with Varied Fear Scores at Twenty - One Months

months had been low reactive, and only 3 percent had been high reactive. Fifty-four percent of all children with four or more fears at fourteen and twenty-one months had been high reactive, and only 10 percent low reactive (see figure 6.4). If a child had no more than one fear at both fourteen and twenty-one months, it was highly probable that this child had been low reactive and very unlikely that he had been high reactive at four months.

A group of thirteen children in Cohort 2 and a group of seven in Cohort 1 (7 percent of all children) showed high fear at all three ages. Twelve were high reactive and only one was low reactive (the remaining seven had been classified as aroused or distressed). Thus, if a child showed high fear at nine, fourteen, and twenty-one months, the odds were twelve to one that that child had been high rather than low reactive. Because a profile of high fear at all three ages was infrequent, we examined each of the thirteen cases in Cohort 2 to see if their four-month behavior was unusual in any way. For ten of the thirteen some aspects of their four-month protocol were atypical, even for high reactives. For example, six infants became extremely irritable and could not be soothed easily. Three infants arched their backs during the initial baseline—an unusual response so early in the battery. Two infants showed an extreme startle reaction to the first trial of the spoken sentences; one of these two showed the most vigorous motor activity to the mobiles of any child in the cohort.

As a comparison, there were twenty children in Cohort 2 and eleven in Cohort 1 (10 percent of both samples) who had no more than one fear across all three assessments. Twenty-four of the thirty-one had been low reactive, and not one had been high reactive. Although boys outnumbered girls slightly (eighteen to thirteen), these unusually fearless children were not very different at four months from the other low reactive infants who were somewhat more fearful. The important fact, however, is that 78 percent of the children who were either consistently high fear or consistently low fear had been classified appropriately as either high or low

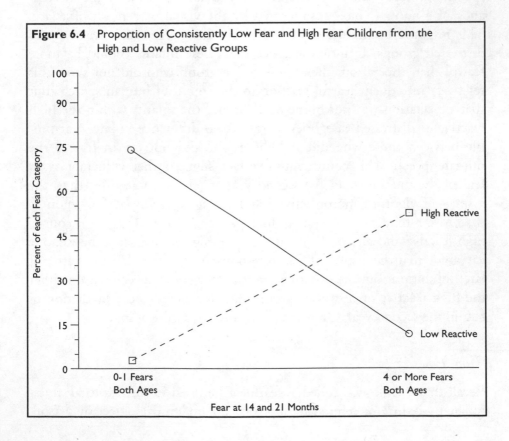

Figure 6.4 Proportion of Consistently Low Fear and High Fear Children from the High and Low Reactive Groups

reactive at four months. Anyone guessing the four-month behavior of these two extreme groups in the second year would have been correct almost four out of five times.

Although the predictive power of the four-month classification was slightly better for children with very low fear scores than for those with high scores, the procedures were designed specifically to elicit fear. Presumably, if we had assessed behavior in the familiar context of the home and coded sociable rather than fearful behavior, we might have found a better relation between high reactivity and low sociability than between low reactivity and high sociability, because most children are sociable in the home setting. The relation between variables is always a function of the measurement context. It is unusual for a functional relation to remain the same across very different situations.

One finding was surprising. A small group of four-month-old infants—about 20 percent—showed an obvious cry of fear to one or both of the speech episodes—the sentences or the syllables—because of the discrepancy of a human voice unsupported by the visual perception of a face. This response occurred almost exclusively among the high reactive and distressed groups. Intuition suggests that these infants should be more fearful than those from the same reactive group who did not show this relatively infrequent fearful reaction to the sound of human speech. But that expectation was not borne out. Among the infants within the high reactive or distressed categories there was no difference in later fear profile between those who did and those who did not cry in fear to the human speech. This counterintuitive fact suggests that vulnerability to fear of the unfamiliar in the second year is related more directly to the display of vigorous motor activity and frequent crying at four months than to the tendency to cry to a discrepancy at this early age. Of course, high reactive and distressed infants had the highest fear score; hence, one can argue that the display of fear in response to the speech is predictive of later inhibition. But the occurrence of the fear cry to speech within either the high reactive or distressed groups did not enhance the prediction of fear in the second year. On occasion, intuition is misleading.

Two Types of Fears

Recall that a child was coded as fearful if he cried in distress to an unfamiliar procedure or refused to approach an unfamiliar object or person.

Each battery had more opportunities for distress fears than for avoidant ones. High reactive infants were vulnerable to both kinds of fear reactions, reflecting a physiological state that renders them especially susceptible to both distress and avoidant responses to discrepancies (there was a positive correlation between the two types of fears). But some children with two or three fears showed avoidant rather than distress fears. They refused to approach the stranger, the robot, or the clown, but they showed no or at most one distress fear. This behavior was most common among the low reactives. Over one-third of the low reactives showed more avoidant than distress fears, while two-thirds of high reactives showed more distress than avoidant fears (see table 6.3). But when we restricted the analysis to children who had three or more fears at fourteen and twenty-one months, most children in all four reactive groups (68 percent) displayed both distress and avoidant fears. That is why most of our analyses use the total fear score. Sixteen percent of the low reactives in this select group displayed only avoidant fears, however, compared with 1 percent of high reactives. Thus, the difference between high and low reactive infants was a bit more salient for distress than for avoidant fears.

There is an analogy in medicine. A proportion of the population can be described as "susceptible to illnesses of the respiratory tract." But physicians find it useful to divide that group into subgroups that have a special vulnerability to asthma, pneumonia, tuberculosis, or the common cold because the genetic, physiological, and environmental bases for vulnerability to these illnesses are different. Most human biologists avoid theorizing about abstract states and prefer to study particular syndromes. Ernest Rutherford once warned the physicists in his laboratory, "Don't let me catch anyone talking about the universe in my department."

These results illustrate the value of a deep analysis of data. We had

Table 6.3 *Mean Number of Distress and Avoidant Fears at Each Age by Reactive Category*

Age (months)		High Reactive	Low Reactive	Distressed	Aroused
9	Distress	1.8	0.4	1.8	0.6
	Avoidant	0.3	0.1	0.1	0.1
14	Distress	2.8	0.8	1.8	1.4
	Avoidant	1.4	0.8	1.1	0.9
21	Distress	1.9	0.8	1.6	1.8
	Avoidant	1.4	1.2	1.5	1.4

established a reasonable, a priori definition of fear that differentiated the reactive groups in a way that was anticipated, implying that our initial assumptions were correct and that further analysis would not reveal much of significance. But separating the fears into those marked by distress compared with those marked by avoidance provided a slightly better differentiation of the two reactive groups and supported the idea that reactive infants are especially disposed to react to unfamiliarity with distress.

Scientists like to believe that their categories are homogeneous and unitary. It is reasonable to assume that failure to approach the clown reflects only a slightly less intense fear state than crying. But the data force us to ask whether reluctance to approach the clown is on a continuum of intensity with screaming on its entrance, or whether avoidance and distress in response to some incentives may reflect distinctive processes in some children.

This is not a trivial issue. The circuits that mediate crying in response to discrepancy are not identical with those that mediate retreat or a reluctance to approach. It is possible that the immediate, sharp cry of fear at the unexpected appearance of a clown requires a physiological profile that is different from the one mediating continued staring at the unfamiliar intruder and reluctance to come closer. Recall from chapter 3 that the basolateral area mediates avoidance in animals, while the central nucleus mediates a defensive-aggressive response. Robert Adamec has suggested that local chemistry within the amygdala influences the probability that an event will evoke greater activity in one or the other of the two major fiber bundles that leave the amygdala—the stria terminalis or the ventral amygdalofugal pathway (VAFP). These two bundles and their targets mediate different behaviors in response to novelty. Extrapolation from the animal evidence suggests that greater activity in the stria terminalis is likely to lead to avoidance; greater activity in the VAFP is more likely to mediate distress. A panic attack may reflect a special physiological state, not just a level of fear that is more intense than the one experienced by a social phobic who must attend a large party; social phobia and panic disorder are different diagnostic categories.

Psychologists are accustomed to thinking in terms of an intensity continuum for an abstract emotional state; hence, there is a bias to reject the possibility of qualitatively different states within what seems to be a unitary emotion. But nature contains persuasive examples of relations between incentives and outcomes in which the processes that mediate phenomena of greater magnitude are not the same as those that mediate events of smaller magnitude. Bohr's seminal insight was to replace the idea of a continuum of energy in the electron shells of an atom with discrete energy states in which some values were absent. The mind tries continually to reduce mental load by grouping large numbers of disparate events into the smallest possible number of categories. There is a human addiction to superordinate concepts that submerge the obvious differences among phenomena that share a small number of qualities so that a maximum number fit into the same class. People find it easier to think of anger as a unitary emotional state that can be indexed by either clenching of the jaw or homicide than to posit two different states of anger. Some physicists believe they will discover the original force that started the universe and that will explain all of matter—the original mover in medieval philosophical treatises. During this era of weak theory in the study of emotional phenomena it may be profitable to treat different behaviors that intuitively seem to be products of the same process as indexes of different states, rather than to assume, reflexively, that they are simply reflecting magnitudes of the same process.

Prediction to Three and One-half Years: Cohort 1

We observed eighty-three of the ninety-four children in Cohort 1 at three-and-a-half years in two situations that usually differentiate inhibited from uninhibited children. In the first, the child and mother were left alone for five minutes in a small room containing six unfamiliar objects (for example, a mask hanging on the wall, a black box, a stool, a ladder lying on the rug). Inhibited children typically played with none or at most one of the objects and, in addition, remained close to the mother for much of the time. Most uninhibited children played immediately with one of the objects, eventually with all of them, and rarely sought contact with the mother. The examiner then entered and invited the child to imitate an action with each of the objects. Inhibited children retreated and did not imitate, while uninhibited children usually implemented every modeled action.

On a later occasion, each child was observed for a half hour in a play situation with an unfamiliar peer of the same sex and age with both mothers present in the room. This procedure is identical to the one described in chapter 4. Inhibited children typically remained close to

Table 6.4 *Stability of Inhibited and Uninhibited Behavior from Fourteen and Twenty-One Months to Three and One-Half Years: Cohort 1*

Mean Fear at 14 and 21 Mos.	Behavior at Three and One-Half Years		
	Uninhibited	Moderate Restraint	Inhibited
High fear	1	10	10
Moderate fear	15	12	6
Low fear	18	10	1

their mothers, were quiet, and rarely initiated a social encounter with the unfamiliar child. Uninhibited children, by contrast, played with the toys, made several approaches to the peer, and rarely sought the mother. The child's behavior in these two situations was used to classify each child as inhibited, uninhibited, or neither. The fear scores at fourteen and twenty-one months predicted these classifications at three-and-one-half years (see table 6.4).

About one-half of the children who had been highly fearful in the second year were classified as inhibited at three-and-a-half years; only one fearful child (a boy) had become uninhibited on this last assessment. The three most inhibited three-and-a-half-year-old girls had been motorically active and extremely irritable at two months and had showed frequent facial grimaces. All three girls had been motorically active at four months, displaying a great deal of tension in their limbs, and two had been very irritable. Their fear scores at fourteen months (10, 6, and 6) were in the top 5 percent of the distribution. Each of the three girls at three-and-a-half years had a small, wiry body build and a narrow face. The mothers reported sleep problems in all three girls and, in two of the three, frequent tantrums at home.

By contrast, 62 percent of the children who had been minimally fearful in the second year were uninhibited at three-and-a-half years; only one child was inhibited. As infants they had been neither highly active nor irritable at two months. If we treat the left diagonals of table 6.4 as reflecting stability of behavioral style, then 48 percent (forty children) retained their behavioral bias, while only 4 percent (two children) behaved in ways that were completely inconsistent with their earlier behavior.

The four-month classifications of reactivity also predicted behavior at three-and-a-half years. Twenty children had been classified as high reactive at four months, twenty-eight as low reactive, sixteen as distressed, and fifteen as aroused; four children could not be classified because of inadequate data. Few infants in the distressed and aroused groups were inhibited at three-and-a-half years; only 10 percent of these children were both highly fearful in the second year and inhibited at three-and-a-half years.

As with the Cohort 2 children, a low reactive classification was a better predictor of uninhibited behavior at three-and-a-half years than high reactivity was with respect to inhibited behavior. One-half of the low reactive infants were uninhibited, and only 14 percent inhibited; 40 percent of the high reactives were inhibited at three-and-a-half years, and 25 percent were uninhibited (see table 6.5).

One-fourth of the high reactive infants were inhibited at fourteen and twenty-one months as well as at three-and-a-half years; one-third of the low reactive infants were uninhibited at all three ages. Thus, a little over one-half of the children from these two categories preserved their expected profiles from fourteen months to three-and-a-half years. Only two children changed in a major way. One low reactive boy who was low fear at fourteen and twenty-one months was inhibited at three-and-a-half years; one high reactive boy who was high fear at fourteen and twenty-one months was uninhibited at three-and-a-half years. This is remarkable preservation of these two reactive profiles.

Only 53 percent of the inhibited three-year-olds, however, belonged to the high reactive category. If an investigator selected twenty shy, timid children from a group of one hundred three-year-olds, only ten or eleven would have been high reactive had they been observed at four months; the others would have acquired their shy, timid profile and therefore would not properly belong in the inhibited temperamental category. Similarly, only four of every ten uninhibited three-year-olds would have been low reactive at four months.

Table 6.5   *Relation Between Reactive Category at Four Months and Behavior at Three and One-Half Years: Cohort 1*

	Behavior at Three and One-Half Years		
Reactive Profile	*Uninhibited*	*Moderate*	*Inhibited*
High Reactive	5	7	8
Low Reactive	14	10	4
Distressed	9	7	0
Aroused	6	6	3

Four infants could not be classified at four months, hence, table 6.4 has four additional cases, noted in bold.

Although intervening experiences must have contributed to behavior at three-and-a-half years, the five high reactive infants who remained fearful on all four assessments differed from the five high reactives who lost their initially fearful profile. Every child in the former group displayed at two months at least one sign of high arousal or dysphoric affect (high muscle tension, facial grimaces, frowns, or frequent fretting), compared with only one child from the latter group. Indeed, every infant who was highly fearful at every age showed either muscle spasticity, grimaces, tongue protrusions, or crying at two months. Recall that ten of the thirteen infants in Cohort 2 who were high fear at all three ages also showed one or two extreme and unusual reactions (such as screaming at the popping balloon or a large startle response to speech).

Brief frowns, grimaces, or pouts in two-month-old infants are reflective of momentary states. Most observers are prone to regard these brief, infrequent facial responses as being of minimal significance in infants this young, products of a room that is too warm, a need to burp, or a state of hunger. It is reasonable to assume that these reactions to temporary conditions have minimal significance for temperament. But that intuition may not be correct. Pouts, grimaces, and facial frowns at eight weeks of age under these laboratory conditions can reveal a stable temperamental characteristic. These reactions may be analogous to a brief lapse of logical coherence in a person's conversation. Such anomalies can be diagnostic of a chronic rather than a transient state.

Some children who experience a parental divorce have more psychological problems two years later than control children who have not experienced the same trauma. Prospective investigations that study children before the divorce occurs, however, often find that those who show serious problems following the divorce also manifested more problems several years before the separation occurred. For obvious reasons, scientists are tempted to assume that the differences between groups who vary in exposure to a stressful experience are a consequent of the stress. They are less open to the possibility that the differences are due, in part, to qualities that existed before the stressful event occurred.

A comparable analysis of low reactive infants in both cohorts who changed their style suggests that environmental events, rather than early characteristics, were more predictive of the phenotype in the second year.

The small number of low reactives who became inhibited had experienced some stress during the second year (for example, a parent had a serious illness, a parent lost a job, a mother went to work for the first time). Sixty-nine percent of the low reactive infants in Cohort 2 who were fearful at twenty-one months were exposed to some stress in the home, compared with 22 percent of those who showed low fear. It appears that the factors that contribute to deviation from the predicted level of fear are primarily environmental for low reactive infants but both biological and environmental for high reactive infants.

Case Illustrations

Before proceeding with further findings, let us take a closer look at two subjects in the study. A description of how each reacted to the various batteries at each age makes clear the differences between the two types of children.

A girl whom we shall call Laura was one of the clearest examples of a high reactive infant who became an extremely inhibited child. At two months, she alternated between babbling and fretting when her mother looked down at her during the initial baseline period; most infants remained quiet under these conditions. Laura became very aroused in response to the first three visual episodes, moving her arms and legs and vocalizing. On some occasions when she reached a high level of motor activity she began to fret, suggesting that she had passed into a state of overarousal. She became so distressed by the fourth trial of the first auditory episode we could not finish the battery.

She was also motorically active during the initial baseline at four months and continued to kick and to vocalize. On the first visual episode, she showed the classic profile of the high reactive infant to the mobiles—she moved her limbs and trunk, and when she reached a high level of arousal on the third trial she began to fret. She arched her back and cried when the second series of mobiles was presented and became so distressed on the third series that we had to stop. She showed a fear face and cried on the third trial of the second speech episode, and we had to terminate the battery because she could not be soothed.

At nine months, Laura was a thin, wiry, blue-eyed infant. She was relaxed during the initial warm-up period but cried when her mother uncovered the moving dinosaur. When the examiner spoke a nonsense phrase as Laura reached for the moving toy, she withdrew in her chair and turned away. The mother reported that Laura cried a lot at home when the mother left the room even temporarily and that she consistently cried on encountering strangers.

Laura was extremely inhibited at fourteen months. She fretted when put down on the rug during the initial warm-up period; less than 5 percent of infants cry during this initial procedure. She cried as the examiner tried to put electrodes on her chest and on the first trial of the wheel, even before any noise was produced. She cried at the application of the blood pressure cuff, refused to put her hand into the cups of liquid, and would not accept any liquid into her mouth. She fretted in response to the examiner's first nonsense utterance accompanying the moving toy and became so upset when the examiner spoke in a stern voice that we had to stop the procedure. In the large playroom, when the stranger entered she retreated immediately to her mother and refused to approach.

At twenty-one months, Laura was still a small, wiry girl with a pale complexion. She touched only two of the five novel toys during the initial five minutes, and she would not imitate any of the examiner's acts. During the warm-up session in the testing room she was talkative and accepted the electrodes and blood pressure cuff. When the examiner modeled the different block constructions, however, she said, "I can't do it" and tried to get out of the chair. When the stranger entered she retreated to her mother and remained close until the stranger left, as she had done at fourteen months. At the clown's entrance, she ran immediately to her mother and, hugging her, sobbed repeatedly, "No, no, no." When the examiner reentered the room with the metal robot, she again ran to her mother, crawled up on her lap, and would not approach.

The mother reported that Laura woke up frequently at night, was still fearful of separation and of strangers, and was shy with most unfamiliar adults.

Anna is a typical example of a low reactive, relaxed, uninhibited girl. At both two months and four months of age, Anna showed infrequent limb activity and no fretting. She was relaxed and minimally fearful at nine months, and the mother reported no problems—neither fear of strangers nor crying at separation.

Anna had no fears at fourteen months. She accepted the electrodes and blood pressure cuff, put her hand quickly into the cups of liquid, laughed at the puppets, and approached both the stranger and the robot within ten seconds. Despite a major renovation in the home, which was restricting the entire family to one-third of their former living space, Anna was showing no unusual behavior at home.

Anna was just as fearless at twenty-one months. She squealed with laughter, greeted the stranger, threw a toy at the clown, and approached the robot immediately. The mother said her behavior in the laboratory was similar to that at home. Anna had no fear of strangers or separation, no shyness with adults, and loved insects.

Sex Differences

Girls were slightly more fearful than boys at every age, but especially at fourteen months (see table 6.6). The sex difference was greatest, however, among the low reactive and distressed infants. Twenty percent of low reactive girls in Cohort 2 increased from low or moderate fear at fourteen months to high fear at twenty-one months, compared with only 6 percent of low reactive boys. Among the distressed infants who showed high fear at both fourteen and twenty-one months, 86 percent were girls. Low

Table 6.6 *Relation of Reactive Category, Ordinal Position, and Sex to Fear at Fourteen and Twenty-One Months: Cohort 2*

| | Mean Fear at 14 Months | | | |
| | Boys | | Girls | |
Four-Month Category	Firstborn	Later-born	Firstborn	Later-born
High Reactive	3.8	4.1	5.2	3.8
Low Reactive	1.1	1.3	1.9	1.9
Distressed	2.2	2.5	3.5	3.2
Aroused	3.4	2.1	1.3	3.3
	Mean Fear at 21 Months			
	Boys		Girls	
Four-Month Category	Firstborn	Later-born	Firstborn	Later-born
High Reactive	3.9	3.0	3.1	3.3
Low Reactive	1.3	1.7	2.5	2.8
Distressed	3.5	1.8	3.3	4.2
Aroused	4.2	2.6	2.1	4.2*

reactive boys were distinctive; they were clearly the least fearful group at every age, with a mean of less than two fears at twenty-one months.

Although the proportion of highly fearful boys and girls was more similar among the high reactives, behavior in response to the clown was an exception; more girls than boys displayed a fear response to this event. The clown elicited the greatest wariness in the largest number of children. Many stared at the intruder a long time and did not approach until the clown invited the child to play with the toy she carried. Although 40 percent of the children did finally approach after the clown invited them, a small group—18 percent—cried in fear as the clown entered the room and ran to the mother.

No other procedure at this age elicited such a clear, almost reflex, distress reaction. Although more high than low reactive infants displayed this reaction (25 percent versus 11 percent), 62 percent of those who cried immediately were girls. It is unlikely that more boys than girls have seen a clown in the past, either at the circus or on television. Hence, this sex difference implies a greater female susceptibility to a fear state in response to an event that has some of the qualities of an innate releaser because it is a serious transformation of the human face.

Although socialization events in the home or surrogate care setting probably contribute to this sex difference, it remains a possibility that biology has some modest influence. Epidemiological surveys always reveal that extreme fearfulness—especially of snakes, mice, and spiders—is less frequent in boys, and a large-scale study on England's Isle of Wight found that diagnoses of anxiety disorders were less common in males than in females. Comparable sex differences exist in animals. Male squirrel monkeys, for example, show fewer alarm calls to threat than females; male rats show less frequent defensive behaviors to threat than do females.

As we have noted, social scientists are prone to see psychological qualities like fear in response to novelty as continua and to assume that the same forces operate over the entire range, so that if high magnitudes on some characteristic predict high fear, then low magnitudes on the same predictor should lead to low fear. The gender asymmetry in very low fear reveals a possible flaw in this assumption. It may be that one neurochemical profile is associated with an unusually fearless temperament but a qualitatively different profile is linked to a highly fearful demeanor; the former may be more prevalent in boys. This idea is in intuitive accord with folk theory. More adolescent males than females take extreme risks involving physical harm, but there is a less striking sex difference in unusually conservative, risk-avoidant behavior. It is known that androgens act on specific neurons in the amygdala and hypothalamus and therefore could influence the probability of fearful behavior. When the amygdala of prepubertal rat pups was removed, males showed dramatic decreases in rough-and-tumble play; the same lesion had no effect on the play of female pups. The minimal fear behavior displayed by some male rats, monkeys, and children could be due in part to a combination of androgenic influences and low excitability of limbic sites acting together to mute the fear states that lead to freezing, retreat, or distress in response to novelty.

Effects of Birth Order

The child's birth order was much less important than gender in predicting fear. There were no consistent differences between first- and later-born children across reactive type, age, and gender (see table 6.6). Later-born girls were more fearful than firstborn girls at twenty-one months, but not at earlier ages. By contrast, later-born boys were less fearful at twenty-one months than firstborn boys.

It is clear that the four-month profile (and, by implication, the infant's temperament) was more potent than either gender or ordinal position in predicting later fear. That fact does not mean that the environment has no influence; it means only that its power is limited by the temperamental characteristics of the infant. A similar conclusion emerged from a study of two pedigrees of Japanese quail chicks bred to be either high or low in fear of the unfamiliar. Although a combination of human handling and an enriched environment designed to make the animals less fearful of novelty was effective in making the normally high-fear strain less fearful, these birds were still more fearful than those in the low-fear strain who did not experience any of the benevolent intervention that reduced avoidance in the high-fear animals. There is no doubt that experience can affect the behavior of animals born with a biological bias to be fearful. But it is difficult to arrange an environment that will make highly fearful animals totally fearless. So, too, with human infants. Later-born, high reactive boys were a little less fearful at twenty-one months than firstborn, high reactive boys, but the former were still far more fearful than low reactive boys of either ordinal position.

Affect at Four Months

We ignored the obvious variation in vocalization and smiling at four months when we classified the infants into one of the four reactive groups because the circuits mediating these behaviors are different from those that are believed to mediate motoricity and crying.

Vocalization and smiling at four months were not highly correlated ($r = 0.2$) and were more frequent among low reactive than among high reactive infants. Vocalization was more common than smiling, but only 2 percent of Cohort 2 showed frequent display of both reactions. Although vocalization did not predict fear across all the infants, the low reactives who were also minimally fearful at both fourteen and twenty-one months vocalized more often than did the low reactives with moderate or high fear at both ages.

Over 40 percent of the infants never smiled, and only 11 percent smiled on four or more trials. Like vocalization, smiling did not predict fear across all infants, but most of those who smiled on four or more trials were low reactive boys. To our surprise, however, low reactive girls did not smile more often than the other girls.

The failure of four-month vocalization, smiling, crying, or motoricity to predict later fear with unusual sensitivity, when each of these responses was considered alone, implies that the quality of affect following arousal—an excited compared with a distressed state—reflects processes different from those that contribute to the ease of becoming aroused. That is why we classified aroused and distressed infants in separate groups. There is no good reason why ease of motor arousal to the colorful mobiles should be correlated with a preference for reacting with smiling and vocal excitement, on the one hand, or fretful distress, on the other. A special vulnerability to distress following arousal might be mediated by amygdalar projections to the cingulate cortex, VAFP, central gray, and the sympathetic nervous system. An excited but nondistressed state is likely to be mediated by other circuits, perhaps projections to the stria terminalis and the septum. Although all high reactive infants are easily aroused, low reactive infants belong to one of two types. Some become excitable and vocalize frequently; others are minimally excitable and neither smile nor vocalize.

As we have noted, vocal excitement or smiling at four months did not predict later fear; in fact, the trend was for highly vocal, smiling four-month-old male infants to have fewer, rather than more, avoidant fears.

Among low reactive infants, boys were more vocal and smiled more often than girls, and these boys were minimally fearful. One of the most vocal four-month-old boys was among the least fearful children.

A group of forty-two children in Cohort 2 (10 percent of the group, nineteen males and twenty-three females) combined either very high or very low four-month vocalization with minimal crying. Hence, most were low reactive (thirty-six of forty-two); the remaining six infants were aroused. These two groups did not differ in fear, smiling, or talking in the second year. But they did differ in level of energy. The term *energy* refers to the tendency in older children to speak in a loud voice, to squeal in delight, and to become restless as the battery proceeded. Thirty-two percent of the highly vocal four-month-olds were judged to possess a high energy level at fourteen and twenty-one months, compared with only 4 percent of the minimally vocal children. When these highly vocal infants smiled in the second year, their smiles were broad with obvious changes in the muscles of the eyes, and often ended in a laugh. The smile of the minimally vocal infants was brief, with little involvement of the eyes. Thus, frequent vocalization at four months, in a group of minimally fearful, nonirritable infants, was associated in the second year with more intense but nondistressed emotional reactivity. In the next chapter we shall see additional support for the claim that ease of arousal is relatively independent of the quality of the affect state that accompanies the heightened arousal.

Later Affect Display: Cohort 2

Each child in Cohort 2 was rated (on a three-point scale) for frequency of vocalization and smiling during the batteries at nine, fourteen, and twenty-one months. Surprisingly, vocalization or smiling at four months did not predict the later display of these responses. Although vocalization did not differentiate the temperamental groups (for both sexes), smiling did. High reactive infants smiled much less often than the other three groups; low reactive and aroused infants smiled most often. The ratio of low to high reactive infants who were frequent smilers at nine, fourteen, and twenty-one months was four to one, in contrast to the two to one ratio for the entire sample.

A comparison of the least frequent smilers in the second year (those infants who received a rating of one at both fourteen and twenty-one

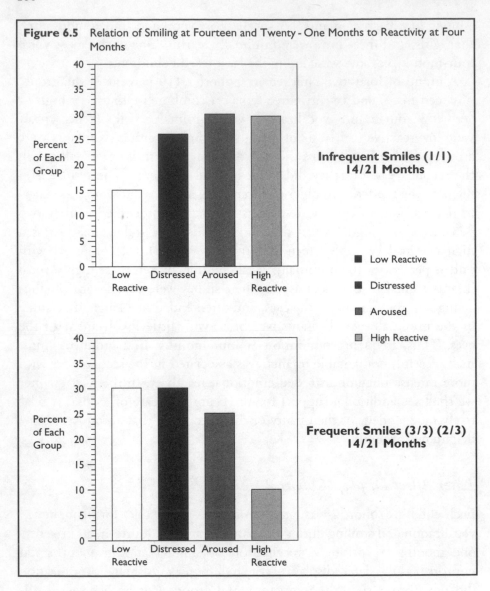

Figure 6.5   Relation of Smiling at Fourteen and Twenty - One Months to Reactivity at Four Months

months) with the most frequent smilers (those who received a rating of three at both ages or ratings of two at one age and three at the other) differentiated the reactive groups more cleanly (see figure 6.5). Twenty-nine percent of the high reactives smiled infrequently, while only 11 percent were frequent smilers. By contrast, 29 percent of low reactives were frequent smilers, and only 16 percent were infrequent. It is not surprising that smiling during the episodes in the second year was inversely related to fear across all children—the more smiling, the less fear. However, more boys than girls were also among the frequent smilers (60 versus 40 percent). Because low reactive boys also vocalized more often than high reactive boys, it appears that display of positive affect better differentiated high from low reactive boys than high from low reactive girls.

It is important to point out that even though high reactive and distressed infants had similar fear scores at twenty-one months, more children from the latter group were frequent smilers, supporting our claim that these two groups are temperamentally different. When we restricted the comparison to those infants who had high fear scores at fourteen months, more distressed than high reactive infants smiled frequently at both fourteen and twenty-one months.

High reactive infants become dour, serious, and fearful as they grow, while low reactives become more joyful and fearless as they mature. Eighteen percent of the children showed a profile that combined low reactivity, low fear, and frequent smiling, while 8 percent showed a profile of high reactivity, high fear, and infrequent smiling. Before the child is two years old, one can see the origins of Galen's sanguine and melancholic temperamental types (see table 6.7).

Further, these two groups differ in facial skeleton in ways that are surprising to us and will be to our colleagues but would not have been to nineteenth-century observers. The infants (of both sexes) who had narrow faces at fourteen and twenty-one months were more often high reactive, highly fearful, and minimally smiling in the second year; the infants with broad faces more often were low reactive, showed low fear, and smiled frequently (see figure 6.6). When the top and bottom quartiles of the index of facial width were compared, 65 percent of those who had

Table 6.7 *Estimates of Prevalence of Temperamental Types*

Begin with 100 healthy, middle-class, Caucasian infants

About 40 will be low reactive	About 22 will be high reactive
25 will be low reactive and low fear at 1 year	14 will be high reactive and high fear at 1 year
18 will be low reactive, low fear, and frequent smiling at 1 year	8 will be high reactive, high fear, and infrequent smiling at 1 year

broad faces were frequent smilers; 71 percent of those with narrow faces were infrequent smilers (see figure 6.7). Perhaps movie directors who cast broad-faced actors and actresses in jovial roles unconsciously sense the audience's expectation that the shape of a person's face is related to his

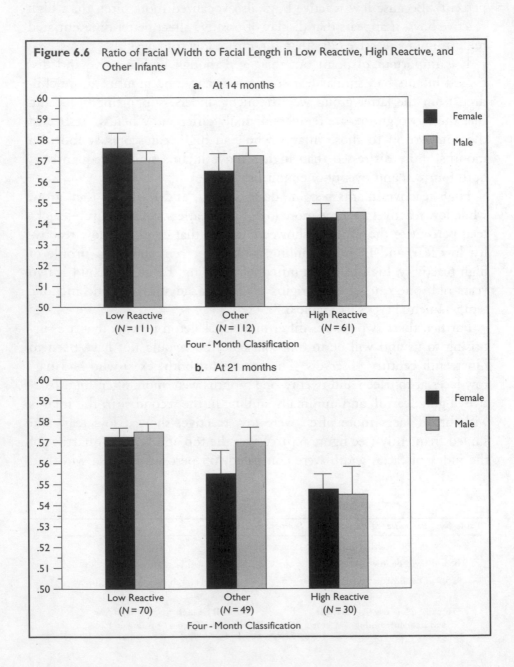

Figure 6.6 Ratio of Facial Width to Facial Length in Low Reactive, High Reactive, and Other Infants

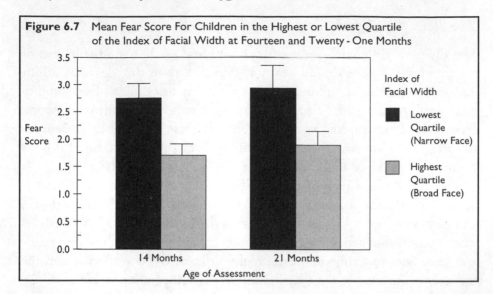

Figure 6.7 Mean Fear Score For Children in the Highest or Lowest Quartile of the Index of Facial Width at Fourteen and Twenty-One Months

mood. Recall Caesar's comment to Antony: "Yond Cassius has a lean and hungry look. He thinks too much; such men are dangerous."

Neither height, weight, nor body mass differentiated the high and low reactive infants, however, and the correlation between the width of the face and body mass was low—only 0.3. Thus, the facial skeleton is revealing a special biological characteristic of the two groups.

The fact that facial skeleton is a significant correlate of the two temperamental groups argues—we believe persuasively—for the influence of genetic mechanisms on features as diverse as facial bone growth, reactivity, affect, and fear of the unfamiliar. We suggested in chapter 5 that the neurochemistry of the neural crest cells may be relevant to this intriguing set of associations. High levels of glucocorticoids (or a high density of receptors) can affect the growth of facial bone. The inbred mice strains for whom growth of facial bone after birth is most vulnerable to the administration of glucocorticoids are also more avoidant to novelty than are strains that are far less vulnerable to the administration of the hormone. Thus, differences in the chemistry of the neural crest might contribute to a cluster of diverse traits that others have noted but not understood. Perhaps the nineteenth-century speculation that the shape of a person's face might reveal a little about his or her personality was not as bizarre as I, and most other twentieth-century psychologists, believed.

The Role of the Home

The dramatic difference between high and low reactive infants in fear of the unfamiliar in the second year adds credibility to the idea that inhibited and uninhibited children inherit different thresholds of excitability in the amygdala and its circuits. Short of direct measurement of neural activity in these children, we have come as close as possible to demonstrating, using the ancient method of indirect proof, that some infants begin life with a bias to develop one or the other of these styles.

The environment is not without influence, however. Almost 40 percent of the high reactive infants did not become highly fearful, despite a profile and demographic background that was similar to those high reactive infants who became inhibited. Because all infants experienced a healthy pregnancy and were born at term without difficulty, it is likely that experience in the first year contributes to the actualization of this temperamental bias.

Doreen Arcus has discovered some of the events in the home that can affect the actualization. A group of twenty-four high reactive infants and twenty-six low reactive infants—all firstborn—were observed in their homes, with the mother present, at five, seven, nine, eleven, and thirteen months. The videotapes from these home visits were analyzed, and the results suggest an interaction between the infant's temperament and home experience. The maternal behaviors that predicted the fear scores for high reactive infants appeared to be produced by different maternal philosophies. Some mothers believe that, most of the time, they should be sensitive and protective of their infants; others award greater importance to helping the child adapt and learn how to cope with minor stresses. The way each mother balances these two imperatives in contemporary American culture determines her behavior with her infant, which in turn influences how fearful the high reactive child will be.

One important predictor was the proportion of time the mother held the infant while it was irritable, especially during the first half year, when mothers hold infants a great deal. The variable was defined formally as the ratio of the time the mother held the infant while it was fretting or crying minus the time the mother held the infant while it was calm divided by the total time the child was held. Obviously, a high ratio reflects the fact that the mother holds the baby when it needs help but not when it doesn't. A similar variable was created for expressions of physical affection toward the infant.

A second relevant practice called limit setting was derived primarily from the later visits to the home at ages nine to thirteen months, after the child was crawling and beginning to stand. Whenever the infant was engaged in any one of a delimited number of transgressions—behaviors defined as dangerous to the infant or others, violations of standards of cleanliness, or acts not healthy for the infant—the mothers' reaction was coded. Examples include reaching for a knife or mouthing an object that might make the baby choke. The variable was defined as the proportion of all transgressions for which the mother issued a firm, direct command or prohibition or blocked the child's access to the forbidden object. Thus, a high score reflected a mother who firmly set strict limits with direct strategies, even though none of the maternal behaviors was harsh. A low score meant the mother was indirect in her limit setting.

The holding and limit setting scores contributed about a third of the variance to the fear score at fourteen months for high reactive infants; it contributed very little variance for low reactive infants. Specifically, high reactive infants growing up with mothers who use firm and direct limit setting and are not always holding them had significantly lower fear scores than high reactive infants with mothers who are less firm and more protective. It appears that mothers who protect their high reactive infants from frustration and anxiety in the hope of effecting a benevolent out-come seem to exacerbate the infant's uncertainty and produce the opposite effect. This result is in greater accord with the old-fashioned behavioristic view than with the modern emphasis on the infant's need for a sensitive parent.

At the end of the twenty-one-month evaluation, all the mothers were interviewed and, as part of that interview, were asked to rank fourteen positive qualities in order of their desirability for the child at five years of age. One of the qualities was obedience to the parents. Every child in the small group of high reactive infants who showed low fear at fourteen and twenty-one months had a mother who regarded obedience as desirable (ranked 1–6). Every mother of a high reactive who placed obedience as relatively unimportant (ranked 7–14) had a child with moderate or high fear. Among the remaining three groups as well, more children with low fear came from homes where the mothers valued obedience.

Montaigne might have smiled upon learning of Arcus's results. He wrote in the *Essays* that parents' natural affection for their children makes them too soft and tender: "Parents are incapable of punishing faults or of letting him be brought up roughly and carelessly, as he should be. . . . If one wants to make him into a man of parts, one must certainly not spare him in youth."

One explanation, admittedly constructed after the fact, is that the mother who requires her eight- to twelve-month-old to meet her socialization demands forces the infant to deal with the mild uncertainty produced by the parent's interference in his behavior. A mother who snaps at a distance "Michael, get away from the lamp" creates a punctate, temporary state of uncertainty in the crawling baby, who did not expect this interruption. Repetitions of this and similar events hundreds of times over the first year permit the growing infant to habituate to the sudden occurrence of the unexpected. When this acclimation is combined with a home environment that, although loving and affectionate, does not reward excessive crying, it may not be surprising that we see a two-year-old who is less likely to cry when the examiner frowns or tries to put a blood pressure cuff around the child's arm.

A high reactive infant reacts to unfamiliarity and challenge with initial avoidance and occasional distress. If the home environment does not partially extinguish that habit, the behavior should persist and such children could be expected to react to the unfamiliar events encountered in the laboratory with crying and avoidance. The infants who had to accommodate to minor frustrations or challenges in the home had opportunities to lose their initially fearful reactions. If their mothers did not come to nurture them every time they cried and, in addition, consistently imposed reasonable demands, such children could have learned to cope with unfamiliar intrusions. As a result, they could be expected to be less fearful in the laboratory.

Low reactive infants typically do not react to unfamiliar challenge with distress or avoidance. The two maternal styles should therefore be expected to exert a less important influence on fear; in fact, these maternal practices did not predict which low reactives would be high and which low fear. Thus, the development of high or low fear depended upon the child's temperament and the home environment. Knowledge of both led to a better prediction of behavior in the second year. Put differently, the maternal behaviors affected high and low reactive infants in different ways.

Once again, a biological analogy is helpful. For the vast majority of infants who can metabolize the common amino acid phenylalanine, which is found in most foods, variation in diet is unrelated to later mental retardation. But for the very small number of infants who cannot metabolize this amino acid, a normal diet leads to mental retardation while a diet with restricted phenylalanine intake prevents serious retardation.

Environments do not influence all children in the same way; this is the fundamental premise in evolution. Rivers containing a high degree of toxic waste will eliminate most species but will have minimal influence on a select few who happen to possess an advantageous genetic constitution. That is why most of the time, short of severe abuse and neglect, we should not ask about the consequences of variation in parental practices, neighborhoods, or school environments on the development of children. The proper question is: How does a particular environment affect a specific temperamental type of child? Galen, too, believed that the temperament at birth interacted with the events of the years that followed.

One more corpus of evidence that would increase our confidence in the conclusion that high reactivity and low reactivity at four months represent early signs of the inhibited and uninhibited categories would be the discovery that high reactive infants, like older inhibited children, possess greater sympathetic reactivity than low reactive infants. We confront that issue in the next chapter.

CHAPTER SEVEN

Infant Reactivity and Sympathetic Physiology

A crystal looks rhythmic from excess of pattern while the fog is unrhythmic in that it exhibits a patternless confusion of detail.

—ALFRED NORTH WHITEHEAD

The infant's reactivity profile at four months proved to be a sensitive predictor of inhibited and uninhibited behavior in the second year. The implication is that the physiological characteristics of these two behavioral styles should also be present in high and low reactive infants. It will be recalled from chapter 5 that the excitability of varied targets of the sympathetic nervous system, including the heart and the pupil, differentiated inhibited from uninhibited school-age children. Further, these differences were in accord with the hypothesis that the two temperamental groups differed in the threshold of excitability of the amygdala and its projections to the sympathetic chain. Hence, it is reasonable to expect that high and low reactive infants should also differ in the responsivity of sympathetic targets. This chapter explores that idea.

As we explore the evidence, it will be helpful to remember the complex relations between peripheral physiology and behavior. Typically, the magnitude of the relation between the two systems does not hit one between the eyes. Even when a particular correlation is significant statistically, the size of the effect is usually modest, and there are often interactions with sex, age, or some other characteristic that is not of direct interest. This fact is disappointing to those who hold the Platonic conception of a hypothetical brain state and radiating from it a cascade of automatically released physiological, emotional, cognitive, and behavioral consequences. Although technical reports rarely say so explicitly, they sometimes imply that the robustness of the relation between a central psychological-physiological state and a behavior should be matched by an equally robust relation to a peripheral physiological response. This ideal is aesthetic but, unfortunately, discordant with the facts. A challenging incentive that induces a brain state often produces a change in behavior or subjective feeling but no change in several peripheral physiological targets, or a change in peripheral physiology but no obvious change in behavior; occasionally, it may produce no change in either behavior or peripheral physiology. We have on many occasions observed a minimal change in heart rate to an event that led the child to assume a wary face and, two seconds later, to cry. As we noted in the preface, mind and body must accommodate to each other, for each has only partial autonomy. On occasion, a person can use psychological devices to prevent a normally threatening event from altering mood or physiology. On less frequent occasions, the psychological strategies are impotent and biology overruns mind. A loose confederation of shared power seems the most accurate way to describe the relations among a brain state, behavior, thought, feelings, and peripheral physiology. We will look first at what we have learned about the relation between reactivity at four months and heart rate reactions to the various laboratory incentives. Be prepared for surprises.

Heart Rate Measures: Cohort 1

In chapter 6, we considered Cohorts 1 and 2 in a single, coherent discussion because the procedures, variables, and results were very similar for the two groups. We gathered some important heart rate information on Cohort 1 infants that was not available for Cohort 2, however, so it is useful to keep the summary of the two cohorts separate.

Heart rate data were collected on several occasions prior to the laboratory observation at four months. The first collection occurred about two weeks prior to the infant's birth, when we recorded fetal and maternal heart rate for fifteen minutes while the mother rested quietly in a supine position in the laboratory. We were able to separate the maternal and fetal heart rate signals for 63 of the 102 infants and computed a mean fetal heart rate across the fifteen-minute epoch.

We also recorded each infant's sleeping heart rate at home at two weeks and again at two, four, and six months. One measure was based on thirty minutes of heart rate gathered while the sleeping infant was held by the mother in an upright posture in order to stimulate sympathetic activity. A second measure came from a longer period of night sleep—two to ten hours—while the infant lay supine in its crib. The sleep data were available for seventy-two infants at two weeks, seventy-six at two months, sixty-one at four months, and sixty-four at six months of age. In addition to the average heart period (the inverse of heart rate) we also implemented a power spectral analysis on each 2.5-minute sample of quiet sleeping heart rate when the infant's breathing was regular. Finally, heart rate was gathered when the alert infants were seen in the laboratory at two, four, nine, fourteen, and twenty-one months.

The influence of the parasympathetic nervous system on the heart, mediated by the vagus nerve, is weak in the first four weeks of life but increases in a major way between two and four months. Because the enhanced vagal activity leads to lower heart rates, while sympathetic activity produces higher rates, any heart rate change is a joint function of the two systems. For this reason, resting heart rate values gathered prior to the enhancement of vagal tone might be a more sensitive index of a particular infant's sympathetic reactivity than heart rate gathered after three months. Maureen Rezendes, in our laboratory, has affirmed the importance of this maturational transition. The increase in vagal activity between ten and thirteen weeks is accompanied not only by lower heart rates but also by increases in motor activity and decreases in crying. It is not surprising, therefore, that there was only modest preservation of the infants' heart rates from two weeks to two, four, or six months. The stability coefficients were a bit higher after four months, but these coefficients, too, were modest, averaging only 0.4. Further, the sleep heart rates were not highly correlated with the heart rates gathered when the children were in an alert state in the laboratory.

THE SIGNIFICANCE OF EARLY HEART RATE

Perhaps the most intriguing discovery was that more high than low reactive infants had high fetal heart rates (over 140 beats per minute [bpm]) a few weeks before birth. The infant who had the highest fetal heart rate (170 bpm) was a high reactive boy. He was irritable at two months and at four months displayed the most vigorous motor activity to the visual episode of any child in the cohort. He was moderately fearful at nine and fourteen months; the noise of the rotating wheel bothered him, and several times he sobbed plaintively, "No, no." At twenty-one months he was exceptionally wary; he cried when the examiner criticized him for failure to complete the difficult block constructions, and he ran to his mother as the clown entered the playroom. The infant with the lowest fetal heart rate (120 bpm) was a low reactive girl who was not fearful. She showed no fears at nine months, was a stolid, not easily perturbed child at fourteen months, and was a relaxed twenty-one-month-old with no distress fears.

The high reactive infants also showed higher two-week sleeping heart rates while being held erect by the mother. This result, which suggests that high reactive infants have greater sympathetic tone, is supported by the spectral analyses of the sleep heart rates. Power spectral analysis is a statistical technique that converts the temporal variability in an epoch of heart periods (the inverse of heart rate) to frequency domains and evaluates the contributions of particular frequency bands to the total heart rate variability. Because the frequencies are associated with different autonomic functions—for example, breathing, blood pressure, and temperature control—spectral analysis permits one to come closer to an estimate of the relative contributions of sympathetic and parasympathetic activity to cardiac function.

There was a greater sympathetic contribution to the erect sleep heart rates of high reactives than of low reactives at both two weeks and two months. Further, the larger the sympathetic contribution to heart rate at two weeks, the more fearful the child was at fourteen and twenty-one months. However, the sympathetic contribution while the infant was supine did not differentiate high from low reactive infants nor high from low fear children. This fact is important because the sympathetic contribution is clearest when the infant is in an erect posture; it is confounded with vagal influence when the infant is supine. The association between the sympathetic contribution and temperament was much smaller at four months and completely absent by six months, presumably because the greater contribution of vagal activity at the older ages disguised the sympathetic influence.

When we combined the fetal heart rates with the spectral analysis at two weeks, three-fourths of the high reactive infants showed both a high fetal heart rate and a large sympathetic contribution to heart rate, while not one low reactive infant met both criteria. Not surprisingly, this small group of high reactive infants was extremely fearful. One girl, the most fearful in the cohort, showed frequent tongue protrusions, facial grimaces, and prolonged motor spasticity at two months and, in addition, was one of the few four-month-olds who cried in fear on seeing the moving mobiles. She also cried in response to the noise of the rotating wheel and screamed on seeing the puppets at fourteen months. At three-and-a-half years, she was unusually timid in the risk room and shy with the unfamiliar girl she was paired with for the play session.

When we combined the spectral analysis at two weeks with behavioral reactivity at four months, infants with both a large sympathetic contribution and high reactivity were very fearful in the second year; infants with a small sympathetic contribution who were low reactive were much less fearful. Further, low reactive infants with a large sympathetic contribution were significantly more fearful than those with a small contribution; high reactives with lower fear scores had a smaller sympathetic contribution than those with higher fear scores. Thus, within each of the two reactivity groups an enhanced sympathetic influence was associated with greater fearfulness in the second year. But the most important result is that heart rate profiles reflecting high sympathetic tone gathered before birth and during erect sleep at two weeks differentiated high from low reactives. This fact suggests that inhibited children are born with a low threshold of excitability in the projections from limbic sites to sympathetic targets in the cardiovascular system and perhaps to others as well.

LATER ALERT HEART RATE

The mean heart rates gathered at four months and older during quiet baseline periods, when no stress was imposed, did not differentiate high from low reactive infants nor high from low fear children. This is not surprising, and other investigators have reported similar results. However, the magnitude of heart rate acceleration in response to selected episodes, especially the rise in heart rate in response to a sour taste, was larger for high reactives. Sour tastes typically produce large increases in heart rate in both animals and humans, larger than those observed in response to other taste qualities. The origin of this sympathetically mediated acceleration is a circuit from the gustatory nerve to the nucleus tractus solitarius (in the medulla) to the parabrachial nucleus (in the pons). One projection from the parabrachial nucleus goes directly to the sympathetic chain, another to the central nucleus of the amygdala and from there to the sympathetic nervous system. High reactive infants also showed a much larger rise in heart rate to the noisy wheel and the examiner's stern criticism at twenty-one months. Thus, the evidence from Cohort 1 affirms the expectation that high reactive infants—like the older inhibited children in chapter 5—possess a more reactive sympathetic nervous system than do low reactives, but after four months resting heart rate does not differentiate the groups as clearly.

Heart Rate Measures: Cohort 2

Cohort 2 was larger than Cohort 1 by a factor of about five, but cardiac data were gathered only when the child was in an alert state at four, nine, fourteen, and twenty-one months. Spectral analyses were not implemented because the infants were not in the sustained quiet state with regular breathing that is required for the analysis. But the much larger sample permits greater confidence in our conclusions. In the discussion that follows heart rate values were deleted for every trial on which an infant fretted, cried, or showed a large change in body posture, like leaning forward, standing up in the chair, or twisting the body. The analyses deal with heart rate activity when the child was in an alert, nonirritable, and relatively quiescent state.

The analyses were always performed separately for boys and girls because girls had slightly higher heart rates at every age. The sex difference was small (1–2 bpm) during the quiet baselines, larger (4–6 bpm) during some of the mildly challenging procedures, and largest in response to the sour taste, as was true for Cohort 1. It is possible that males and females possess slightly different neurochemistries in those limbic and brain stem sites that control change in heart rate.

CHANGE IN BASELINE RATES

Although high reactive boys had higher initial baseline heart rates at four and nine months than did low reactives, the baseline heart rates at fourteen and twenty-one months did not differentiate these two groups, and baseline rates failed to differentiate the two groups of girls at any age. The failure of baseline heart rates to distinguish consistently between the two temperamental groups of girls, together with their lack of stability over age, are in accord with what was found for Cohort 1 and with the suggestion that, with age, variation in quiet, resting heart rate is not closely associated with these temperamental categories.

But changes in baseline rates were informative. More high than low reactive children had a higher and less variable baseline heart rate at twenty-one than at fourteen months, even though the two groups had similar baseline values at fourteen months. Because over three-fourths of all the infants had a lower baseline at twenty-one than at fourteen months, it appears that more high reactives were in a state of sympathetic arousal as the twenty-one-month battery began. A lower and more variable heart rate with age is mediated by parasympathetic activity; therefore the reversal of the expected age trend among some high reactive infants suggests competition from the sympathetic nervous system. Further, more high than low reactives showed an increase in heart rate (about 4 bpm) from the first to the final sitting baseline at fourteen months. This finding, too, suggests that more high reactives became sympathetically aroused over the course of the battery as an accompaniment to their higher fear score.

EXTREME HEART RATES AND ACCELERATION

The highest heart rates attained by the adolescents in chapter 5 better discriminated the two temperamental groups than did heart rate at rest, average heart rate across all the trials of a particular episode, or the average heart rate across all the episodes. Similarly, the highest heart rate on any one of the three trials when lemon juice was placed on the fourteen-month-old's tongue better differentiated the high from low reactives in Cohort 1 than did the mean heart rate across all three trials. Other investigators have come to a similar conclusion regarding extreme values. The highest heart rate attained to cognitive stress and to exercise were better predictors of adult heart rate outside the laboratory than the average heart rate over a series of different cognitive stressors. Similarly, the largest change in a number of varied physiological targets better differentiated states of fear from anger than did mean values. And the peak frequency of distress calls distinguished closely related species of monkeys more clearly than did the average frequency.

Some behavioral scientists believe that baseline values should be especially revealing because a person's cognitive ability prior to a mental task often predicts quality of performance on the task; the implication is that baseline characteristics reflect a significant personal quality. By contrast, physiologists are more likely to treat the maximal reaction to an imposed stress as a more sensitive index of the person's physiology. The physician evaluating a patient's risk for cardiac arrest will pay special attention to the highest heart rate and blood pressure attained under extreme physical exertion and less attention to the values recorded when the patient is sitting quietly in a chair. For the same reason, the appearance of a few very fast or very slow waves in a one-hour EEG is a better index of possible epilepsy or brain lesion than the average power in the EEG over a half hour. Similarly, if a patient who has been logical and coherent throughout the session with his therapist suddenly turns on the latter, who has been pressing him, and states with anger, "You can't question me that way, I'm Napoleon," that single, bizarre statement in an otherwise sane hour of conversation will tempt the therapist to ascribe a complex set of personality characteristics to the patient.

Social scientists have preferred average over peak values on the assumption that the mean is the most accurate estimate of whatever hypothetical process or processes produce a scatter of scores. This presumption rests on the premise that the total range of scores is due to the operation of the same mechanism or mechanisms. But if one set of processes mediates one part of the distribution and a different set mediates another, the mean will be a misleading summary of the data. The most important influence on body temperature in a group of healthy, relaxed persons sitting in a room at 70 degrees Fahrenheit is an endogenous control mechanism in the hypothalamus. But consider a sample of fifty nurses working in a tropical hospital and fifty patients in the malaria ward of that hospital. The mean body temperature of about 101 degrees across all one hundred persons will be misleading because it represents two different distributions—one from the fifty healthy staff and another from the fifty fevered patients. David Magnusson has criticized the reflex reliance on popular statistical decisions without prior reflection on the nature of the problem at hand.

There are few behaviors or physiological measures for which the total range of scores is the product of the same mechanisms. Even the performances of college students sitting in a quiet laboratory deciding if they saw a red square, green circle, or blue triangle, as each is flashed briefly on a monitor, are influenced by variation in visual acuity, capacity for sustained attentiveness, and motivation to perform well. These three processes probably contribute differentially to performances that are of modest, compared with unusually high, accuracy over the sixty-minute session.

There are at least two independent influences on the magnitude of cardiac change to an incentive: the anatomical and physiological characteristics of the cardiovascular system, on the one hand, and, on the other, susceptibility to being affected psychologically by the particular incentive. If these two characteristics are inherited independently—a reasonable assumption—and no more than 20 percent of children are born with both an autonomic and a psychological vulnerability to challenge, then the top 25 percent of heart rate values might be a more sensitive index of this type of child than the mean value. Perhaps that is why only one-third of the inhibited thirteen-year-olds, but fewer uninhibited youth, had high heart rates in response to challenge, while the mean heart rate did not differentiate the two temperamental groups.

Each child's heart rate was averaged over epochs within each episode, usually ten seconds in duration, and we selected the highest and lowest mean heart rate from all of the child's epochs on each of the batteries. Each child had a single high and low rate for each battery. Most four-month-olds had their highest mean heart rate in response to the moving mobiles and their lowest heart rate while listening to the sentences or syllables. At fourteen months, the highest mean heart rate usually occurred in response to the sour taste and the lowest to the wheel, rather than to the more obviously discrepant procedures. Each child's maximal and minimal heart rates were a bit more stable over time than the baseline values, were unrelated to the child's body size or build, and differentiated the two reactive groups at four months. Thirty-two percent of high reactives, but only 13 percent of low reactives, had both maximal and minimal four-month heart rates in the highest quartile of each distribution; that is, more high reactives, of both sexes, had high values for both the maximal and minimal rates. By contrast, 31 percent of low reactives but only 14 percent of the high reactives had values in the lowest quartile for both the maximal and minimal heart rates. At fourteen and twenty-one months, however, the maximal and minimal heart rates did not separate the groups.

In chapter 6, we estimated that eighteen of every hundred infants should be low reactive at four months and low fear and frequent smiling at fourteen months. If we add the criterion of a low minimal heart rate at four months, then fifteen of every hundred infants would meet the four criteria. We also estimated that eight infants in every hundred should be high reactive with high fear and infrequent smiling in the second year. If we add the criterion of a high maximal heart rate at four months, six of every hundred would meet all four criteria. Thus, twice as many infants possess the features of an uninhibited compared with an inhibited temperament.

The magnitude of increase in heart rate to particular episodes was also informative. At both nine and fourteen months the high reactive girls, but not boys, showed larger rises in heart rate in response to the sudden appearance of the unfamiliar adult. At nine months an unfamiliar woman dressed in ordinary clothes entered the room, walked slowly toward the infant, and when she was about a foot away, spoke to the child. At fourteen months, the stranger wore a white laboratory coat and a gas mask, a very discrepant event. Many children showed a small drop in heart rate in response to the strangers, characteristic of a state of attention. But more high than low reactive girls accelerated on both occasions; 45 percent of the high reactives, but only 22 percent of the low reactive, girls showed accelerations of at least 2 bpm at both ages. The rise in heart rate was small because the mother was present in the room.

The magnitude of cardiac acceleration to the sour taste also differentiated the two groups, as it did for Cohort 1. About one-third of the high reactive girls, but only 10 percent of the low reactives, showed large accelerations to the sour taste at fourteen months; 38 percent of the high, compared with 16 percent of the low, reactive girls had large accelerations to the sour taste at both fourteen and twenty-one months. Although the high and low reactive girls had similar heart rates to the first administration of the lemon juice, 60 percent of high reactive girls, but only 40 percent of low reactives, showed an acceleration of at least 2 bpm over the succeeding two administrations. That is, the high reactive girls were more likely to attain their highest heart rate on the second or third trial. This fact implies either that high reactive girls had a more excitable sympathetic circuit from the amygdala or parabrachial nucleus to the sympathetic axons serving the heart or that high reactive girls developed a stronger state of aversion to the anticipation of the second or third administrations of the unpleasant liquid and, as a result, displayed an enhanced acceleration.

The difference in magnitude of acceleration to the sour taste was not as dramatic for boys, in part because more high reactive boys than girls refused to accept the lemon juice on their tongue. Some cried or turned away and, as a result, no heart rate data could be gathered. It is possible that these resistant boys would have shown large accelerations.

Although high heart rates, resulting from large accelerations in response to the strangers and sour taste, distinguished high from low reactive girls, very low heart rates better discriminated the two groups of boys. The average of the lowest heart rate attained during the batteries at four, fourteen, and twenty-one months was significantly smaller for low than for high reactive boys; the low reactive boys had the lowest baseline heart rates at every age (see figure 7.1). Recall that very low heart rates were also characteristic of the uninhibited male adolescents. Among the boys with very low heart rates at four, fourteen, and twenty-one months, 68 percent were low reactive and 32 percent high reactive. The difference between the two groups of boys was especially significant in response to the spoken sentences at four months. About one-third of the low reactive, compared with 15 percent of the high reactive, boys were in the lowest quartile of the distribution of minimal heart rates. In addition, more low than high reactive boys attained heart rates lower than 120 bpm to the flashing lights at nine months, which produced an unusual degree of quieting and prolonged attentiveness.

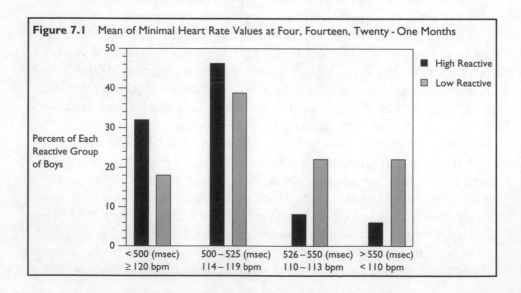

Figure 7.1   Mean of Minimal Heart Rate Values at Four, Fourteen, Twenty - One Months

The most consistent result is that about one-third of high reactive girls showed very high heart rates and about one-third of low reactive boys showed very low heart rates. But there is an important difference in meaning between the following two sentences:

1. High reactive girls have higher average heart rates to selected challenges than low reactive girls.
2. One-third of high reactive girls compared with 10 percent of low reactive girls display high heart rates to selected challenges.

Sentence (2) is the more correct description and, as we noted in chapter 5, is matched by studies of adult patient groups. Usually only 20–40 percent of a patient population with anxiety disorder show large changes in heart rate or blood pressure to a challenge.

THE RELATION OF HEART RATE TO FEAR

Although very high or very low heart rates at four months and the size of heart rate changes to particular intrusions in the second year differentiated the high and low reactives, neither baseline, maximal, minimal, nor heart rate change at any age was associated consistently with level of fear (recall that we had eliminated all heart rate trials on which the child cried); the same was true for Cohort 1. There were, however, three exceptions to this general claim.

The small group of low reactives whose level of fearfulness increased from fourteen to twenty-one months had higher maximal heart rates at four months than those who remained minimally fearful. Further, low reactives with a high and stable baseline heart rate at fourteen months, compared with low reactives with a low and variable heart rate, had more avoidant fears at fourteen and twenty-one months. Finally, high reactive girls with large accelerations to the sour taste had more avoidant fears than high reactive girls with small accelerations. Nonetheless, it is fair to conclude that neither heart rate nor variability in an alert infant older than four months is a particularly sensitive correlate of fear in the second year. Heart rate in older infants seems to be reflecting an affect state that, as we shall see, is more clearly related to mood.

HEART RATE AND SMILING

The prevalence of very low heart rates among low reactive boys implies that heart rate might be related to affectivity, for in the second year low reactive boys smiled most often. This hypothesis appears to have promise, for the boys with low minimal heart rates at four months were the most frequent smilers in the second year. Their low heart rates were typically attained during one or both of the auditory episodes when the infants were listening quietly to the spoken sentences or syllables. One small group of boys who attained exceptionally low heart rates while listening to the taped female voice speak short sentences became the most vocal and smiling children in the second year.

The low reactive boys who smiled frequently in the second year had lower minimal heart rates at every age than did low reactives who smiled infrequently. A similar difference was found with Cohort 1. Among low reactive boys with very low heart rates at four months, 40 percent smiled several times during the battery at two months of age, compared with only 16 percent of low reactive boys with high four-month heart rates. This association was absent among high reactives and was less striking among the girls. There was one interesting exception to this last conclusion. Although heart rate variability during the minute of quiet baseline, considered alone, was not associated with either the fear or affect scores, a small group of low reactive girls (11 percent) had a low and highly variable heart rate at both four and fourteen months, and another small group of low reactive girls (13 percent) had a high and minimally variable heart rate at those two ages. The former group smiled more often in the second year.

In addition, the small group of high or low reactive infants (4 percent of high and low reactives) who smiled the most at both fourteen and twenty-one months had more variable heart rates during the initial baseline at fourteen months than the 15 percent who showed minimal smiling. Thus, for children for whom the frequency of smiling was at either extreme, a highly variable resting heart rate was associated with positive affect, while a stable heart rate was linked to a more serious mood. Most of the former children were low reactive; most of the latter were high reactive. It is important to point out, however, that this relation held only for children who had extreme values on the two measures. The correlation between heart rate variability and smiling for all children was only .10.

Our faith in the claim that a low and variable heart rate is associated with a more joyful mood is enhanced by the discovery of a similar relation in the large group of twins, discussed earlier, whose development is being studied at the Institute of Behavioral Genetics at the University of Colorado. The fourteen-month-old twins who smiled frequently in the home during both the administration of tests and a free-play session, whether classed as inhibited or uninhibited, had lower heart rates in the laboratory than those children who smiled infrequently.

The adolescents described in chapters 4 and 5 also showed an association between heart rate and smiling. We examined each adolescent's tendency to show an initial heart rate acceleration (the first two trials) on three procedures: listening to digits and words that had to be remembered and solving anagram problems. An increase in heart rate of at least 2 bpm (about 10 msec.) between trials 1 and 2 of each episode was treated as a rise in heart rate. Seven adolescents showed rises that large to the three episodes, while thirteen showed no acceleration to any of these episodes. Inhibited and uninhibited youth were represented equally in both groups, but 43 percent of those who accelerated were subdued and rarely smiled, compared with 15 percent of those who did not accelerate at all.

Thus, the affect state that is characterized by frequent, spontaneous talking and smiling is linked with minimal sympathetic tone on the heart in both adolescents and younger children. It is possible that the dour, serious mood and sympathetic reactivity are products of a central limbic state that blocks the relaxed mood required for frequent smiling and laughing and, in addition, exerts an excitatory influence on sympathetic ganglia that serve the cardiovascular system. It is reasonable to suggest that projections from the amygdala are participants in the creation of this state.

Ten percent of low reactive boys and 6 percent of low reactive girls showed a combination of three qualities: low fear and frequent smiling in the second year and a consistently low heart rate. Not one high reactive infant showed this trio of characteristics. Three low reactive boys were distinctive in having consistently low minimal heart rates; their rate at twenty-one months was less than 90 bpm, compared with the average of 110 bpm for the remaining boys. These three boys smiled more often than any other children during the nine-month battery and were unusual in the display of laughter, vitality, and fearlessness during the second year.

Two of these boys continued to be highly affective at fourteen and twenty-one months. The third became a bit subdued at fourteen months, perhaps because of tension in the home; a relative who lived nearby had become psychotic, and the family was worried about him.

These low reactive–low fear–low heart rate–high smiling boys may represent a special temperamental category and an example of the concept of emergenesis introduced in chapter 2. A small proportion of infants inherit the genes that determine biological sex and make a contribution to low reactivity, low fear, frequent smiling, and a low heart rate. Each of these five characteristics is likely to be influenced by different groups of genes; hence, a child who possesses all five features must inherit all of the relevant genes—a low probability event. The analogy is a tall woman with extraordinary stamina, exceptional musical talent, and a soprano voice—another low probability event.

Thus, subtypes exist within the high and low reactive groups. For some questions these less frequent subtypes can be ignored; for others it will be useful to regard them as uncommon temperamental categories. We turn again to biology for an analogy. When the phenomenon of interest is form of reproduction, biologists are likely to treat all mammals as a category distinct from all reptiles. But when the question involves life span or social relationship to humans, biologists will divide the mammals into subgroups—for example, rodents compared with canines. The fineness of any categorization depends upon the investigator's theoretical purposes. If prediction of fear is of primary interest, then reactivity at four months is clearly the most relevant quality. But if one wishes to predict affectivity, too, heart rate is a relevant feature, and it becomes useful to divide the low reactives into smaller subgroups.

The most important conclusion is that high or low heart rate or magnitude of heart rate change, considered alone, is as much a reflection of the child's temporary state as an enduring characteristic and should not be used as a defining index of reactivity. About one-third of high reactive girls attained high heart rates because of large heart rate accelerations; one-third of low reactive boys attained very low heart rates. But many high reactive children who became inhibited (about 25 percent) had low heart rates; many low reactive–uninhibited children (about 20 percent) had high heart rates; and many children from both reactive groups had heart rate values typical of most infants of their age and sex. A similar result was noted for the adolescents.

Thus, heart rate measures, especially after two months, should be regarded—like eye color or facial skeleton—as a modest correlate of reactivity, but not as a necessary characteristic of either category, presumably because the sympathetic control of heart rate depends on factors that can be relatively independent of those that contribute to reactivity. The assumption that the excitability of the amygdala contributes to both fearful behavior and a reactive sympathetic nervous system is not inconsistent with the fact that heart rate and fear are independent. The projections from the amygdala to the ventromedial hypothalamus probably facilitate a behaviorally fearful profile, but the projections to the lateral hypothalamus facilitate a reactive sympathetic nervous system. There is no reason to assume similar levels of excitability in the circuit from the lateral hypothalamus to the sympathetic nervous system and the circuit from the ventromedial hypothalamus to the motor systems that mediate fearful behavior. Hence, fearfulness and heart rate could be independent, even though both are mediated by the reactivity of the amygdala and its projections.

Asymmetry of Facial Temperature

We turn now to a second reaction that is a consequence of sympathetic activity. The surface temperature of the forehead is due primarily to the state of constriction of arterioles under the skin that are sympathetically controlled by axons that travel from the cervical ganglion to the face. Constriction of these arterioles, mediated by alpha adrenergic receptors, reduces blood flow and, as a consequent, produces surface cooling. This is one of the important ways mammals cope with cold stress, for the vasoconstriction decreases the loss of body heat to the outside air. The arterioles on the face probably do not contain the beta receptors that can mediate vasodilation and surface warming, although the hands and fingertips do contain both alpha and beta receptors. The sympathetic innervation of the skin is independent of the sympathetic control of heart rate or blood pressure; usually there is a minimal relation between changes in skin temperature and changes in other sympathetic targets.

Small changes in facial temperature can reflect a momentary change in emotional state. Two- to four-month-old infants displayed a drop in forehead temperature when the mother left them alone or when a stranger replaced the mother, suggesting that sympathetic constriction of the arterioles can accompany a temporary state of uncertainty. Further, more extremely shy than extremely sociable women showed facial cooling of .10° C or greater while trying to solve a series of difficult anagram problems.

Most studies of skin temperature measure a small area on the middle finger of the nondominant hand, rather than the forehead, and also find a drop in temperature when subjects are stressed in some way. For example, the finger temperature of adults who were watching a surgical film decreased about 0.4° C. Similarly, adults who expected to be shocked while performing a motor task showed a drop in finger temperature of about 0.3° C. Adults who tried to simulate a state of fear or to imagine what they would do in a frightening situation also showed cooling on the finger and forehead.

It is important to note that when finger temperature is measured on both hands, the left is typically cooler than the right. It will be recalled from chapter 2 that more adults show greater EEG activation on the left, compared with the right, frontal area. But when infants or children are in situations normally productive of fear, EEG activation is greater on the right than on the left side. More important, fearful, inhibited three-year-olds, compared with fearless, uninhibited ones, show greater EEG activation on the right than on the left frontal area. And infants who are both high reactive at four months and fearful in the second year show greater right-sided activation in the frontal area at both nine and fourteen months. Low reactive, high smiling infants who become minimally fearful show greater activation of the left frontal area.

The association between fearful behavior and greater activation on the right side can be explained if we assume that right, compared with left, frontal activation is associated with a greater susceptibility to a state of fear to the unfamiliar, perhaps because of higher concentrations of norepinephrine in the right hemisphere. This idea is in accord with evidence indicating that ligation of the middle cerebral artery on the right hemisphere is followed by a decrease in norepinephrine in both the cortex and brain stem; no such change is noted following ligation of the middle cerebral artery on the left side. Further, depletion of norepinephrine in rat pups reduces the animals' usual withdrawal to novelty, implying that norepinephrine in the right hemisphere plays a greater role in the reaction to novelty than it does in the left hemisphere. It is of interest that the ten Sprague-Dawley rats, from a total of sixty, who were the most emotional when placed in a novel environment had significantly larger amounts of norepinephrine in the brain than the ten least emotional rats.

ASYMMETRIC REACTIVITY IN THE SYMPATHETIC NERVOUS SYSTEM: OTHER STUDIES

A surprising fact discovered during the last twenty years is that the sympathetic nervous system is slightly more reactive on the right than on the left side of the body. For example, stimulation of the right stellate ganglion in dogs leads to a tachycardia that is absent following stimulation of the left stellate ganglion. Scientists who discovered a similar phenomenon in human patients concluded, "There are different patterns of right- and left-sided sympathetic cardiac innervation in man, and the right stellate ganglion has a much greater influence on heart rate than does the left stellate ganglion." Further, inactivation of the right hemisphere by intracarotid injections of amobarbitol in human patients led to cardiac deceleration, while inactivation of the left hemisphere was associated with an acceleration, suggesting that increased activity on the right side of the brain is associated with increased sympathetic influence on the heart.

Moreover, the anatomical connections from the amygdala and hypothalamus to the sympathetic ganglia on the same side of the body appear to be stronger than those to the ganglia on the opposite side. Retrograde tracing of connections from the autonomic nervous system to the hypothalamus in rats, cats, and monkeys (*Macaca fasicularis*), following injections of horseradish peroxidase into the spinal cord, revealed labeling of a distinct group of neurons in the hypothalamus of all three species. The largest number of labeled neurons was found in the paraventricular nucleus on the side of the injection, as compared with the opposite side. This result is in accord with the finding that electrical stimulation of the hypothalamus of anesthetized cats produces greater nasal vasoconstriction on the same side as the stimulating electrode than on the opposite side.

As we noted earlier, cerebral asymmetry in processing information is related to the family of states normally called anxiety or fear, on the one hand, or happiness or joy, on the other. In one series of studies, right-hemisphere processing of an emotional film (a surgical operation) led to a higher heart rate than did left-hemisphere processing of the same film or right-hemisphere processing of a neutral film. In addition, subjects processing the films with the right hemisphere judged both emotional and neutral films as more unpleasant than did subjects processing the same films with the left hemisphere. Another study found that right-hemisphere processing of an emotionally stressful film was accompanied by larger rises in systolic and diastolic blood pressure than processing by the left hemisphere. A subsequent report from the same laboratory discovered that increases in salivary cortisol occurred with right-hemisphere processing of an emotional film but not with right-hemisphere processing of a neutral film or with left-hemisphere processing of either the emotional or the neutral film.

There is also asymmetry in the magnitude of the skin conductance response to slides of angry or happy faces, which served as conditioned stimuli for an unconditioned stimulus of shock. This measure reflects degree of sweating on the skin surface. When the two different faces were presented tachistoscopically to the right or left hemisphere during extinction of the skin conductance response, the largest responses occurred when angry faces were projected to the right hemisphere.

An injection of sodium amobarbitol into the right carotid artery is accompanied by an increase in laughter and an elated mood; an injection of the same drug into the left carotid leads to unresponsiveness or crying. These facts are in accord with clinical reports suggesting that damage to the right hemisphere—for example, as the result of a stroke—is often followed by indifference or inappropriate elation, while damage to the left hemisphere is often followed by a depressed, dysphoric, or anxious mood.

Finally, the magnitude of the eye blink component of the startle reflex to a loud noise is greater when the sound is delivered to the left ear than when it is delivered to the right ear. Because of the greater contralateral transmission of auditory stimulation, this result is "consistent with the hypothesized right hemisphere dominance in the affective modulation of the startle response."

The entire corpus of data summarized, together with extensive reviews of this domain, suggests a functional association between asymmetry of activity in those brain areas that influence the sympathetic nervous system and variations in behavior and physiology that are assumed to accompany the affect states associated with fear.

FACIAL TEMPERATURE

The final procedure administered to the children at twenty-one months evaluated facial temperature using a thermography scanner. The child sat unconstrained on the mother's lap during the thermographic recordings, with the lens of the scanner placed two feet from the child's face. The battery consisted of four brief episodes during which a total of twelve images were recorded.

The first discovery was that a comparison of the mean temperatures of the right and the left forehead (across all twelve images) revealed a slightly cooler temperature on the left side—as is true for the fingers of the two hands. When the criterion for asymmetry was set at a difference of at least .10° C, 37 percent of the children were cooler on the left forehead, 20 percent were cooler on the right, and the remaining subjects showed no asymmetry. These proportions are remarkably similar to EEG indexes of asymmetry in frontal activation, implying that the two phenomena are related.

It is reassuring that 54 percent of the adolescents described in chapter 4, both inhibited and uninhibited, were cooler on the left forehead, while only 9 percent (four children) were cooler on the right. The four adolescents with a cooler right forehead had been classified as inhibited in the second or third year. Even four-month-old infants show a bias for a cooler left forehead.

One possible basis for the lateral asymmetry in both EEG activation and forehead temperature is a difference in reciprocal activity between selected structures in the limbic area and cortex. Afferent feedback from the body organs served by the sympathetic nervous system courses through the nucleus tractus solitarius in the medulla on its way to the hypothalamus and amygdala. The density of neural traffic in the ipsilateral reciprocal circuit between the amygdala and the frontal cortex might influence both degree of EEG activation as well as constriction of arterioles of the forehead. Because of an association between the side of greater cerebral activity and constriction of the arterioles on that side, greater neural traffic in the loop on the right side should be associated with EEG activation on the right and a cooler right forehead; greater traffic in the loop on the left side would be associated with greater left-sided activation and a cooler left forehead. The evidence suggests that most children and adults have greater neural activity in the loop on the left side.

Although the difference in temperature between the left and right sides of the forehead, when considered alone, was not highly related to reactivity, it was associated with smiling in both sexes and with number of distress fears in girls. More children who smiled frequently in the second year had a cooler left than right side; more children who smiled infrequently

Table 7.1   *Proportion of Left and Right Asymmetry Groups Showing Low, Moderate,*
             or High Levels of Smiling in the Second Year: Cohort 2

Mean Smiles, 14 and 21 months		Left Side[a] Cooler N = 141	Right Side Cooler N = 97
Low	(Mean ≤ 1.5)	40%	55%
Moderate	(Mean = 2.0)	32%	29%
High	(Mean ≥ 2.5)	28%	16%

[a]Asymmetry by total or changed asymmetry; both sexes.

were cooler on the right side (see table 7.1). A small group of nineteen children were very frequent smilers at four, fourteen, and twenty-one months; fourteen of these children (74 percent) were cooler on the left, and only three were cooler on the right side. This same relation also occurred in Cohort 1; children who smiled frequently were more often cooler on the left forehead.

In addition, Cohort 2 girls with a cooler right forehead had a mean of 2.0 distress fears, compared with 1.3 for those with a cooler left side. Two-thirds of the girls with a cooler right forehead had frequent distress fears, compared to only one-third of the girls with a cooler left forehead (see table 7.2). Forty-two percent of the girls in Cohort 1 with four or more distress fears at fourteen months also had a cooler right forehead, compared with 22 percent of those with no more than one distress fear. Further, not one girl with a cooler right forehead had been classified as low reactive. The relation between temperature asymmetry and smiling and distress fears enhances our confidence that asymmetry of temperature on the forehead is associated with the ease of assuming a distressed or a happy mood. It is relevant that one-half of the adolescent females who smiled frequently during the two-hour laboratory session had a cooler left forehead,

Table 7.2   *Proportion of Girls with Left or Right Asymmetry with Low versus High Distress*
             Fears: Cohort 2

Mean Distress Fears at 14 and 21 Months	Left Side Cooler[a]	Right Side Cooler
Low (≤ 1.0)	63	36
High (≥ 1.5)	37	64

[a]Asymmetry defined by total or changed asymmetry.

compared with 28 percent of those who smiled infrequently. All four of the adolescents with a cooler right side, who had been classed as inhibited in the second year, smiled infrequently during the laboratory battery.

Finally, the children with a high and stable heart rate on the first baseline at fourteen months (but not at four and twenty-one months) were more likely to be cooler on the right side; children with a low and variable heart rate were more likely to be cooler on the left side. When we combined a high, stable heart rate on the initial fourteen-month baseline with the total asymmetry index favoring a cooler right side and a low, variable heart rate with the index favoring a cooler left side, the two groups differed in their four-month heart rates. The children with a low, variable fourteen-month heart rate and a cooler left side (12 percent of all high and low reactive children) had attained lower minimal heart rates at four months than the complementary group (7 percent of high and low reactive children). The two groups also differed in heart rate reaction to the sentences, syllables, and mobiles at four months, but not to the initial baseline (see figure 7.2).

It may come as no surprise that the children who smiled at least once

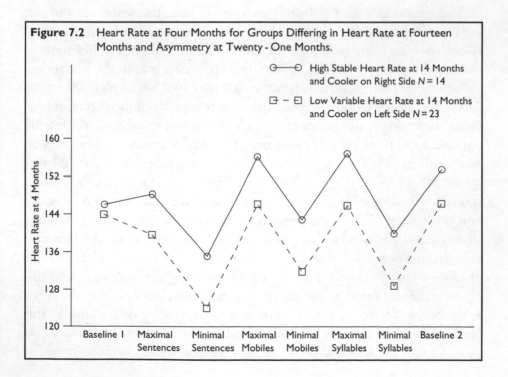

Figure 7.2 Heart Rate at Four Months for Groups Differing in Heart Rate at Fourteen Months and Asymmetry at Twenty - One Months.

○——○ High Stable Heart Rate at 14 Months and Cooler on Right Side N = 14

◻ – ◻ Low Variable Heart Rate at 14 Months and Cooler on Left Side N = 23 at four months more often came from the group with a low, variable heart rate and a cooler left side, compared with those who had a high, stable heart rate and a cooler right side (58 percent versus 39 percent). As early as four months some infants reveal in a smile to their mother or to speech a special temperamental quality that is independent of behavioral reactivity, gender, or fear but seems linked to a happy mood and lower sympathetic reactivity in the cardiovascular system.

CASE STUDIES

The two twenty-one-month-old girls in Cohort 2 with the largest total asymmetries favoring a cooler right forehead (.42 and .46° C) were fearful. One girl had been high reactive at four months; the other had been classified as distressed (low motor–high cry). The formerly high reactive girl became so distressed during the second auditory episode at four months that the session had to be terminated. This girl cried when the electrodes and blood pressure cuff were applied, and when the stranger and clown entered the playroom, she ran to her mother, remaining frozen during the few minutes each intruder was in the room.

The second girl cried in fear in response to both the sentences and the syllables at four months. She clung to her mother in the risk room at twenty-one months, and when the clown entered, she ran to her mother and would not leave her during the time the clown was in the playroom, sobbing repeatedly "I can't" when the clown invited her to play.

The girl from Cohort 1 with the largest total asymmetry favoring a cooler right side (a difference of .35° C) was one of the three most fearful children at all three ages. She had been classified as aroused when she was four months old. During the battery at two months, she displayed frequent tongue protrusions, which are a sign of motor tension. At four months, she showed increasing arousal across the trials of each episode, and during the mobiles she showed an extreme degree of motor rigidity in her arms; on two of the trials, her body became rigid. At fourteen months, she displayed nine fears—placing her in the top 1 percent of the group—crying in response to the wheel, resisting the sour taste and the blood pressure, refusing to imitate the examiner, and crying when the examiner spoke to her in a stern voice. At twenty-one months, she became frozen in the risk room and cried in fear when the examiner took a mask from the wall and asked her to put it on. As at fourteen months, she cried on the application of the electrodes and the blood pressure cuff and screamed as the clown entered the room.

The two boys with the largest total asymmetry values favoring a cooler right forehead (asymmetry values of .36 and .30° C) were also subdued and wary. One boy, classified as aroused at four months because he was high motor–low cry, was moderately fearful at fourteen months and smiled infrequently on all assessments. At twenty-one months, he refused to accept the tastes or the blood pressure cuff, cried in response to the stranger and the robot (less than 1 percent of twenty-one-month-olds cried in response to both), and fled to his mother when the clown entered. The mother reported that he had become aggressive at home, pulling hair and hitting, and that it was difficult for him to "wind down." This boy had sensitive skin, kept a comfort blanket, and became upset when either parent criticized him in raised voice.

The second boy with a very cool right forehead was high reactive at four months, showed frequent fears at both fourteen and twenty-one months, and did not smile once during the fourteen-month battery. He was extremely irritable at twenty-one months, refusing the electrodes, blood pressure cuff, and olfactory stimulation. His mother also reported that he had sensitive skin and needed a comfort toy.

The two girls in Cohort 2 with the largest total asymmetry scores favoring a cooler left forehead (.60 and .52° C) were considerably more affective and much less fearful. One girl, who was low reactive, was a bit wary at twenty-one months but smiled and laughed throughout most of the battery. The second girl was low motor–high cry at four months, and at twenty-one months she was fearless and relaxed and smiled frequently.

The Cohort 1 girl with the coolest left forehead (difference of .32° C) was a low reactive infant with very few distress fears at each age. At two months and four months, she smiled frequently, especially to the human voice. She was an easy infant at nine months, even smiling when her mother left her for a brief separation. She never fretted or cried during the entire battery. At fourteen months, she continued to smile frequently and had only one distress fear. At twenty-one months, she talked continually during the battery, was relaxed, laughed at the rotating wheel, and occasionally issued squeals of joy.

The Cohort 1 boy with the most extreme total asymmetry favoring a cooler left side (.52° C) was low reactive but highly vocal at four months. He showed low fear at every age—a rare category—and was among the most frequent smilers on every assessment. At twenty-one months, he talked continually and laughed during the battery. His mother described him as easy to soothe and as a "wonderful boy." This boy is a classic example of a low reactive–high smiling–low fear child; it cannot be a coincidence that his left-sided asymmetry was among the largest of any child.

A Synthesis

There are three important results in this complex texture of details. First, more high than low reactive infants in both cohorts showed signs of enhanced sympathetic activity in the cardiovascular system, especially prior to four months. The most persuasive sources of evidence were the higher fetal and two-week sleep heart rates and the enhanced power in the low frequency band of the spectral analysis at two weeks and two months. It seems unlikely that a family environment could have shaped a reactive sympathetic system in the first fourteen days of life in healthy infants born to economically secure mothers who experienced an easy pregnancy and delivery. Reactivity at four months was a much better predictor of later fear than was heart rate, however; the early behavior provided a more sensitive index of an inhibited style than did peripheral cardiac physiology.

The twin sample in the University of Colorado studies, described in chapter 5, provided an unexpected but relevant discovery. The index of inhibition at fourteen months was more heritable than was heart rate. Intuition suggests that a physiological feature that reflects one of the underlying features of inhibition should be more heritable than a behavioral quality, but each peripheral physiological target is under diverse influences, some of which have little to do with the processes that mediate inhibition. Presumably if one had access to events in the amygdala and its first order synapses, measurements of the activity of these structures would be as heritable as behavior.

Behavioral inhibition was also more stable than heart rate. For both the twin as well as the nontwin groups, inhibited behavior was better preserved from fourteen to twenty-one months than heart rate or heart rate change—correlations of 0.4 versus 0.2–0.3. A subject's momentary state seems to be a more critical determinant of heart rate than of inhibited behavior. The heart, skin, and pupil are influenced by a large number of diverse factors. Hence, there is greater lability in a peripheral physiological system and, therefore, less stability over time. Consider as an analogy the stability of a person's comprehension vocabulary over a five-year period, which is about 0.8–0.9. It is unlikely that EEG or PET measures of neural activity in the language areas of the brain would be as stable over five years as the vocabulary score. When a large number of separate systems must cooperate to produce a particular response, the stability of the final coherent outcome is often greater than the stability of any one of the components.

Second, the child's sex influenced the relation of physiology to behavior. The low reactive boys who smiled frequently had lower heart rates than all other groups of children. High heart rates discriminated high from low reactives better for girls, while very low heart rates were more differentiating for boys. Because a high concentration of opioids can dampen sympathetic influence on the heart, it is possible that the low reactive boys with low heart rates inherit unusually high levels of opioids and/or a greater density of opioid receptors in central or medullary sites.

Let us suppose that a consistently low heart rate reflects less activity in relevant parts of the sympathetic nervous system and therefore less feedback from these peripheral sympathetic targets to the medulla, amygdala, and frontal cortex. The conscious perception of bodily activity is one component of the conscious state of fear, as William James and Carl Lange argued. When feedback from sympathetic targets is reduced the brain may be in a special state that permits a child to smile and to laugh easily. If this state, which is associated with a cooler left forehead and greater EEG activation in the left frontal area, is difficult to attain because of excessive feedback from sympathetic targets, a child is more likely to be affectively subdued.

The profile that combined low reactivity, low four-month heart rate, low fear, frequent smiling, and a cooler left forehead characterized a small group of boys who behaviorally were exuberant and full of vitality. One boy is prototypic. He smiled during the initial baseline at four months when his mother was looking down at him, but remained relaxed with minimal limb activity during the entire four-month battery. He squealed with joy at most of the nine-month episodes; he even smiled when the examiner frowned and spoke to him with a stern voice. He approached both the stranger and the robot in less than ten seconds and laughed or smiled in response to most of the twenty-one-month procedures, including the examiner's criticism. Most low reactive boys did not show this intensely joyous profile; no high reactive child came close.

The fact that less than 10 percent of this large sample possessed this combination of five characteristics has implications for current practices in psychological and physiological research. The vast majority of laboratory studies of children or adults contain fewer than forty unselected volunteers. Laboratory studies of patients typically have smaller samples. If some temperamental categories comprise 5 to 10 percent of the population, samples this small will contain fewer than four subjects with one of the profiles, and an investigator is unlikely to detect them. Indeed, some scientists might exclude these subjects because of their deviant scores. Consider a biologist interested in behavioral differences among dogs who assessed the first forty animals that pet owners brought to her laboratory. The sample would be unlikely to include a greyhound, a toy Pekingese, or a wolfhound. A single greyhound in a group of hybrid mutts might even be treated as aberrant and removed from the analyses.

Thus, the continued use of small samples acts to support a defense of continuous dimensions rather than categories. The relation between heart rate and the behavioral variables was complex and distinctly non-linear. For example, most of the time there was no significant relation, across all the children, between heart rate (or heart rate variability) and smiling. The children at the extremes on both reactions, however, were clearly different from others. There were more low reactives among those who smiled a great deal and had very variable heart rates; more high reactives showed the opposite profile.

Relations among most psychological and biological variables are rarely linear. There is no relation for some ranges, while for others there is a clear relation. This is a general principle in science. Consider, as an illustration, the relation between body weight, on the one hand, and health, popularity, or speed of running, on the other. If a scientist based her conclusion on the first thirty adult women who volunteered for such a study and all the volunteers happened to weigh between 110 and 140 pounds, she would find no relation between weight and any of the other three characteristics. If, however, she assessed three hundred subjects, it is likely that the sample would contain some very heavy and some very light subjects and these two groups would differ in their health, speed of running, and popularity. The relation between any two phenomena is rarely the same for all ranges of the variables. Conclusions about functional relations must always specify a range. Theoretically interesting relations are likely to be restricted to subjects who have extreme values; a volunteer sample of thirty subjects is unlikely to reveal these relations. For this reason, progress in understanding personality and temperament will follow the recruitment of much larger samples and the use of more varied procedures than are currently the practice.

The third important result to emerge from our research is that infants seem to inherit two independent qualities: ease of arousal, on the one hand, and the valence of the state that follows arousal, on the other. Motor activity and vocalization to events like those presented on our four-month battery provide two indexes of ease of arousal, a concept close in meaning to Rothbart's idea of reactivity. Smiling or distress, associated with either left or right asymmetry of frontal activation and a low or high heart rate, reflect the valence, or the quality, of the affective state that follows the arousal. High reactive infants are easily aroused and usually move into a state of distress following the heightened arousal. Low reactive children, by contrast, do not become aroused easily. On those occasions when they do, about 15 percent are biased to assume a state we might call unusually happy or joyful. The children in this group tend to have very low and variable heart rates. But ease and valence of arousal are not highly correlated in a large group of unselected infants. Only 10 percent of low reactive infants showed a combination of a low and variable heart rate and a cool left forehead. Thus, ease of arousal, valence of arousal, and degree of sympathetic influence on the heart are relatively independent processes in large samples of children.

Peter Lang and his colleagues at the University of Florida believe that ease and valence of arousal are separate characteristics in adults as well. Adults viewing pleasant and unpleasant pictures reported experiencing different degrees of arousal. When subjects felt highly aroused, they showed large changes in skin conductance, but reports of high arousal occurred in response to both the pleasant and the unpleasant pictures. Smiling and a large change in heart rate were more closely related to the valence of arousal; these reactions occurred more often in response to the pleasant rather than the unpleasant pictures.

It may not be a coincidence that 16 percent of the adults in Lang's study showed a combination of both high sympathetic reactivity and minimal smiling. These two features are salient characteristics of inhibited children, who we now know make up about 20 percent of large volunteer samples. By contrast, 33 percent of the adults displayed both low sympathetic reactivity and frequent smiling, a proportion remarkably close to our estimate of 35–40 percent for low reactive–uninhibited children. We must now devise more sensitive ways to measure ease and valence of arousal to varied classes of events in infants, children, and adults. It is not clear how best to accomplish that goal, but at least we have a surer grasp of the next questions to ask.

CHAPTER EIGHT

Implications

What heredity determines are not fixed characters but developmental processes.
—T. DOBZHANSKY

The two temperamental biases explored in the previous chapters have implications that extend beyond a person's degree of reserve or spontaneity with strangers. They also touch a number of phenomena that rest on differential susceptibility to particular emotional states. One of the most obvious involves the ease with which the moral emotions of anxiety, shame, and guilt are experienced when someone violates a personal or community standard of behavior. Occasionally, the intensity or chronicity of fear, anxiety, or guilt spills beyond the level most treat as expectable for our species, and the victim is diagnosed as abnormal. Galen also noted that a melancholic temperament is especially vulnerable to the bouts of fear and depression that modern clinicians classify as pathological. Even though most inhibited and uninhibited children will never require psychiatric care, their adult personality styles will be influenced by their inherited physiology; therefore, an understanding of personality is enhanced by recognizing the contribution of temperament. Perhaps the most speculative implication is the possibility that geographically separated ethnic groups differ in the prevalence of particular temperaments. This chapter explores these four ideas.

Temperament and Conscience

Restraint on the actions that society regards as violations of its moral code usually involves both an emotional state and a conscious imposition of control; the latter used to be called *will*. Although parents—and later teachers and peers—shape both restraining processes simultaneously through modeling, threat, and punishment, the two are not perfectly correlated. The dissociation is particularly clear in the contrast between principled and conventional standards. The former—for example, a standard on avoiding cruelty—always involves an emotional reaction; as a result, these imperatives are violated less often. Conventional standards—remaining silent in the theater, for example—rely less on anxiety or guilt to mediate restraint and, therefore, are honored less consistently and violated at minimal emotional cost.

Most three-year-olds know that hitting another person and destroying property are wrong, and they experience anxiety, fear, or shame following expression or contemplation of these forbidden acts. Later, they will experience guilt. Children vary, however, in the intensity and duration of their emotional reactions to violations of local standards. Most psychologists have assumed this variation to be primarily a function of family experience. Parents who set firm standards and used the threat of love withdrawal were supposed to create children with the most intense levels of anxiety, shame, and guilt. If, in addition, the children were trained to inhibit the expression of asocial responses, they would become civil youth.

Kant believed that people varied inherently in their potential for guilt; that is one reason why he based morality on reason. Kant assumed that all humans were able to rely on their God-given rationality to inform their will and therefore to control asocial behavior. He was less certain that all adults were able to experience the level of guilt necessary to protect society from serious misconduct. Recall that the salient features of Galen's melancholic type were sadness, guilt, and self-reproach.

Anxiety and guilt over violations of moral standards are mediated by some of the same limbic circuits that mediate high reactivity and inhibition. Thus, inhibited children might be more susceptible to these moral emotions and biologically prepared to feel more intense guilt or anxiety over asocial behavior. If such children grow up in home environments that insist on obedience, they should show signs of unusually strict standards on the behaviors that their families regard as inappropriate.

There is support for this idea. Grazyna Kochanska first determined which of fifty-eight middle-class children—one-and-a-half and three-and-a-half years old—were inhibited and which uninhibited and observed each mother to find out if she reasoned with her child when she made requests or simply demanded obedience, relying on her authority to require conformity. When these children were eight to ten years old, they were asked to complete a set of stories and to infer the feelings of the protagonists in the stories. The children who had been inhibited six years earlier and, in addition, had mothers who used reasoning when they disciplined, rather than demanding compliance, told more stories indicative of a relatively strict conscience. Among the children who were uninhibited, however, the mother's use of either reasoning or an authoritarian style was unrelated to the strictness of the child's conscience. There was an interaction between the child's original temperament and the mother's disciplinary style; that is, the inhibited children were affected by the parental socialization style more clearly than the uninhibited ones. This result is analogous to Doreen Arcus's discovery that the fear of high reactive infants was influenced by the mother's willingness to impose socialization demands in the first year, while the fear of low reactive infants was not.

All children come to realize that they will feel discomfort when they anticipate punishment for actions that others disapprove. For inhibited children, whose physiology makes them especially vulnerable to this uncertainty, expectation of punishment or criticism may be particularly aversive. As a result, they should be expected to avoid acting in ways that will provoke these emotions. Hence they should be especially receptive to adopting the standards of their family and community and acquiring a conscience that is less permissive of moral error. Among Israeli children living on a kibbutz, the few who had achieved bladder control early (by age three) had a more fearful personality than the larger number who had not yet achieved control. The former children woke up frequently at night and showed obvious signs of anxiety over wetting their beds.

The laboratory behaviors of inhibited children are illustrative. In one episode in the fourteen-month battery the examiner uncovered a rotating toy and, after the child had reached for it, spoke a nonsense phrase in a sharp voice with a frown on her face. The timing was such that the examiner's reaction seemed to chastise the child for reaching for the toy. A majority of high reactive children stopped reaching at once, withdrew in the chair, and assumed a facial expression of wariness; some cried. Although many low reactive children stopped reaching, they were unlikely to become wary and rarely cried. Some low reactives looked at the examiner and vocalized, as if protesting her rebuke to them; a few even smiled. It was rare for high reactive children to treat the examiner's rejecting behavior as if it were a joke.

During the twenty-one-month battery, the examiner first modeled two simple constructions from blocks and asked the child to imitate her. Almost all children did so successfully. On the next two trials the block constructions were difficult; only one child was able to do them. After the child had tried but failed to match the model, the examiner assumed a frown and said, in a disapproving tone of voice, "Oh, no, (child's name), oh, no." The rebuke led many high reactive children to assume a serious facial expression; a few cried. But some uninhibited children smiled, as if the examiner's disapproval did not generate any apprehension. These reactions to the examiner's chastisements imply that inhibited children are more vulnerable to uncertainty following adult disapproval. It is not surprising, therefore, that the mothers of high reactive infants were likely to report that their children were unusually sensitive to punishment, both at home and in day care settings.

Uninhibited children, by contrast, may experience a diluted fear of adult punishment and therefore may feel a less urgent need to conform to family standards. In homes that do not punish yelling, aggression, or destruction of property in a consistent manner, these children may acquire a permissive superego. One-fourth of the uninhibited boys were unusually aggressive with other children and, according to the mothers, "afraid of nothing." If these boys encounter environments in the future where asocial behavior is punished and there are few models for aggression, there is little danger that they will become chronically asocial or delinquent adolescents. But if they live in homes that are permissive of aggression and play in neighborhoods rampant with crime, they may be at some risk for delinquency. David Magnusson is probably correct when he suggests that some boys are temperamentally vulnerable to a delinquent career but not because there are genes for crime. Rather, the biology affects the experience of fear of punishment.

The possibility that some temperamental types feel the pinch of conscience less harshly than others poses an ethical dilemma for modern societies. Adults in small isolated villages in Latin America, Indonesia, or Africa rely on surveillance by all as an important basis for continuous protection against stealing, property damage, and attack. Those living in large cities must rely more often on each person's internalized conscience and the assumption that all children are capable of acquiring a similar intensity of moral emotion to norm violations.

Two popular explanations of adolescent criminality in the United States are that early experiences in the home did not teach the child right from wrong and that harsh treatment produced chronic anger and hostility. The first explanation, which is essentially cognitive, is not qualitatively different from the reason why some children know more state capitols than others. The second ignores the low level of crime in Puritan New England towns in the seventeenth century.

If a small group of children experience minimal anxiety, fear, and guilt over stealing or aggression because of a combination of temperament and experience, rather than simply because of insufficient tutoring or a harsh home life, some people might urge implementation of a new type of McNaughton rule. Recall that the present rule says that a person who does not know an act was illegal cannot be tried for breaking the law. Do we need a rule for the small number who have the necessary knowledge but have an impaired capacity to experience the emotions that serve as a governor for most of us?

Although a larger proportion of males than females find it relatively easy to violate family and community norms on aggression, only a small proportion of low reactive, fearless two-year-old boys, probably no more than 1 percent across all family circumstances, will ever commit a serious criminal act. Even among older children who are excessively aggressive, less than one-third become antisocial adults. Given these odds, the most sensitive diagnostic procedures would lead to more incorrect than correct predictions. If psychologists desiring to predict later delinquent behavior developed a perfect diagnostic test for selecting extremely uninhibited one-year-old children who also had low sympathetic tone, it is estimated that they would detect about twenty boys from every thousand children tested. But probably only one or two of these twenty is likely to become a chronic or violent delinquent; hence the scientists would be wrong nineteen out of twenty times.

Temperament and Psychopathology

It is likely that inhibited and uninhibited temperaments make a modest contribution to the later appearance of behaviors clinicians regard as pathological. A small proportion of inhibited children are probably at greater than average risk for the development of generalized anxiety disorder, social phobia, panic, or agoraphobia. These symptoms are not common in children, even among those who have been subjected to a trauma. Of forty school children who were kidnapped and then terrorized for about two days, only ten developed a syndrome called posttraumatic stress disorder. On February 24, 1984, a Los Angeles sniper in a building across the street from an elementary school fired at a group of children on the playground. One child was killed and thirteen were injured; a siege followed that lasted several hours. About one month later a group of psychologists and psychiatrists talked with the children to determine which ones were suffering from the extreme stress. Thirty-eight percent of the children were judged to be anxious, but an equal proportion—39 percent—were not. The primary quality that differentiated the anxious from the nonanxious children was a prior avoidant personality among the former group. The children who were uninhibited before the shooting event experienced far less fear. Similarly, only 40 percent of college students living in the San Francisco area had nightmares following a nearby earthquake. Only some young physicians making their first presentations at grand rounds, a stressful exercise, had an increase in epinephrine and norepinephrine. Some showed no change in biochemistry from the beginning to the end of their presentation. Thus, it is a stubborn fact that only some individuals react with the psychology and physiology of fear to what seems to an observer to be an extremely stressful event.

THE EVIDENCE FOR DIAGNOSING PATHOLOGY

At present, diagnoses of psychopathology are based almost completely on patients' verbal descriptions of their feelings and behavior. When the patient is a child, diagnosis is based on descriptions supplied by the parents. As we have seen, this is a special form of evidence. Recall that conclusions about the sources of concern among Americans—whether jobs, schools, pollution, or nuclear war—depend on how the question is asked.

A diagnosis of American schools provides an example of the relation between the source of evidence and a judgment. The mathematics and reading achievement scores of American children are seriously lower than those of children in Japan and in many countries of Europe. Yet a majority of American parents tell interviewers they are satisfied with the quality of their children's instruction and academic progress. If we relied on the parental reports we would conclude that there are no serious problems with American schools. If, on the other hand, we compared the literacy levels and mathematics achievement scores at high school graduation in the United States with those of other nations, we would arrive at a very different diagnosis of the quality of American education.

A similar conclusion holds for estimates of psychopathology. Assignment of a child to a diagnostic category is a professional judgment, based on verbal description, that the child's behaviors and emotions are deviant and, further, that the patient or the patient's family is worried about the symptoms. The dissatisfaction is as important for the diagnosis as the child's actual behavior, for the possession of a set of traits need not be highly correlated with satisfaction or dissatisfaction over their possession. Two men may have exactly the same compulsive symptom—they frequently check their back pockets to ensure that their wallets are still there—but the more reflective, introspective man is likely to decide that his concerns are not rational. The less introspective one may accept his behavior as reasonable, especially if he lives in a city where stealing is common. The recognition that one is behaving irrationally is an important fact, but since both men have the same symptom one can argue that both of them are obsessive-compulsive, with one having insight and one not. The criterion of insight is not applied across all psychiatric diagnoses. If a man had a delusion that God had selected him for a special mission he would be diagnosed as paranoid, even if he did not believe his ideas were abnormal.

Similarly, if two ten-year-old children were equally shy but one was doing well in school, had a close friend, and was involved in a hobby, while the other was doing poorly in school and had no friends or hobby, the latter would be diagnosed as having an anxiety disorder, but the former may not. Extreme shyness is not treated as pathological in all societies. Many shy adolescents in twelfth-century France chose to enter monasteries; few were advised to consult a physician. And in 1807, Jane Austen wrote to her sister complaining, "What is become of all the shyness in the world? . . . Shyness and the sweating sickness have given way to confidence and paralytic complaints."

A second, more complex issue is the basis for the diagnosis. The verbal description of symptoms is the essential component, but people who are not aware that their behavior or mood is deviant are likely to minimize their symptoms when they are asked to describe them, while those who believe that they are deviant are likely to exaggerate their symptoms. Thus, the belief that one is behaving or feeling in an abnormal fashion will influence the description of those qualities to another person.

When a newspaper or magazine reports that the National Institute of Mental Health conducted a survey of two hundred thousand Americans and found that 3 percent of the population has social phobia—feeling very anxious with strangers and trying to avoid meeting new people—the estimate is based on the adults' answers to half a dozen questions posed by an unfamiliar interviewer, often a graduate student, either in person or on the telephone. Adults who have a sharp increase in heart rate or sweating when they meet strangers but are not aware of these changes—or, if they are, do not interpret them as reflecting anxiety—will not be diagnosed as having social phobia. The diagnosis also excludes people who feel apprehensive with strangers but are reluctant to admit it to an unfamiliar voice on the telephone. Further, anxiety over meeting strangers is a heterogeneous category. If a random sample of adults are asked, "Are you shy with strangers?" about 40 percent will answer in the affirmative because many people feel slightly uncomfortable initially when they meet people they do not know. Yet we know that no more than 20 percent of children begin life with a temperamental bias to be inhibited. Therefore, most adults who say they are shy were not temperamentally inhibited children.

The reliability of the diagnosis is also a problem. Two trained people studying typed or recorded interviews with adults will agree 90 percent of the time that a person who reports no fears at all is not suffering from anxiety disorder. But when a person tells an interviewer he occasionally feels anxious at parties, independent judges will not always agree on a diagnosis of anxiety disorder. In one study of 361 adults independent judges agreed on the diagnosis of social phobia in 12 cases but disagreed in 15 cases.

One reason for the modest agreement is that the diagnosis of anxiety disorder necessarily involves a judgment of the degree to which the emotions interfere with daily functioning. That judgment is difficult to make. A woman who says she feels anxious occasionally when her husband is away on a long business trip but adds that she handles this tension well is usually not diagnosed as having anxiety disorder. The patient's evaluation of her ability to cope with the dysphoric feelings enters into the diagnosis. Put plainly, if two women experience the same level of physiological discomfort and conscious concern with their husbands' absences but one intellectualizes the worry and the other remains preoccupied with her husband's safety, only the second woman will be diagnosed as having anxiety disorder.

Further, diagnoses are occasionally indifferent to the realistic sources of fear or anxiety in the environment. A woman with a premature four-month-old infant, an unemployed husband, and a mother dying of cancer has three major sources of worry that will lower her threshold for becoming concerned over an accident to her absent husband. Psychiatry has become unusually pragmatic over the past twenty-five years. Clinical psychiatrists are appropriately concerned with the emotional states of their patients, and much of the time the therapy will be administration of a drug. Drugs are indifferent to the specific cause of anxiety, and many psychiatrists and psychologists have become equally indifferent to the psychological origins of a patient's current state. Although this pragmatic perspective may be efficient it hampers deeper understanding.

During most of this century, professionals assumed that intrapsychic conflict and unconscious psychological processes were the basic causes of symptoms. On reflection, this view is a bit odd because it was ascendant during a period of economic depression when many Americans were under severe economic stress and were anxious for realistic reasons. Nonetheless, psychoanalytic theory insisted that the intrafamilial experiences of childhood, especially events surrounding sexuality and anger, were the basic causes of symptoms. Technical papers in the early issues of the journal *Psychosomatic Medicine* assumed that anxiety and guilt surrounding sex, anger, and dependence were the primary causes of allergies, ulcers, and high blood pressure, not the death of the spouse. Only if the death generated guilt would symptoms develop.

This premise lasted until the late 1960s, when the social conditions of poor minority groups were forced upon American consciousness. The plight of the poor was captured in vivid scenes on television screens and in Sunday supplements. As an accompaniment to the new concern with life conditions, psychologists and sociologists developed instruments to measure the potentially stressful events that humans endured—death of a loved one, loss of a job, marital strife, and daily frustrations. There is even a scale of everyday hassles. This new attitude assumes that the major conditions that alter mood and provoke pathology are serious losses and life disappointments. How did this change in perspective occur?

First, historical events tested and rejected Freud's assumption that guilt over sexual and hostile ideas and emotions was the primary cause of psychopathology. The resulting theoretical vacuum made it easier for real events to replace psychological ones.

A second reason for a concern with life events has been the increased interest in physical health among the middle class. Many adults expect their lives to contain psychological tension, frustration, and anxiety because they work in large bureaucracies, commute long distances in urban areas, and are forced to adjust to a lifestyle with both spouses working. A majority cannot do much about these daily frustrations; hence, uncertainty over these realities has decreased. But there is something everyone can do about personal health. The dramatic decrease in mortality from infectious diseases like pneumonia, tuberculosis, and diphtheria leaves the diseases of aging, cancer, and cardiovascular disease as the major causes of death and incapacitation. The public is told regularly that proper diet and exercise can postpone the onset of these diseases. The unvoiced extrapolation is that mental illness can also be prevented by altering one's concrete life conditions.

A third factor is an increasing tendency in our society to externalize the causes of a person's current status. At the turn of the century, success and failure were regarded as the consequences of individual effort and skill. If a person became a doctor, lawyer, professor, or vice president, it was assumed that she must have applied native talents with persistence. One who remained an unskilled laborer was considered to lack sufficient intellectual ability or motivation.

The civil rights movement and the promotion of affirmative action programs in both the corporate and academic worlds have weakened the assumption that personal qualities are the sole determinants of a life itinerary. Most people are conscious of the fact that important external forces are not under their control. For example, arbitrary cut-off scores on college and professional entrance examinations can frustrate a legal or medical career. It should be remembered that at the turn of the century a moderately intelligent high school graduate with a reasonable grade record and letters of recommendation from a few teachers could enter medical school by simply sending in the first year's tuition.

A final historical factor involves the sociology of science. The younger cohort of scientists in departments of psychology and sociology, who are eager to publish in order to gain promotion, must obtain federal funding to support their research. Contemporary review committees have become more positivisitic over recent years and less tolerant of theoretical ideas describing processes that cannot be measured reliably. Questionnaires and interviews that ask informants about life events have face validity— after all, most people who tell an interviewer that they lost their jobs last week are probably telling the truth. Thus, these methods seem safer and journal referees assume their validity. As a result, this form of inquiry has become popular, and its large number of practitioners have, by consensus, affirmed the validity of this strategy of research. The result is a group of social scientists who have come to believe that frustrations and disappointments are the primary causes of mental illness. Failure to get into law school is seen as the cause of a depression, not a guilt-prone personality that reacts to loss with sorrow because of a temperamental bias or childhood separation from a parent.

John Bowlby's recollection of an experience as a trainee in child psychoanalysis, when Melanie Klein was supervising his treatment of an anxious boy, conveys this secular change. One day the young boy Bowlby was treating was unusually anxious. When Bowlby tried to find out why, he learned that the boy's mother had deserted him a few days earlier. When Bowlby had his supervisory session with Klein, he told her of the importance of the maternal desertion. According to Bowlby, Klein replied, "Dr. Bowlby, we are not concerned with the actual experiences of the child; we are only concerned with the fantasy."

But it remains a stubborn fact that only a minority react to loss of a job or a loved one with serious psychological symptoms. For most, there is a temporary increase in anger or sadness, which runs its course, and the person adapts. This is the human condition. Every life is punctuated with disappointments; pathology develops in only a few. Hence, it is necessary to go beyond the event and ask about the stable psychological and biological characteristics of the person who develops the symptom.

Adults who believe they can handle stress show a smaller adrenal reaction in the laboratory to sustained loud noise than those who feel they cannot cope with stress well, even when all the subjects are able to control the level of the noise. Psychology is the vehicle that carries the external frustration to the physiological channels. When a bridge is weak structurally, either because of its age or because of poor construction, it may crack under the weight of a very heavy truck. But because bridges are supposed to carry heavy loads, all of us understand that the cause we seek for the broken bridge is not an immediate one—the overloaded truck—but the historical causes. So, too, with human mental illness. The death of a spouse does alter a person's mood, and some widows and widowers become temporarily depressed. But in order to understand prolonged depression we must also inquire into the biological predisposition for that mood and the sequence of prior experiences that prepared the person for the change in emotional state. I do not question the necessity and utility of relying on a patient's report of feelings and symptoms as one basis for diagnosing pathology. But if supplementary information were gathered, psychiatry might have different diagnostic categories and different estimates of the prevalence of mental illnesses.

Dyslexia offers a nice example of the theoretical advances that are possible when new methods provide novel evidence. Twenty years ago, dyslexia was defined as a serious disorder of reading in an otherwise intelligent, healthy child. The primary observation was behavioral—severe retardation in reading text. The advent of PET technology permitted scientists to assess the differences in metabolic activity in response to the component skills that are involved in reading. Some dyslexics show special profiles of metabolic activity in the temporal lobe when they have to create rhymes, although their brain activity appears normal when they have to judge the correctness of the grammar of a sentence. Should this finding prove valid, professionals will redefine one form of dyslexia as primarily a phonological disorder and secondarily as a reading problem. This kind of progress is likely to occur for many currently popular pathological categories. If American adolescents were administered both a standard psychiatric diagnostic interview and the laboratory battery described in chapters 4 and 5, different categories of pathology would be invented and there would be different estimates of the prevalence of varied anxiety disorders. The current estimates of the number of Americans infected with the HIV virus are many times larger than the number of cases of AIDS because the former is based on a laboratory analysis of blood, not just the patient's report of illness.

WHAT HAVE WE LEARNED?

Most of our knowledge of psychopathology is based on answers given in interviews and our inferences; therefore, we must use that information as best we can. What, in fact, do we know? An epidemiological study of 18,000 adults in different cities representative of American society reveals that 9.7 percent of women and 4.7 percent of men have an anxiety disorder characterized by admission of muscle tension, restlessness, shortness of breath, heart palpitations, dry mouth, dizziness, flushes, feeling on edge, difficulty concentrating, or trouble falling asleep, as well as chronic feelings of worry and/or phobias of insects, animals, high places, railroad crossings, bridges, or confined spaces. A similar sex difference occurs in all similar evaluations; about twice as many females as males—among children as well as adults—report prolonged periods of intense anxiety and fear. This difference was present in seventeenth-century England. Richard Napier, a seventeenth-century English physician who specialized in mental problems, recorded in meticulously kept notes that more women than men came to him with complaints of mental anguish due to troubled love relations, marital problems, or loss of a loved one. A fourth source of worry—economic problems—was reported equally often for men and women.

The diagnosis of panic disorder, based on sudden, unexpected increases in heart rate, sweating, tension, disturbed breathing, chest pain, and the feeling that one is about to faint, accompanied by a fear that one is dying or going crazy, is less common. It occurs in about 1–2 percent of women and less than 1 percent of men. Although infrequent, panic also occurs in school-age children. A fear of leaving home—called agoraphobia—usually follows a series of panic attacks leading a person to fear an unexpected attack on the street or in a car.

Anxiety, phobias, and panic are more frequent among adults who are economically less secure and have not attended college. Only 4.6 percent of middle-class adults are diagnosed with anxiety disorder, compared with 10.5 percent of lower-middle- and lower-class adults. Even though the prevalence is low, in this case the class difference may be the partial result of life circumstances. Economic insecurity is a major cause of worry in many American families. In addition, poor urban residential areas pose more frequent dangers of physical attack than middle-class neighborhoods. A continuing preoccupation with steady employment, family debt, and sidewalk attacks will make some people vulnerable to other targets of fear. The fact that panic attacks are reported by 1.2 percent of lower-class adults but by only 0.2 percent of middle-class adults—a six-fold differ-ence—may be a partial consequence of differential exposure to these real-istic dangers. But over 90 percent of adults exposed to the same stressful conditions do not have panic attacks.

There is a surprising sameness to the prevalence of anxiety disorders in extraordinarily diverse settings. The incidence is under 10 percent in New Haven, Connecticut; Edinburgh, Scotland; London, England; Can-berra, Australia; and Uganda, even though poverty, crime, and social unrest are higher in New Haven and Uganda than they are in Canberra.

Scientists interested in the degree to which heredity controls anxiety disorders often base their estimates on studies of twins. One such study estimates the heritability of anxiety disorder to be 0.4, similar to the heri-tability of an inhibited temperament. The first- and second-degree adult relatives of very fearful children are also more likely to have anxiety disor-der (40 percent) than the relatives of hyperactive children (28 percent) or control children with no symptoms (18 percent). About one in five sib-lings of very fearful children are themselves unusually anxious or fearful.

The heritability of specific phobias—0.6—is a bit higher than it is for generalized anxiety disorder. Some phobias, especially of blood and of injections, that begin during late childhood persist into adulthood. The less frequent diagnosis of panic is also under genetic control, although the heritability is lower—0.3. About one-third of identical twins whose co-twin has panic attacks is likely to develop panic—a degree of concordance that is slightly lower than that for schizophrenia. For every ten families with a panic patient, five or six will have at least one other adult relative—parent, aunt, uncle, or grandparent—with the same symptom. Thus, genetic factors do contribute to the development of varied adult anxiety disorders. It is equally clear that the mode of inheritance is complex; the majority of genetically related relatives of fearful children are not diag-nosed as anxious, and childhood stress is always a contributing factor.

It is not clear whether inhibited children are at special risk for panic attacks, social phobia, a phobia of animals, blood, or heights, or whether these children are at equal risk for all three diagnoses. When panic, depressed, and social phobic patients were asked to recall whether they were shy or fearful as children, all three groups admitted to more fre-quent signs of childhood inhibition than adults without any of these symptoms. Therefore, inhibited children may be equally likely to develop anxiety disorder, social phobia, panic, or depression.

It is important to appreciate, however, that the vast majority of inhibited, anxious, or phobic children do not become panic patients later in life. In one study, only 7 percent of forty-five school-age children with school phobia became adults with panic and/or agoraphobia. Because the prevalence of panic or social phobia in the population is low (less than 5 percent), an almost perfect test that correctly predicted 90 percent of all people who would develop panic and correctly eliminated 90 percent of those who would not develop the symptom would be correct in only about one-third of the cases it predicted would develop the symptom. The prediction would be incorrect for two out of every three persons. But prediction of a shy, restrained adult personality from early inhibition, which is not a psychiatric diagnosis, is much more accurate than prediction of the less frequent, psychiatric category of anxiety or panic disorder.

It is natural to focus on the risk status of the inhibited child, for intense anxiety is debilitating and maladaptive in modern society. But uninhibited children are also at risk, for different problems. Most students of psychopathology in children agree on two complementary clusters of symptoms that have acquired the names *internalizing* and *externalizing*. Children in the former group are anxious, guilty, worried, or phobic. One of the adolescent girls who had been classified as inhibited at age two could not control the urge to tell her parents each night before bedtime that they should remember to wear their seatbelts when they went to work the next day. Children in the externalizing group are described as impulsive, aggressive, hyperactive, or asocial, and evidence points to a genetic contribution in some of these children. Inhibited children are more likely to be internalizing; uninhibited children more likely to be externalizing.

An inhibited temperament may protect a child living in a high-risk environment from becoming asocial. David Farrington of Cambridge University has found that shy, inhibited seven-year-olds living in London neighborhoods with high rates of crime are less likely to become chronic delinquents than are outgoing, uninhibited boys living in the same neighborhoods.

A larger than expected proportion of boys with serious conduct disorder have low levels of dopamine-beta-hydroxylase, an enzyme necessary for the last metabolic step in the production of norepinephrine. If one consequent of brain norepinephrine is lower thresholds of arousal in those areas that mediate fear and guilt, perhaps these uninhibited, asocial boys have a high threshold for experiencing any of the moral emotions following delinquent behavior. But, as we have suggested, the lower level of anxiety experienced by uninhibited adolescents represents a risk only if they grow up with permissive families in neighborhoods where aggression and crime are common and where provocations for asocial behavior occur regularly. If not, these boys may become successful politicians, generals, or business executives—roles that also require muted levels of fear, anxiety, or guilt.

Personality and Temperament

Although the two temperamental categories contribute a little to the likelihood of later psychiatric symptoms, the more secure prediction from childhood to adolescence and adulthood involves vocational and marital choice and styles of relating to others—in short, to personality rather than to psychopathology.

Many inhibited adolescents recognize an uncomfortable feeling of tension when they have to meet unfamiliar people, confront challenge or danger, or adopt an overly competitive stance. These adolescents are likely to avoid choosing vocations where these emotions are provoked and the appropriate behaviors required. Inhibited adolescents, if they are fortunate enough to have a choice, will select jobs that permit them to work alone, to remain in control of the immediate future, and to avoid possible physical harm, loss of resources, and the feeling of humiliation following task failure. Thus, inhibited adolescents are unlikely to become test pilots, salespeople, investment bankers, CEOs, or trial lawyers. If they are college graduates, inhibited youth are apt to select careers in mathematics, art, writing, and computer programming—challenging activities that permit them to control novelty and titer the daily level of uncertainty. Uninhibited youth will choose the vocations inhibited adolescents usually avoid, such as lawyer, surgeon, stockbroker, entrepreneur, and politician. These occupations demand an ability to be relaxed, comfortable, and confident with strangers and a willingness to confront unpredictable risk with minimal tension.

The personality profiles most closely related to inhibited and uninhibited temperaments are introversion and extroversion, and Jung's descriptions of the introvert and extrovert capture likely adult outcomes of the two childhood temperaments. The introvert has a natural tendency to move away from the world to thought, imagery, and reflection; the extrovert engages the world with energy and zeal. (Recall the cases of Tom and Ralph from chapter 5.) Jung liked the introvert, celebrating his sensitivity to feelings and love of ideas; at times he came close to describing the extrovert as a brute. Ideas, Jung claimed, are the primary bases for action for the introvert; for the extrovert, reality dominates. The introvert likes to base decisions on abstract principles; the extrovert's evaluation is more flexible, often local to a particular situation.

Percy Bridgman, the physicist credited with the philosophy called operationalism, illustrates the deep conviction introverts often award to their beliefs. According to his biographer, Bridgman was a shy, retiring person; on one occasion he decided not to contribute to an exhibit at the annual meeting of the American Association for the Advancement of Science because, "On seeing the exhibit I was overcome with shyness at the unpretentiousness of my offering and decided it was better not to show it." Bridgman's loyalty to empirical truths, rather than formal ones, was challenged by Einstein's theory and the rise of quantum mechanics, both of which gave mathematical meanings to the more concrete experiences of length and location in space. Operationalism was Bridgman's attempt to make the specific laboratory procedure an inherent component of the meaning of a scientific concept. But, as Jung would have anticipated, Bridgman insisted that a belief in the truth of any statement had a subjective component. Data, no matter how impeccable, required the faith of an individual reflecting on all the evidence. Thus, history distorted Bridgman's philosophy by folding his views in with the logical positivists who wished to eradicate all subjectivity from an evaluation of what is true. Bridgman resisted quantum mechanics and relativity because their concepts did not match his subjective intuitions, which he trusted—as it turned out, to excess.

American society is suspicious of the introverted isolate with one or two friends who avoids social gatherings. Kant would have been surprised by this contemporary prejudice. He was of the opinion that "separation from all society is regarded as sublime. . . . To be sufficient for oneself, and consequently to have no need of society, without at the same time being unsociable, is something bordering on the sublime."

The relation between inhibited and uninhibited temperaments and the other four popular personality factors described in chapter 2—agreeableness, conscientiousness, emotional stability, and curiosity—is much less clear. The information before us does not imply that these two types of children will differ on those four abstract qualities. But that conclusion should not be surprising. The two temperaments should not dominate, imperialistically, all facets of adult personality. It is amazing that the profiles of the second year have the power they appear to command.

Ethnicity and Temperament

There is a possibility that the prevalence of various temperamental types may differ slightly among the world's ethnic groups. We noted in chapter 1 that reproductively isolated populations across the world possess different frequencies of particular genes. For example, northern Europeans, compared with Asians, have a much higher incidence of the gene associated with an Rh negative blood type—15 percent versus 1 percent. But Asians have a higher frequency of one of the mutations linked to a vulnerability to bladder cancer and lack an enzyme needed to metabolize alcohol; hence, they are likely to show facial flushing after consuming a small amount of alcohol. In addition, Asians lack the enzyme needed to tolerate the sugar lactose present in milk. More relevant to our studies is the fact that when a drug that lowers the reactivity of the sympathetic nervous system (by blocking beta receptors) is given to Chinese and Caucasian adults, the former display a lower heart rate and blood pressure than the latter, implying different metabolism of the drug. Every introductory textbook in human genetics mentions that Jews are more vulnerable to Tay-Sachs syndrome, while adults of African pedigree are especially vulnerable to sickle-cell anemia. Variation in the prevalence of these rare diseases is the product of selective mutations maintained by thousands of years of reproductive isolation. It is reasonable, therefore, to assume that DNA sequences with implications for temperament also appeared in isolated human populations, perhaps even genetic changes related to the categories of high and low reactive infants.

Although this idea is not popular among social scientists, who prefer to believe in maximal similarity among human groups, comparisons of Asian and Caucasian children have suggested that Asian infants are less easily aroused by stimulation. Over twenty years ago, Freedman and Freedman reported that newborn Asian-American infants, compared with European-Americans, were calmer, less emotionally labile, and more easily consoled when distressed. They wrote, "The European-American infants had a greater tendency to move back and forth between states of contentment and upset. . . . The Chinese-American newborns tended to be less changeable, less perturbable, tended to habituate more readily and tended to calm themselves or to be consoled more readily when upset."

Chinese-American infants living in Boston were less active and far less vocal in response to visual and auditory events during the first year than Caucasians living in the same neighborhoods. Japanese infants were less likely to display intense distress to inoculation and took twice as long as Caucasian infants to cry when their arms were restrained. Further, a group of Chinese, Japanese, Filipino, and Hawaiian children living in Honolulu were less reactive to stimulation at three to four months than Caucasian infants from the same city. Gordon Bronson noted, "It was only among the Caucasian group that the more highly reactive infants were to be found."

These differences in the first year have a parallel in older children. The parents of school-age Thai children, compared with Caucasian-Americans, were more concerned with their children's low energy, low motivation, and forgetfulness; the parents of the Caucasian children reported more concern with disobedience, aggression, and hyperactivity. Although these differences have been interpreted as reflecting only cultural variation in socialization, temperament might make a small contribution to these profiles.

Support for this claim comes from a comparison of Asian and Caucasian four-month-old infants. John Hendler and Sheila Greene in Dublin and Wang Yu-Feng in Beijing administered the same battery we gave to Cohort 2 (see chapter 6) to 106 Irish infants born to parents who themselves were born in Ireland and to 80 Chinese infants whose parents were born in the People's Republic of China. Most of these mothers were, like the Boston group, well educated and remained at home during the infants' first four months.

The Caucasian infants—from both Dublin and Boston—had much higher levels of motor activity, irritability, and vocalization than the Chinese infants, by a factor of 4 for motor activity and vocalization and a factor of 5 for crying. Only frequency of smiling, which was low for all infants, was similar for the two ethnic groups. Significantly more Caucasian than Chinese infants were high reactive; significantly more Chinese than Caucasian infants were low reactive. Indeed, the typical Chinese infant was far less reactive than the average low reactive American infant. It is relevant to note that Asian psychiatric patients require lower doses of some psychotropic drugs than do Caucasians with the same diagnosis, indicating lower levels of limbic arousal in the Asian patients.

This evidence invites speculation on the differences in the classic philosophies of Asians and Europeans. Post-reformation Christian philosophy, which is more clearly a product of northern rather than southern Europe, emphasizes the inherently dysphoric mood of human beings. The commentaries on human nature by Martin Luther and John Calvin emphasize the anxiety, fear, and guilt that is endemic to the human condition and the extraordinary effort necessary to control these gnawing, unpleasant emotions. As a professor of biblical theology in Wittenberg in his early thirties, Luther wrote, "Should it not be enough for miserable sinners eternally damned by original sin to be oppressed by all sorts of calamity through the law of the Ten Commandments? Must God add suffering to suffering even through the Gospel and also threaten us with his righteousness in his wrath for the Gospel too?"

John Calvin, who probably suffered from an obsessive-compulsive disorder and was chronically anxious as both an adolescent and an adult, confessed, "The thought repeatedly occurs to me that I am in danger of being unjust to God's mercy by laboring with so much anxiety to assert it, as if it were doubtful or obscure." Calvin saw anxiety everywhere and brooded about its place in human affairs, believing that humans could never escape their fears: "We cannot be otherwise than continuously anxious and disturbed." Calvin was certain that humans must struggle continually with the fear of impending danger; total freedom from anxiety was impossible because humans were simply unable to obliterate dark thoughts of the future. One of Calvin's biographers, William Bouwsma, notes that Calvin's belief that freedom from anxiety was the most desirable of all states reflects a stoic view of beatitude emanating from his own chronic dysphoria. It may not be a surprise that Kretschmer described Calvin's face as "of an extreme schizothymic form. . . . [It was a] very long face, [with a] long sharp nose" (see figure 8.1).

Buddhist philosophy, more attractive to Asians, emphasizes attainment of serenity as the ideal life goal. A person approaches this state by ridding the self of all desire because frustrated wishes are the primary cause of a state of unhappiness that most scholars translate as "suffering." But the emotional states of sadness, frustration, regret, or even anger, which accompany either the inability to gain a desired goal or the loss of a satis-

Figure 8.1 John Calvin

From the monograph by Prof. D. Benrath, "Calvin und das Genfer Reformationswerk" in Werkshagen's *Der Protestantismus.*

fying one, are very different from the states of anxiety or guilt that accompany anticipation of danger, criticism, punishment, or self-reproach. Put simply, anxiety and sadness are different emotions.

The Buddhist imperative urges elimination of wishes for material and sensory pleasures so that one can attain a tranquility only possible when a conscious awareness of the world and of the self is temporarily obliterated. The complete detachment from self and from others, which is necessary to gain Nirvana, is captured in a story reported by Charles Eliot:

> A monk was meditating under a tree when his former wife came and laid his child before him saying: "Here, monk, is your little son, nourish me and nourish him." The monk took no notice and sent her away. The Buddha, seeing this, said: "He feels no pleasure when she comes, no sorrow when she goes: him, I call a true Brahman released from passion."

The desirability of eliminating states of affective arousal is linked to a passive rather than an active attitude toward the world. It is hard to imagine many European philosophers or statesmen celebrating the virtue of a detached quiescence, as Lao-tzu did over two thousand years ago:

Strength and power lie below, weakness and softness stand above
In all of the world nothing is more pliant than water.
And yet it has no equal in resiliency against that which is hard.
That which is weaker conquers that which is strong;
That which is soft conquers that which is hard. . . .
There is nothing better than limitation.

Compare Lao-tzu with Pierre Janet, the French psychiatrist whose writings informed Freud:

Sadness is always a sign of weakness and sometimes of the habit of living weakly. The investigations of pathological psychology has shown us the evil of sadness, and, at the same time, have evidenced a very important thing: the value of work and of joy.

Most scholars who have commented on these very different philosophical views on the nature of being human have emphasized only cultural determinants. Social scientists have assumed further that the differences in modal personality profiles between Asians and Europeans are derivatives of the adoption of one or the other of these two philosophies. I am tempted, however, to agree with Daniel Freedman, who speculated that temperament might make a small, but nonetheless real, contribution to the attractiveness of one or the other of these two ideological positions. Stated more boldly than is warranted, if a large number of adults are experiencing high levels of anxiety, guilt, and fear because of their temperament, a philosophy that urges them to be serene, free of emotion, and detached from others may meet some resistance because the ideal state of perfection does not come close enough to their conscious feeling tone and therefore will seem unattainable. By the same token, a philosophy that accepts chronic anxiety, melancholy, and fear as definitive of the human condition will seem invalid to those whose consciousness is fed by a lower level of limbic arousal. Being freed from all dysphoria may seem a real possibility to this latter group. Perhaps nature and nurture come together to influence even the preferred philosophical assumptions of an isolated cultural group.

For readers who find it difficult to imagine how the chemistry of the brain could have anything to do with the attractiveness of an ethical stance, I point out that some facts have required counterintuitive explanations. The observations and inferences of Galileo and Kepler implied that the earth was circling the sun—a conclusion I still find counterintuitive. Although scientists are now certain that the African and South American continents were once joined, this suggestion was rejected soundly when it was first announced. Perhaps the most difficult ideas to accept come from quantum mechanics. A stream of electrons is beamed at a partition containing two separated slits placed in front of a rear surface. Intuition dictates that any one electron should go through either one slit or the other and that therefore the pattern of energy on the rear surface struck by the electrons should have two distinct areas corresponding to the positions of the slits, in the partition. But, to the surprise of physicists, an interference pattern, not two discrete areas, appears on the rear surface. The puzzle is deepened because if the scientist puts an electron detector near the two slits, the interference pattern vanishes. The mathematics that will explain these enigmatic observations requires the counterintuitive assumption that all the electrons went through both slits and took all possible paths before striking the rear surface. Surely, acceptance of that idea is more difficult than the modest proposal that inheriting a particular temperamental bias might affect one's philosophical preferences. Theodore Bullock, an eminent neuroscientist, wrote, "The measure of value of a hypothesis . . . is not its plausibility or compatibility with a subset of facts, or its presumed validity, but its heuristic potential—how much it suggests for the next stage of investigation."

Should these speculations prove valid, they have no political or legal implications whatsoever. Women have higher basal metabolic rates and less muscle mass than men, but our society sees no reason to use those differences as a basis for awarding or restricting their power. Unfortunately, we live in a historical moment when ethnic and racial variations are imbued with unusually strong emotion and all such differences are evaluated reflexively as good or bad. Wittgenstein understood the independence of ethics and facts; some have suggested that the *Tractatus* was written in order to make that division explicit. Science has enriched our lives, made labor easier, and contributed to human health and longevity. But science is not to be used as the sole, or even the primary, basis for our laws or morality. Humans differ in an unknown number of genetically based characteristics. This diversity is to be regarded as a set of interesting facts about nature and never exploited as an argument for the awarding of differential privilege.

The pragmatic spirit of Americans resists celebrating knowledge that is not put to some useful purpose, even though Congress has voted many millions of dollars to place instruments in the sky that will observe distant galaxies and inform us about the earliest moments of the universe. As I have written elsewhere, the procedures of science provide one of the most powerful ways to illuminate the nature of the world. The propositions that are constructed from the mysterious marriage of the concrete and the imagined can bring clarity, comprehension, and, on occasion, a feeling that combines delight, awe, wonder, and serenity into an emotion for which we have no name. But still we ask for more. Not satisfied with the gift of understanding, we demand that the fruits of empirical research be applied in some way, and especially that they tell us what we ought to do when alternative ethical positions require us to choose one action over another. However, facts alone cannot support a moral proposition. Facts may prune the tree of morality; they cannot be its seedbed.

CHAPTER NINE

Reflections

Facts do not speak.
　　　　　—JULES-HENRI POINCARÉ

Galen did not speculate on the infant profiles of melancholic and sanguine adults, but I suspect he would have been pleased with the fact that a cautious or relaxed reaction to novelty is preserved from very early childhood to adolescence. The predictive power of the four-month behavioral profiles was unanticipated when we began this work fifteen years ago. The intensity of motor activity and distress in sixteen-week-old infants in response to colorful moving mobiles, human speech, and a cotton swab dipped in dilute alcohol reflect central physiological processes that lie at the foundation of inhibited and uninhibited temperaments. This discovery is simultaneously the most surprising and significant in this long research journey.

About two of every ten healthy Caucasian infants inherit a physiology that biases them to be both aroused and distressed by stimulation early in the first year and initially avoidant of unfamiliarity in the second and third years. About four of ten infants inherit a physiology that permits them to be relaxed at four months and relatively fearless in early childhood. The suggestion that these two temperaments are under some genetic control is based on the degree of behavioral similarity of identical twins and the modest but consistent associations with sympathetic reactivity, asymmetry of cerebral activation, facial structure, body build, eye color, and atopic allergies. It is difficult to imagine the environmental experiences that could produce, in infants growing up with well-educated, economically secure, affectionate parents, the combination of a high sleeping heart rate at two weeks, vigorous limb movements and crying in response to a mobile at sixteen weeks, and, at twenty-one months, cries of fear at the application of heart rate electrodes, a blood pressure cuff, and the entrance of a clown. It is more credible to argue that these longitudinal coherences reflect, in part, stability in the excitability of the amygdala and its projections to motor, autonomic, cortical, and brain stem centers.

Genes are not omnipotent, however, and they necessarily share power with experience. Over one-third of the high reactive infants were not exceptionally shy or fearful in the second year; a few were fearless. The home observations indicated that a mother's actions affected the probability that a high reactive infant would become inhibited. A nurturing parent who consistently protected her high reactive infant from minor stresses made it more, rather than less, difficult for the child to control an initial urge to retreat from strangers and unfamiliar events. The equally accepting mothers who made mundane, age-appropriate demands for cleanliness and conformity helped their high reactive infants tame their timidity. Chess and Thomas anticipated this discovery in their discussion of the goodness of fit between the child's temperament and the parents' ideals and actions. Parents who do not become anxious or threatened by extreme timidity in their children will neither overprotect them nor become angry with them and will thereby help to create a less anxious adolescent.

These discoveries should not be surprising. The idea of natural selection rests on an interaction between the inherited characteristics of an animal and its environment. The ecological changes that occurred sixty million years ago created an environment ill suited for dinosaurs but better tailored for mice. The interactions between temperament and family experience, which developmental scientists expect, are difficult to prove because they require extensive observations of the social environment and the child. Of course, interactions with experience need not involve temperament; they can include social class, medical history, ordinal position, or gender. Most of the time there is no uniform effect of a particular environment. All children raised in poverty do not become school dropouts; all firstborns with kind professional parents do not become high-achieving adults. A premature infant raised in a nurturant, stable, middle-class home has a good chance of achieving normal intellectual potential; the same infant raised in an economically disadvantaged family is less likely to do so. The addiction to seeking uniform outcomes of particular experiences has prevented developmental scientists from discovering less frequent but equally dramatic interactions. Whether a therapeutic program is directed at crack babies or aggressive ten-year-olds, a benevolent intervention will be helpful for some, but rarely for all.

We found many examples of interactions that involved the child's biological sex. About 15 percent of low reactive girls who were also minimally fearful at nine and fourteen months became very fearful at twenty-one months; very few low reactive boys showed a pattern of increased timidity. It is likely, of course, that parents unconsciously treat sons and daughters in different ways and produce the larger number of older fearful girls. The differences between the sexes were most striking when we compared boys and girls on a cluster of characteristics, rather than a single feature. About 15 percent of boys, but only 5 percent of girls, displayed a combination of low reactivity, very low heart rate, and consistently low fear. A small group of low reactive boys with very low heart rates and frequent bouts of laughter became the most uninhibited children. Some behaved as if nothing short of serious physical harm could frighten them. I suspect these boys belong to a special temperamental category within the larger low reactive group.

One such boy, who showed minimal fear at every age, was bubbling with energy on every assessment. He ran around the room, unrestrained, during the free-play periods. Unlike most fourteen-month-olds, who initially stare at the robot for fifteen or twenty seconds, he ran toward it immediately. When he was twenty-one months, his mother complained that he hit and bit other children, threw things around the house, and is excessively stubborn. During the peer play observation at three-and-a-half years, he talked continuously, ran across the room screaming, and shoved the other boy on several occasions. This degree of unrestrained behavior was uncommon among boys, but it never occurred in any girl. We are tempted to suggest that the central physiological profile of boys enhances the behavioral consequences of those genes that contribute to low reactivity, low sympathetic tone, and uninhibited behavior.

Geneticists have discovered that the same gene can produce different outcomes depending upon whether its source is the mother or the father.

Thus, it is possible that the long chain of biological products that is traceable to the genes that determine biological sex influences the quality of the profile we call low reactive–uninhibited.

Although it is not always necessary to ask the evolutionary question regarding the adaptiveness of every stable trait, the presence of high and low fearful members in all mammalian species suggests that both styles must have adaptive features in order to survive over generations. The animal—or child—who is cautious to discrepancy is less likely to risk harm by impulsively approaching an unfamiliar object. On the other hand, the bold individual is more likely to gain resources that are limited. Steven Suomi, of the National Institute of Child Health and Human Development, reports that some fearful rhesus living on the small island of Cayo Santiago are liable to starvation because they wait until the other animals have had their turn at the food stores placed daily by research staff; on some occasions all the food is gone when the bolder animals leave. On the other hand, some of the fearless animals die of wounds incurred in attacking a stronger animal. Thus, the advantages associated with each temperament are balanced by disadvantages in a different context. There are no free lunches.

What Names Should We Use?

Philosophers ask three fundamental questions about natural phenomena: What is it? How do we determine what it is? What are its functional consequences? We suggest that, for temperament, the answers to these questions are: Temperament is an inherited profile of behavior, affect, and physiology that is best discovered by observing directly the young child's psychological and biological reactions to specific incentives and charting how these initial biases lead to distinctly different envelopes of behavior and mood that are moderately stable over later childhood and adolescence.

The assumption of a moderately stable central physiological pattern that is expressed in varied behavioral forms with growth requires more than one descriptive term. Even though all tadpoles that survive metamorphosis become frogs, biologists use different names for the two developmental stages. One of the problems affecting the sciences that use language rather than mathematics to describe functional relations is that most languages do not have good ways to describe transitional states. This is especially serious in psychology because the behavioral development of animals and humans is characterized by transitions. This problem frustrates research on temperament. Some of the children classified as inhibited or uninhibited at twenty-one months had changed behaviorally by seven or thirteen years. Two formerly uninhibited girls had become moderately shy by age seven. Should we classify these girls as inhibited, uninhibited, or neither? A formerly inhibited child was a sociable and spontaneous adolescent but retained her high heart rate. There is no simple way to communicate these changed profiles. That is why Gottlob Frege claimed that language cannot always capture a particular thought.

When we began this research we relied only on the behavior of the two-year-old as the basis for classification. It seemed reasonable to name one profile *inhibited* and its complement *uninhibited*. We learned that the two types possess different physiologies, although each implicates the excitability of the amygdala and its projections. Because we do not have direct evidence on the excitability of these anatomical circuits, it is prudent to continue to choose constructs for the profiles that are based primarily on psychological rather than physiological features.

Because not all high reactive infants became inhibited two-year-olds, and some shy, fearful two-year-olds were not high reactive infants, we need to distinguish among these outcomes. We propose that the terms *inhibited type* and *uninhibited type* refer to the two contrasting hypothetical genotypes inferred from features displayed in early infancy—especially high or low reactivity at four months, but including high or low sympathetic tone in the first two months. The term *inhibited* refers to the actualization of a shy, timid, fearful profile in the second year in children who are an inhibited type; *uninhibited* refers to the appearance of bold, sociable, outgoing behavior in two-year-old children who are an uninhibited type. Not all inhibited types become inhibited children. Some infants who showed all the early signs of the inhibited type—high fetal heart rate, high heart rate at two weeks, high reactivity at four months—were not very fearful in the second year. We estimate that about 20 percent of Caucasian infants are inhibited types, but only 10–15 percent become inhibited in the second year. It is probably not a coincidence that about 15 percent of school-age children have a diagnosis of anxiety disorder, with more girls than boys assigned to this category.

The distinction between the concepts of an inhibited or uninhibited type and an inhibited or uninhibited child is analogous to the distinction between genotype and phenotype or between potential and actualized forms. All low-pressure areas in the Caribbean in late August do not become hurricanes. All children born with the central nervous system needed for exceptional musical talent do not become musicians; among those who do, some become composers, some pianists, others vocalists.

We stress the behavioral over the physiological features because each of the peripheral biological signs was only modestly correlated with the behavioral categories. Neither heart rate, blood pressure, temperature asymmetry, body build, eye color, nor susceptibility to allergies was an extremely sensitive sign of either of the temperamental types, and none was as good as behavioral reactivity at four months in predicting inhibited or uninhibited behavior. The biological features we measured are analogous to seasonal migration as a defining characteristic of some birds. Flying south in the winter is characteristic of many birds, but not of all. We regard reactivity at four months as a primary feature of the inhibited type, not only because it predicts fearful behavior but also because it probably reflects varying thresholds of excitability in limbic sites. If there were no theoretical connection between the four-month behavior and the limbic thresholds, the former would not be regarded as a primary feature.

Finally, we require names for the inhibited or uninhibited children who later lose most of the defining behavioral characteristics of their category—for example, the inhibited children who at adolescence appear relaxed, sociable, and even bold. Although this outcome is uncommon, a few adolescents fit this description. Physicians use the term *in remission* for formerly depressed patients who have recovered normal function. We suggest that the terms *formerly inhibited* and *formerly uninhibited* refer to older children who were inhibited or uninhibited in early childhood but lost, presumably through experience, most of the behavioral signs of their category.

An inhibited child might display at age ten only one of the many features that are potential derivatives of the inhibited type, such as shyness with strangers, timidity toward physical challenge, excessive worry over school grades, preoccupation with the health of a parent, minimal spontaneous affect, a phobia of animals, a tense musculature, or a guarded style of interaction. The last two features are the most common in older children who had been inhibited at age two but were no longer exceedingly shy or fearful. Every adolescent who is an inhibited type need not possess all of the features that define the younger inhibited child. The external appearances of the neck in mice, giraffes, and humans are very different, yet all three species have seven vertebrae in the neck, traceable to the early origins of the vertebral column.

The concepts of a new domain of scholarship called fuzzy logic is helpful in deciding on the proper categorization of children who change their demeanor with development. In classic Aristotelian logic, a person either belongs or does not belong to a particular category; there is no way to denote partial membership. A woman cannot be partially pregnant. This is the law of the excluded middle. Fuzzy logic, however, permits partial membership in a category; one can meaningfully state that a particular child is 50 percent inhibited if she possesses one-half of the characteristics that define the category. That does not mean that the child will behave in a timid way 50 percent of the time.

The category *race horse* provides a useful analogy. Only a small proportion of all horses possess the many biological features that permit them to run at unusually fast speeds and to be amenable to training for commercial racing. A race horse who wins the triple crown probably has all the features of the category—for example, an optimal arrangement of skeleton and muscle mass, stamina, invulnerability to fear, resistance to illness, and a level of docility that is optimal for training. The race horses who possess only the first two of these characteristics would be classified in fuzzy logic as one-third race horses. However, the horses who have none of the features belong to a qualitatively different category of *non–race horses*. The perspective provided by fuzzy logic seems to fit nature well; a robin has more of the features of the category *North American bird* than does a penguin.

Let us assume, as an illustration, that excitability of the amygdala, reactivity of the peripheral sympathetic nervous system, high reactivity at four months, and fearful behavior in the second year represent two physiological and two psychological features that define the category *inhibited type*. These four features are probably inherited independently in a large unselected population. Remember that high sympathetic tone, as reflected in a high and stable heart rate, was related to a serious, dour affect state, but not to fearfulness. Thus, a child could be 25, 50, 75, or 100 percent an inhibited type. Only a very small proportion of children are high reactive, are highly fearful, and have a consistently high heart rate, blue eyes, narrow face, and a cooler right forehead.

The perspective of fuzzy logic implies that the concept *inhibited type* consists of a family of related genotypes, rather than a single genetic pattern. The high reactives who became extremely fearful in the second year had some biological characteristics that differentiated them from high reactives who became only moderately fearful. The former group had a narrower face and a cooler right forehead, suggesting that they were biologically different from their less fearful high reactive colleagues. The sociable, spontaneous adolescent who had been inhibited at age two is a phenotype who, like a retired race horse, has lost most of the defining characteristics but might retain some aspects of the physiology derived from his genetic constitution.

Jung held a similar view. All introverted types did not become or remain shy adults; some even acquired a sociable demeanor. Thus, the inhibited and uninhibited classifications in older children, adolescents, and adults require historical information, even though some psychologists argue that classification of people by their earlier qualities has minimal advantages. Temperamental types, they believe, should be classified functionally, either by their current style of social interaction or by ease of adaptation. This argument, which is defensible, would yield temperamental categories different from the ones we have described. For example, it would group together all shy ten-year-olds who behave similarly with older strangers, whether their shyness derived from being an inhibited type or was the product only of past experience. Yet, as we have seen, the complete psychological and physiological profiles of the such children are not identical and are potentially distinguishable.

Because the theoretical meaning of the term *inhibited child* involves a biological, behavioral, and emotional profile, the behavioral displays actualized in a specific context should not be regarded as conceptually separate from the biological characteristics that mediate the fearful responses. The idea of an inhibited child combines both behavior and biology. The independence of an entity—the child—and its functions was a major node of disagreement between Alfred North Whitehead and Bertrand Russell. Russell believed that the two ideas were independent; Whitehead insisted that they were a unity. Consider the thought, "Lions stalk gazelles." Russell would have argued that the predicate "stalk" was applicable to a variety of animals and could be treated as an independent function. Whitehead would have claimed that lions stalk in a very particular way, different from that of hyenas; hence, the original idea should not be parsed into one class of agents and another of actions. I side with

Whitehead, as do all who believe that the mood of the agent who "kisses" is different for an actor who is a child, a lover, or a grandmother. I believe that the social behavior of inhibited children in varied, unfamiliar situations is not exactly like the behavior of those who acquired their shy, timid demeanor through experience. The former group smile less often and have much greater muscle tension. Hence, it may be unwise to treat the predicate "is shy with others" as a function that is separable from the type of person displaying it.

Psychology possesses a large number of terms that name only surface characteristics, in part because, in comparison with biology, it does not have the advantage of rigorous theory and powerful methods. The most popular concepts in personality refer to qualities like sociable, agreeable, anxious, depressed, or conscientious. Understanding the origins of these qualities is frustrated by the mystery surrounding their developmental origins and physiological correlates. Almost every behavioral phenotype has two or more distinct etiologies. Even delusions and hallucinations, the defining symptoms of schizophrenia, can occasionally be the product of an acute illness or drug toxicity. Historical information permits differentiation of these varied types.

The preference for a historical or a functional classification depends on the use to which the classification will be put. Chickens are classified as birds by zoologists, as Sunday dinner by families, as a commodity by investors, and as a source of salmonella infection by pathophysiologists. Each categorization has a useful purpose. Our interest is in understanding the development of individual variation in mood and behavior. Because some shy, introverted adults were reactive infants and some were not, we wish to distinguish between these two types. If all one knows is that an adult is introverted, it is not possible to determine which developmental route was taken. It is a cardinal assumption in developmental biology that one cannot infer developmental mechanisms from looking only at final forms.

When a scientific domain is immature and underlying mechanisms are unknown, investigators have no choice but to invent categories defined primarily by similarity in surface characteristics. Hence, objects that appear different are usually placed in separate categories. Aristotle treated turtles and snakes as very different forms, but when the evolutionary origins of these species became known, their classifications were reshuffled. The tension over a reliance on early history is also seen in controversies among biologists who argue about the characteristics to be used in assigning an animal to a species and determining its emergent evolution. Nature is permissive with respect to the language we choose to name the forms in her garden of delights. She only insists that we respect the integrity of the forms that we move back and forth between our verbal inventions.

What Changes with Development?

A critical but unresolved issue is whether formerly inhibited children who had signs of limbic reactivity when younger (for example, high sympathetic tone on the heart) might also change their physiology as they became less fearful. It is not possible to answer this intriguing question with certainty. We know there can be major changes in behavior without substantial changes in autonomic physiology. Half of the twenty-two high reactive infants in Cohort 1 were very fearful in the second year, whereas the other half displayed low or moderate fear, yet the two groups showed similar patterns of heart rate, heart rate acceleration, asymmetry of forehead temperature, and diastolic blood pressure. And some of the inhibited two-year-olds who became sociable adolescents retained their limbic excitability. Thus, even though experience can alter surface behavior, the psychological change is not always accompanied by an alteration in physiology. It is also true, however, that some formerly inhibited adolescents did show a substantial decrease in autonomic reactivity as they became bolder.

Further, animal research reveals clearly that physiology is malleable to experience. Human handling of rat pups for a brief period each day during the first three weeks of life alters permanently the chemistry of the hippocampus. When male rats were stressed by the introduction of new males into the living area each day, they showed a larger increase in adrenal steroids to a novel event than did rats who had lived under low stress. Presumably the prior stressful experience had altered the animals' physiology.

If stressful experiences can alter brain neurochemistry—and perhaps even genes through the influence of molecules like cortisol on the DNA in the nucleus—then chronic reduction of uncertainty could affect the biology of inhibited children. Geneticists tell us that genes turn on and off during a lifetime. If an inhibited child acquired effective coping reactions that permitted her to gain control over her uncertainty, a change in the excitability of limbic circuits might occur. We noted that some inhibited two-year-old children did show a decrease in both fearful behavior and sympathetic reactivity as they grew. Thus, there is no determinism in the early temperamental bias; no genetic conductor coordinating all the players in one unchanging melody.

Throughout the analyses we affirmed what others have reported—namely, that the intercorrelations of the behavioral variables that index the two temperaments were higher than the comparable correlations among the peripheral, physiological measurements. For example, the relations among latency to talk and to play and amount of time spent close to the mother in the laboratory setting were correlated about 0.4 to 0.5, but the correlations among heart rate, blood pressure, pupillary dilation, and temperature asymmetry were lower. No single biological variable was as predictive of inhibited or uninhibited behavior in the second year as high or low reactivity at four months, although aggregating across several physiological reactions did distinguish between the two groups. Further, the predictive relation between infant and child behavior was more robust than the comparable relations between physiological variables measured in infancy and in later childhood. Why is this so?

One answer is that coherent behavioral systems are more stable than the smaller, separate components contributing to the whole. I suspect that the speed of a gazelle running from a predator—which involves the combination of activity in the brain and large muscle groups—is more stable from day to day than separate measures of neural activity and muscle potential. A principle of organization theory is that as one ascends from fundamental components to larger entities that combine the former, the stability of the increasingly complex structure is enhanced. The economic productivity of all of American society is more stable from year to year than the productivity of any one county.

Why, then, should psychologists be concerned with physiology? What information does biology contribute? One answer is that knowledge of physiology provides clues to a deeper understanding of behavior. The course of the symptoms of malaria was known before any scientist detected malaria parasites in the blood. Once the life cycle of the parasite was understood, the explanation of the course of the disease became richer and more satisfying. The fact that a proportion of high reactive and inhibited children show large rises in heart rate in response to challenge, as well as right-sided activation in the EEG, permits more exact inferences about the role of the nervous system and limbic sites in particular. Without the biological data, these hypotheses would seem less reasonable. Even though a high heart rate at two weeks cannot be used alone to predict high reactivity and inhibited behavior with exceptional sensitivity, the fact that more high reactive infants had high sleeping heart rates at this early age adds credibility to our interpretation. Linguists do not need to know that there is an increase in connectivity in the left hemisphere between one and three years of age in order to predict the lawful increase in the sophistication of children's speech. But an understanding of that lawful phenomenon is helped by knowing that there is a major change in the neurophysiology of the language area at this time.

Some readers may be surprised by this modest evaluation of the significance of physiological evidence for classifying temperaments. One reason for the surprise is that the history of physics over the last four centuries presents such a persuasive model of how a successful science develops. Many scientists, from diverse domains, have assumed that a similar historical sequence must characterize the growth of all the sciences. The popular view is that one group of scientists first works out a number of valid principles that apply to observable phenomena. These discoveries are later used by other investigators who develop more fundamental principles that explain the invisible, but presumably more basic, events that account for the observable ones. For example, Newton discovered the laws of motion for stones as well as planets. Three centuries later, Einstein, reflecting on the new evidence from laboratory studies of radiation, challenged Newton's claim that space and time were absolute. Over the next two decades, physicists like Heisenberg, Schrödinger, Bohr, and Born created the mathematics of quantum mechanics that explains atomic events. Physicists believe that the equations of quantum mechanics represent the foundation of the phenomena Newton described, as well as the basis for the invisible events produced by electrons, protons, and neutrons inside an atom.

A similar, but slightly less obvious, historical sequence occurred in genetics. Darwin first described the phenomena of animal evolution, and Mendel inferred some of the laws that explain the inheritance of characteristics in plants. Less than a century later, molecular biologists discovered the tiny chemical structures that mediate both the appearance of new species and wrinkling in peas. Once again, the discovery of fundamental principles for observable phenomena was followed by the uncovering of more basic principles that explained both the invisible and the visible events.

These histories have led most scientists, as well as others, to assume that an identical sequence is occurring in psychology at the present time. Technical journals, as well as the responsible media, report dramatic advances in our understanding of the neurochemistry and neurophysiology of the brain. Complex machines like MRI and PET reveal how metabolically active a brain area becomes following stimulation, and pharmacologists are gaining insight into the chemistry of the receptors on the surface of neurons that are provoked into activity by the release of molecules by presynaptic neurons.

Unlike physics and genetics, however, psychology has not had its Newton or Darwin. Hence, there is not a set of principles that explain a large number of psychological phenomena. The closest psychology comes to deep principles for observed behavior are the discoveries of Pavlov, Hull, Miller, and Skinner involving classical and operant conditioning of new habits in animals. These discoveries are not to be belittled, but there are no principles of comparable power for emotions, reasoning, language, or memory. Scientists working on the invisible chemical and electrical phenomena that occur in synapses and neural circuits have leapt ahead of those who are trying to infer fundamental psychological principles. Some might claim that this uneven advance is unimportant; a few might contend that psychology might skip the century or so of research needed to discover the fundamental principles of molar behavior. But this state of affairs is not welcome and is a little dangerous. I make this claim because the scientists who invented quantum mechanics and molecular biology took their direction from the facts of the observable phenomena. Try to imagine the content of molecular biology without Darwin or Mendel.

Neuroscientists have temporarily moved ahead of psychology and are making fundamental discoveries of great importance. But the observable behavioral events to which these individual discoveries apply are often unclear. Because psychologists have not worked out deep, valid principles about anxiety, anger, or guilt, it is difficult to relate the neuroscience evidence to these emotions. Moreover, without the constructs provided by psychological principles, study of the invisible chemical and electrical events lacks the guidance that these principles could provide.

If psychology had discovered a large number of valid principles for emotions, these principles could give direction to neurochemical investigations, and sooner, rather than later, scientists would discover the functional relations between the invisible microevents in the synapse and the observable behavioral ones.

I do not minimize the significance of the neuroscientists' discoveries, but the big prize is understanding the relation between molecular and behavioral events. Each domain is moderately autonomous, and it is unlikely that science can skip the phase of discovering psychological principles. That is why temperamental categories will always have a psychological aspect.

A temperamental profile is an emergent phenomenon that is not totally reducible to physiological processes, even though physiology makes a contribution to it. The physical concept of entropy provides an analogy. Entropy refers to the degree of energy disorder in a large system. A log has less entropy before it is burned than while it is burning. But entropy is not a characteristic of any atom in the log; it is an emergent quality derived from very large numbers of atoms joined together under special conditions. So, too, is a temperamental profile an emergent quality that is not reducible to any single biological system.

The gathering of biological data is not always motivated by a desire to reduce behavior to physiology; it serves theoretical understanding. I suspect that there will never be a time when scientists will be able to use only biological measurements to predict social behavior without the addition of some psychological information. I make that claim because physiological measures will necessarily have ambiguous meaning until the investigator knows something of the subject's history and psychological state. No profile of PET, EEG, or plasma chemistry has an unambiguous significance independent of the person's past experiences, current activity, and psychological state. We have learned a great deal about the role of brain function in visual perception; but no physiologist is prepared to state what an animal is perceiving, or what stimulus is in the animal's visual field, by looking only at the pattern of electrical discharge on an oscilloscope. All matter is composed of electrons, neutrons, and protons, but butter and beeswax are very different substances.

Temperament is a psychological construct, with behavior and emotion as its primary referents. We probe biology in order to understand the psychological profile and to differentiate similar surface profiles that are not abetted by temperamental mechanisms.

Categories and Continua Revisited

Throughout most of this book I have contrasted high with low reactive infants or inhibited with uninhibited children and have not compared each of these extreme groups with more typical children. This issue deserves discussion. An expert who is asked about the cause of tornadoes assumes that the interrogator intends a contrast with everyday weather, not with hurricanes. The answer to why a tornado and not a hurricane will contain special features that are absent from the answer to why a tornado and not ordinary July weather. Put formally, an explanation of the occurrence of p assumes a particular contrast event, whether q, r, s, or t. The cause of p rather than q can be different from the cause of p rather than r.

The reasons why 1 percent of American families are wealthy (say, incomes over $200,000) rather than poor (incomes under $10,000) are not the same as those that explain why 1 percent are wealthy and over 50 percent of families earn between $25,000 and $75,000 annually. In the first comparison, years of education, place of residence during childhood, ethnicity, and race are significant factors in the account. These factors are far less important in the second comparison, because a large number of American families who earn between $25,000 and $75,000 have graduated from high school, live in the suburbs, and are white. In this comparison temperament, personality, schools attended, motivation, parental practices, friendships, and luck become more important elements in the explanation.

This issue of which groups are being compared is ignored when a quality is regarded as continuous and differences in wealth, health, or mood are presumed to be the product of variation in one or more continuous processes. Some psychologists and parents regard shyness as being at one extreme of a continuum that has sociability at the other end. Hence, the appropriate contrast to the 15–20 percent who are extremely shy are the 80 percent who are not excessively shy, rather than the small group of extremely sociable children we call uninhibited. But extreme shyness is not on a continuum with extreme sociability; each is a distinct qualitative category. We have described some of the features that differentiate the two extreme types. We have not named the features that distinguish the inhibited from the average child; these may be different. Of course, not all why questions require specifying a comparison. There is, we assume, a correct explanation of why dinosaurs became extinct, even though we do not yet have that answer. When the evidence is in, scientists may be able to classify inhibited and uninhibited children absolutely, rather than relative to one another. When that time comes, the answer to "Why is this child inhibited?" will not depend on an implied comparison. But until that happy time, it will be necessary to stipulate the comparison group.

This issue invites a re-examination of the tension between categories and continua in describing behavior, emotion, and ability. We raised this idea in chapter 2, but we now have more information. In classical psychoanalytic theory, *personality* had a specific meaning; it referred to the structure of affects, motives, unconscious conflicts, and symptoms that were the product of a particular life history in a person with an inherited level of libido. These bold ideas assumed a large number of varied life histories that funneled down to a small number of personality types, each particularly vulnerable to special symptoms. But each personality type was defined by the entire structure of behavior, emotion, symptoms, libido, and life history. Although psychoanalytic theory has lost most of its loyal adherents over the last quarter century, some psychologists and psychiatrists, even those who are not particularly friendly to the theory, continue to retain this complex, but useful, definition.

The new cohort of investigators, who have become more positivistic, define personality most often in terms of current self-reported behaviors and emotions. Life history, temperament, and physiology are less important components of the most popular personality constructs. This view invites the assumption that all the variation in a particular profile—for example, extroversion—is a product of the same basic mechanisms. The preference for placing each individual on a number of continuous psychological (or biological) dimensions, rather than assigning some people to categories, rests on the premise that all the variation in a quality like sociability is derived from the same underlying processes. A shy person is presumed to have less of whatever a sociable person possesses in abundance. I favor the view that the extremes of sociability and shyness are mediated by different processes. Predicting which adolescents will become drug users is most accurate when the investigator treats the chronic drug user as a member of a distinct qualitative category, and far less accurate when the risk for drug use is seen as a continuous trait.

David Magnusson agrees. Only a small proportion—about 12 percent—of a large group of ten-year-old boys engaged in criminal activity as both adolescents and adults. And this distinct group had lower levels of adrenaline in their urine at age ten than males who were only asocial as adolescents. But Magnusson argues that there is not a linear relation between a continuous disposition that one might call "degree of criminality" and concentration of adrenaline. The strategy of conceptualizing both the behavior and the physiology as continua must be complemented with an approach that makes a type of individual, defined by characteristic profiles of reaction, the unit of observation.

One basis for the claim that high and low reactive infants belong to distinct categories and are not extremes on a continuum of ease of arousal comes from the developmental outcomes of the other two groups of infants. It is not clear whether infants who displayed low motor activity but frequent crying—the distressed group—are more or less aroused than the smaller group of infants who were very active motorically but did not cry at all. The categorical solution assumes that the four reactive groups we posited in chapter 6 inherited qualitatively different neurochemistries. The excitability of the basolateral and central areas of the amygdala are modulated by different chemistries that are probably inherited independently. High motor activity with frequent crying presumes a low threshold of reactivity in both the basolateral and central areas. High motor activity combined with infrequent crying presumes a low threshold only in the basolateral area.

It is also important that within the high or low reactive groups there was no relation between degree of motor activity or frequency of crying and subsequent level of fear. If a four-month-old infant had been categorized as high reactive because she showed extreme motor activity on six trials and crying on at least two episodes of the battery, she was as likely to be highly fearful as one who had considerably higher motor and cry scores. This result was surprising and is inconsistent with the idea of a continuum of arousal or reactivity. As we noted in chapter 7, ease of arousal and quality of arousal are separate characteristics. The four-month-old must pass a certain threshold of arousal and also be biased to become irritable when aroused in order to display vigorous motor activity as well as crying in response to stimulation. Once an infant has passed those critical thresholds, he or she behaves in the second year like most high reactive infants, regardless of the magnitudes of motor activity and irritability displayed.

Some psychologists might argue that crying, not motor activity, is the important predictor of later fear. That suggestion is vitiated by the discovery that high reactive infants differed from the distressed children who had low motor and high cry scores in qualities other than fearfulness. The former were unlikely to smile and laugh, their fears were often expressed as distress cries, and they showed large accelerations of heart rate to the sour taste. The distressed children smiled often, had smaller accelerations to the sour taste, and their fears were more often displayed in the form of reluctance to approach an unfamiliar person or object. The fact that these two groups differed on a number of qualities other than total fear score implies that they belong to qualitatively different groups.

Another persuasive argument for the utility of categories is the relative independence of motor activity, irritability, vocalization and smiling. Few of the correlations among these responses in infants growing up in Boston, Dublin, or Beijing were larger than 0.4; most were smaller. Only when we combined some of the variables to create categories did coherent clusters emerge. This is the biologist's strategy. Body size, fur coloration, basal metabolic rate in the winter months, and predatory aggression are generally independent features across all mammals. But a small group of mammals are large, have dark fur, have a low basal metabolic rate in winter, and are aggressive in the spring and summer months. Grizzly bears are defined by a correlated cluster of relatively independent variables.

As we have seen, subtypes exist within the larger reactivity groups. Ten percent of the low reactive boys had very low heart rates, smiled frequently, were fearless, and had a cooler left forehead; not one high reactive boy showed this combination. But the correlations among reactivity, heart rate, smiling, fear, and asymmetry across the entire sample were low. Thus, forehead asymmetry assumed a special significance only within the low reactive, low fear, high smiling boys. Among macaque monkey species, size is correlated with aggressivity and a combination of these two features differentiates these related groups. But aggressivity is not correlated with size across all mammals; giraffes and elephants are less aggressive than hyenas and pumas. A species is characterized by a patterned hierarchy of features; the significance of any one feature depends on the species. A particular characteristic (for example, irritability, a narrow face, or heart rate acceleration) will not have the same significance in all individuals. A narrow face is a better correlate of extreme inhibition within high reactive infants than it is in the general population. It is an error to regard any one feature as having the same theoretical meaning across all persons, even if the sample is limited, as it is in our case, to middle-class Caucasian children.

One reason for the continued reliance on continua is the absence of powerful theory to guide the grouping of people into types. It took us several years to discover the four infant reactive types, and I am not certain we would have inferred these four categories by thought alone. We would not have discovered them by applying a factor analysis to the four-month motor and cry scores and the fear and affect data gathered at fourteen and twenty-one months. When we performed such an analysis, the first factor was best interpreted as high fear, but the four-month motor and cry scores were not highly correlated with that factor, and the analysis did not reveal the four reactive types. When we added several heart rate variables to the matrix and performed a second factor analysis, the heart rate variables now emerged as the first factor, because of their high intercorrelations, but no behavioral or affect variable had high loadings on this factor.

Empirical measures that produce continuous distributions are easy to obtain and to manipulate statistically. It is therefore tempting to rely on them during this pretheoretical era. But sole reliance on statistical procedures like regression, path analysis, factor analysis, and analysis of covariance, which assume that relations are linear and that individuals differ only in the magnitude of what are assumed to be continuous processes, can distort nature in a serious way. The assumption of a continuum is a mathematical abstraction imposed on nature that seems to deny what is obvious in our ordinary observations of the external world, as well as the domain of particle physics. The external world comes in discrete units— a tree, a branch, a bird, and a beak. One must blur that scene seriously in order to produce an apparent continuum of color, light, and form.

We have noted many times that a relation between a pair of variables did not hold for all children or for the total range of scores. For example, for the entire group there was no significant correlation ($r = .10$) between the variability of the child's baseline heart rate and the frequency of smiling at fourteen months. However, the approximately 5 percent of children who smiled very frequently in the second year—a qualitatively distinct group—had a lower and more variable heart rate than the small group who smiled minimally. An investigator not receptive to the hypothesis of discrete groups within a larger sample might conclude from the low correlation between the two responses that they were unrelated. The relation between magnitude of heart rate acceleration to the sour taste and reactivity was very robust for girls, but weaker for boys; the relation between a low four-month heart rate and later smiling was much stronger for boys than for girls.

The need for restriction in our generalizations is so common it approaches the status of a general principle. Generality of a functional relation across all categories (of humans or animals) or ranges of measures is the exception, not the rule. Of course, without a priori guides to parse the samples into types or to determine the correct ranges, investigators are reluctant to use post hoc decisions that are unacceptable to colleagues. But investigators should remain open to the possibility of categories within a large sample as they examine their evidence.

Are There Other Temperamental Categories?

A small group of infants—about 10 percent—displayed unusually high levels of energy as they thrashed their arms and legs but did not fret or cry at four months; they were classified as aroused. These infants vocalized and smiled frequently in the second year, occasionally laughing with zeal. This quality is difficult to name, for it is not captured simply by activity level. Other children run a lot but do not possess the enthusiasm and vibrancy that is distinctive of these children. The term *vitality* comes closest.

A complementary class, also about 10 percent, displayed very low energy and appeared to observers as listless. Some were irritable during the first six months and resembled the low motor–high cry group. As two-year-olds they were quiet and emotionally subdued, and they rarely displayed the intense fear to novelty characteristic of high reactive infants. They were more often avoidant and reluctant to approach unfamiliar people or objects. Galen might have regarded them as the early form of the phlegmatic temperament.

The excitability of the hippocampus, which plays an important role in the detection of subtle discrepancies, could form the foundation of still another temperamental type. Activity of the hippocampus is monitored, in part, by levels of CRH and cortisol and the density of receptors for these molecules. Thus, it is possible that children who possess an excitable hippocampus might belong to a temperamental group characterized by an unusual sensitivity to events that are only subtly different from past experience.

One important function of the frontal cortex is to inhibit voluntary action, and dopamine is essential for implementation of this restraint. Children with phenylketonuria (PKU), a rare inherited disease associated with lower levels of dopamine in the frontal area, are more impulsive on certain problem tasks. These facts raise the possibility of an impulsive temperamental type based on a special neurochemistry of dopamine metabolism in the frontal area. Each of these suggestions of other temperamental categories is speculative; future research will determine their validity.

Some temperamental types will be extremely rare. One child showed the following unique developmental profile. He frowned six times during the two-month assessment, sometimes between stimulus presentations. Spontaneous frowns are rare at all times and especially so during the quiet intervals between stimuli, when nothing is in the infant's perceptual field. This boy also frowned frequently and retained a sad facial expression for periods as long as thirty seconds during the four-month assessment. He was motorically inactive to the mobiles but on one trial showed a facial expression of fear followed by a sharp scream. No other four-month-old behaved this way to this episode. After he cried in fear on a subsequent visual episode, he could not be calmed and we had to terminate the session. He was classified at four months as low motor–high cry, but the frequent frowns, sad facial expressions, and sharp cry of fear in response to the mobiles suggested that he belonged to a special, rare group.

This boy was unusually irritable during the nine-month assessment, fretting at every provocation and remaining wary throughout the battery. His behavior in response to the puppets was informative, for he always turned his head to the left as the recorded voice was transmitted through the centrally located speaker, suggesting an asymmetry favoring the right hemisphere; he also consistently raised his left arm toward the visual stimulus at two months. He cried when the stranger entered the playroom—a reaction that occurs in less than 5 percent of nine-month-old children—and his mother reported that he was very restless and a poor sleeper.

The boy's profile continued to be idiosyncratic at fourteen months. He maintained a sad facial expression throughout the ninety minutes, had several uncontrolled tantrums, vocalized in short, explosive bursts, and often showed a pained facial expression without an accompanying cry or fret—a silent expression of angst. Although his fear score was high, the most salient aspects of his profile were the explosive outbursts and silent but pained facial expression. He was willful when he returned to the laboratory at twenty-one months, resisting the placing of electrodes and ripping them off as they were applied. He refused the administration of almost every episode by screaming in order to force termination, and he showed a cooler right forehead. His mother acknowledged that he had become more aggressive lately—"He walks up and bites you"—adding that he cries consistently when she takes him out of the house.

When we saw him at three-and-a-half years he was calmer, not shy with the examiner, and displayed no unusual behavior during the ninety-minute session. One month later, however, in the play situation with an unfamiliar boy of the same age, he showed a combination of initial shyness along with a single act of impulsive aggression that was uncommon. As the session started, he stayed close to his mother, staring at the other child, as inhibited children often do. The wariness lasted for about five minutes, after which he left his mother, went to center of the room, and began to punch and kick a large inflated toy. Several minutes later he seized a toy the other boy was holding and retreated with it to his mother. About five minutes later—about fifteen minutes into the session—when the other boy was inside a plastic tunnel, he picked up a wooden pole and began to strike the tunnel with vigor in the place where the boy was sitting. The force of the blow made the other boy cry. This unprovoked act of aggression to an unfamiliar peer is a rare event in this laboratory context with a parent present.

I have described this case in detail because of the lessons it can teach. Psychologists appreciate that temporary moods in unusual situations can provoke atypical reactions that are not stable characteristics of a child. Stanley Milgram's classic studies of obedience made this point clearly. Hence, psychologists are properly cautious about inferring stable personal qualities from a few rare behaviors in an atypical situation and mistakenly ascribing a person's actions to pervasive internal qualities rather than the nature of the situation. However, this boy showed unique reactions on every assessment—frequent frowning at two months, a fear cry in response to the mobiles at four months, extreme inhibition at nine months, silent expressions of distress at fourteen months, uncooperativeness at twenty-one months, and finally, at three-and-a-half years, an act of unprovoked aggression toward another child. Although the aggressive response is rare statistically (I have seen it only twice in over several hundred play sessions of this type), it was the only deviant act in that session. Most psychologists observing this child for the first time would probably dismiss the striking of the other child as reflecting greater than normal frustration on that particular day. The mother was not concerned with her son's development and did not request any additional information or help. But I believe that the impulsive act of aggression reflects a deep quality and that this boy is a member of a rare temperamental category.

These categories have not been discovered because they are infrequent. Clinicians have found it helpful to distinguish between profiles that are statistically rare and those that are common, with the usual assumption that the former—like autism—are partly genetic in origin. These rare categories are not likely to be present in the small samples psychologists recruit. As noted in chapter 7, only 6 percent of the infants were high reactive, fearful, infrequent smilers, with high heart rates. The typical psychological sample of thirty subjects might contain no, or perhaps only one, individual with this profile. Thus, current practices in psychology mitigate against discovering these children. A medical examination of a random sample of forty adults would probably find no cases of Huntington's disease, schizophrenia, or a host of other valid disease categories. This principle holds for all inquiries into nature. A geological survey of randomly selected areas of a hundred square miles is unlikely to find any fault lines in tectonic plates; a survey of most hundred square miles of ocean will fail to find one whale. Physicists have to examine billions of energy profiles produced by a linear accelerator in order to find a particular subatomic particle.

The significant entities in nature are not distributed with equal frequency across all locales. Indeed, psychologists who study human behavior are unusual among natural scientists in their working assumption that the important aspects of human nature will be present in any volunteer sample of three dozen people living within twenty miles of the laboratory. This prejudice stems in part from the wish to deny important differences in human cognitive, emotional, and behavioral characteristics. That denial may be in the service of an admirable political philosophy, but it is obstructing theoretical advance. If some temperamental categories have a prevalence of about 5 percent, scientists should recruit a minimum of two hundred subjects in order to find at least ten individuals who belong to a specific group.

A second reason why these less frequent categories have not been found is traceable to the choice of statistical methods. As we have noted, a factor analysis of the continuous variables of motor activity, crying, fear, smiling, and magnitude of heart rate change did not yield a factor that describes the 6 percent of our sample who are high reactive infants with a high heart rate at four months and high fear and low smiling in the second year, because the correlations among these variables in a large, unselected sample are low. Gordon Bronson, over twenty years ago, explored the phenomenon of childhood fear in an insightful report that acknowledged that some infants were prone to show caution to novelty. Because his samples typically contained less than forty infants, however, he could not distinguish between the temperamentally inhibited child and the fearful one who had acquired a similar profile.

The qualities that will define future temperamental categories may be far less salient to parents than shyness or sociability. Consider the boy described earlier. Parents are unlikely to report that their two-month-old infant usually moves his left arm rather than his right when excited or notice the occurrence of brief facial frowns at eight weeks of age. The temperamental categories that are defined by those reactions will have to be inferred from careful, direct observations combined with insightful hunches about the psychological and physiological features of particular profiles. We do not know enough at the present time to rely on only one strategy. One day, scientists with a deeper knowledge of behavior, neurochemistry, and physiology will detect these rarer types of children.

Progress in neurobiology will aid the discovery of new temperaments, for future scientists will regularly gather information on central brain states while children are engaged in particular challenges. When this time comes, biological variables will be more consistent features, along with behavior, of an individual's temperamental category. The biological data will also lead to the splitting of behavioral phenotypes into subgroups with different central states. Thus, the number of temperamental types will increase in a major way, requiring theorists to organize the types in accord with etiology, links to psychopathology, or socially desirable behaviors, much as diseases have been assigned to categories like infectious, autoimmune, and cancer (for etiology), as well as degree of disability, age of onset, course, and type of cure. I suspect that most of the temperamental types will be associated with inherited differences in neurochemistry, but a small number may be the product of a distinct anatomy. Others will be the consequences of prenatal events that affected the brain's growth. In time, the many temperamental types may be assigned to categories based on their origins. There will be neurochemical temperaments, anatomical temperaments, and prenatal temperaments. When this level of progress is attained, Down's and Williams' syndromes may be folded in with other temperamental types that are rare, genetic anomalies involving both anatomy and chemistry of the brain. The inhibited and uninhibited types may be like the common cold, frequent and of less dramatic consequence than bipolar depression or schizophrenia. Scientific inquiry begins with the obvious and ends with the most amazing.

Internal Tone

Afferent feedback from the body—heart, gut, lungs, and muscles— ascends to the brain after first converging, in turn, on the medulla, pons, and central area of the amygdala to arrive finally at the frontal cortex and form the foundation of a conscious perception of an internal body tone. This private perception does not enjoy a large set of descriptive terms capable of communicating to others exactly what is being felt. The problem becomes immediately clear if one tries to construct sentences that describe one's current internal feelings. The perception of body tone, like the olfactory sense, is verbally impoverished compared with the richer language available to describe what we see and hear. Most languages do not have many words that can capture the olfactory experience of cinnamon, a spring rose, a forest in late October, or the sensations coming from the stomach or heart. People usually communicate olfactory sensations by referring to an object that has a distinct aroma, rather than using adjectives that describe the sensory quality per se. It is probably relevant that auditory and visual information synapse on the lateral nucleus of the amygdala, while smell, taste, and sensations from the heart and gut synapse on the corticomedial or central areas. It is likely that in order for sensory information to become easily accessible to language it must first synapse on the lateral nucleus. Information from our bodies does not.

The dependence of modern industrial societies on speech and writing has persuaded many that words are valid representations of experience. If a psychiatrist asks, "Were you afraid of crowds as a child?" and the patient answers in the affirmative, the former assumes that the patient experienced a special dysphoric state. But that assumption may be flawed. Words are judgments, and judgments are not always linked closely to feelings. I believe I would answer in the affirmative if someone asked, "Were you angry when Saddam Hussein invaded Kuwait?" even though I am not certain I was angry at the time. Because I judged the aggressive action as unfairly hostile in intent, I know I should have felt angry. Every use of affect language does not imply the existence of a feeling by the speaker. Wittgenstein and Frege both argued that the impotence of language to describe feelings was due in part to the fact that every sentence assumes a comparison context. Language is not autonomous in the same way as my perception of a tree or a cramp. When a woman is asked about her feelings toward her husband, she may unconsciously compare a set of alternative ideas referring to tension, anger, fear, disappointment, or uncertainty. The feeling tone in consciousness, however, is less often the result of a referendum on several choices.

The imperfect relation between words intended to describe feelings and the feelings themselves has an analogue in an equally imperfect relation between a daily chronicle of events, as reported in a newspaper, and the historian's narrative written years later. The narrative imposes a judgment on the events that is in the service of coherence. Hayden White writes, "This value attached to narrativity in the representation of real events arises out of a desire to have real events display the coherence, integrity, fullness, and closure of an image of life that is and can only be imaginary. . . . Does the world really present itself to perception in the form of well-made stories . . . that permit us to see the end in every beginning? . . . Could we ever narratize without moralizing?"

Every sentence that tries to describe the feelings in consciousness is simultaneously a judgment that combines the information with past experience, the social context, and some minimal anticipation of what might follow a particular description. Conversations also require logic, consistency, familiar words, and politeness; none of these constraints is relevant to feeling tone. Indeed, it is remarkable that language tells us anything significant about conscious feelings.

Language is like a ritualized dance before a wedding. The actions of the dancers—the movements of arms, trunk, legs, and head—are symbols that are analogous to words. But symbols are not to be confused with the feelings of the bride and groom being celebrated. Psychiatrists and psychologists want to make inferences about feelings, not words, for their therapeutic interventions are directed at changing the person's emotions, not their verbal reports. But we rely on words because they are easier to access than feelings. In so doing we are like the person searching under the street light for the keys that were lost in the park because that is where the light is brightest.

The absence of both accurate language for and reliable behavioral and physiological signs of internal body tone have tempted most investigators to ignore these perceptions and, further, to assume that body tone is essentially the same in most people. Jung did not agree, suggesting to Freud that individuals differed in their consciousness—an idea that Freud rejected.

T. S. Eliot, a shy, quiet child who became an introverted adolescent, possessed a consciousness that, I suggest, was different from most. Through poetic images he found ways to express the feeling tone that is inaccessible to everyday language, as in *The Waste Land,* the poem that first brought him fame:

April is the cruellest month, breeding
Lilacs out of the dead land, . . .
And the dead tree gives no shelter, the cricket no relief,
And the dry stone no sound of water. . . .
I will show you fear in a handful of dust.

The Hollow Men, written in 1925, also contains a melancholic mood:

We are the hollow men
We are the stuffed men
Leaning together
Headpiece filled with straw. Alas!
Our dried voices, when
We whisper together
Are quiet and meaningless
As wind in dry grass
Or rats' feet over broken glass
In our dry cellar.

Try to empathize with one of Anne Sexton's "Love Poems":

I have a black look I do not
Like. It is a mask I try on.

I migrate toward it and its frog
Sits on my lips and defecates.

The imagery in Sylvia Plath's poems reflects a similar consciousness:

The air is a mill of hooks
Questions without answers,
Glittering and drunk as flies
Whose kiss stings unbearably
In the fetid wombs of black air under pines in summer

or

This is the light of the mind, cold and planetary
The trees of the mind are black. The light is blue.
The grasses unload their griefs on my feet as if I were God.
Prickling my ankles and murmuring of their humility.
Fumy, spiritous mists inhabit this place.

Plath's diary entry for November 3, 1952, while she was an undergraduate at Smith College, described an internal tone not attainable by everyone:

I am afraid. I am not solid, but hollow. I feel behind my eyes a numb, paralyzed cavern, a pit of hell, a mimicking nothingness. . . . I look at the hell I am wallowing in, nerves paralyzed, action nullified—fear, envy, hate; all the corrosive emotions of insecurity biting away at my sensitive guts.

We have discovered that about one-third of inhibited children have a highly reactive sympathetic nervous system; hence, they might experience unusually salient feedback from sympathetic sites in the body to the amygdala and cortex. The resulting conscious perception of body tone might have unique consequences for these inhibited children as well as for highly anxious introverts. Recall that low reactive boys who smiled, laughed, and vocalized most often in the second year had very low heart rates and a cooler left forehead.

If a proportion of inhibited children are likely to experience a body tone that is slightly uncomfortable and learn that unfamiliar situations enhance that feeling, they will learn to avoid such situations. Additionally, the dysphoric tone requires an explanation. Adolescents and adults are likely to interpret a dysphoric tone as indicating a source of worry and will adopt behaviors intended as defenses against the imagined dangers. The reader will have recognized in this discussion the nineteenth-century diagnosis of neurasthenia, as well as the current category of generalized anxiety disorder. Adults with this diagnosis report feeling anxious about potential harm, failure, rejection, or disaster, while recognizing a lack of rational support for these worries. Their mood is not always a product of repressed sexual conflict, as Freud claimed, nor of stressful social conditions, as sociologists argue, but occasionally the result of feedback from an overly reactive sympathetic nervous system. This suggestion retains that part of the James-Lange argument that feedback from the body can contribute to an emotional state of fear without contradicting Walter Cannon's devastating critique of James's strong position that all emotions were derivative of peripheral feedback. Individuals may also differ in feedback from other body sites, each making a contribution to consciousness. For example, because males have a greater ratio of muscle mass to body weight than females, feedback from the muscles might be more salient for men than for women, and the perception of body tone by men might be subtly different from that of women. Simon Le Vay has suggested that the tone associated with sexuality may be different in gay men and straight men.

The family of body tones each of us lives with is so completely hidden from others and so far beyond measurement that it does not enter into our theorizing about the causes of variation in mood and behavior. The biology that is one of the vital components of temperament probably affects perceived body tone. These perceptions resist facile description, but like the invisible hands of a puppeteer they influence actions. It is here that temperament's darkest shadow may fall.

These ideas are not being pursued in contemporary research for two major reasons. First, modern science is appropriately positivistic. There is no reliable way to measure the perception of body tone other than by asking people how they feel, and we have argued that most people do not have adequate language to describe these feelings. Internal tone is not captured by measurements of central or peripheral physiological activity, for conscious tone is an integrated product of more than activity in the heart, gut, and muscles. The electrical properties of the signal that a bat sends as it flies toward an insect are not identical to the brain's integrated reaction to the feedback from a moth target. The conscious state produced in two people with heart rates of 130 bpm following exercise need not be similar because individuals vary in the filtering quality of the medulla.

Second, the strong egalitarian premise in the West is unfriendly to the idea of fundamental differences in consciousness because consciousness is where will, and, therefore, freedom of choice, resides. If some people experience a consciousness that is dysphoric they may not be sufficiently free to select the best action. John Searle suggests that consciousness is at the core of our humanity and mental life. If individuals experience different consciousnesses because of inherent physiological biases, the unity of our species is subject to question—a blasphemous idea. Humans accept major differences in musical talent, athletic skill, and good health, but these sources of variation are unimportant compared with human consciousness. The possibility that people experience different body tones implies an obstacle to communication and the uncomfortable thought that all are not equally capable of understanding or having empathy for another. The inability of two adults to communicate their feelings is as fundamental to the harmony of society as the inability of two animal groups to interbreed—remember, the competence to interbreed is a primary criterion of a species. It is not surprising, therefore, that there is resistance to awarding too much importance to differences in body tone. If a chronically jovial mood is, in part, the product of a tone derived from an inherited physiology—this idea does not have the same meaning as the statement that individuals vary in their physiology—then jovial adults have an unfair advantage. A happy mood, we would like to believe, has to be earned, awarded, or scavenged from bits of good fortune. If it is simply a gift of nature awarded in the beginning, surely there is injustice.

How Much Control Do We Have?

Although temperamental ideas provoke uncomfortable thoughts about biological differences among racial and ethnic groups, they present a more serious threat to the idea of free will. The most consistent assumption in Western culture, traceable to the Greeks and implicit in the motto "Live free or die" on New Hampshire license plates, is that each of us is in control of and responsible for our actions. This is our solution to the problem of preventing strong emotions, especially anger, jealousy, envy, and sexual passion, from provoking behaviors that require monitoring. The solution adopted by many societies, ancient and modern, is to link every child and adult into a set of close interdependent relations so that fear of criticism and rejection by group members guarantees restraint on actions that passions demand. That solution works.

Western culture, however, placed the restraint within the individual. The Greeks nominated reason as the source of restraint; for Christians it was will. The medieval Church insisted that people who became mentally disturbed because of possession by the devil permitted the contamination and were therefore responsible for their ill fortune.

Because we would like to believe that the mind controls the body, we prefer to assume that each person should be able to monitor his or her moods as well as actions. Some chronically tense people conclude that they are immature or unintelligent if they cannot control their feelings. A recent biography of Ludwig Wittgenstein makes clear that his temperament kept him in a state of dysphoria for most of his life. The suicides among his brothers imply a genetic component to his chronic melancholia. But Wittgenstein did not acknowledge that possibility in any of his letters or diary entries. Indeed, he came to the opposite conclusion, for he wrote in despair in his early fifties that he was still prone to moods of anxiety that he attributed to his lack of wisdom. His diary entry for April 1, 1942 reads, "I have suffered much but I am apparently incapable of learning from my life. I suffer still just as I did many years ago. I have not become any stronger or wiser."

Charles Whitman climbed a tower at the University of Texas in 1966 and shot his rifle indiscriminately at people below. He had told a psychiatrist about his uncontrollable violent impulses and, prior to his display of violence, wrote:

I don't really understand myself these days. Lately, I have been a victim of many unusual and irrational thoughts. These thoughts constantly recur, and it requires a tremendous mental effort to concentrate. I talked to a doctor once for about two hours and tried to convey to him my fears that I felt overcome by overwhelming violent impulses. After one session I never saw the doctor again, and since then I have been fighting my mental turmoil alone. After my death I wish that an autopsy would be performed to see if there is any visible physical disorder. I have had tremendous headaches in the past.

An autopsy revealed a walnut-size tumor pressing against Whitman's amygdala.

How much conscious control did Wittgenstein or Whitman have? At one extreme are well-functioning adults who, over the course of a few weeks, have become deeply depressed for the first time and cannot, without professional help, regain their former gentle mood. There is agreement that these unfortunate people did not have control over the acute onset of their deep lethargy and sadness. By contrast, we assume that a person who just insulted a neighbor could have controlled that act, and we hold him responsible. But the middle ground, where Wittgenstein lived, is ambiguous. Can most adults who are suspicious, angry, depressed, or worried gain control over those emotions? Our answer has social consequences, for our attitudes and reactions toward others depend on our interpretation of their behavior. If I believe a colleague can control his angry outbursts, I feel moral outrage and become irritated with him when he violates a community norm of civility. If, on the other hand, I believe that his biology or past history makes it unusually difficult for him to suppress his hostility, I become somewhat more forgiving. That is why we do not hold young children responsible for actions that in an adolescent would invite severe sanctions.

The increasing public awareness of temperamental biases will render the ascription of blame more acute. For example, in July 1993 newspapers around the nation reported that Dean Hamer of the National Cancer Institute had discovered a genetic basis for some cases of male homosexuality. The implication added by many journalists, but not by Hamer, was that these men were driven to their sexual orientation by forces completely outside their control. I do not cite this event to convey a pejorative attitude toward a gay lifestyle, only to point out that the attraction to genetic explanations of complex behavior is linked too closely with a determinism that makes a mockery of human evaluation and choice.

The separate threads of naturalism, biological determinism, and individual liberty have become intertwined in the fabric of contemporary American philosophy. The consequence of the mutual support of each view is a permissive posture toward any impulse that a person believes is inherent in his makeup. Yielding to that impulse permits the individual to feel he is being loyal to the beatitude of naturalism and the imperative to resist any imposition of external restraint on actions that feel "right." But Americans are not consistent in their application of these standards. Male primates—including men—are naturally promiscuous. Yet no state legislature is being bombarded with letters demanding that husbands be permitted complete sexual license. The community understands that the natural forces that push for sexual pleasure can be controlled without exacting a serious psychological price. Similarly, chimpanzees and gorillas naturally deceive other members of their species, but there is no howl of complaint when a stockbroker is jailed for lying to a customer about the sales of a new company. Yes, deceit does come easily, but so does control of dishonesty.

The nature of modern society has persuaded many that they have little control over events that their grandparents believed were within the sphere of personal will. Historical events during the last half century have eroded the nineteenth-century view that will has a position in the psychic anatomy as significant as thought and emotion. Many Americans are prepared to excuse many actions in others, including robbery, fraud, and murder, as not always within their limited sphere of control. We are told that conditions in urban ghettos generate a mood of hopelessness and anger that cannot be suppressed; hence, many have become willing to excuse acts of violence that would have enraged nineteenth-century New Yorkers.

Attributing causes to external forces has even permeated our interpretation of amoral behavior among well-educated adults with intellectual talent. For example, the committee appointed by the Dean of Harvard Medical School in 1982 to investigate a young scientist who admitted to fabricating his results concluded that competitive conditions in the laboratory could contribute to acts of fraud. This judgment came dangerously close to declaring that sane, intelligent adults are not to be held completely responsible for behaviors they know to be seriously amoral if they happen to work in a setting that is full of temptation.

Because all of us live with temptations, this argument comes close to declaring that adults should not always be expected to have the ability—that is, the will—to control violations of community standards even if they do not happen to share them. The public expects, as it should, that scientists are bound to the same set of ethical responsibilities that apply to all members of the society. It is dangerous to claim that temptations of fame, promotion, or money can overwhelm a scientist's judgment and provoke an act of fraud for which he or she is not totally responsible.

A more serious example of this new view is beginning to permeate our interpretations of parental abuse of children. A few commentators have excused cruel parental acts by citing poverty, isolation from friends and family, or drug addiction. After all, the argument goes, how can anyone expect a young mother living alone in a small apartment with few financial resources and no friends to control her anger when her infant will not stop crying? Several years ago, an American judge excused a mother who had murdered her infant, arguing that a woman's hormonal status after birth is abnormal. But all infants are occasionally difficult to soothe and have been so since our species appeared. Javanese mothers are also annoyed by the piercing cry of a demanding infant, but they seem better able to check their anger, and few Javanese find that surprising. Historians and anthropologists have discovered very few societies, in the past or present, in which the rate of physical abuse of children was as high as it is now in some urban areas of the United States and Europe. It should not be newsworthy that a mother can tolerate her infant's demanding screams and monitor her own angry outbursts. Such control is well within the capacity of almost every adult.

How should we evaluate adolescents or adults whose temperamental bias makes it easier for them than for others to exhibit unchecked aggression? Should we be more forgiving of outbursts in these persons than in equally irascible people who acquired their angry mood? This is an ethical, not a scientific issue. Western thought since Locke has regarded psychological characteristics as sculpted primarily by experience and therefore subject to will, even though the tantrum of a chronically abused child may be as difficult to restrain as the depressed mood of an adult who inherited this predisposition.

There were approximately 20,000 homicides in the United States in 1992. If we restrict the discussion to people between ages fifteen and fifty, the homicide rate is still lower than one in seventy thousand, less than the deaths due to cancer in adults over fifty years of age. Thus, homicides are rare events. Nonetheless, I have always assumed, as I believe most people do, that shooting or stabbing another is a deliberate act. Some respected criminologists, however, contend that most adults who have committed their first homicide will never commit another. They claim further that some acts of murder require the joint occurrence of a great many events (for example, a bar, a hard day at work, too many drinks, and a hostile patron who teased the murderer once too often). If any one of the above conditions had not been met—the teasing had been on the street rather than in the bar, the aggressor had had an easy day at work or had had one beer instead of five, or the hostile patron had not been present—there would not have been a homicide. This example returns us to the issue of the deliberateness of behavior.

Acts vary in the thought that precedes them. As we have noted several times, an observer's judgment of the volitional quality of a behavior determines the evaluation of the agent and the action, especially when the act violates community standards. If an observer believes the act was deliberate, the agent is judged responsible; if it was not, there is a willingness to excuse the agent. Our attitude toward the murderer in the bar is dependent in part on whether we believe there was any conscious planning before the aggression occurred.

The grimace of an eight-week-old is clearly not deliberate; a driver swerving off the road is a bit more deliberate. How shall we regard the murder in the bar? Let us pull the knot tighter and ask: Under what extenuating conditions would we excuse a legally sane adult of adequate intelligence who raped and killed a woman, made up fraudulent data in a scientific study, set fire to a house, or stole perfume from a store because we believed the person was unable to inhibit the action? I find it difficult to think of many extenuating circumstances. If this claim seems overly harsh to some readers—it would not to Galen or to eighteenth-century men and women—then we must acknowledge a profound secular change in our interpretation of human behavior since the Second World War. Honest concern with and guilt over the plight of unempowered people and those under unusual stress have generated an understandable reluctance to blame the victim. The writer of an article in an issue of the AARP Bulletin excused a middle-class woman who left her aging mother in a hospital with no identifying address as an inevitable, morally acceptable consequence of the younger woman's inability to cope with her parent. This permissiveness is surprising, given the fact that middle-aged women have been caring for their parents since the human family emerged.

Different historical forces have produced pollution of our air and water and the realization that our illnesses are not always due to a moral lapse or negligence in monitoring our diet and sleep. The dramatic advances in medical genetics remind us that the development of high blood pressure, cancer, Alzheimer's disease, or schizophrenia are not due only to how deliberately virtuous, gentle, and sane a life we have led. Thus, many have become persuaded that a similar principle should be applied selectively to selfish, cruel, or criminal acts. I believe that the premise that many adults do not have the power to control their behavior is dangerous.

To imply that humans are hairless versions of silver-backed gorillas is tantamount to denying one of the sturdiest functions that accompanied the evolution of Homo sapiens. Put plainly, so that there is no confusion, every sane adult of average intelligence has the ability to moderate his or her asocial actions. Any neighbor, judge, or jury who excuses fraud, stealing, or murder because of life conditions, excessive frustrations, or unusual provocations not only denies our nature but, more seriously, contributes to a community mood that will only exacerbate the problem this permissiveness is trying to ameliorate.

The contemporary appeal of the externalization of blame, combined with an enthusiasm for having continuous access to one's emotions, affirms the human desire to act in accord with how one feels at the moment and to dilute the necessity of monitoring actions with ethical judgments. It is not obvious that this new attitude of freedom of expression is either healthier for the person or more adaptive for society than the conviction that one of the unique products of our evolution is the capacity to select and control our behavior. Remember, God told Adam and Eve after they ate from the tree of knowledge that they, but none of the animals, would know the difference between right and wrong. Although the poet-philosopher Lucretius accepted temperamental variation, he was also certain that the "lingering traces of inborn temperament that cannot be eliminated by philosophy are so slight that there is nothing to prevent men from leading a life worthy of the gods."

The acceptance of temperamental factors in the nineteenth century was not threatening, for it was most often applied to the few who had a pathological diagnosis of depression, mania, or delusions. If a schizophrenic told a judge he had killed a homeless man because God told him to rid the world of vagrants, the judge would not hold him responsible but would pity a person whose biology had eroded his will. It is obvious that a schizophrenic is qualitatively different from the majority of the populace, and therefore to declare that the patient inherited a special constitution does not add salt to the wound. But contemporary applications of temperamental biases are intended to apply to everyone. Every individual has some neurochemical profile and therefore everyone belongs to at least one temperamental group. No one is excluded from some constitutional bias that contributes to an aspect of his or her mood and behavior. Thus, it is reasonable to ask: Should everyone be required to be in continuous control of all of their behavior?

One answer begins from an easy vantage point. A small number of individuals possess a central nervous system that creates feeling states that cannot be controlled. Sylvia Plath, Anne Sexton, Ludwig Wittgenstein, and William James experienced dark moods that they tried unsuccessfully to subdue. In their cases, will lost to temperament. Few will argue that these creative people are to be criticized for their long periods of dysphoria. Similarly, no one faults the small proportion of adults who experience sudden autonomic surges, a racing heart, perspiration on the face, suffocation, and the terror of a panic attack. Nor do we blame the children who, despite effort, have difficulty learning to read rapidly or to dance with grace. We acknowledge that these qualities lie outside of will.

But the idea of will was not intended to apply to blue moods, sudden terror, or artistic talents. The concept was intended to apply to the control of aggression, deceit, dishonesty, and exploitative sexuality. Will is relevant only to restraint on action, not to the control of emotion or the development of exceptional talent. No one can control feeling hungry, but everyone can control the theft of food. No one can control anger all of the time, but one can inhibit striking another. Humans cannot control sexual arousal, but they can control rape. Thus, will is not undermined by temperament. We need not excuse murder or rape by noting low serotonin levels in the cerebrospinal fluid of the aggressor. Serotonin may make a small contribution to the frequency of a wish and the intensity of the accompanying emotion, but will still sits in the sizable moat between feeling and action, checking all émigrés for their credentials. An acceptance of temperamental biases does not excuse asocial behavior.'

The popularity of any of the large number of ideas that have some scrap of truth depends not so much on the quality of the evidence or the grace and logic of the argument, but on the mood of the community to whom it is addressed. That mood is difficult to predict because it fluctuates with historical conditions. If the generation of French born at the turn of the century had not been feeling uncomfortable levels of guilt over their behavior during the Nazi occupation of their country, Sartre's suggestion that the past is irrelevant—an attitude viewed as immoral by victims of persistent prejudice—would not have been celebrated and existentialist philosophy would not have attained its brief moment on center stage. If the extreme behaviorists had not promoted the proposition that a two-year-old's first sentences were totally dependent on the occurrence of adult rewards for speaking, the nativist position charted by Chomsky and his students would not have gained its initial momentum.

We are witness to a debate about the efficacy of will because earlier scholars awarded it complete sovereignty and contemporary science is demonstrating its occasional impotence. Both positions have their spheres of validity. The view that is likely to predominate for a generation or so will depend on future events that must remain unknowable. However, because biology is in such rapid ascendance it is likely that the temperamental argument will become unduly persuasive—but only for a while.

Nonetheless, an uneasiness still hovers over the mundane events that fill each day's interactions in families and with friends. Consider a couple in which one spouse is continually concerned with dirt in the house. The compulsive partner criticizes the other whenever the latter makes crumbs, comes into the house with dirty shoes, or spills tea on the table. Let us turn the gain up a little by adding that this thirty-five-year-old adult is also dour of mood and worries continually about auto accidents, bacteria in the water, burglars at night, and being exploited by shopkeepers. We have described the profile psychiatrists call obsessive-compulsive disorder, which has a genetic component, although the mode of inheritance is likely to be complex. Nonetheless, we can ask whether this person should be held accountable by the spouse for the myriad daily behaviors that are frustrating and provoke anger. Are these actions a failure of will?

Suppose further that the partner of the obsessive-compulsive cannot reveal deep, tender feelings, laugh heartily, or relax in intimacy. This profile frustrates the compulsive spouse who wishes a tenderness that the other seems unable to provide. Should this partner be held responsible for the suppressed personality? If we answer no, then perhaps the frustrated partner—be it a lover or a spouse—should be accepting of the other.

Most of us begin each day with the twin assumptions that everyone has an obligation to be aware of the needs of the other and, second, all who are sane possess the ability to be loyal to that imperative. Hence, justifiable anger is generated if someone fails that obligation. The concept of temperament has its most ambiguous implications in these everyday cases. If a temperamental bias can create psychic states that, on occasion, render will temporarily impotent, we can pose the ethical question: Is a spouse or friend obligated to accept such frustrating behavior in another, or is a person justified in becoming angry with a partner who seems to violate an imperative that most accept? This question can be decided only by taking an ethical position; it lies outside of the facts. I am unsure, even though I do not criticize everyone who cannot learn differential equations, does not laugh heartily at jokes, or cannot achieve a playful mood.

At the moment, we must live with ambiguity on this issue. This conclusion does not mean we should adopt an automatic permissiveness toward all profiles that are influenced by temperament. I have no doubt that in the next half century scientists will find that a small proportion of murderers, obsessives, and risk-takers have a neurochemistry different from most of the population. But these facts that the future promises do not imply that the wills of these individuals were totally compromised by their biology. It is here that we must stop and say no more, at least at present. We must live with the uncertainty and, as Wittgenstein urged, be silent. He failed to add, but I trust he intended, silent but reflective.

NOTES

CHAPTER ONE: *The Idea of Temperament: The Past*

PAGE 3, BECAME MORE PREVALENT: R. E. Siegel, *Galen's System of Physiology and Medicine* (Basel: Karger, 1968); R. E. Siegel, *Galen on Psychology, Psychopathology, and Function and Diseases of the Nervous System* (Basel: Karger, 1973). The Renaissance physicians and philosophers rejected Galen's decision to make the observable qualities of heat and moisture primary. Paracelsus (1493–1541) asserted that each object had a single primary substance, which was invisible and which determined its essence. Paracelsus believed that these primary substances were related to sulphur, salt, and mercury.

PAGE 4, CLIMATE OF THE REGION OF THE NILE: M. W. Dols, *Medieval Islamic Medicine* (Berkeley: University of California Press, 1984).

PAGE 4, A. Stewart, *Our Temperaments* (London: Crosby Lockwood, 1887).

PAGE 4, "IN COMPARISON WITH THE TEUTONIC RACES": A. Bain, *On the Study of Character* (London: Parker Son and Bourn, 1861), p. 218.

PAGE 4, EXTREMELY LOW INCIDENCE: L. L. Cavalli-Sforza, "Genes, People, and Language," *Scientific American* 265 (1991):104–11.

PAGE 4, ORIGINATED IN NORTH AFRICA: B. P. Dohrenwend et al., "Socioeconomic Status and Psychiatric Disorders," *Science* 255 (1992):946–52.

PAGE 5, BUT NOT BECAUSE HE WAS A MELANCHOLIC TYPE: See M. Yosida, "The Chinese Concept of Nature," in *Chinese Science*, ed. S. Nakayama and N. Sivin (Cambridge: MIT Press, 1973), pp. 71–90; M. Porkert, *The Theoretical Foundations of Chinese Medicine* (Cambridge: MIT Press, 1974); A. C. Gaw, "Psychiatric Care of Chinese-Americans," in *Culture Ethnicity and Mental Illness*, ed. A. C. Gaw (Washington, D.C.: American Psychiatric Press, 1993), pp. 245–80. The lack of interest in temperament among Chinese commentators might also be traced to the Confucian premise that all humans are equal in their original endowment and become different through experience. Donald Munro has suggested that this view was a reaction to a prior era of hereditary privilege in China. See D. J. Munro, *The Concept of Man in Early China* (Stanford: Stanford University Press, 1969).

PAGE 6, RURAL MALAY COMMUNITIES: C. Laderman, *Taming the Wind of Desire* (Berkeley: University of California Press, 1991).

PAGE 7, "WHICH ONE RECEIVES FROM OUR PARENTS": R. Burton, *Anatomy of Melancholy* (London: G. Bell, [1621] 1923), p. 241.

PAGE 8, "A REGULATIVE PRINCIPLE": A. Roback, *The Psychology of Character*, 2d ed., (New York: Harcourt Brace, 1931), p. 450.

PAGE 9, F. J. Gall, *On the Organ of the Moral Qualities and Intellectual Faculties and the Plurality of the Cerebral Organs,* trans. W. Lewis (Boston: Marsh, Copen and Lyon, 1835); J. G. Spurzheim, *Phrenology* (Boston: Marsh, Copen and Lyon, 1834). Roger Cooter, in *The Cultural Meaning of Popular Science* (Cambridge: Cambridge University Press, 1984), points out that Gall's premise that psychological functions are localized in the brain is an accepted tenet in modern neuroscience. It was Gall's second premise, that the shape of the skull revealed these functions, that was satirized, especially after 1860, when quacks began to exploit this idea with the public by promising people psychological diagnoses. Cooter suggests that during the earlier period of greater acceptance of phrenology in Britain, it was the skilled working class and artisàns, not the upper class, who were enthusiastic about phrenology because it may have rationalized their upward mobility as a biological inevitability.

PAGE 9, G. Combe, *The Constitution of Man* (Boston: Couter and Hendee, 1829).

PAGE 10, J. Simms, *Physiognomy Illustrated,* 8th ed. (New York: Murray Hill, 1887).

PAGE 10, J. A. Fowler, *A Manual of Mental Science for Teachers and Students* (New York: Fowler & Walls, 1897).

PAGE 10, G. Draper, *Human Constitution* (Philadelphia: Saunders, 1924).

PAGE 10, C. Lombroso, *Crime and Its Causes* (Boston: Little Brown, 1911).

PAGE 10, E. Kretschmer, *Physique and Character,* 2d ed., trans. W. J. H. Sprott (New York: Harcourt Brace, 1925). Kretschmer's ideas survive in a modern study revealing that bipolar depressives have broader faces and deeper chests than members of other psychiatric categories. See R. J. Brown et al., "Multivariate Analysis of Anthropometric and Psychometric Variables in Probands with Affective Disorders and Their Families," *Neuropsychobiology* 1 (1975):87–105.

PAGE 11, W. H. Sheldon, *The Varieties of Human Physique* (New York: Harper, 1940). See also R. N. Sanford et al., "Physique, Personality, and Scholarship," *Monographs of the Society for Research in Child Development* 8 (1943):1–705; R. N. Walker, "Body Build and Behavior in Young Children," *Monographs of the Society for Research in Child Development* 27 (1962):1–94.

PAGE 11, E. A. Hooton, *Crime and the Man* (Cambridge: Harvard University Press, 1939).

PAGE 11, FORCED UNDERGROUND FOR SEVERAL DECADES: When Gordon Allport reviewed the literature on personality traits in 1927 ("Concepts of Trait and Personality," *Psychological Bulletin,* 24:284–93), he did not discuss temperament. Ten years later, however, in his famous text (*Personality* [New York: Henry Holt, 1937]), he explicitly acknowledged the importance of temperamental factors, although he restricted its influence to emotional phenomena.

PAGE 12, IT SEEMS TRANSPARENTLY TRUE: Most historians fail to mention the fact that Locke accepted the role of temperament for selected traits. He wrote, "Some men by unalterable frame of their constitution are stout, others timorous, some confident, others modest and tractable" (*Some Thoughts Concerning Education,* Section 101, in *On the Conduct of Understanding*). Also, "Amongst men of equal education, there is greater unequality of parts," Essay VII.

PAGE 12, Z. Y. Kuo, "Psychology Without Heredity," *Psychological Review* 31 (1924):427–48.

PAGE 15, "BECAUSE I HAVE TO WRITE": J. P. Sartre, *The Words*, trans. B. Frechtman (New York: George Braziller, 1964).

PAGE 16, ADD AND SUBTRACT: K. Wynn, "Addition and Subtraction by Human Infants," *Nature* 358 (1992):749–50.

PAGE 19, I. P. Pavlov, *Lectures on Conditioned Reflexes*, vol. 1, trans. and ed. W. H. Gantt (New York: International Publishers, 1928).

PAGE 20, "LIBERATE ENERGY": J. Breuer and S. Freud, *Studies in Hysteria*, Standard ed. (London: Hogarth, [1893–1898] 1956), p. 198. It is relevant that Freud was primarily interested in the variation within people; Galen was equally interested in the differences among cultural groups living in geographically separate places—for example, Egypt, Greece, and Asia Minor.

PAGE 20, THE PROFILE OF THE INTROVERT: C. Jung, *Memories, Dreams, Reflections*, trans. A. Jaffe (New York: Vintage, 1961).

PAGE 21, RESPONSIBLE FOR THESE BEHAVIORS: Galen accepted the Greek explanation of hysteria as due to a wandering uterus, which could be caused by chronic sexual frustration. Galen described his successful treatment of a woman who had fits of muscle contraction; he masturbated her to orgasm. Cited in J. Roccatagliata, *A History of Ancient Psychiatry* (New York: Greenwood, 1986), p. 204.

PAGE 21, TO LIFE IMPRISONMENT INSTEAD OF DEATH: See E. F. Torrey, *Freudian Fraud* (New York: HarperCollins, 1992), for a fuller exposition.

PAGE 22, FOR MOST OF THIS CENTURY: J. C. Ballenger et al., "Three Cases of Panic Disorder with Agoraphobia in Children," *American Journal of Psychiatry* 146 (1989):922–24.

PAGE 22, "AND ORIGINALLY RELATIONAL": A. Fogel, *Developing Through Relationships* (Chicago: University of Chicago Press, 1993), p. 4.

PAGE 23, W. McDougall, *Introduction to Social Psychology* (London: Methuen, 1908).

PAGE 23, T. F. Szasz, *The Myth of Mental Illness* (New York: Harper and Row, 1961).

PAGE 24, J. P. Scott and J. Fuller, *Genetics and the Social Behavior of the Dog* (Chicago: University of Chicago Press, 1965).

PAGE 24, M. E. Goddard and R. G. Beilharz, "A Multivariate Analysis of the Genetics of Fearlessless in Potential Guide Dogs," *Behavior Genetics* 15 (1985):69–89.

PAGE 24, FOR A GREAT MANY SPECIES: See D. T. Corey, "The Detectors of Exploration and Neophobia," *Neuroscience and Biobehavioral Reviews* 2 (1978):232–53, for an excellent review of novelty avoidance in animals.

PAGE 24, FOR A SHORT PERIOD: D. A. Carbonaro et al., "Behavioral and Physiological Responses of Dairy Goats to Isolation," *Physiology and Behavior* 51 (1992):297–301.

PAGE 24, MUCH LESS TIMID: R. Greenberg, "The Role of Neophobia in Determining the Degree of Foraging Specialization in Some Migrant Warblers," *The American Naturalist*, 122 (1983):444–53.

PAGE 25, IT DOES JUST THAT: R. Greenberg, "Differences in Neophobia Between Naive Song and Swamp Sparrows," *Ethology* 91 (1992):17–24.

PAGE 25, PERIODS OF IMMOBILITY: A. D. Mills and J. M. Faure, "Diversion Selection for Duration of Chronic Immobility and Social Reinstatement Behavior in Japanese Quail (*Coturnix Japonica*) Chicks," *Journal of Comparative Psychology* 105 (1991):25–38.

PAGE 25, ON THE TEMPERAMENT OF THE ANIMAL: F. Launay et al., "Effects of CRF on Isolated Japanese Quails Selected for Fearfulness and for Sociality," *Physiology and Behavior* 54 (1993):111–18.

PAGE 25, FROM THE SAME STRAIN: E. B. Olson and W. P. Morgan, "Rat Brain Monoamine Levels Related to Behavioral Assessment," *Life Sciences* 30 (1982):2095–2100.

PAGE 25, ULCERS FOLLOWING SIMILAR RESTRAINT: P. G. Henke, "Potentiation of Inputs from the Posterolateral Amygdala to the Dentate Gyrus and Resistance to Stress Ulcer Formation in Rats," *Physiology and Behavior* 47 (1990):659–64; see also N. Pradhan, S. Arunasmitha, and H. B. Udaya, "Behavioral and Neurochemical Differences in an Inbred Strain of Rats," *Physiology and Behavior* 47 (1990):705–8; S. Cabib et al., "Behavioral and Biochemical Changes Monitored in Two Inbred Strains of Mice During Exploration of an Unfamiliar Environment," *Physiology and Behavior* 47 (1990):749–57.

PAGE 26, HIGHER BLOOD PRESSURE: D. A. Blizard, B. Liang, and D. K. Emmel, "Blood Pressure, Heart Rate, and Plasma Catecholamines Under Resting Conditions in Rat Strains Selectively Bred for Differences in Response to Stress," *Behavioral and Neural Biology* 29 (1980):487–92.

PAGE 26, PHYSIOLOGY, AND BEHAVIOR: C. T. Snowdon, C. L. Coe, and A. Hodun, "Population Recognition of Infant Isolation Peeps in the Squirrel Monkey," *Animal Behavior* 33 (1985):1145–51.

PAGE 26, LINKED TO FEARFULNESS: S. J. Suomi, "Early Stress and Adult Emotional Reactivity in Rhesus Monkeys," in *The Childhood Environment and Adult Disease*, Ciba Foundation Symposium 156 (Chichester: Wiley, 1991), pp. 171–88.

PAGE 26, WERE THE MOST AGGRESSIVE: A. S. Clarke, W. A. Mason, and G. P. Moberg, "Differential Behavioral and Adrenocortical Responses to Stress Among Three Macaque Species," *American Journal of Primatology* 14 (1988):37–52; A. S. Clarke and W. A. Mason, "Differences Among Three Macaque Species in Response to an Observer," *International Journal of Primatology* 9 (1988):347–63.

PAGE 26, ALMOST NORMAL SOCIAL BEHAVIOR: G. P. Sackett et al., "Social Isolation Rearing Effects in Monkeys Vary with Genotype," *Developmental Psychology* 17 (1981):313–18.

PAGE 27, POTENTIALLY VULNERABLE TARGET SYSTEM: S. Cohen et al., "Chronic Social Stress, Affiliation, and Cellular Immune Response in Nonhuman Primates," *Psychological Science* 3 (1992):301–4. S. B. Manuck et al. ("Individual Differences in Cellular Immune Response to Stress," *Psychological Science* 2 [1991]: 111–15) found that men with high sympathetic tone showed a more compromised immune response following stress than men with low sympathetic reactivity.

PAGE 29, SOME IMPOSSIBLE: P. Marler, "The Instinct to Learn, in *The Epigenesis of Mind*, ed. S. Carey and R. Gelman (Hillsdale, N.J.: Erlbaum, 1991), pp. 37–66; C. R. Gallistel et al., "Lessons from Animal Learning for the Study of Cognitive Development," in *Epigenesis*, ed. S. Carey and R. Gelman, pp. 3–36.

PAGE 29, REVIEW OF CHILDREN'S PHOBIAS: J. M. Berecz, "Phobias of Childhood," *Psychological Bulletin* 70 (1968):694–720.

PAGE 29, ONLY NINETEEN YEARS LATER: R. McNally, "Preparedness and Phobias, *Psychological Bulletin* 101 (1987):283–303.

PAGES 29–30, H. Eysenck, *The Structure of Personality* (London: Methuen, 1953).

PAGE 30, A. Thomas and S. Chess, *Temperament and Development* (New York: Brunner Mazel, 1977).

PAGE 30, S. Diamond, *Personality and Temperament* (New York: Harper, 1957).

PAGES 30–31, ATTENTION SPAN AND PERSISTENCE: Thomas and Chess, *Temperament.*

PAGE 31, WHO HAD HAD AN EASY TEMPERAMENT: A. Thomas and S. Chess, "Temperamental Follow-Up to Adulthood," in *Temperamental Differences in Infants and Young Children*, Ciba Foundation Symposium 89 (London: Pitman, 1982), pp. 168–75.

PAGE 32, S. Weinberg, *Dreams of a Final Theory* (New York: Pantheon, 1992).

PAGE 37, WITHIN AND OUTSIDE THE ORGANISM: Even the gene for eye color in Drosophila does not always produce the same eye color in the mature flies; the outcome depends upon the position of the DNA fragment on the chromosome. See R. Lewis, T. Hazelrigg, and G. M. Rubin, "Effects of Genomic Position on the Expression of Transduced Copies of the White Gene of Drosophila," *Science* 229 (1985):558–61.

CHAPTER TWO: *What Is Temperament?*

PAGE 39, A. R. Damasio, D. Tranel, and H. C. Damasio, "Somatic Markers and the Guidance of Behavior," in *Frontal Lobe Function and Dysfunction*, ed. H. Levin, H. Eisenberg, and A. Benton (New York: Oxford, 1991), pp. 217–29.

PAGE 39, "TO BEG THE SUCCOUR OF INSTINCT": C. S. Peirce, *Reasoning and the Logic of Things*, ed. K. L. Ketner (Cambridge: Harvard University Press, [1898] 1992), p. 111.

PAGE 41, AGREE ON FOUR CRITERIA: H. H. Goldsmith et al., "Round Table: What Is Temperament?" *Child Development* 58 (1987):505–29.

PAGE 42, 40 PERCENT STATE THAT THEY ARE SHY: P. A. Pilkonis and P. G. Zimbardo, "The Personal and Social Dynamics of Shyness," in *Emotions in Personality and Psychopathology*, ed. C. E. Izard (New York: Plenum, 1979), pp. 133–60.

PAGE 42, CONSTITUTE THE PRIMARY TEMPERAMENTAL TYPES: C. R. Cloninger, "A Systematic Method for Clinical Description and Classification of Personality Variants," *Archives of General Psychiatry* 44 (1987):573–88.

PAGE 42, THREE MAJOR TEMPERAMENTS: A. H. Buss and R. Plomin, *A Temperament Theory of Personality Development* (New York: Wiley, 1975).

PAGE 42, ON BOTH QUALITIES: M. A. Bruch et al., "Shyness and Sociability Reexamined," *Journal of Personality and Social Psychology* 57 (1989):904–15.

PAGE 43, DIFFERENT KINDS OF PEOPLE: L. R. Goldberg, "The Structure of Phenotypic Personality Traits," *American Psychologist* 48 (1993):26–34.

PAGE 43, R. D. Davis and T. Millon, "The Five Factor Model for Personality Disorders," *Psychological Inquiry* 4 (1993):104–9.

PAGES 44–45, WILL NOT EMERGE AS A FACTOR: In addition, slight changes in the items of the questionnaire can have dramatic effects on the resulting factors extracted. If a psychologist added to a personality questionnaire four questions dealing with an avid interest in professional sports, that interest would emerge as a factor, and the addition could lead to a different solution to the unchanged items dealing with personality.

PAGE 46, THE DOMAIN OF ADULT TEMPERAMENT OR PERSONALITY: Another problem is that when people take more than one questionnaire in the same session, their responses to the first survey can influence the answers to the second. If a person first fills out a questionnaire dealing with moods of depression, he will, on a subsequent questionnaire, report a different mood than if he had initially filled out a questionnaire dealing with another content. See J. R. Council, "Context Effects in Personality Research," *Current Directions in Psychological Science* 2 (1993):31–34.

PAGE 46, OF THIS FIRST DEVELOPMENTAL STAGE: M. K. Rothbart, "Temperament in Childhood: A Framework," in *Temperament in Childhood*, ed. G. A. Kohnstamm, J. E. Bates, and M. K. Rothbart (Chichester: Wiley, 1989), pp. 59–76.

PAGES 47–48, J. Strelau, "The Regulative Theory of Temperament as a Result of East-West Influences, in *Temperament in Childhood*, ed. Kohnstamm, Bates, and Rothbart, pp. 35–48; J. Strelau, *Temperament, Personality, Activity* (New York: Academic Press, 1983).

PAGE 48, J. Gray, *The Neuropsychology of Anxiety* (Oxford: Oxford University Press, 1982).

PAGE 49, VITAL PART OF THE DEFINITION: The dramatic advances in molecular biology are leading to a redefinition of the word *animal*. In my youth, I was given a functional definition—any organism that feeds, moves, and responds to stimuli. It is now being suggested that an animal is an organism with a particular spatial pattern of gene expression; this is a very different structural definition. See J. M. W. Slack, P. W. H. Holland, and C. F. Graham, "The Zootype and the Phylotypic Stage," *Nature*, 301 (1993):490–92

PAGE 50, N. Fox, personal communication, 1992.

PAGE 50, BASIC FEELINGS AND EMOTIONS: C. Fourier, *The Passions of the Human Soul* (London: H. Bailliere, 1851).

PAGE 51, THAN THE WILD VARIETIES: D. Kruska, "Mammalian Domestication and Its Effect on Brain Structure and Behavior," NATO ASI Series, vol. G17, in *Intelligence and Evolutionary Biology*, ed. H. J. Jerison and I. Jerison (Berlin: Springer-Verlag, 1988), pp. 211–50.

PAGE 51, MOSSY FIBER TERMINALS: W. E. Crusio, H. Schwegler, and J. H. F. Van Abeelen, "Behavioral Responses to Novelty and Structional Variation of the Hippocampus in Mice," *Behavioral Brain Research*, 32 (1989):81–88.

PAGE 51, AND BEHAVIORAL AVOIDANCE OF NOVELTY: F. M. Clark and H. K. Proudfit, "Anatomical Evidence for Genetic Differences in the Innervation of the Rat Spinal Cord by Noradrenergic Locus Ceruleus Neurons," *Brain Research* 591 (1992):44–53.

PAGE 51, LESS EFFECTIVE OPIOID PROCESSES: J. A. McCubbin et al., "Opioidic Inhibition of Circulatory and Endocrine Stress Response in Cymologous Monkeys," *Psychosomatic Medicine* 55 (1993):23–28.

PAGE 52, DISLIKE OF UNFAMILIAR FOODS: J. L. Rapoport et al., "Newborn Dopamine-beta-hydroxylase, Minor Physical Anomalies, and Infant Temperament," *American Journal of Psychiatry* 134 (1977):676–79.

PAGE 53, SEVERE CONDUCT DISORDER: G. A. Rogeness et al., "Near Zero Plasma Dopamine-beta-hydroxylase and Conduct Disorder in Emotionally Disturbed Boys," *American Academy of Child Psychiatry* 4 (1986):521–27.

PAGE 53, OR NONCRIMINALS: D. P. Farrington, "Implications of Biological Findings for Criminological Research," in *The Causes of Crime*, ed. S. A. Mednick, T. E. Moffitt, and S. A. Stack, (New York: Cambridge University Press, 1987), pp. 42–64.

PAGE 53, WHILE SITTING QUIETLY IN A CHAIR: D. Kindlon et al., "Longitudinal Study of Heart Rate, Its Relationship to Stable and Unstable Patterns of Fighting Behavior, Family Disorder, and Pubertal Status" (Unpublished paper, Harvard School of Public Health, 1993).

PAGE 53, "LESS CAPABLE OF EXPERIENCING FEAR": P. H. Venables, "Autonomic Nervous System Factors in Criminal Behavior," in *Causes of Crime*, ed. Mednick, Moffitt, and Stack, pp. 110–30.

PAGE 53, ACTIVATION IN THE EEG: A. Raine, P. H. Venables, and M. Williams, "Relationships Between Central and Autonomic Measures of Arousal at Age 15 Years and Criminality at Age 24 Years," *Archives of General Psychiatry* 47 (1990):1003–1007.

PAGE 54, SERVING THE LEFT HEMISPHERE: R. G. Robinson, and J. T. Coyle, "The Differential Effect of Right vs. Left Hemisphere Cerebral Infarction on Catecholamines and Behavior in the Rat," *Brain Research* 188 (1980):63–78.

PAGE 54, SHOW GREATER ACTIVATION ON THE RIGHT SIDE: R. J. Davidson et al., "Approach-withdrawal and Cerebral Asymmetry," *Journal of Personality and Social Psychology* 58 (1990):330–41.

PAGE 54, FEAR AND SADNESS, ON THE OTHER: W. Heller, "The Neuropsychology of Emotion," in *Psychological and Biological Approaches to Emotion*, ed. N. C. Stein, B. Leventhal, and T. Trabasso (Hillsdale, N.J.: Erlbaum, 1990), pp. 167–211.

PAGE 54, INCREASED WORRY, ANXIETY, OR DEPRESSION: G. Gainotti, "Emotional Behavior and Hemispheric Side of Lesion," *Cortex* 8 (1972):41–55; R. G. Robinson and B. Szetela, "Mood Change Following Left Hemispheric Brain Injury, *Annals of Neurology* 9 (1981):447–53.

PAGE 55, INTENSITY OF THE EMOTION: G. L. Ahern et al., "Right Hemisphere Advantage for Evaluating Emotional, Facial Expressions," *Cortex* 27 (1991):193–202.

PAGE 55, PROCESSING IT WITH THE LEFT: S. J. Dimond, L. Farrington, and P. Johnson, "Differing Emotional Responses from Right and Left Hemispheres, *Nature* 261 (1976):690–92.

PAGE 55, SUFFERED LEFT HEMISPHERE DAMAGE: M. K. Mandal, S. C. Tandon, and H. S. Asthana, "Right Brain Damage Impairs Recognition of Negative Emotions," *Cortex* 27 (1991):247–53.

PAGE 55, DIFFERENT AFFECT STATES: J. S. Reilly et al., "Babies' Faces: Affective Facial Expression in Infants with Focal Brain Damage" (Unpublished paper, University of California, San Diego, 1992). It is of interest that most of a group of infant chimpanzees who were extremely irritable at two days of age were left-handed at three months, while a majority who were right-handed had been minimally irritable at two days of age. See W. D. Hopkins and K. A. Bard, "Hemispheric Specialization in Infant Chimpanzees (Pan Troglodytes)," *Developmental Psychobiology* 26 (1993):219–35.

PAGE 56, M. D. Hauser, "Right Hemisphere Dominance for the Production of Facial Expression in Monkeys," *Science* 261 (1993):475–77.

PAGE 57, THEIR CHILDREN WERE TWENTY-ONE MONTHS OLD: M. K. Pyles, H. R. Stolz, and J. W. MacFarlane, "The Accuracy of Mothers' Reports on Birth and Developmental Data," *Child Development* 6 (1935):165–76; M. R. Yarrow, J. D. Campbell, and R. V. Burton, "Recollections of Childhood," *Monographs of the Society for Research in Child Development* 35 (1970), no. 5.

PAGE 57, G. W. Allport, *Personality* (New York: Henry Holt, 1937).

PAGE 57, DIFFERENT PLACES IN THE BRAIN: J. Hart and B. Gordon, "Neural Subsystems for Object Knowledge," *Nature* 359 (1992):60–64.

PAGE 57, CATEGORIZING PEOPLE, OBJECTS, AND EVENTS: C. E. Osgood, "Studies on the Generality of Affective Meaning Systems," *American Psychologist* 17 (1962):10–28; C. E. Osgood, G. J. Suci, and P. H. Tannenbaum, *The Measurement of Meaning* (Urbana: University of Illinois Press, 1957). The intimate relation between knowledge and method is seen in this classic—but unfortunately rarely cited—work on connotative meaning, published thirty-seven years ago. Imagine a group of scientists wishing to know whether most people in a culture impose the same set of descriptive concepts on a large and varied set of objects and people. The investigators could decide to ask several hundred adults directly, "What ideas come to mind when you think of a woman, man, general, criminal, cup, carrot, or cheesecake?" Most of the replies would probably be functional, referring to the activities of the people and the actions in which the objects participated. Osgood, Suci, and Tannenbaum used a very different method, however, and uncovered a different answer. They created a list of adjectives, each with an antonym—for example, *big-small, soft-hard, pretty-ugly*—and asked large numbers of adults to rate, on a seven-point scale for each pair of opposite adjectives, a large number of diverse nouns referring to people and objects. Factor analysis of the answers showed that most people relied on three concepts, which Osgood called evaluation, potency, and activity. Put more plainly, the subjects unconsciously asked whether the people and objects they were rating were good or bad, strong or weak, active or passive. But that discovery was a function of the method the investigators used. Psychologists who talked with people or observed their behavior probably would not have come up with this discovery. Questionnaires designed to measure temperament in children ask parents to describe the behaviors of their children, not their private emotional connotations to those behaviors. If Osgood, Suci, and Tannenbaum discovered a basic truth about the human mind, then parental answers will be influenced by this perspective, and most parents will impose an evaluative dimension on the words they use to describe their children. The question "Is your child afraid of strangers?" is less likely to yield an affirmative reply if the parent regards a fear of strangers as an undesirable trait. Children who are described by their mother as fearful are likely to have a parent who does not regard that quality as highly undesirable. The use of questionnaires to assess temperament in children is colored by the parent's emotional reactions to the child's personality. Thus, the meaning of the classification "fearful child" when based on parents' answers to a questionnaire is different from the meaning of the same phrase when it is based on direct observations of the child. See H. H. Goldsmith, "Studying Temperament via Construction of TBAQ" (Unpublished paper, University of Wisconsin, 1993).

PAGES 57–58, TRAITS MEASURED BY THE QUESTIONNAIRE: F. M. Ahern et al., "Family Resemblances in Personality," *Behavior Genetics* 12 (1982):261–80.

PAGE 58, THAN DO COLLEGE-EDUCATED PARENTS: D. Spiker, P. K. Klebanov, and J. Brooks-Gunn, "Environmental and Biological Correlates of Infant Temperament" (Paper presented at International Society for Infant Studies meeting, Miami, Fla., May 1992).

PAGE 58, OR MOTHERS FREE OF DEPRESSION: J. M. Green et al., "Mothers' Perception of Their Six-Week-Old Babies," *Irish Journal of Psychology* 12 (1991):133–44. See also T. Field, C. Morrow, and D. Adelstein, "Depressed Mothers' Perceptions of Infant Behavior," *Infant Behavior and Development* 16 (1993):99–108.

PAGE 58, COME FROM PARENTAL REPORT: J. S. Reznick, J. Robinson, and R. Corley, "Genetic and Environmental Effects on Intelligence in the Second Year" (Unpublished paper, Yale University, 1993).

PAGE 58, ATTENTION TO EVENTS: H. H. Goldsmith, "Temperament," in *Handbook of Emotion*, ed. M. Lewis and J. Haviland (New York: Guilford Press, 1993), pp. 353–64.

PAGE 60, GENETIC CONTRIBUTION TO INTROVERSION: J. M. Horn, R. Plomin, and R. Rosenman, "Heritability of Personality Traits in Adult Male Twins," *Behavior Genetics* 6 (1976):17–30.

PAGE 60, SAME MEANING TO ALL INFORMANTS: R. Schweder, "The Cultural Psychology of the Emotions," in *Handbook of Emotions*, ed. M. Lewis and J. Haviland, pp. 417–434.

PAGE 61, G. Frege, *Posthumous Writings* (Chicago: University of Chicago Press, 1979).

PAGE 61, "FROM THE FEELING ITSELF": G. T. Ladd, *Psychology* (New York: Scribner, 1895), p. 165.

PAGE 61, MUCH PHYSIOLOGICAL CHANGE: M. Fredrikson, K. Klein, and A. Ohman, "Do Instructions Modify Effects of Beta Adrenoceptor Blockade or Anxiety?" *Psychophysiology* 27 (1990):309–17.

PAGE 63, "MAY BE SEVERELY FLAWED": R. Seifer et al., "Infant Temperament Measured by Multiple Observations and Mother Report," *Child Development* 63 (1992):16. See also B. E. Vaughn et al., "Maternal Characteristics Measured Prenatally Are Predictive of Ratings of Temperamental Difficulty on the Carey Infant Temperament Questionnaire," *Developmental Psychology* 23 (1987):152–61.

PAGE 63, AVERAGED ONLY ABOUT 0.2: M. H. Bornstein, J. M. Gaughran, and D. Segui, "Multivariate Assessment of Infant Temperament," *International Journal of Behavioral Development* 14 (1991):131–51. There is also a poor relation between descriptions of nine-month-olds by mothers and by fathers, as well as a poor relation between the parents' descriptions and laboratory observations of infants encountering a stranger or a visual cliff. See H. H. Goldsmith and J. J. Campos, "The Structure of Temperamental Fear and Pleasure in Infants," *Child Development* 61 (1990): 1944–64.

PAGE 63, UNFAMILIAR EVENTS PRESENTED IN THE LABORATORY: J. Rosicky, "The Assessment of Temperamental Fearfulness in Infancy" (Paper presented at the meeting of the Society for Research in Child Development, New Orleans, La., March 1993).

PAGE 63, "OR CHARACTERISTICS OF YOUNG CHILDREN": D. Spiker et al., "Reliability and Validity of Behavior Problem Checklists as Measures of Stable Traits in Low Birth Weight, Premature Preschoolers," *Child Development* 63 (1992):1481–96; the quote is from p. 1490.

PAGE 63, BETWEEN TWO DIFFERENT INFORMANTS WAS LESS THAN 0.3: T. M. Achenbach, *Assessment and Taxonomy of Child and Adolescent Psychopathology* (Newbury Park, Calif.: Sage, 1985). Agreement is no better when peers, teachers, and school-age children judge various behavioral traits, including fearfulness. Although all three informants believe some children are fearful, they do not agree on who they are. See R. N. Walker, "Some Temperamental Traits in Children as Viewed by Their Peers, Their Teachers, and Themselves," *Monograph of the Society for Research in Child Development* 32 (1967), no. 6.

PAGE 64, "ALMOST NEVER THE RULE": R. G. Klein, "Parent-Child Agreement in Clinical Assessment of Anxiety and Other Psychopathology," *Journal of Anxiety Disorders* 5 (1991):182–98; the quote is from p. 195.

PAGE 68, A. Kleinman, *Rethinking Psychiatry* (New York: Free Press, 1988).

PAGE 68, CANNOT BE PLACED ON A CONTINUUM OF AROUSAL: When data on a large number of physical features were gathered on adults with different psychiatric diagnoses as well as their first-degree relatives, a canonical analysis that treated the physical variables as continuous did not distinguish among the psychiatric categories. But a discriminant analysis that assigned each person to one of four clinical groups revealed that the bipolar depressives had a significantly different profile—a wide face and deep chest. Thus, an important fact emerged only when the individuals were treated as categories. See R. J. Brown et al., "Multivariate Analyses of Anthropometric and Psychometric Variables in Probands with Affective Disorders and Their Families," *Neuropsychobiology* 1 (1975):87–105.

PAGE 69, "PHYSIOLOGIC RESPONSE PATTERNS AS WELL": R. Hoehn-Saric and D. R. McLeod, "The Peripheral Sympathetic Nervous System," *Psychiatric Clinics of North America*, 11 (1988):375–86; the quote is from p. 383.

PAGE 69, OTHER CELLS IN THE VICINITY: M. P. Jung and S. Yamane, "Sparse Population Coders of Faces in the Inferotemporal Cortex," *Science*, 256 (1992):1327–31; C. M. Leonard et al., "Neurons in the Amygdala of the Monkey with Responses Selective for Faces," *Behavioral Brain Research* 15 (1985):159–76.

PAGE 70, P. Duhem, "Quantity and Quality," in *The Aim and Structure of Physical Theory* (Princeton: Princeton University Press, 1954).

PAGE 71, ANY THEORETICALLY REASONABLE CONTINUUM: M. Myrtek, *Constitutional Psychophysiology* (New York: Academic Press, 1984).

PAGE 71, D. Magnusson, *Individual Development from an Interactive Perspective* (Hillsdale, N.J.: Erlbaum, 1988); R. A. Hinde and S. A. Dennis, "Categorizing Individuals," *International Journal of Behavioral Development* 9 (1986):105–19.

PAGE 71, D. T. Lykken et al., "Emergenesis," *American Psychologist* 47 (1992): 1565–77.

PAGE 71, WITH A FREQUENCY OF 0.20: C. C. Li, "A Genetical Model for Emergenesis," *American Journal of Human Genetics* 41 (1987):517–23.

PAGE 72, P. E. Meehl, "Factors, Taxa, Traits, and Types," *Journal of Personality* 60 (1992): 117–74.

PAGE 73, PREDICTION OF CHILDHOOD ABILITY IS MUCH IMPROVED: L. S. Siegel, "A Reconceptualization of Prediction from Infant Test Scores," in *Stability and Continuity in Mental Development,* ed. M. H. Bornstein and N. A. Krasnegor (Hillsdale, N.J.: Erlbaum, 1989), pp. 90–100.

PAGE 74, "QUALITATIVELY, NOT QUANTITATIVELY": E. Mayr, *The Growth of Biological Thought* (Cambridge: Harvard University Press, 1982), pp. 54–55.

CHAPTER THREE: *The Family of Fears*

PAGE 78, OF THE PRIMARY AFFECTS: R. A. Shweder, "The Cultural Psychology of the Emotions," in *Handbook of Emotions,* ed. M. Lewis and J. Haviland (New York: Guilford, 1993). Claparede begins his chapter for the 1927 Wittenberg College symposium on emotions with "The psychology of affective processes is the most confused chapter in all psychology." E. Claparede, "Feelings and Emotions," in *Feelings and Emotions,* ed. M. L. Reymert (Worcester, Mass.: Clark University Press, 1928), pp. 124–39. The quote is from p. 124.

PAGE 79, FEATURES OF EACH EMOTIONAL STATE: As cognitive science has penetrated the domain of emotions, the nature of the physiology associated with an emotion has been subtly replaced by the incentive event as the primary criterion for classifying emotions. One recent book suggests that emotions should be parsed into four classes depending upon whether the incentive is (1) a present event, (2) anticipation of a future event, or (3) an agent or (4) an object. A. Ortony, G. L. Clore, and A. Collins, *The Cognitive Structure of Emotions* (New York: Cambridge University Press, 1988). Of course, many cultures also differentiate emotions by the incentive that produces them. In some parts of Micronesia, two states of anger, named with different words, are based on whether the cause is another person's violation of community norms or the person's own failure. See C. Lutz, *Unnatural Emotions* (Chicago: University of Chicago Press, 1988).

PAGE 79, THEY ALSO DIFFER IN PHYSIOLOGY: David Barlow, who has written extensively on anxiety, agrees that anxiety, defined as a state of apprehension regarding the future, is qualitatively different from the fear states of the panic patient. Barlow believes that a combination of temperamental vulnerability and childhood experiences, characterized by lack of control over undesired events, produces anxious adults. Thus, contemporary theorists replace conflict over sex and hostility with a more cognitive notion of "impaired control" as the experiential contribution to neurosis. D. H. Barlow, "The Nature of Anxiety," in *Chronic Anxiety,* ed. R. M. Ropee and D. H. Barlow (New York: Guilford, 1991), pp. 1–28.

PAGE 80, VISCERAL INFORMATION IN AN ENVIROMENTAL CONTEXT: G. Mandler, *Mind and Emotion* (New York: Wiley, 1975).

PAGE 81, VERY DIFFERENT FEELINGS: J. C. Selner, *Teaching of St. Augustine on Fear as a Religious Motive* (Baltimore: St. Mary's University, 1937).

PAGE 81, TO LOVE THE DEITY: J. Bunyan, *A Treatise of the Fear of God* (Oxford: Clarendon Press, [1679] 1981).

PAGES 81–82, R. May, *The Meaning of Anxiety* (New York: Ronald Press, 1950).

PAGES 81–82, S. A. Kierkegaard, *The Concept of Dread*, 2d ed. (Princeton: Princeton University Press, [1844] 1957).

PAGES 81–82, M. Heidegger, "The Principle of Identity," in *Identity and Difference*, trans. J. Stambaugh (New York: Harper and Row, 1969).

PAGES 81–82, J. P. Sartre, *Being and Nothingness* (New York: Philosophical Library, [1943] 1957).

PAGE 82, P. Lagerqvist, "The Eternal Smile," in *The Eternal Smile* (New York: Hill and Wang, 1971).

PAGE 82, A MALAY TRIBE OR A TIBETAN VILLAGE: S. H. Potter, "The Cultural Construction of Emotion in Rural Chinese Social Life," *Ethos* 16 (1988):181–208.

PAGE 83, VULNERABILITY TO FEAR: S. Freud, *Inhibitions, Symptoms, and Anxiety* (London: Hogarth, [1926] 1948). The quotes are from pp. 133 and 105.

PAGE 86, DOES NOT SHOW THE ENHANCED STARTLE: J. M. Hitchcock and M. Davis, "Fear Potentiated Startle Using an Auditory Conditioned Stimulus," *Physiology and Behavior* 39 (1987):403–8.

PAGES 87–88, NATURE OF THE MEASUREMENTS: A similar conclusion holds for statements on human memory. A patient called H. M. had large areas of his temporal lobe removed to alleviate epilepsy. As a result, he became amnesic. But the seriousness of his memory impairment depended upon how his memory was assessed. If H. M. were shown a single picture and had to say later if he had seen it in the past, his recall was poor. But if he were shown two pictures, one of which he had seen and one not, his memory performance was much better and similar to that of normal adults. D. M. Freed, and S. Larkin, "Rate of Forgetting in H. M.," *Behavioral Neuroscience* 102 (1988):823–27.

PAGE 88, SUBJECTIVE FEELING STATE: The case for parsing the state of fear into separable components is helped, I believe, by a reminder that a century ago scientists believed that the visual perceptions of a person were also a unity. We now know that form, color, depth, and movement are initially processed by different collections of neurons in varied sites in the brain; only later are these different qualities integrated. M. Livingstone and D. Hubel, "Segregation of Form, Color, Movement, and Depth," *Science* 240 (1988):740–49.

PAGE 88, OR EFFICIENTLY THAN OTHER ANIMALS: D. H. Overstreet, A. H. Rezvani, and D. S. Janowsky, "Maudsley Reactive and Nonreactive Rats Differ Only in Some Tasks Reflecting Emotionality," *Physiology and Behavior* 52 (1992):149–52.

PAGES 89–90, AND GENERALIZE TO OTHER NOVEL SITUATIONS: R. E. Adamec and T. Shallow, "Lasting Effects on Rodent Anxiety of a Single Exposure to a Cat," *Physiology and Behavior.* In press.

PAGE 90, AWARD THIS STATE TO INVERTEBRATES: I. M. Marks, *Fears, Phobias, Rituals* (Oxford: Oxford University Press, 1987). For a clear historical summary of the instinct controversy, see S. Diamond, "Four Hundred Years of Instinct Controversy," *Behavior Genetics*, 4 (1974):237–52.

PAGE 90, PRODUCE IMMOBILITY: G. J. Gagliardi, G. G. Gallup, and J. C. Boren, "The Effect of Different Pupil to Eye Size Ratios on Tonic Immobility in Chickens," *Bulletin of the Psychonomic Society* 8 (1976):58–60.

PAGE 90, UNUSUAL SHAPE AND FORM OF MOVEMENT: When slides of snakes and spiders are used as conditioned stimuli prior to the administration of electric shock, compared with the presentation of flowers, there is a greater conditioning of heart-rate change to the biologically appropriate fearful patterns than to the neutral ones. The effect was potentiated for subjects who said they were afraid of snakes and spiders. D. W. Cooke, R. L. Hodes, and P. J. Lang, "Preparedness and Phobia," *Journal of Abnormal Psychology*, 95 (1986):195–207. A recent survey of the fears of almost 1,000 Australian children seven to eighteen years old indicated that snakes, rats, and spiders discriminated the sexes better than other targets of fear. All three have some qualities of innate releasers. See E. Gullone and N. J. King, "The Fears of Youth in the 1990s," *Journal of Genetic Psychology* 154 (1993):137–53.

PAGE 90, I. M. Marks, *Fears*. The quote is from p. 40.

PAGE 91, G. T. Ladd, 1895.

PAGE 91, PHYSIOLOGICAL STATE AND/OR BEHAVIORAL REACTION: J. LeDoux et al., "Different Projections of the Central Amygdalar Nucleus Mediate Autonomic and Behavioral Correlates of Conditioned Fear," *Journal of Neuroscience* 8 (1988):2517–29.

PAGE 91, NOT DUE TO INNATE PROCESSES: S. Rachman and C. G. Costello, "The Etiology and Treatment of Children's Phobias," *American Journal of Psychiatry* 118 (1961):97–101.

PAGE 91, SIGNS OF FEAR OF THE OBJECT: S. Mineka and M. Cook, "Immunization Against the Observational Conditioning of Snake Fear in Rhesus Monkeys," *Journal of Abnormal Psychology* 95 (1986):307–18.

PAGE 92, DUE TO A BRAIN DISTURBANCE: M. Prince and J. J. Putnam, "A Clinical Study of a Case of Phobia," *Journal of Abnormal Psychology* 7 (1912):259–76.

PAGE 92, THOSE EXPERIENCED IN THE PAST: A special set of neurons in the inferior temporal cortex, adjacent to the hippocampus and amygdala, responds to visual stimuli that are discrepant, and these cells habituate as the stimulus becomes familiar. See E. K. Miller, L. Li, and R. Desimone, "A Neural Mechanism for Working and Recognition Memory in Inferior Temporal Cortex," *Science* 254 (1991):1377–79.

PAGE 92, MALAISE, LETHARGY, AND A LOSS OF ENERGY: In Malaysia the stigmatized syndrome called *latah* seems more complex; those suffering from *latah* may exhibit the symptoms of echolalia. Some observers have suggested that this behavior is one way for the person to inform the community that he is under stress. B. J. Good, and A. M. Kleinman, "Culture and Anxiety," in *Anxiety and Anxiety Disorders*, ed. A. H. Tuma and J. D. Maser (Hillsdale, N.J.: Erlbaum, 1985), pp. 297–328.

PAGE 92, "REMAINED IN THAT STATE UP TILL THIS TIME": W. MacEwen, "Short Communications," *Glasgow Medical Journal* (1872): 80.

PAGE 93, SIGNS OF GOD'S WRATH: K. Park and L. J. Daston, "Unnatural Conceptions," *Past and Present* 92 (1981):20–54. Buddhist views on human nature emphasize the singular significance of unfamiliarity. An event is the occasion for a release of energy. If the event is unfamiliar, a misperception of danger may occur and a fear state will follow.

PAGE 94, DOES NOT APPEAR BEFORE THIS TIME: When members of a species of monkey called vervet encounter a novel food source or an unfamiliar human, two-year-old animals approach both targets more quickly than younger or older monkeys. See L. A. Fairbanks, "Risk Taking by Juvenile Vervet Monkeys," *Behavior* 124 (1993):57–72. Two years in the life of a monkey is roughly equal to six or seven years in the human child. Reflection on children's behavior affirms that first graders are more impulsive than two- or twelve-year-olds. Perhaps important maturational changes in the primate brain lead to a brief period of fearlessness in the five- to six-year-old child.

PAGE 94, EXHIBITING THREAT POSTURES: G. P. Sackett, "Monkeys Reared in Isolation with Pictures as Visual Input," *Science* 154 (1966):1468–72.

PAGE 94, AND THEREFORE PREDICTABLE: M. R. Gunnar, L. Leighton, and R. Peleaux, "Effects of Temporal Predictability on the Reactions of One Year Olds to Potentially Frightening Toys," *Developmental Psychology* 20 (1984):449–58.

PAGE 95, "THE CHILD IS APT TO FEAR": J. Sully, "Studies in Childhood VIII: Fear," *The Popular Science Monthly* 47 (1895):1–11. The quotes are from p. 10 and p. 2.

PAGE 95, FROM THE STATE OF ANXIETY: The pattern of cerebral blood flow using PET methods reveals different degrees of cerebral activity when adults are experiencing anxiety and when persons with a phobia of snakes are watching films of snakes and experiencing the fear state. See M. Fredrikson et al., "Regional Cerebral Blood Flow During Experimental Phobic Fear," *Psychobiology* 30 (1993):126–30. Further, the physiological profile of patients with blood injury phobia is different from that of people who have simple phobias or social phobia. See R. Hoehn-Saric and D. R. McLeod, "Somatic Manifestations of Normal and Pathological Anxiety," in *Biology of Anxiety Disorders*, ed. R. Hoehn-Saric and D. R. McLeod (Washington, D.C.: American Psychiatric Press, 1993), pp. 177–222. Gordon Bronson also distinguished between wariness—the temperamental vulnerability to fear of novelty—and a fear state that was learned. See G. W. Bronson and W. B. Pankey, "On a Distinction Between Fear and Wariness," *Child Development* 48 (1977):1167–83.

PAGE 95, A DIFFERENT, ALBEIT RELATED, STATE: R. S. Kahn and C. Moore, "Serotonin in the Pathogenesis of Anxiety," in *Biology*, ed. Hoehn-Saric and McLeod, pp. 61–102.

PAGE 95, FEAR OF LEAVING HOME: J. M. Murphy, "Abnormal Behavior in Traditional Societies," in *Handbook of Cross Cultural Human Development*, ed. R. H. Munroe, R. L. Munroe, and B. B. Whiting (New York: Garland, 1981), pp. 809–26.

PAGE 96, UNFAMILIAR ANIMAL FROM THE SAME SPECIES: P. Marler, "On Animal Aggression," *American Psychologist* 31 (1976):239–46.

PAGE 96, DECREASE IN DEFENSIVE-AGGRESSIVE BEHAVIOR: E. D. Kemble, D. C. Blanchard, and R. J. Blanchard, "Effects of Regional Amygdaloid Lesions on the Flight and Defensive Behaviors of Wild Black Rats (*Rattus rattus*)," *Physiology and Behavior* 48 (1990):1–5. Further, rats with lesions in the basolateral area showed impaired active avoidance learning and no conditioned freezing. See C. A. Lorenzini et al., "Effects of

Nucleus Basolateralis Amygdalae Neurotoxic Lesions on Aversive Conditioning in the Rat," *Physiology and Behavior* 49 (1991):765–70.

PAGE 97, IS A SMALLER CENTRAL AREA: D. Kruska, "Mammalian Domestication and Its Effect on Brain Structure and Behavior," in *Intelligence and Evolutionary Biology*, ed. H. J. Jerison and I. Jerison, NATO Series vol. 17 (Heidelberg: Springer-Verlag, 1988), pp. 211–50.

PAGE 97, DESERVE DISTINCT STATUS: Rats who were subjected to inescapable shock in a distinct context failed to show conditioned freezing after the amygdala was removed, but they still displayed a failure to escape, which had been regarded as simply a result of more intense fear. Thus, two behaviors that had been viewed as derivatives of fear and part of the behavioral inhibition system appear to be mediated by different neural circuits. See S. F. Maier et al., "The Role of the Amygdala and Dorsal Raphe Nuclei in Mediating the Behavioral Consequences of Inescapable Shock," *Behavioral Neuroscience* 107 (1993):377–88.

PAGE 98, J. A. Gray, *The Neuropsychology of Anxiety* (Oxford: Clarendon, 1982).

PAGE 102, IF THIS EVENT IS UNFAMILIAR: The claim that the hippocampus and amygdala are provoked by discrepancy is supported by an unusual study with human subjects. An adult with electrodes implanted in both the hippocampus and the amygdala heard a series of two different tones. The more discrepant tone occurred 20 percent of the time; the other was heard 80 percent of the time and was therefore more familiar. Although the hippocampus and amygdala displayed an increase in electrical activity to both the infrequent and frequent tones, the potentials were larger to the less frequent, less familiar stimulus. The same effect was noted when adults looked at simple line designs; the less frequent design produced a larger electric potential. See E. Halgren et al., "Endogeneous Potentials Generated in the Human Hippocampal Formation and Amygdala by Infrequent Events," *Science* 10 (1990):803–5.

PAGE 104, THAN THE VOICE OF ONE WHO IS FEARFUL: Computer programs devised by Philip Lieberman of Brown University evaluate the change in variability accompanying the altered muscle tension in the muscles and, by inference, a state of fear in the speaker.

PAGE 104, ARE PRESUMED TO ACCOMPANY FEAR: B. S. Kapp, J. P. Pascoe, and M. A. Bixler, "The Amygdala," in *Neuropsychology of Memory*, ed. L. R. Squire and N. Butters (New York: Guilford, 1984), pp. 473–88.

PAGE 104, NIBBLE AT THE EAR OF A CAT: D. C. Blanchard and R. J. Blanchard, "Innate and Conditioned Reactions to Threat in Rats with Amygdaloid Lesions," *Journal of Comparative and Physiological Psychology* 81 (1972):281–90.

PAGE 104, REDUCE ULCERATION: P. G. Henke, "The Amygdala and Restraint Ulcers in Rats," *Journal of Comparative and Physiological Psychology* 94 (1980):313–23.

PAGE 105, THAN IN THE LEFT AMYGDALA: R. L. Lloyd and S. Cling, "Delta Activity from the Amygdala in Squirrel Monkeys," *Behavioral Neuroscience* 105 (1991):223–29.

PAGE 105, DO NOT SHOW THIS AUTONOMIC REACTION: A. Ohman, "Fear and Anxiety as Emotional Phenomena," in Lewis and Haviland, *Handbook*, pp. 511–36.

PAGES 105–6, MAGNITUDE OF CHANGE IN THE BIOLOGICAL VARIABLES: M. Fredrikson, O. Sundin, and M. Frankenhaeuser, "Cortisol Secretion During the Defence Reaction in Humans," *Psychiatric Medicine* 47 (1985):313–19.

PAGE 106, TO THE FRONTAL CORTEX: G. Paxinos, *The Human Nervous System* (New York: Academic, 1990).

PAGE 106, J. Searle, *The Rediscovery of Mind* (Cambridge: MIT Press, 1992).

PAGE 106, "THINE HEART SHALL MEDIATE TERROR": Cited in D. B. Mumford, *Biological Psychiatry* 160 (1992):92–97.

PAGE 106, BOTH FEAR AND DESIRE: R. R. Dejarlais, *Body and Emotion: The Aesthetics of Illness and Healing in Nepal and the Himalayas* (Philadelphia: University of Pennsylvania Press, 1992).

PAGE 107, SIGNAL-TO-NOISE RATIO IN THE SENSORY CORTEX: C. E. Jahr and R. A. Nicoll, "Noradrenegic Modulation of Dendrodendritic Inhibition in the Olfactory Bulb," *Nature* 297 (1982):227–29.

PAGE 107, DETECT EACH HEARTBEAT WITH UNUSUAL ACCURACY: C. H. Rous, G. E. Jones, and K. R. Jones, "The Effect of Body Composition and Gender on Cardiac Awareness," *Psychophysiology* 25 (1988):400–407.

PAGE 107, DETECTION OF THEIR HEART BEATS: A. Ehlers and P. Breuer, "Increased Cardiac Awareness in Panic Disorder," *Journal of Abnormal Psychology* 101 (1992): 371–82.

PAGE 108, MORE SALIENT STATE OF CONSCIOUS FEAR: Studies of mice indicate that both alpha and beta adrenergic receptors in the brain can mediate withdrawal to novelty. See A. L. Gorman and A. J. Dunn, "Beta-adrenergic Receptors Are Involved in Stress Related Behavioral Changes," *Pharmacology, Biochemistry, and Behavior* 45 (1993):1–7. Further, CRH can increase norepinephrine levels in the brain. See H. Emoto et al., "Corticotropin Releasing Factor Activates the Noradrenergic Neuron System in the Rat Brain," *Pharmacology, Biochemistry, and Behavior* 45 (1993):419–22.

PAGE 108, See R. E. Adamec, "Individual Differences in Temporal Lobe Sensory Processing of Threatening Stimuli in the Cat," *Physiology and Behavior* 49 (1991):455–64; and "Anxious Personality in the Cat," in *Psychopathology and the Brain*, ed. B. J. Carroll and J. E. Barrett (New York: Raven, 1991), pp. 153–68. See also R. E. Adamec and D. McKay, "The Effects of CRF and Alpha-helical CRF on Anxiety in Normal and Hypophysectomized Rats" (Unpublished paper, Memorial University, St. Johns, Newfoundland, 1993). This study demonstrated that injection of CRF into the rat's cerebral ventricles induced withdrawal from novelty, independent of any effects on the pituitary adrenal axis.

PAGE 109, GAINS CONSIDERABLE SUPPORT: P. G. Henke, "Recent Studies of the Central Nucleus of the Amygdala and Stress Ulcers," *Neuroscience and Biobehavioral Reviews* 12 (1988):143–50.

PAGE 110, REPLACES FEAR OF DIRECT ENCOUNTER WITH THE UNFAMILIAR: R. G. Klein and C. G. Last, *Anxiety Disorders in Children* (London: Sage, 1989). Robert Levy's description of Tahitians suggests that adults feel uncomfortable when meeting a stranger—the term is *ha'ama*—but the emotion is due to an anticipation of being judged in an undesirable light. Thus, the same word is used when someone enters one's home when it is not clean. The feeling generated by an anticipation of punishment, called *arofa*, is used when the agent knows he has violated a community standard. Americans would probably use the term *embarrass* for the first instance and *anxiety* for the second. Fear of unfamiliar events is called *meha meha* and comes close to the English phrases *fear of the uncanny* and *fear of possible harm*. See R. I. Levy, *Tahitians* (Chicago: University of Chicago Press, 1973).

PAGE 110, NOT OF AN UNEXPECTED EVENT: P. Janet, "Fear of Action as an Essential Element in the Sentiment of Melancholia," in *Feelings and Emotions*, ed. M. L. Reymert (Worcester, Mass.: Clark University Press, 1928), pp. 297–309.

PAGE 112, Mayr, *Growth*.

PAGE 112, AND CAREFUL ATTENTION TO DETAIL: The continual discovery of exceptions to general principles is characteristic of biology. Until recently, most scientists assumed that, among mammals, males typically mated with genetically related females in order to maximize their reproductive success. Male pilot whales, however, appear to be an exception. See B. Amas, C. Schlotterer, and D. Tautz, "Social Structure of Pilot Whales Revealed by Analytical DNA Profiling," *Science* 260 (1993):670–72.

CHAPTER FOUR: *The Beginnings*

PAGE 114, "CHARACTERISTICS OF THE INDIVIDUAL": J. Kagan and H. A. Moss, *Birth to Maturity* (New York: Wiley, 1962), p. 277. A longitudinal study of subjects from the Berkeley Longitudinal Study found that very shy boys entered into marriage, parenthood, and occupational role later than did sociable children. Shy girls were less likely to remain in the work force after marriage. See A. Caspi, G. H. Elder, and D. J. Bem, "Moving Away from the World," *Developmental Psychology* 24 (1988):824–31. In addition, Gordon Bronson, who analyzed a corpus of longitudinal data, found that boys who were very fearful and shy during infancy became shy, timid eight-year-olds. See G. W. Bronson, "Fear of Visual Novelty," *Developmental Psychology* 2 (1970):33–40.

PAGE 114, J. I. Lacey and B. C. Lacey, "Verification and Extension of the Principle of Autonomic Response Stereotype," *American Journal of Psychology* 7 (1958):50–73.

PAGE 114, E. Gellhorn, *Physiological Foundations of Neurology and Psychiatry* (Minneapolis: University of Minnesota Press, 1953); M. A. Wenger "The Measurement of Individual Differences in Autonomic Balance," *Psychosomatic Medicine* 3 (1941): 427–34.

PAGE 115, EFFECTS OF DAY CARE: J. Kagan, R. B. Kearsley, and P. R. Zelazo, *Infancy* (Cambridge: Harvard University Press, 1978).

PAGE 115, R. Smith, *Inhibition* (Berkeley: University of California Press, 1992).

PAGE 117, EXAMPLES OF THIS STYLE: The complexity of the phenomena of human psychological functioning and their natural tie to philosophy leads creative minds interested in philosophical matters to select psychology rather than physics or chemistry for graduate training. The breadth of an original curiosity about broad philosophical themes has the advantage of a fuller appreciation of theory, but it has the disadvantage of tempting young scholars to impose a philosophical imperative on observations. Jean Piaget provides an illustration. As Fernando Vidal points out in his forthcoming book *Piaget Before Piaget*, the young Piaget had been influenced by Henri Bergson's philosophy and the biological data on the evolution of snails. Before he was twenty years old, he tried to unite these ideas, coming to the tentative conclusion that human reasoning evolved gradually and continuously over time, as snails have evolved into new species, given enough time and geographical isolation. If developmental changes in human reasoning were analogous to evolutionary changes in the shapes of the shells of fresh water snail species, one should be able to study the infant—analogous to the original snail of several hundred million years ago—and see the origins of later thought. By tracking the child's mental growth, one would understand how adult reasoning emerged out of the young child's inferences.

But if this analogy fails, and I believe it does, then study of the infant and young child would reveal little about adult human reasoning. Study of the fertilized zygote reveals nothing of the physiology of the newborn because of dramatic transformations over the course of fetal development. Had Piaget asked, "What is the infant like?" instead of "What reactions in the infant are analogous to thought in the adult?" he might have written a different theory.

PAGE 117, P. W. Bridgman, *The Logic of Modern Physics* (New York: Macmillan, 1927).

PAGES 117–18, D. Magnusson, "Back to the Phenomena," *European Journal of Personality* 6 (1992):1–14; the quote is from pp. 5 and 11.

PAGE 118, "NOT A PRESCRIPTION FOR MAKING DISCOVERIES": Cited in G. Holton, *The Advancement of Science and Its Burdens* (Cambridge: Harvard University Press, 1986), p. 169.

PAGE 118, A. Jaffe and F. Quinn, "Theoretical Mathematics," *Bulletin of the American Mathematical Society* 29 (1993): no. 1, pp. 1–14. The quote is from p. 8.

PAGE 118, INFINITE VARIETY OF NATURE: H. Georgi, Personal letter to the author, 1993.

PAGE 120, IMPLYING THAT THE UNITY IS BROKEN: L. Svensson, C. Harton, and B. Linder, "Evidence for a Dissociation Between Cardiovascular and Behavioral Reactivity in a Spontaneously Hypertensive Rat," *Physiology and Behavior* 49 (1991):661–65.

PAGE 121, WHEN THE QUESTION WAS OPEN-ENDED: H. Schuman and J. Scott, "Problems in the Use of Survey Questions to Measure Public Opinion," *Science* 236 (1987):957–59.

PAGE 121, TO ASK THE SAME QUESTION: Gigerenzer has shown that the claims by Tversky and Kahneman that humans cannot reason well about probability are a result of how the problem is framed to the subject. See G. Gigerenzer, "The Bounded Rationality of Probabilistic Mental Models," in *Rationality*, ed. K. I. Manktelow and D. E. Over (London: Routledge, 1993), p. 14.

PAGE 122, HIS HEART RATE AND BLOOD PRESSURE: Myrtek, *Constitutional Psychophysiology*.

PAGE 123, HISTORY MIGHT HAVE BEEN DIFFERENT: S. Diamond, *Personality and Temperament* (New York: Harper, 1957).

PAGE 123, ISOLATION FROM THE PEER GROUP: W. Emmerich, "Continuity and Stability in Early Social Development," *Child Development* 35 (1964):311–32.

PAGE 124, THE RESPONSE SELECTED: T. C. Schneirla, "An Evolutionary and Developmental Theory of Biphasic Processes Underlying Approach and Withdrawal," in *Nebraska Symposium on Motivation: 1959*, ed. M. R. Jones (Lincoln: University of Nebraska Press, 1959), pp. 1–44.

PAGE 124, MORE EXTREME IN THEIR BEHAVIOR: This strategy of studying extremes is also useful in studying the effect of social class on pregnancy among unmarried adolescents. The probability of becoming pregnant is high for those living in the poorest third of Black neighborhoods in Chicago, but the difference between the middle third and the best third of the Black neighborhoods is trivial. See S. E. Mayer and C. Jencks, "Growing Up in Poor Neighborhoods," *Science* 243 (1989):1441–45.

PAGE 126, THE SUBJECTS SAID THEY WERE EXPERIENCING: G. C. Curtis, Personal communication, 1992. See also R. M. Nesse et al., "Endocrine and Cardiovascular Responses During Phobic Anxiety," *Psychosomatic Medicine* 47 (1985):320–32.

PAGE 126, ON THE BEHAVIOR THAT FOLLOWS FOOT SHOCK: W. F. Supple, R. N. Leaton, and M. S. Fanselow "Effects of Cerebellar Vermis Lesions on Species Specific Fear Responses, Neophobia, and Taste Aversion in Rats," *Physiology and Behavior*, 39 (1987):579–86.

PAGE 128, STRATEGY WAS STRAIGHTFORWARD: C. Garcia-Coll, J. Kagan, and J. S. Reznick, "Behavioral Inhibition in Young Children," *Child Development* 55 (1984):1005–9. The 117 children were selected from a larger group of 305 whose mothers had been interviewed by telephone regarding their children's behavior. The mothers' descriptions of their children were used to select those who were likely to be minimally or maximally fearful in the laboratory.

PAGE 129, CORRELATION ACROSS THE TWO SESSIONS WAS .63: In general, correlation coefficients larger than 0.30 should be taken seriously. Not all unprotected sexual encounters lead to pregnancy; the estimated correlation between such occurrences of sexual intercourse and subsequent pregnancy is between 0.2 and 0.3—but that is still high enough to take seriously.

PAGE 130, APPROACHES TO THE UNFAMILIAR PEER: For details, see J. Kagan, J. S. Reznick, and N. Snidman, "Biological Bases of Childhood Shyness," *Science* 240 (1988):167–71.

PAGE 130, OBJECTS IN A SMALL, UNFAMILIAR ROOM: The objects were a beam set at an angle of 30 degrees to the floor, a large black box with a circular hole and handle, and a set of bars that were mounted so that the child's feet would have to leave the floor if she chose to play on them.

PAGE 130, IN THE CHILD'S OWN KINDERGARTEN CLASSROOM: A large number of observers who were unfamiliar with the child's classification visited the child's school on two occasions and coded whether the child was alone or interacting with peers or a teacher as well as the activity the child was pursuing.

PAGE 132, SECOND-GRADERS ARE EXTREME SOCIAL ISOLATES: K. H. Rubin, "The Waterloo Longitudinal Project," in *Social Withdrawal, Inhibition, and Shyness in Childhood*, ed. K. H. Rubin and J. B. Asendorpf (Hillsdale, N.J.: Erlbaum, 1993), pp. 291–314.

PAGE 132, STARING AT ANOTHER ANIMAL FROM A DISTANCE: S. Suomi, Personal letter to the author, 1993.

PAGE 133, OBJECTS, PEOPLE, AND EVENTS: See J. Kagan, J. S. Reznick, and J. Gibbons, "Inhibited and Uninhibited Types of Children," *Child Development* 60 (1989):838–45.

PAGE 133, THE ORIGINALLY INHIBITED OR UNINHIBITED CHILDREN: The children who had been classified as inhibited in the second year made only thirty-two spontaneous comments with the examiner and seventeen spontaneous comments with the peers, compared with sixty-six and fifty-five comments for the uninhibited children. One-fourth of the originally inhibited children were extremely quiet with the examiner; not one originally uninhibited child even approached that degree of restraint in conversation. See also D. C. Murray, "Talk, Silence and Anxiety," *Psychological Bulletin* 75 (1971):244–60.

PAGE 133, AS OTHER PSYCHOLOGISTS HAVE NOTED: Jens Asendorpf found that latency to the first spontaneous utterance and proportion of time silent were sensitive indexes of inhibited behavior. See J. Asendorpf, in "Beyond Temperament," ed. Rubin and Asendorpf, pp. 265–85. See also M. E. Evans, "Communicative Competence as a Dimension of Shyness," in the same volume, pp. 189–212.

PAGE 133, T. W. Deacon, "The Neural Circuitry of Primate Calls and Human Language," *Human Evolution*, 4 (1989):367–401. Further, there is good evidence that the anterior cingulate area is involved in voluntary speech and vocalization; see D. Von Cramon and U. Jurgens, "The Anterior Cingulate Cortex and the Phonatory Control in Monkey and Man," *Neuroscience and Biobehavioral Reviews* 7 (1983):423–25.

PAGE 134, Rubin, "The Waterloo Project."

PAGE 136, LESS WELL ON THIS SECOND TEST: For example, early in the laboratory session at seven and a half years, each child heard a narrated story and subsequently was given eighteen pictures to arrange so that they matched the chronology of the story they had just heard. Four difficult tests were then administered in order to create a state of uncertainty. A second, parallel story was then narrated, and the child was asked to arrange a different set of eighteen pictures to match the second story. The two temperamental groups had similar memory scores on the first story, before the imposed stress. But the inhibited children made more errors than the uninhibited ones on the second story following the stressful tests.

PAGES 136–37, STROOP INTERFERENCE TEST: J. R. Stroop, "Factors Affecting Speed in Serial Verbal Reactions," *Psychological Monograph* 50 (1938):38–48.

PAGE 137, THREATENING AND NONTHREATENING WORDS: See R. J. McNally et al., "Cognitive Processing of Trauma Cues in Rape Victims with Posttraumatic Stress Disorder," *Cognitive Therapy and Research* 16 (1992):283–95; A. D. Arnold and J. M. Cheek, "Shyness, Self-preoccupation, and the Stroop Color Word Test," *Personality and Individual Differences* 7 (1986):1–3.

PAGE 137, WHILE NAMING THE COLORS OF THE THREAT WORDS: The variable was the difference between the number of threat words and the number of positive emotional words that were among the fourteen longest latencies (top quartile) ($t = 1.9$, $p < .05$).

PAGE 138, MEANINGFUL ANXIETY SYNDROME: J. Biederman et al., "Psychiatric Correlates of Behavioral Inhibition in Young Children of Parents With and Without Psychiatric Disorders," *Archives of General Psychiatry* 47 (1990):21–26; J. F. Rosenbaum et al., "Further Evidence of an Association Between Behavioral Inhibition and Anxiety Disorders: Results from a Family Study of Children from a Non-clinical Sample," *Journal of Psychiatric Research* 25 (1991):49–65.

CHAPTER FIVE: *The Physiology of Inhibited and Uninhibited Children*

PAGE 140, TEMPORARILY ACTIVE METABOLICALLY: Even though many scientists are hoping that this new technique will provide a sensitive and accurate index of psychological state, an uncritical optimism may be premature. When patients with a phobia of snakes were shown pictures of these feared objects, they showed an increase in metabolic activity in visual association areas but decreased activity in the brain areas that one would most expect to be activated by an unexpected fearful stimulus, especially the temporal and amygdalar area and the orbital frontal cortex. See G. Wik et al., "A Functional Cerebral Response to Frightening Visual Stimulation," *Psychiatry Research: Neuroimaging*, in press.

PAGE 141, R. C. Tryon, "Genetic Difference in Maze Learning Ability in Rats," *39th Yearbook of the National Society for the Study of Education*, Part I (Bloomington, Ind.: Public School Publishing Company, 1940), pp. 111–19; L. V. Searle, "The Organization of Hereditary Maze Brightness and Maze Dullness," *Genetic Psychology Monographs* 39 (1949):279–325.

PAGE 142, LIMITATIONS ON CERTAINTY THAT THIS CHOICE ENTAILED: The choice of organism for study can be of singular significance. Mendel originally chose a plant species with unusual genetics. Had he not shifted to peas, he would not have discovered the first basic principles of heredity. Experimental embryology also made substantial advances when scientists replaced the amphibian embryo with that of the chick. The nervous system of the chick is built with a more elaborate design and lends itself to a more rigorous analysis of its neural structures. See R. Levi-Montalcini, "The Nerve Growth Factor 35 Years Later," *Science* 237 (1987):1154–62.

PAGE 142, "OVERREACTIVE SYMPATHETIC NERVOUS SYSTEM": J. A. Barre, cited in G. Guillain, *J. M. Charcot* (New York: Hoeber, 1959), p. 158.

PAGE 142, "EXCESSIVE BLUSHING AND PALING": J. Breuer, and S. Freud, *Studies in Hysteria* (New York: Nervous and Mental Disease Publishing Company, [1895] 1937), p. 180.

PAGE 142, IN ADDITION, SEEM TO BE HERITABLE: K. A. Matthews et al., "Are Cardiovascular Responses to Behavioral Stressors a Stable Individual Difference Variable in Childhood?" *Psychophysiology* 24 (1987):464–73; J. R. Turner, "Individual Differences in Heart Rate Response During Behavioral Challenge," *Psychophysiology* 26 (1989): 497–505.

PAGE 143, A SMALL INCREASE IN CORTISOL: E. van Borell and J. F. Hurnik, "Stereotypic Behavior, Adrenocortical Function and Open Field Behavior of Individually Confined Gestating Sows," *Physiology and Behavior* 49 (1991):709–13.

PAGE 143, ACTIVITY IN THE FACE AND LEGS: D. R. McLeod, R. Hoehn-Saric, and R. L. Stefon, "Somatic Symptoms of Anxiety," *Biological Psychiatry* 21 (1986):301–10.

PAGE 144, LIMBIC AROUSAL AND PSYCHOLOGICAL STRESS: R. H. Rahe et al., "Psychological and Physiological Assessments on American Hostages Freed from Captivity in Iran," *Psychosomatic Medicine* 52 (1990):1–16.

PAGE 144, SYMPATHETIC ACTIVITY TO THE SAME CHALLENGE: P. J. Mills et al., "Temporal Stability of Task Induced Cardiovascular, Adrenergic, and Psychological Responses," *Psychophysiology* 30 (1993):197–204.

PAGE 144, CORRESPONDING CHANGE IN HEART RATE: It appears that local circuits associated with each sympathetic target can influence the reactivity of that target independent of brain activity. See L. G. Elfvin, B. Lindh, and T. Hokfelt, "The Chemical Neuroanatomy of Sympathetic Ganglia," *Annual Review of Neuroscience* 16 (1993): 471–507.

PAGE 145, NOT SUPPORTED BY THE FACTS: Even when neurons in a cat's hypothalamus that lead to defensive behavior are stimulated and plasma measures of norepinephrine and epinephrine rise, the increases in heart rate and blood pressure are relatively small. The correlation between epinephrine output of the medulla and the rise in heart rate was only .44. Thus, even when the scientist is experimentally controlling the central state, the peripheral response is not closely yoked to that state. See S. L. Stoddard et al., "Plasma Catecholamines Associated with Hypothalamically Elicited Defense Behavior," *Physiology and Behavior* 36 (1986):867–73.

PAGE 145, H. Weiner, *Perturbing the Organism* (Chicago: University of Chicago Press, 1992), p. 72. See also J. C. Curtis and D. A. Glitz, "Neuroendocrine Findings in Anxiety Disorders," *Neurologic Clinics* 6 (1988):131–48. College women were told they would be given easy, moderately difficult, or very difficult memory items. The subjects' heart rates and blood pressures were measured when they estimated the difficulty of the next test item to be administered as well as during the task. The largest increase in systolic blood pressure occurred when the women said they were maximally involved in the task, not when they expected a difficult test item. Because the relation between the magnitude of increase in heart rate and blood pressure was larger for the moderately difficult items than for the hardest items, it is likely that the subjects withdrew some effort from the very hard items. As a result, the changes in sympathetic responses were muted. See R. A. Wright, R. J. Contrada, and M. J. Patone, "Task Difficulty, Cardiovascular Response, and the Magnitude of Goal Valence," *Journal of Personality and Social Psychology* 51 (1986):837–43.

PAGES 145–46, YOKED TO A PARTICULAR PSYCHOLOGICAL STATE: A nice example of the independence of heart rate and blood pressure is the fact that in conditioning procedures in which a tone is followed by shock, a conditioned increase in blood pressure occurs only if the tone reliably predicts the occurrence of the shock. A conditioned rise in heart rate, however, occurs whether or not the tone and shock are contingent or occur randomly. See J. Iwata and J. E. Le Doux, "Dissociation of Associative and Nonassociative Concomitants of Classical Fear Conditioning in the Freely Behaving Rat," *Behavioral Neuroscience* 102 (1988):66–76.

PAGE 147, THAN DID THE UNINHIBITED CHILDREN: A study of eight-year-old twins revealed that shy children showed larger heart rate accelerations to a cognitive test and that 40–60 percent of the variance in heart rate could be explained by genetic factors. D. I. Boomsma and R. Plomin, "Heart Rate and Behavior of Twins," *Merrill Palmer Quarterly* 32 (1986):141–51.

PAGE 147, PHASES OF EACH EPISODE: The phases ranged from five to thirty seconds; the baselines were averaged over sixty seconds.

PAGE 148, DISCRIMINATOR OF DIFFERENT STRAINS OF ANIMALS: J. D. Newman, "Investigating the Physiological Control of Mammalian Vocalizations," in *The Physiological*

Control of Mammalian Vocalization, ed. J. D. Newman (New York: Plenum, 1988), pp. 1–6. Further, the stability of systolic blood pressure over a two-week period was higher when the child was physically stressed than when sitting quietly. H. L. Tavas and J. F. Salis, "Blood Pressure Reactivity in Young Children," *Journal of Developmental and Behavioral Pediatrics* 13 (1992):41–45.

PAGE 148, A. F. Ax, "The Physiological Differentiation between Fear and Anger in Humans," *Psychosomatic Medicine* 15 (1953):433–42.

PAGE 148, HAVE HIGH VALUES ON BOTH MEASURES: Chi square = 4.8, $p < .05$.

PAGE 148, RESPONSE TO CHALLENGE: On the final baseline we compared the mean heart rate while sitting with the highest rate attained during any one of the six ten-second epochs while the adolescent was standing. Fifty-eight percent of inhibited youth but 26 percent of uninhibited youth had large rises of heart rate (20 to 25 bpm; chi square = 7.5, $p < .01$).

PAGE 149, MEDIATE THE STARTLE REFLEX: M. Davis, "Pharmacological and Anatomical Analysis of Fear Conditioning Using the Fear Potentiated Startle Paradigm," *Behavioral Neuroscience* 100 (1986):814–24.

PAGE 150, THAN WHEN THE ADULT FEELS SAFE: C. Grillon et al., "Fear Potentiated Startle in Humans," *Psychophysiology* 28 (1991):588–95.

PAGE 150, P. J. Lang, M. M. Bradley, and B. H. Cuthbert, "Emotion, Attention, and the Startle Reflex, *Psychological Review* 97 (1990):377–98.

PAGE 150, 32 PERCENT VERSUS 16 PERCENT: Chi square = 4.2, $p < .05$.

PAGE 151, THE PITCH PERIODS OF SPOKEN UTTERANCES: Computer programs written by Philip Leiberman of Brown University permit one to quantify changes in the variability of the pitch periods. (The actual index is the standard deviation of the normalized distribution of twice the difference between two successive pitch periods divided by the sum of the periods.)

PAGE 151, TRACEABLE TO THE CENTRAL NUCLEUS OF THE AMYGDALA: Women who admitted to high anxiety, compared with low-anxiety women, displayed more frequent bursts of muscle activity in various sites on the body, but there was no correlation among levels of muscle tension across the different body sites. See A. J. Fridlund et al., "Anxiety and Striate Muscle Activation," *Journal of Abnormal Psychology* 95 (1986):228–36.

PAGE 151, CORTISOL LEVELS FROM FIVE TO SEVEN YEARS WAS LOW: It is possible that inhibited children with high cortisol levels at age five who became much less inhibited secreted less cortisol at seven. Daily exposure to the same stress in rats leads to an adaptation and a decreased response of the pituitary adrenal axis to a stressor. See A. Armario et al., "Response of Anterior Pituitary Hormones to Chronic Stress," *Neuroscience and Biobehavioral Reviews* 10 (1986):245–50. Among children three to six years of age, the more fearful, shy children showed an increase in salivary cortisol from the beginning of a play session to the end of the session, while the more aggressive children showed a drop in cortisol. See D. A. Granger, K. Stansbury, and B. Henker, "Preschoolers' Behavioral and Neuroendocrine Responses to Challenge," *Merrill Palmer Quarterly*, in press.

PAGE 152, STRIKE ONE BETWEEN THE EYES: See Kagan, Reznick, and Snidman, "Biological Bases." for details. An unpublished study of children seven to seventeen years of age who had been referred for psychological problems revealed that the most anxious and inhibited children showed larger rises in cortisol following a stressful laboratory procedure than did the children whose profiles were characterized by low anxiety. See D. A. Granger, J. R. Weisz, and D. Kauneckis, "Neuroendocrine Reactivity, Internalizing Behavioral Problems, and Control Related Cognitions in Clinic Referred Children and Adolescents." (Unpublished paper, Department of Psychology, University of California, Los Angeles, 1993).

PAGE 152, "ARE NOT HOMOGENEOUS": Hoehn-Saric and McLeod, "Somatic Manifestations," p. 210.

PAGE 153, COHERENT, INTEGRATED CHARACTERISTIC OF FITNESS: B. Wallace, *Fifty Years of Genetic Load* (Ithaca: Cornell University Press, 1991).

PAGE 153, WHILE VIEWING A THREATENING SCENE: This suggestion is affirmed by the fact that adult men react to different stressors with a maximum response in different bodily systems. To difficult arithmetic items, there is a major increase in respiratory rate, to cold water there is a large rise in diastolic blood pressure, and to exercise there is a large increase in heart rate. Each stress creates a different arousal state and a different physiological profile. See M. Myrtek and S. Spital, "Psychophysiological Response Patterns to Single, Double, and Triple Stressors," *Psychophysiology* 23 (1986):663–71.

PAGE 154, S. Epstein, "The Stability of Behavior," *American Psychologist,* 35 (1980):790–806.

PAGE 155, R. P. Abelson, "A Variance Explanation Paradox," *Psychological Bulletin* 97 (1985):129–33; the quote is from p. 133.

PAGE 156, R. J. Davidson and N. A. Fox, "Frontal Brain Asymmetry Predicts Infants' Response to Maternal Separation," *Journal of Abnormal Psychology* 98 (1989):127–31.

PAGE 156, IN SPEECH THAN THE RIGHT: Patients who have had their left frontal lobe removed (with a resulting greater dominance of the right hemisphere) make few spontaneous comments. Patients who have had their right frontal lobe removed make an excess number of spontaneous comments. See B. Kolb and L. Taylor, "Affective Behavior in Patients with Localized Cortical Excisions," *Science* 214 (1981):89–91.

PAGE 157, STORY OF DR. JEKYLL AND MR. HYDE: A. Harrington, *Medicine, Mind, and the Double Brain* (Princeton, N.J.: Princeton University Press, 1987).

PAGE 157, UNINHIBITED CHILDREN SHOWED GREATER ACTIVATION ON THE LEFT SIDE: R. J. Davidson R. Finman, A. Straus, and J. Kagan, "Childhood Temperament and Frontal Lobe Activity" (Unpublished manuscript, University of Wisconsin, 1991).

PAGE 161, THE RELATIVES OF THE UNINHIBITED CHILDREN: J. Kagan et al., "Temperament and Allergic Symptoms," *Psychosomatic Medicine* 53 (1991):332–40.

PAGE 161, ARE ALSO MORE PRONE TO HAY FEVER: I. R. Bell et al., "Is Allergic Rhinitis More Frequent in Young Adults with Extreme Shyness?" *Psychosomatic Medicine* 52 (1990):517–25; I. R. Bell et al., "Vascular Disease, Risk Factors, Urinary Free Cortisol, and Health Histories in Older Adults," *Biological Psychology* 35 (1993):37–49. See also L. A. Schachner and R. L. Hansen, *Pediatric Dermatology* (New York: Churchill Livingstone, 1988). Given the tendency for inhibited children to show greater activation of the right hemisphere, it is of interest that lesioning the left fronto-parietal cortex in C3H/HE mice reduces the capacity of the animal's immune system to respond to an antigen, while lesions of the right enhance mitogenesis. See P. J. Neveu et al., "Modulation of Mitogen Induced Lymphoproliferation by Cerebral Neocortex," *Life Science* 38 (1986):1907–13. The interaction of a temperamental susceptibility to stress and reactivity of the immune system is illustrated in a study of two groups of men. One group displayed high sympathetic tone, while the other showed low tone before any stress was imposed. Both types of men then experienced very difficult cognitive tests. Only the men who entered the laboratory with high sympathetic reactivity showed a compromised immune response to an antigen; the men with low sympathetic tone did not. S. B. Manuck et al., "Individual Differences in Cellular Immune Response to Stress," *Psychological Science* 2 (1991):111–15.

PAGE 162, FEARLESS CHILDREN WERE BROWN-EYED: A. Rosenberg and J. Kagan, "Iris Pigmentation and Behavioral Inhibition," *Developmental Psychobiology* 20 (1987): 377–92; A. Rosenberg and J. Kagan, "Physical and Psychological Correlates of Behavioral Inhibition," *Developmental Psychobiology* 22 (1989):753–70. Kenneth Rubin and D. Roth of the University of Waterloo have replicated this association in Toronto schoolchildren. Approximately 40 to 45 percent of North American children have blue eyes. The relation of eye color to inhibition does not hold during the first year, because eye color is still changing during the first few years of life.

PAGE 162, CINDERELLA'S STEPSISTERS: D. Arcus, "Vulnerability and Eye Color in Disney Cartoon Characters," in *Perspectives on Behavioral Inhibition*, ed. J. S. Reznick (Chicago: University of Chicago Press, 1989), pp. 291–97; Chi square = 8.7 p < .01.

PAGE 162, WITH GRAY FUR (LINKED TO THE AGOUTI GENE): C. E. Keeler, "The Association of the Black (Non-Agouti) Gene with Behavior," *Journal of Heredity* 33 (1942):371–84; C. A. Cottle and E. O. Price, "Effects of the Non-Agouti Pelage Color Allele on the Behavior of Captive, Wild Norway Rats (Rattus Norvegicus)," *Journal of Comparative Psychology* 101 (1987):390–94.

PAGE 162, THAN THOSE WITH LIGHTER COATS: E. O. Price, "Behavioral Aspects of Animal Domestication," *The Quarterly Review of Biology* 59 (1984):11–32. When amphibian embryos are stressed during metamorphosis, the HPA axis is activated and the Pars intermedia shows hyperfunction, resulting in a failure to stimulate the pigment cells. As a result, the animal skin is lighter. A. A. Voitkevich, "Interrelation of the Nervous and Endocrine Regulation of Melanocytes," in *Structure and Control of the Melanocytes*, ed. G. Della Porta and O. Muhlback (Berlin: Springer-Verlag, 1966), pp. 44–52.

PAGE 162, THAN DO UNINHIBITED CHILDREN: The actual measure was the ratio of width to length of face. Ratios less than .50 appeared to observers to be narrow; ratios greater than .60 appeared broad. These values represent approximately the top and bottom 20 percent of the distribution of values.

PAGES 162–63, RATED AS THE MOST AGGRESSIVE CHILDREN: R. Walker, "Body Build and Behavior in Young Children," *Monographs of the Society for Research in Child Development* 27 (1962), no. 3.

PAGE 163, FOR DUTCH CHILDREN: P. F. Verdonck and R. N. Walker, "Body Build and Behavior in Emotionally Disturbed Children," *Genetic Psychology Monographs* 94 (1976):149–73.

PAGE 163, NOT ONE MESOMORPHIC BOY WAS THAT CAUTIOUS: J. Kagan, "Body Build and Conceptual Impulsivity in Children," *Journal of Personality* 34 (1966):118–28.

PAGE 163, BREEDS WITH A LOWER RATIO: D. Lester, "Body Build and Temperament in Dogs," *Perceptual and Motor Skills* 56 (1983):590.

PAGE 163, PREVALENT AMONG SOUTHERN EUROPEANS: H. V. Meredith, "Variation in Body Stockiness Among and Within Ethnic Groups at Ages from Birth to Adulthood," in *Advances in Child Development and Behavior* vol. 20, ed. H. W. Reese (New York: Academic Press, 1987), pp. 1–60.

PAGE 163, ABOUT SIXTY TO A HUNDRED THOUSAND YEARS AGO: L. L. Cavalli-Sforza, P. Menozzi, and A. Piazza, "Demic Expansions and Human Evolution," *Science* 259 (1993):639–46.

PAGE 163, MAJOR NEUROTRANSMITTER OF THE SYMPATHETIC NERVOUS SYSTEM: Norepinephrine leads to an increase in basal metabolic rate and, as a consequent, an increase in core temperature. Because individuals with a greater ratio of body surface to weight lose more body heat, ectomorphs would require a higher basal rate than mesomorphs. See J. Bligh, *Temperature Regulation in Mammals and Other Vertebrates* (New York: American Elsevier, 1973).

PAGE 164, PROPENSITY TO FEAR OF THE UNFAMILIAR: Gerbils who have light-colored fur and pink eyes react to experimental imposition of a cold temperature with more frequent shaking of the body (in order to raise body temperature), while gerbils with black fur display this behavior less frequently. R. Wong and P. Gray-Allen, "Coat Color Genes and Cage Behavior Affect Care of the Body Surface Behavior of Meriones Unguiculatus," *Behavior Genetics* 22 (1992):125–34. The increase in basal metabolic rate produced by the activity of norepinephrine is greater in strains of fish that normally live in very cold waters (for example, the Arctic). Laboratory comparisons of Arctic cod with strains from warmer waters revealed that the former had higher oxygen consumption, showed greater activity in laboratory pools, and appeared to the investigator to be more fearful of capture. G. F. Holton, "Metabolic Cold Adaptation of Polar Fish," *Physiological Zoology* 47 (1974):137–52.

PAGE 164, NOT ALL OF WHICH ARE DESIRABLE: J. P. C. Dumont and R. M. Robertson, "Neural Circuits," *Science* 233 (1986):849–52.

PAGE 164, PIGMENTATION AND THE GROWTH OF FACIAL SKELETON: J. M. Gardner et al., "The Mouse Pink Eye Dilution Gene," *Science* 257 (1992):1121–24.

PAGE 164, PROTOTYPIC INHIBITED CHILD: The fates of neural crest cells are monitored by local chemical events, especially glucocorticoids, which affect the balance of sympathetic and parasympathetic neurons in the autonomic nervous system. See A. J. Doupe, "Role of Glucocorticoids and Growth Features in the Development of Neural Crest Derivatives" (Ph.D. diss., Harvard University, 1984). See also D. J. Anderson, "Molecular Control of Cell Fate in the Neural Crest," *Annual Review of Neuroscience* 16 (1993):129–58. It is also relevant that albino mice, who have no pigment in eye or fur, are less exploratory in a novel, open field than other strains—another link between the genes controlling melanin production and those controlling the behavioral reaction to unfamiliarity. See J. C. DeFries, J. P. Hegmann, and M. W. Weir, "Open Field Behavior in Mice," *Science* 154 (1966):1577–79.

PAGES 164–65, D. K. Belyaev, "Destabilizing Selection as a Factor in Domestication," *Journal of Heredity* 70 (1959):301–8.

PAGE 166, IS INFLUENCED BY GENETIC FACTORS: R. Plomin and D. C. Rowe, "Genetic and Environmental Etiology of Social Behavior in Infancy," *Developmental Psychology* 15 (1979):62–72.

PAGE 166, DO NOT HAVE THIS GENETIC ANOMALY: L. Kron et al., "Anorexia Nervosa and Gonadal Dysgenesis," *Archives of General Psychiatry* 34 (1977):332–35.

PAGE 167, A. Matheny, "Developmental Behavior Genetics: The Louisville Study," in *Developmental Behavior Genetics: Neural Biometrical and Evolutionary Approaches*, ed. M. E. Hahn et al. (New York: Oxford University Press, 1990), pp. 25–38.

PAGE 167, FOR SHY, FEARFUL BEHAVIOR: H. H. Goldsmith and I. I. Gottesman, "Origins of Variation in Behavioral Style," *Child Development* 52 (1981):91–103.

PAGE 167, AGGREGATE INDEX OF INHIBITION: J. L. Robinson et al., "The Heritability of Inhibited and Uninhibited Behavior," *Developmental Psychology* 28 (1993): 1030–37.

PAGE 168, FROM THE MODERATELY SHY CHILD: The degree of distress to maternal separation at fourteen, twenty, and twenty-four months was also heritable—coefficients ranged from .63 to .81.

PAGE 168, "ARE PRONE TO BECOME MORBIDLY OBESE": R. A. Price and A. J. Stunkard, "Commingling Analysis of Obesity in Twins," *Human Heredity* 39 (1989):121–35; the quote is from p. 133.

CHAPTER SIX: *Early Predictors of the Two Types*

PAGE 171, NOVEL, UNFAMILIAR EVENTS: E. J. Rolls and G. V. Williams, "Neuronal Activity in the Ventral Striatum of the Primate," in *The Basal Ganglia II*, ed. M. B. Carpenter and A. Jayarama (New York: Plenum, 1987), pp. 349–56; H. J. W. Nauta, "The Relationship of the Basal Ganglia to the Limbic System," in *Handbook of Clinical Neurology*, vol. 5, ed. P. J. Vinken, G. W. Bruyn, and H. L. Kluwans (New York: Elsevier, 1986), pp. 19–31.

PAGE 172, CHANGES IN MOTOR ACTIVITY: B. A. Vogt and H. Barbas, "Structure and Connections of the Cingulate Vocalization Region in the Rhesus Monkey," in *The Physiological Control of Mammalian Vocalization*, ed. J. D. Newman (New York: Plenum, 1988), pp. 203–28; J. D. Newman, "The Primate Isolation Call and the Evolution and Physiological Control of Human Speech," in *Language Origins: A Multidisciplinary Approach*, ed. J. Wind et al. (The Hague: Kluwer, 1992), pp. 301–21; J. D. Newman, "The Infant Cry of Primates," in *Infant Crying*, ed. B. M. Lester & C. F. Z. Boukydis (New York: Plenum, 1985), pp. 307–23.

PAGE 172, EVIDENCE FROM OTHER LABORATORIES: Mice from three related strains differ in motor activity during the pre- and perinatal periods. See N. Kodama, "Behavioral Development and Strain Differences in Perinatal Mice," *Journal of Comparative Psychology* 107 (1993):91–98.

PAGE 173, POSSESS AN EXCITABLE AMYGDALA: L. LaGasse, C. Gruber, and L. P. Lipsitt,

"The Infantile Expression of Avidity in Relation to Later Assessments," in *Perspectives on Behavioral Inhibition*, ed. J. S. Reznick (Chicago: University of Chicago Press, 1989), pp. 159–76.

PAGE 173, NINE-MONTH-OLDS: A. P. Matheny, M. L. Reise, and R. S. Wilson, "Rudiments of Infant Temperament," *Developmental Psychology* 21 (1985):486–94; M. L. Reise, "Temperamental Stability Between the Neonatal Period and 24 Months," *Developmental Psychology* 23 (1987):216–22.

PAGE 173, LATER IN THE FIRST YEAR: G. W. Bronson, "Infants' Reactions to Unfamiliar Persons and Objects," *Monograph of the Society for Research in Child Development* 37 (1972), no. 3. An independent longitudinal study of newborns followed to the preschool years revealed that males who were irritable as newborns were subdued as two- to three-year-olds. See R. K. Yang and C. F. Halverson, "A Study of the Inversion of Intensity Between Newborn and Preschool Age Children," *Child Development* 47 (1976):350–59.

PAGE 173, IN THE FIRST OR SECOND YEAR: C. van den Boom, "Neonatal Irritability and the Development of Attachment," in *Temperament in Childhood*, ed. G. A. Kohnstamm, J. E. Bates, and M. K. Rothbart (New York: Wiley, 1989), pp. 299–318.

PAGE 174, EACH FOUR-MONTH-OLD INFANT: The four-month batteries were slightly different for Cohorts 1 and 2; the following description is for Cohort 2. The mother first looked down at the infant for one minute, smiling, and then moved to a chair out of the infant's sight. The examiner placed a speaker baffle with a schematic face attached to the front surface to the right and about ten inches from the infant's face, and the infant heard a tape recording of a woman speaking eight different sentences, each about six seconds long, with five seconds of silence between each utterance. For example, one of the sentences was, "Hello, baby, how are you today?" The speaker was removed, and the examiner, standing in back of the infant, moved a series of mobiles back and forth in front of the infant's face. One mobile had a single colorful toy, the second mobile had three toys, and the third mobile had seven colorful objects. Each mobile was moved back and forth for twenty seconds, and each mobile was shown three times (for a total of nine trials). The examiner then presented a cotton swab, which had been dipped either in water or in dilute butyl alcohol, to the infant's nostrils for five seconds. The swab was dipped in water on the first trial, in butyl alcohol for trials 2, 3, and 4, and on the final trial in water again. The speaker baffle was again placed in front of the infant, who now heard a female voice speaking three different syllables (*ma, pa, ga*) at three different loudnesses, for a total of nine trials. The examiner then popped a balloon about three inches behind the child's head. Finally, the mother returned and stood in front of her child once again, smiling but not talking, for one minute.

PAGE 175, UNHAPPY FACIAL EXPRESSION: We computed a quantitative index of each child's motor activity by summing the occurrence of movements of both arms, both legs, and hyperextension of the arms or legs; each such occurrence was awarded one point. In addition, each occurrence of bursts of both arms or legs (two or more movements in quick succession) or arching of the back was awarded two points. Movements of the legs—flexing, extending, and kicking—made the largest contribution to the motor activity score; arching of the back and arm movements occurred less often.

The index of crying was the number of seconds the child cried across the battery (mean was eight seconds). An index of fretting and fussing was the number of trials on which these two responses occurred (mean was seven). The indexes of vocalization and crying were also based on the number of trials on which each response occurred (mean for vocalization was twelve trials; mean for smiling was one trial).

PAGE 175, WERE CALLED HIGH REACTIVE: Only 10–15 percent of infants displayed an extreme distress reaction to a heel stick during the opening days of life and to an inoculation at two months. The authors noted that only these high reactive newborns remained highly reactive at two months, supporting the idea of a category of infant. See J. Worobey and M. Lewis, "Individual Differences in the Reactivity of Young Infants," *Developmental Psychology* 25 (1989):663–67.

PAGE 176, MADE BY DIFFERENT CODERS: The high reactive infants had significantly higher scores than the low reactives on every one of the motor activity and irritability variables ($p < .001$ for most comparisons). For example, the mean score for leg movements was 35 for high reactives and 19 for low reactives; for arching of the back, 6.3 for high reactives compared with 2.2 for low reactives; for duration of crying, 13.3 seconds for high reactives and 0.7 seconds for low reactives; and for extreme spasticity, 4.0 for high reactives and 1.5 for low reactives. Typically, the high reactives had values two to three times those of the low reactives.

PAGE 177, LIMBIC FUNCTION BY FOUR MONTHS: Maureen Rezendes, who observed a small group of infants at seven, ten, thirteen, and sixteen weeks, discovered major changes in motor behavior and crying between ten and thirteen weeks of age. Attentive parents also recognize an increase in motor activity and a dramatic decrease in irritability between two and four months. Less obvious to parents are the decreases in asymmetric facial grimaces, mediated by brain stem activity, and the enhanced parasympathetic influence on the heart. As we shall see, the behavioral profiles at four months, after this transition, were better predictors of the two temperamental profiles in the second year than was behavior at eight weeks.

PAGE 177, THESE STRESSFUL EVENTS: M. Lewis, personal communication, 1992.

PAGE 178, RATHER THAN DIFFERENCES IN TEMPERAMENT: A description of the batteries at nine, fourteen, and twenty-one months follows.

Nine-Month Battery

(1) The child and mother played together in a small room, in order to acclimate the child to the testing situation.

(2) The examiner entered and placed electrodes for the recording of heart rate on the child's body.

(3) The child was then placed in a seat and a one-minute, quiet, resting heart rate was gathered.

(4) The examiner brought in an open metal wheel. She spun it for six trials, each thirty seconds in duration. On the first trial, there were no objects in the wheel. For trials 2–5, she added an increasing number of plastic objects, so that when the wheel spun, it made noise. On the sixth trial, the wheel was empty.

(5) The mother then sat in the chair the examiner had occupied and presented a

moving toy dinosaur to the child on two trials. On the first trial, she smiled as she presented the toy. On the second trial, she assumed a frown on her face.

(6) The mother and child then went into an adjoining room, and the child was put in a highchair. The child saw the following sequence for seven trials. In the right half of the visual field, a pair of lights alternated, and several seconds later a toy bear appeared on the left side banging a drum.

(7) The child then saw one of a pair of puppets made of papier-mâché alternately in the right or left half of the visual field. One puppet had a painted smile; the other a painted frown. As the puppet appeared, the child heard a nonsense syllable spoken by a female voice in a friendly tone (to accompany the smiling puppet) or a stern, angry tone (to accompany the puppet with the frown). This was repeated for ten trials.

(8) The child and mother then returned to the original testing room. The child saw a toy car roll down an incline and strike a pile of blocks on five trials.

(9) The examiner then uncovered a rotating toy and after a fixed interval smiled and spoke a nonsense syllable in a friendly voice. On the next trial, she uncovered a different rotating toy but this time frowned and issued the same nonsense syllable with a stern, angry voice.

(10) A second resting baseline heart rate was obtained.

(11) The examiner then left, and a few seconds later an unfamiliar woman dressed in ordinary street clothes entered and approached the child slowly and quietly. When she was within one foot of the child, she spoke to the child briefly and then left.

(12) The mother, child, and examiner then went to a large playroom in a different part of the building. The child and mother played in the large room with age-appropriate toys for five minutes.

(13) A different unfamiliar woman then entered, holding a small toy. She sat on the rug looking down for one minute; for the second minute she played with the toy; for the third minute she spoke to herself; and for the fourth minute she invited the child to approach and play with her toy. The stranger then left.

(14) A radio-controlled car was then placed on the rug and was moved about on the rug for thirty seconds.

(15) The examiner then entered with a small robot and invited the child to approach it.

Battery at Fourteen Months

(1) The child and mother were brought to the same small testing room and played for five minutes.

(2) The examiner then entered and placed electrodes on the child.

(3) One minute of quiet, resting heart rate was taken.

(4) One minute of heart rate was taken while the child was standing.

(5) The same wheel used at nine months was presented again for a total of six trials.

(6) A blood pressure cuff was placed on the child's right arm, and two sitting and two standing blood pressures were obtained.

(7) The examiner then displayed each of six acts and invited the child to imitate her.

On three of the six trials, the examiner put her finger into a small container containing either water, red fluid, or black fluid and invited the child to do the same.

(8) The examiner requested that the child accept on his tongue a drop of water. On the next three trials a sweet solution was used, and on the final three trials a solution of dilute lemon juice.

(9) The examiner then uncovered the same rotating toy used at nine months. For the first two trials, she smiled and uttered the nonsense syllable with a friendly voice. On the second two trials, she frowned and uttered the nonsense syllable with a stern voice.

(10) Sitting and standing baseline heart rates were then obtained.

(11) The examiner then left, and an unfamiliar woman dressed in a white laboratory coat and wearing a gas mask approached. She silently walked toward the child, and when she was within one foot of the child, she spoke and then left.

(12) The child was then taken to the adjoining testing room and saw the same puppet procedure that was used at nine months.

(13) The child and mother were then taken to the same large playroom used at nine months and allowed to play for five minutes.

(14) A stranger entered, and the procedure used at nine months was repeated.

(15) The stranger then rose and went to a corner of the room and opened a cabinet containing a large metal robot. After revealing the robot, the examiner stood for one minute quietly and then invited the child to approach her. The stranger then left.

(16) Several seconds later she returned wearing a black cloth over her head and shoulders. She was quiet for one minute and then invited the child to approach her.

Battery at Twenty-one Months

(1) Initially, the child and mother were taken to a small room they had never visited before and left alone for five minutes. The room contained five unfamiliar objects—a large black box with a hole, some chimes hanging from the ceiling, a piece of wood shaped in the form of a trapezoid, a small stool that if climbed would allow the child to stand on a cabinet, and a Hallowe'en mask attached to a post. After five minutes, the examiner entered and carried out a specific action with each of the five objects named above and invited the child to imitate her.

(2) The mother, child, and examiner then went to the small testing room that had been used at nine and fourteen months, and the mother and infant were allowed to acclimate for five minutes. The examiner then entered and placed electrodes on the child's body.

(3) Baseline sitting and standing heart rates were gathered as they were at fourteen months.

(4) Sitting and standing blood pressures were then obtained, as they were at fourteen months.

5) The examiner then administered a sharp, loud, high rising sound intended to startle the child.

(6) The examiner then brought in the same wheel that had been used at nine and

fourteen months, and the child was exposed to five trials; for trials 1 and 5 the wheel was empty; for trials 2, 3, and 4 plastic objects were placed in the wheel.

(7) The examiner then administered the same sequence of plain water, sweet water, and dilute lemon juice as described for the fourteen-month battery.

(8) The examiner invited the child to imitate some block constructions. For trials 1 and 2 the constructions were easy, and the child was successful. For trials 3 and 4 the constructions were difficult (only two children were able to complete them). After a fixed period of time during which the child was unsuccessful, the examiner frowned and said in a stern voice, "Oh no, (child's name), oh no." The child was then given a fifth trial with an easy block construction, which all children completed.

(9) A second startle stimulus was administered.

(10) The examiner then dipped a cotton swab in butyl alcohol and placed it under the child's nose on three trials.

(11) Sitting and standing baseline heart rates and sitting and standing blood pressures were obtained as at fourteen months.

(12) The mother and child were then brought to the same large playroom used at nine and fourteen months and allowed to play for five minutes.

(13) A stranger entered repeating the procedure described at the two earlier stages.

(14) After the stranger left, a woman dressed in a red clown costume and wearing a red-and-white mask entered. The clown spoke as she entered, and after thirty seconds of talking, she invited the child to approach her.

(15) Finally, after the clown left, the examiner returned with a radio-controlled metal robot. The robot was silent for the first minute, then began to issue lights, sounds, and movement, and the examiner invited the child to approach and touch the robot. The intercoder reliability for the scoring of fear was 0.89.

PAGE 178, IN MORE THAN TWO-THIRDS OF THE CHILDREN: John Rosicky of the University of Oregon has found that only 20–30 percent of one-year-olds display fear across a variety of discrepant events. See J. Rosicky, "The Assessment of Temperamental Fearfulness in Infancy" (paper presented at a meeting of the Society for Research in Child Development, New Orleans, March 1992).

PAGE 179, THE STRANGER, THE ROBOT, AND THE CLOWN: Reluctance to imitate the examiner when she put her hand in the cups of clear, red, or black liquid was coded as an avoidant fear because it implied apprehension over an action that may have been punished at home. Fear was coded only if the child failed to imitate the examiner on all three trials, not just one trial.

PAGE 179, FOR THE TWO COHORTS AT THE THREE AGES: The sample seen at nine months in Cohort 2 was smaller because the data from Cohort 1 revealed that this age did not provide a sensitive index of fear. The sample at twenty-one months is 20 percent smaller than the one at fourteen months because we did not assess some distressed and aroused infants as a result of a heavy testing schedule. Thus, the different sample sizes are not due to differences in parental willingness to cooperate.

PAGE 179, For table 6.2 the standard deviations for the fear scores were 1.9 at nine months and 2.3 at fourteen and twenty-one months.

PAGE 180, THIS FEARFUL REACTION OVER THE NEXT SIX MONTHS: There is also an increase in fear to other unfamiliar events between ten and twelve months (see J. L. Jacobson, "Cognitive Determinants of Wariness Toward Unfamiliar Peers," *Developmental Psychology* 16 [1980]:347–54) and to the perception of lack of control over an event (see M. R. Gunnar, "Control, Warning Signals, and Distress in Infancy," *Developmental Psychology* 16 [1980]:281–89).

PAGE 182, THE STABILITY AND PREDICTABILITY OF FEAR: A total of 95 children from Cohort 1 and 209 children from Cohort 2 were observed at all three ages—nine, fourteen, and twenty-one months. A total of 364 Cohort 2 children were observed at both fourteen and twenty-one months. Because Cohort 2 was much larger than Cohort 1, we will concentrate on this group in the presentation of results; the results were very similar for the two cohorts.

PAGE 182, CONTINUED HIGH FEAR AT FOURTEEN AND TWENTY-ONE MONTHS: A total of twelve of the twenty Cohort 2 children who showed high fear at nine months also showed high fear at fourteen and twenty-one months; only two showed low fear. Two-thirds of the Cohort 1 children with high fear at nine months also showed high fear at fourteen months.

PAGE 183, INTERMEDIATE LEVELS OF FEAR AT EACH AGE: Analysis of variance of the fear scores was significant at each age ($F = 13.5$, $p < .001$ at nine months; $F = 36.2$, $p < .001$ at fourteen months; $F = 8.4$, $p < .01$ at twenty-one months). There was no significant sex difference at any age, but a significant reactivity by sex interaction at twenty-one months ($F = 3.4$, $p < .05$). Post hoc t tests revealed that at fourteen months high and low reactives were significantly different from distressed and aroused groups ($p < .01$). Of course, high and low reactive infants were significantly different from one another at every age ($t = 5.1$, $t = 10.0$, $t = 4.4$ at nine, fourteen, and twenty-one months). Most children were seen at both fourteen and twenty-one months; hence, an analysis of the relation of the four-month reactive categories to fear over this interval is instructive. Over one-third of the high reactives showed high fear at both ages, compared with 4 percent who showed low fear. By contrast, 39 percent of the low reactives were low fear and 10 percent high fear at fourteen and twenty-one months. The other two groups were intermediate.

PAGE 184, AND ONLY 10 PERCENT LOW REACTIVE: Chi square $= 51.0$, $p < .0001$.

PAGE 184, HIGH FEAR AT ALL THREE AGES: It is probably not a coincidence that a longitudinal study of over one hundred French infants followed from birth to the middle of the second year revealed that 8 percent were extremely shy and fearful at eighteen months—a value that is very close to the 7 percent of Cohort 2 who were highly fearful at all three ages. See S. A. Dargassies, *The Neuromotor and Psychoaffective Development of the Infant* (Amsterdam: Elsevier, 1986).

PAGE 184, HIGH RATHER THAN LOW REACTIVE: Had we used only the quantitative frequencies, and not the reactivity categories, the infants who received high motor and cry scores would have shown more fearful behavior than those with low values. A regression equation that used these quantitative indexes of motor activity and irritability to predict fearful behavior resulted in a significant multiple correlation. But prediction from the linear regression was a little less powerful than the prediction based on the categorical judgments of reactivity.

PAGE 187, BETWEEN THE TWO TYPES OF FEARS: r = .38, .29, .13 at nine, fourteen, and twenty-one months, respectively.

PAGE 187, USE THE TOTAL FEAR SCORE: The stability correlations for distress and avoidant fears were just a bit lower than those for the total fear score (0.34 for avoidant fears and 0.37 for distress fears, compared with 0.44 for all fears across the period between fourteen and twenty-one months).

PAGE 187, FOR DISTRESS THAN FOR AVOIDANT FEARS: Goldsmith and Campos also report that distress cries to a stranger or to the visual cliff are not associated with avoidance behavior to these events in a volunteer group of nine-month-old infants. See H. H. Goldsmith and J. J. Campos, "The Structure of Temperamental Fear and Pleasure in Infants," *Child Development* 61 (1990):1944–64. The distinction between the two kinds of fears was least obvious at nine months, primarily because many children were not capable of locomotion and avoidant fears were infrequent. Nonetheless, even at this early age, the largest difference in fearful behavior between high and low reactive infants involved distress fears to prohibition (30 versus 13 percent), puppets (17 versus 5 percent), lights (17 versus 2 percent), the mother frowning (17 versus 3 percent), and the approach of a stranger (13 versus 2 percent).

The difference in distress fears between high and low reactive groups was greatest at fourteen months, especially to the stranger who entered the playroom with a black cloth over her head (27 percent of the high reactives cried, compared with 2 percent of the low reactive children), prohibition (55 versus 18 percent) and puppets (45 versus 13 percent). The episode that best differentiated the high from the low reactive infants at twenty-one months was the clown (29 percent of high reactives versus 9 percent of low reactives cried in fear to the clown). But, as we have noted, the difference between the two groups was minimal for avoidance fear of the stranger with the black cover (27 versus 32 percent) and the robot (49 versus 36 percent) at fourteen months; and, at twenty-one months, the clown (30 versus 37 percent) and the robot (23 versus 27 percent).

PAGE 191, FROM THESE TWO CATEGORIES: Only eight inhibited three-year-olds had been high reactive at four months; the others belonged to one of the other three categories. Only fourteen uninhibited three-year-olds had been classified as low reactive at four months.

PAGE 193, OF THOSE WHO SHOWED LOW FEAR: In addition, only 36 percent of the mothers of low reactives who became fearful indicated that they regarded obedience as a highly desirable quality when their child was older, compared with 61 percent of the low reactive children who showed low fear.

PAGE 195, 6 PERCENT OF LOW REACTIVE BOYS: A very small number of children had scores that were very deviant from their expected fear scores. Only four high reactives had zero or one fear at fourteen and twenty-one months (three boys and one girl), and only six low reactives had four or more fears at both ages (four girls and two boys). The motor and cry scores of these children were not different from those of the rest of the infants in their respective categories. Thus, their unexpected behavior in the second year could not have been predicted from their four-month reactions. Even facial width was not deviant; two of the four high reactives with low fear had narrow faces. Gender was the best predictor of these anomalous fear scores and in a direction that would be expected.

PAGES 195–96, MEAN OF LESS THAN TWO FEARS AT TWENTY-ONE MONTHS: Four percent of the children in Cohort 2 seen at fourteen and twenty-one months showed no fears at both ages; eight were low reactive boys, but only three were low reactive girls. Among the seventy children who showed either no fears or one fear at both fourteen and twenty-one months (20 percent of the group) 41 percent were low reactive boys; the remaining children were distributed among the other seven groups (combination of two genders by four reactive groups). Chance dictates that 12.5 percent of each of the eight groups should contain consistently low fear children.

PAGE 196, IS LESS FREQUENT IN BOYS: R. J. Rose and W. B. Ditto, "The Developmental Genetic Analysis of Common Fears from Early Adolescence to Early Adulthood," *Child Development* 54 (1983):361–68. See also Y. Wang et al., "An Epidemiological Study of Behavior Problems in School Children in Urban Areas of Beijing," *Journal of Child Psychology and Psychiatry* 30 (1989):907–12; E. Gullone and N. J. King, "The Fears of Youth in the 1990s," *Journal of Genetic Psychology* 154 (1993): 137–53.

PAGE 196, ANXIETY DISORDERS WERE LESS COMMON IN MALES THAN IN FEMALES: M. Rutter et al., "Research Report: Isle of Wight Study," *Psychological Medicine* 6 (1976): 313–32.

PAGE 196, ALARM CALLS TO THREAT THAN FEMALES. L. J. Crepau and J. D. Newman, "Gender Differences in Reactivity of Adult Squirrel Monkeys to Short Term Environmental Challenges," *Neuroscience and Biobehavioral Reviews* 15 (1991): 469–71.

PAGE 196, TO THREAT THAN DO FEMALES: D. C. Blanchard et al., "Sex Effects in Defensive Behavior," *Neuroscience and Biobehavioral Reviews*, in press.

PAGE 197, PLAY OF FEMALE PUPS: M. J. Meaney, A. M. Dodge, and W. W. Beatty, "Sex Dependent Effects of Amygdalar Lesions on the Social Play of Prepubertal Rats," *Physiology and Behavior* 26 (1981):467–72. The corticomedial and basolateral areas of the amygdala have receptors for androgens; their activity is apt to be different for the sexes.

PAGE 197, HIGH OR LOW IN FEAR OF THE UNFAMILIAR: R. B. Jones, A. D. Mills, and J. M. Faure, "Genetic and Experiential Manipulation of Fear Related Behavior in Japanese Quail Chicks (Coturnix Japonica)," *Journal of Comparative Psychology* 105 (1991): 15–24.

PAGE 198, THAN AMONG HIGH REACTIVE INFANTS: $t = 2.17$, $p < .05$ for smiling; $t = 2.31$, $p < .05$ for vocalizing.

PAGE 198, MODERATE OR HIGH FEAR AT BOTH AGES: $t = 2.75$, $p < .01$.

PAGE 198, FOUR OR MORE TRIALS WERE LOW REACTIVE BOYS: The Cohort 1 boys also smiled more than the girls at four months, and more low than high reactive infants smiled frequently at both two and four months.

PAGE 198, EASE OF BECOMING AROUSED: Not even crying at four months had a high predictive relation to fear ($r = .16$ for fear at fourteen months; $r = .04$ for fear at twenty-one months).

PAGE 198, STRIA TERMINALIS AND THE SEPTUM: In squirrel monkeys, purring and chattering calls, which reflect a self-confident, challenging attitude, are controlled by the stria; calls of alarm which accompany flight and fear, are mediated by the ventral amygdalofugal fibre bundle. See U. Jurgens, "Amygdalar Pathways in the Squirrel Monkey," *Brain Research* 241 (1982):189–96.

PAGE 199, AT NINE, FOURTEEN, AND TWENTY-ONE MONTHS: A rating of one reflected little or no vocalizing or smiling, typically fewer than four smiles and fewer than six vocalizations. A rating of two reflected five to ten smiles and seven to fifteen vocalizations; these responses had to occur on at least two episodes. A rating of three reflected frequent smiling and vocalization; these responses had to occur on more than half of the episodes. Smiling and vocalization increased for all children between nine and fourteen months and for some children between fourteen and twenty-one months. As at four months, vocalization and smiling were only modestly associated ($r = 0.3$).

PAGE 200–201, AND ONLY 16 PERCENT WERE INFREQUENT: Chi square = 3.8, $p < .05$.

PAGE 201, THE MORE SMILING, THE LESS FEAR: The correlation between smiling and fear was −.30 at fourteen months and −.32 at twenty-one months ($p < .001$), and smiling was moderately stable from fourteen to twenty-one months ($r = .26$, $p < .001$). Smiling in the second year also differentiated, within the high and low reactive groups, between the children who were highly fearful and those who were minimally fearful. Within high reactives, smiling at twenty-one months differentiated those with high fear at both fourteen and twenty-one months from those with low fear ($t = 2.2$, $p < .05$). Within the low reactives, smiling at both fourteen and twenty-one months differentiated between those with low fear at both ages compared with those with moderate or high fear ($t = 2.1$, $p < .05$ at fourteen months; $t = 2.4$, $p < .01$ at twenty-one months).

PAGE 201, DOUR, SERIOUS, AND FEARFUL AS THEY GROW: It is of interest that the administration of clonodine, a drug that increases the activity of norepinephrine in the brain of ten-day-old rats, leads to an increase in distress vocalizations. But administration of the same drug one week later, when the rats are seventeen days old, leads to a marked decrease in distress calls. We have noted that high reactive infants showed frequent distress at four months but in the second year were subdued and serious. One week in the life of a rat is comparable to about one year in the human infant. Both the excessive distress at four months and the later affective restraint in the second year could be due to higher norepinephrine levels in the brain. See P. Kehoe, "Ontogeny of Adrenergic and Opioid Effects on Separation Vocalization in Rats," in *The Physiological Control of Mammalian Vocalization*, ed. J. D. Newman (New York: Plenum, 1988), pp. 301–20.

PAGE 201, SANGUINE AND MELANCHOLIC TEMPERAMENTAL TYPES: It is of interest that an observational study of American and Israeli children, aged two to fifteen years, who were either high or low in frequency of smiling in response to the smile of an examiner revealed that the mothers of the infrequent smilers also smiled infrequently during social interaction and were less affectively expressive than the mothers of children who smiled frequently. See Y. E. Babad, I. E. Alexander, and E. A. Babad, "Returning the Smile of the Stranger," *Monographs of the Society for Research in Child Development* 48 (1983), no. 5.

PAGE 201, WERE LOW REACTIVE, SHOWED LOW FEAR, AND SMILED FREQUENTLY: The variable was the ratio of the width of the face at the bizygomatic (high cheekbone) to the length of the face. Most fourteen-month-old infants had ratios between .51 and .59, with a mean of .56. High reactives had significantly smaller ratios than low reactives; infrequent smilers (at fourteen and twenty-one months) had smaller fourteen-month ratios than frequent smilers. Low reactive frequent smilers had a mean ratio of .57, compared with .52 for high reactive infrequent smilers ($t = 3.20$, $p < .01$). When we limited the comparison to those with very narrow faces at fourteen months (ratio ≤ .50), compared with those with very broad faces (ratio ≥ .60), each group making up about 20 percent of the entire cohort, the former had higher fear scores at fourteen months ($t = 3.00$, $p < .05$) and at twenty-one months ($t = 3.12$, $p < .01$) and lower smile ratings at fourteen months ($t = 2.18$, $p < .05$) and twenty-one months ($t = 2.15$, $p < .05$). When we restricted the analysis to the ten children with the narrowest (ratio ≤ .46) versus the ten with the broadest (ratio ≥ .65) at fourteen months (each is 3.5 percent of the sample), 40 percent of the former were high fear at both fourteen and twenty-one months, compared with no child in the broad-faced group.

PAGE 203, STRAINS THAT ARE FAR LESS VULNERABLE: W. R. Thompson, "The Inheritance of Behavior," *Canadian Journal of Psychology,* 7 (1953):145–55; B. E. Walker and F. C. Fraser, "The Embryology of Cortisone Induced Cleft Palate," *The Journal of Embryology and Experimental Morphology* 5 (1957):201–9.

PAGE 205, HOMES WHERE THE MOTHERS VALUED OBEDIENCE: Thirty-eight percent of the children with low fear at fourteen and twenty-one months had mothers who ranked obedience in ranks 1 through 6, compared with 26 percent of the mothers of children with moderate or high fear (total $N = 362$; chi square = 4.9, $p < .05$).

PAGES 205–6, "NOT SPARE HIM IN YOUTH": M. de Montaigne, *Essays* (Harmondsworth, Eng.: Penguin, [1580] 1958), p. 58.

PAGE 206, IN DIFFERENT WAYS: Analogous interactions are often found in two strains of animals who are cross-fostered to a mother of a different strain. The treatment will affect one strain but not the other. See S. C. Maxson and A. Trattner, "Interaction of Genotype and Fostering in the Development of Behavior of DBA and C57 Mice," *Behavior Genetics* 11 (1981):153–65.

CHAPTER SEVEN: *Infant Reactivity and Sympathetic Physiology*

PAGE 208, NOT OF DIRECT INTEREST: Adult men and women differ in the relation of heart rate and blood pressure to different types of stressors, and women show a faster latency to peak muscle tension in the heart than do men. See B. E. Hurwitz et al., "Differential Patterns of Dynamic Cardiovascular Regulation as a Function of Task," *Biological Psychology* 36 (1993):75–95.

PAGE 209, DISCORDANT WITH THE FACTS: The suggestion that brain processes and psychological states interact finds support in work with animals. The superior colliculus is a collection of neurons that receives visual information from the retina and passes it on to the thalamus and cortex. Some neurons in the superior colliculus also respond to sounds, however. If a cat hears a tone in a lighted room, a proportion of neurons in the colliculus will respond to the tone. But after a blindfold is placed over the cat's eyes so that it cannot see any light, the neurons that responded earlier to the tone do not respond at all. That is, the response of these neurons to the tone depends on the state created by the visual input. Put differently, the reaction to a particular stimulus depends on the state of the brain at the time a new stimulus arrives. If high reactive or inhibited children are in different physiological states when they are in an unfamiliar place, the new event may lead to a special response in inhibited children that does not occur in uninhibited children. See B. E. Stein and M. A. Meredith, *The Merging of the Senses* (Cambridge, Mass.: MIT Press, 1993).

PAGE 209, THOUGHT, FEELINGS, AND PERIPHERAL PHYSIOLOGY: H. Weiner, *Perturbing the Organism* (Chicago: University of Chicago Press, 1992). See also R. Hoehn-Saric and D. R. McLeod, "The Peripheral Sympathetic Nervous System," *Psychiatric Clinics of North America* 11 (1988):375–86; G. Burnstock and C. H. V. Hoyle, *Autonomic Neuroeffector Mechanisms* (Paris: Harwood, 1992). The latter authors point out that autonomic neurons can release, in addition to norepinephrine, several transmitters and they are influenced by peptides as well. Further, it has been discovered that subpopulations of cells involving sympathetic targets are chemically coded with a high degree of specificity. Hence, local circuits, almost like reflexes, influence sympathetic organs like the heart with little or no central control. These are autonomous circuits. See L. G. Elfvin, B. Lindh, and T. Hokfelt, "The Chemical Neuroanatomy of Sympathetic Ganglia," *Annual Review of Neuroscience* 16 (1993):471–507.

PAGE 210, IN A MAJOR WAY BETWEEN TWO AND FOUR MONTHS: R. M. Harper et al., "Polygraphic Studies of Normal Infants During the First Six Months of Life," *Pediatric Research* 10 (1976):945–51.

PAGE 210, DECREASES IN CRYING: M. O. Rezendes, "Behavioral and Autonomic Transitions in Early Infancy" (Ph.D. diss., Harvard University, 1993).

PAGES 210–11 FEW WEEKS BEFORE BIRTH: Mean of 145 bpm for high reactives versus 135 bpm for low reactives ($p < .10$). Sixty-three percent of low reactives (fifteen of twenty-four) had fetal heart rates below the median of the whole group, compared with 18 percent (two of eleven) of high reactives (chi square = 5.9; $p < .05$).

PAGE 211, WHILE BEING HELD ERECT BY THE MOTHER: High reactives had a mean of 149 bpm versus 144 bpm for low reactives ($F = 5.1$, $p < .05$). Every high reactive infant with adequate data had a two-week sleep heart rate equal to or higher than 140 bpm, compared with 60 percent of the low reactives ($p < .01$ by the Exact Test). In addition, 45 percent of the high reactives, compared with 28 percent of low reactives, were also above the median value for the sleep heart rate at two months. Finally, every high reactive had a mean sleep heart rate across the data gathered at two weeks and two months greater than 135 bpm, compared with only one-half of the low reactives.

PAGE 211, TO CARDIAC FUNCTION: There are two major peaks in the heart rate spectrum. One is a high frequency peak, parasympathetic in origin, that occurs once every two seconds and is associated with breathing. This parasympathetic activity increases in magnitude over the first six months of life and centers at about 0.25 Hz in older children. The low frequency peak, which occurs about twice per minute, represents fluctuations in vasomotor tone associated with cyclical changes in blood pressure and temperature. The low frequency band, which is more constant over age and centers at about 0.04 Hz, is primarily under sympathetic control, especially when the child is in an erect posture, but it is monitored by both sympathetic and parasympathetic activity when the child is supine or sitting.

We identified for each sample of heart rate the two boundary frequencies from the respiratory peak in the spectrum of the respiratory wave form and calculated the power between these two frequencies. We shall call the power in this band vagal or parasympathetic power. We shall call the power in the low frequency band, from 0.02 to 0.10 Hz, sympathetic power.

PAGE 211, AT BOTH TWO WEEKS AND TWO MONTHS: High reactives had a mean low power value of 13,165 and 12,808, compared with 5,430 and 6,292 for low reactives ($F = 2.9$, $p < .05$ at two weeks. $F = 4.0$, $p < .05$ at two months).

Panic patients also have more power in the low frequency band of the spectral analysis of heart rate when they are standing, as do the high reactive infants. See V. K. Yeragani et al., "Decreased Heart Rate Variability in Panic Disorder Patients," *Psychiatry Research* 46 (1993):89–103.

PAGE 211, THE MORE FEARFUL THE CHILD WAS AT FOURTEEN AND TWENTY-ONE MONTHS: The correlation between the sympathetic contribution at two weeks and fear at fourteen months was .52 ($p < .001$); the correlation with fear at twenty-one months was .36 ($p < .05$).

PAGE 212, MET BOTH CRITERIA: A high fetal heart rate was defined as a rate > 140 bpm, and high sympathetic power was defined by a value > 11,000. The difference between the high and low reactives was significant at $p < .01$.

PAGE 212, WHO WERE LOW REACTIVE WERE MUCH LESS FEARFUL: A total of twenty-three infants showed one or the other of these two contrasting profiles. The fear scores for twenty-two of the twenty-three infants were in accord with the expectation that the former would show high fear and the latter low or moderate fear. This result is in accord with that of Nathan Fox, who has reported that fourteen-month-olds with high vagal tone were the most sociable, uninhibited children. See N. A. Fox, "Psychophysiological Correlates of Emotional Reactivity During the First Year of Life," *Developmental Psychology* 25 (1989):364–72.

PAGE 212, TO SYMPATHETIC TARGETS: Tiffany Field has reported that alert newborns with high sleeping heart rates show minimal facial expressiveness to an adult displaying expressions of surprise, sadness, and joy. We noted in chapter 4 that high reactives are less expressive facially than low reactives. See T. Field, "Individual Differences in the Expressivity of Neonates and Young Infants," in *Development of Nonverbal Behavior in Children*, ed. R. Feldman (New York: Springer-Verlag, 1982). In addition, newborns with high heart rates cried more during a standard examination than those with low heart rates. See G. Spangler and R. Scheubeck, "Behavioral Organization in Newborns and Its Relation to Adrenocortical and Cardiac Activity," *Child Development* 64 (1993):622–33.

PAGE 212, OTHER INVESTIGATORS HAVE REPORTED SIMILAR RESULTS: The long-term stability of heart rate to challenge is greater than resting heart rate. See J. K. Murphy, B. S. Alpert, and S. S. Walker, "Stability of Ethnic Differences in Children's Pressor Responses During Three Annual Examinations," *American Journal of Hypertension* 4 (1991):630–34. Further, despite the fact that handling infant rat pups permanently alters limbic excitability, handled and nonhandled adult rats differed only in the magnitude of increase in corticosteriods to stress, not in baseline values. See M. J. Meaney et al., "The Effects of Neonatal Handling on the Development of Adrenocortical Response to Stress," *Psychoneuroendocrinology* 16 (1991):85–103.

PAGES 212–13, IN RESPONSE TO OTHER TASTE QUALITIES: J. F. Campbell et al., "Responses of Single Units of the Hypothalamic Ventromedial Nucleus to Environmental Stimuli," *Physiology and Behavior* 4 (1969):183–87.

PAGE 213, FROM THERE TO THE SYMPATHETIC NERVOUS SYSTEM: T. E. Finger, "Gustatory Nuclei and Pathways in the Central Nervous System," in *Neurobiology of Taste and Smell,* ed. T. E. Finger and W. L. Silver (New York: Wiley, 1987), pp. 331–53.

PAGE 213, EXAMINER'S STERN CRITICISM AT TWENTY-ONE MONTHS: The difference between high and low reactives in magnitude of heart rate acceleration to these episodes was significant when differences in baseline heart rate were controlled ($p < .05$ for all three comparisons).

PAGE 213, A MORE REACTIVE SYMPATHETIC NERVOUS SYSTEM THAN DO LOW REACTIVES: A similar conclusion follows from a comparison of two strains of rats (Wistar Kyoto and Brown Norway) on whom plasma levels of epinephrine and norepinephrine were obtained while the animals were undisturbed in their cages—baseline resting—and when they were stressed by shock. The two strains had very similar levels of epinephrine and norepinephrine while unstressed in the cage, but the Wistar Kyoto animals had much higher levels than the Brown Norway rats following shock. Thus, only the values obtained following stress differentiated the two groups. See R. McCarty, R. F. Kirby, and P. G. Garn, "Strain Differences in Sympathetic-Adrenal-Medullary Responsiveness and Behavior," *Behavioral and Neural Biology* 40 (1984):98–113.

PAGE 213, CONFIDENCE IN OUR CONCLUSIONS: The maximal sample sizes are 92 high and 128 low reactives at four months; 66 high and 96 low reactives at nine months; 95 high and 141 low reactives at fourteen months, and 76 high and 121 low reactives at twenty-one months.

PAGES 213–14, AT FOUR AND NINE MONTHS THAN DID LOW REACTIVES: $t = 2.85$, $p < .01$ at four months; $t = 2.03$, $p < .05$ at nine months for low versus high reactive boys. In addition, among boys, more high reactives showed a large drop in heart rate (> 6 bpm) to the first trial of the spoken sentences (chi square = 5.0, $p < .05$), because they were startled by the sudden, unexpected onset of the auditory event (75 percent of high reactive boys versus 46 percent of low reactive boys).

PAGE 214, LACK OF STABILITY OVER AGE: The correlations between the baseline values at four months and succeeding ages ranged from 0.2 to 0.4 for the high reactive infants and 0.1 to 0.2 for the low reactives. The preservation of baseline heart rate from fourteen to twenty-one months was better, especially for girls ($r = 0.5$ for girls and 0.2 for boys). The cross age stability of heart rate to selected challenging episodes was similar.

PAGE 214, HIGHER AND LESS VARIABLE BASELINE HEART RATE AT TWENTY-ONE THAN AT FOURTEEN MONTHS: Forty-two percent of the high reactives had a higher baseline heart rate at twenty-one than at fourteen months (chi square = 3.7, $p < .10$). The measure of variability was the standard deviation of all of the heart periods during the one-minute epoch. The larger the number, the greater the vagal or parasympathetic influence on the heart. This measure was only modestly associated with absolute heart rate (*r* averaged 0.4), with lower rates always associated with a more variable heart rate.

PAGE 214, SERIES OF DIFFERENT COGNITIVE STRESSORS: D. W. Johnston, P. Anastasiadis, and C. Wood, "The Relationship Between Cardiovascular Responses in the Laboratory and in the Field," *Psychophysiology* 27 (1990):34–44.

PAGE 214, FEAR FROM ANGER THAN DID MEAN VALUES: A. F. Ax, "The Physiological Differentiation between Fear and Anger in Humans," *Psychosomatic Medicine* 15 (1953): 433–42.

PAGES 214–15, THAN DID THE AVERAGE FREQUENCY: J. D. Newman, "The Primate Isolation Call in the Evolution and Physiological Control of Human Speech," in *Language Origins*, ed. J. Wind (Boston: Kluwer, 1992) pp. 301–21.

PAGE 215, FROM THE FIFTY FEVERED PATIENTS: If an investigator measured the height of one thousand children who were either ten, eleven, twelve, thirteen, or fourteen years old, he would find a relatively smooth linear function. By contrast, if he measured the same thousand children once a year across the same four-year period and calculated the largest and smallest annual increase in height, he would find the growth spurt that characterizes adolescence. The first strategy might not reveal the growth spurt as clearly, because children show the spurt at different times during the period between ten and fourteen years. Megan Gunnar of the University of Minnesota collected a large number of samples of saliva from preschool children across a period of several months. The presence of a small number of peak values of salivary cortisol, which was associated with greater intrasubject variability, more clearly differentiated behavioral groups than the average cortisol level of a child across all of his or her samples.

PAGE 215, Magnusson, "Back to Phenomena."

PAGE 216, THIS TYPE OF CHILD THAN THE MEAN VALUE: Only about 15 percent of subjects showed large rises in heart rate and blood pressure to stress. J. LeBlanc et al., "Plasma Catecholamines and Cardiovascular Responses to Cold and Mental Activity," *Journal of Applied Physiology* 47 (1979):1207–11.

PAGE 216, RATHER THAN TO THE MORE OBVIOUSLY DISCREPANT PROCEDURES: The nature of the episode had a more potent effect on cardiac activity than did the infant's reactivity or sex. Each battery contained a number of psychologically discrepant procedures (the mother frowning at the infant, the examiner speaking in a stern voice, a puppet appearing accompanied by a voice with a harsh tone, an unfamiliar woman in a white laboratory coat and gas mask approaching the child). Most of the time, these unexpected, unfamiliar events did not produce maximal heart rates. We ranked the five episodes at fourteen and twenty-one months that produced the highest heart rates in most of the children through acceleration. At fourteen months, these were the sweet and sour tastes, the wheel, the stranger, and the puppets; At twenty-one months, they were the sweet and sour tastes, the wheel, criticism during the block task, and the sudden loud noise. Differences among the children in average resting heart rate are not of relevance, because the ranking of the five highest rates was performed within each child's protocol.

The sweet and sour tastes produced the highest heart rates in over 90 percent of the children; the noisy wheel was also effective in producing high heart rates in a large number of children. Neither the tastes nor the wheel are, strictly speaking, unfamiliar stressors that generate a great deal of fear. Many more children became wary when the examiner criticized them for not modelling the difficult block construction, but 40 percent of the children showed no important change in heart rate (< 2 bpm) to the examiner's criticism; fewer than 5 percent showed a heart rate change that small to the sweet or sour tastes. The reaction to a drop of dilute lemon juice, which is a biologically optimal incentive for cardiac acceleration, was a better correlate of reactivity at four months than magnitude of heart rate change to criticism or a stranger wearing a white laboratory coat and gas mask.

Most scientists assume, as we did originally, that the state of fear to the unfamiliar should generally be accompanied by a rise in heart rate. But the body is not as closely yoked to the mind as we had assumed. Children as well as adults differ in how well they can cope with a psychological intrusion. If an animal has some control over a stressor (for example, electric shock), there is less sympathetic activation than if the animal can do nothing to prevent the painful event. See A. Tsuda and M. Tanaka, "Differential Changes in Noradrenaline Turnover in Specific Regions of Rat Brain Produced by Controllable and Uncontrollable Shock," *Behavioral Neuroscience* 99 (1985):802–17. Some inhibited children acquire reactions that keep uncertainty under control; as a result, they do not always show a rise in heart rate to challenge or discrepancy. See G. Stemmler, *Differential Psychophysiology* (New York: Springer-Verlag, 1992) for similar conclusions.

PAGE 216, LOWEST QUARTILE FOR BOTH THE MAXIMAL AND MINIMAL HEART RATES: Chi square = 11.6, $p < .01$. For Cohort 1 infants, too, 45 percent of high reactives had high heart values for both the maximal and minimal scores (greater than 164 and 127 bpm); 31 percent of low reactives had low values for both variables (less than 157 and 127 bpm); chi square = 5.0, $p < .05$.

PAGE 217, MEET THE FOUR CRITERIA: The criterion for a low minimal heart rate at four months was a value less than 130 bpm; a high value for the maximal rate was greater than 140 bpm.

PAGE 217, 2 BPM AT BOTH AGES: Chi square = 5.2, $p < .05$. See also G. Bohlin and B. Hagekull, "Stranger Wariness and Sociability in the Early Years," *Infant Behavior and Development 16* (1993):53–67.

PAGE 217, BECAUSE THE MOTHER WAS PRESENT IN THE ROOM: There is a larger increase in heart rate in response to a stranger when the mother is absent. See J. J. Campos et al., "Cardiac and Behavioral Interrelationships in the Reaction of Infants to Strangers," *Developmental Psychology* 11 (1975):589–601.

PAGE 217, LARGE ACCELERATIONS TO THE SOUR TASTE AT FOURTEEN MONTHS: The mean accelerations from the initial baseline were 69 versus 59 msec. for high versus low reactives ($p < .05$). Two-thirds of the high reactive girls had accelerations from the baseline greater than 60 msec. (at least 15 bpm) compared with 41 percent of the low reactive girls. When the acceleration of heart rate was based on the difference between the initial trial, when water was administered, and the trial of highest heart rate to a sour taste, the result was similar: 67 percent of high reactive girls had large accelerations, compared with 37 percent of low reactive girls; these differences controlled for the heart rate to the initial baseline.

PAGE 217, LARGE ACCELERATIONS TO THE SOUR TASTE AT BOTH FOURTEEN AND TWENTY-ONE MONTHS: Chi square = 4.1, $p < .05$. The stability of the maximal heart rate to the sour taste from fourteen to twenty-one months was 0.4. In addition, high reactive girls had larger accelerations to the first appearance of the puppets at fourteen months ($t = 2.23$, $p < 05$). One-quarter of the high reactive girls had accelerations ≥ 6 bpm, compared with 3 percent of the low reactive girls (chi square = 8.0, $p < 01$).

PAGE 218, WAS SIGNIFICANTLY SMALLER FOR LOW THAN FOR HIGH REACTIVE BOYS: Twenty-one percent of low reactives had a mean rate < 110 bpm, compared with 8 percent of high reactives (three boys). The average minimal heart rate across all three ages was 114 bpm for low reactive boys versus 118 for high reactive boys ($t = 2.19$, $p < .05$).

PAGE 218, ESPECIALLY SIGNIFICANT IN RESPONSE TO THE SPOKEN SENTENCES AT FOUR MONTHS: Low reactive boys attained lower minimal heart rates at four months to the sentences ($t = 2.16$, $p < .05$), the syllables ($t = 1.99$, $p < .05$), and butanol ($t = 2.15$, $p < .05$). At nine months low reactive boys had lower heart rates to the wheel ($t = 1.95$, $p < .05$), and to the lights ($t = 2.27$, $p < .01$). See also J. Kagan and J. S. Reznick, "Task Involvement in Cardiac Response in Young Children," *Australian Journal of Psychology* 36 (1984):135–47.

For forty high reactive and forty-two low reactive infants, salivary cortisol was gathered at home on three mornings early in the day when the infants were five months and again when they were seven months of age. The mean cortisol levels at five and seven months, which were only modestly related, were between 3,000 and 6,000 pmol/l for most children. There was no relation between average cortisol level at the two ages and either sex, reactivity, smiling, fear, or heart rate across all eighty-two children. But when the analysis was restricted to low reactive boys, two interesting facts emerged. First, low reactive boys with high cortisol levels had more distress fears than those with low cortisol levels (four of the seven children with high levels had one or more distress fears in the second year compared with only one of seven boys with low cortisol levels). Further, low reactive boys with high cortisol did not attain heart rates as low as those with low cortisol levels. This result was clearest at fourteen months, when four of seven boys with low cortisol had heart rate values greater than 525 msec. (114 bpm), compared with only one of the boys with high cortisol levels. Finally, all seven boys with low cortisol levels were relaxed and much less energetic than the typical low reactive boy. The fact that low cortisol was associated with a lower heart rate is theoretically reasonable, but this relation occurred only in low reactive boys. Thus, the important implication is that no single physiological index has the same meaning across different types of children. It is necessary to examine variation in physiological measures within sex or within sex and reactivity groups. Cortisol levels in healthy young children are influenced by so many different factors that no value has a univocal significance independent of these other constraints.

PAGE 219, THOSE WHO REMAINED MINIMALLY FEARFUL: Twenty-one percent of low reactives with consistently low fear had minimal four-month heart rates (less than 115 bpm), while only one child who increased in fear from fourteen to twenty-one months had a minimal heart rate that low. Among low reactive girls, who more often increased in fear, the thirteen girls who went from low fear at fourteen months to three or more fears at twenty-one months showed a minimal four-month heart rate of 133 bpm; the twenty low reactive girls who remained low fear at both ages had a minimal four-month heart rate of 126 bpm ($t = 1.78$, $p = .08$).

PAGE 219, MORE AVOIDANT FEARS AT FOURTEEN AND TWENTY-ONE MONTHS: The index of variability of heart rate was the standard deviation of the interbeat intervals for the one minute of baseline. Twenty-nine percent of low reactives with a high and stable baseline heart rate at fourteen months had two or more avoidant fears at fourteen months, compared with 7 percent of those with a low and variable heart rate (chi square = 6.9, $p < .01$). Thirty-eight percent of those with a high and stable baseline heart rate at fourteen months had two or more avoidant fears at twenty-one months, compared with 21 percent of those with a low and variable baseline heart rate (chi square = 3.1, $p < .10$). A high stable baseline heart rate as the session begins may reflect a state of heightened uncertainty that contributes to more avoidant fears, but not to more distress fears. This relation holds only among low reactives, however. Support for the claim that heart rate and variability during the baseline reflects a temporary affect state is found in the fact that heart rate variability was not very stable from fourteen to twenty-one months ($r = .34$ for girls and .06 for boys). Thus, most children who were high and stable at fourteen months were not high and stable at twenty-one months.

PAGE 219, IS MORE CLEARLY RELATED TO MOOD: Older children who showed high heart rate variability while watching a film about two boys frightened by a stranger lurking outside the home showed less distress and more obvious facial expressions of interest and concern than those with low heart rate variability. These behavioral qualities are characteristic of uninhibited children; hence, one would expect them to show greater variability of heart rate. See R. A. Fabes, N. Eisenberg, and L. Eisenbud, "Behavioral and Physiological Correlates of Children's Reactions to Others in Distress," *Developmental Psychology* 29 (1993):655–63.

PAGE 220, WERE THE MOST FREQUENT SMILERS IN THE SECOND YEAR: Sixty-one percent of the boys (from all four reactive groups) who were frequent smilers in the second year had low minimal heart rates at four months (< 120 bpm), compared with 25 percent of the infrequent smilers (chi square = 8.2, $p < .01$). This difference also held for each of the reactive groups considered separately. The high vocal boys at fourteen and twenty-one months also had low minimal heart rates at fourteen months compared with the quiet boys ($t = 2.06$, $p < .05$).

PAGE 220, SPOKEN SENTENCES OR SYLLABLES: Chi square = 9.5, $p < .01$; $t = 2.09$, $p < .05$ for the difference between the two groups of boys for the minimal heart rate to sentences. The two groups of girls also differed in minimal heart rate to the female voice speaking syllables ($t = 2.41$, $p < .01$). The low reactive boys who had large differences between the highest and lowest heart rate to the sentences (> 10 bpm) also smiled more at fourteen months than the low reactive boys with smaller difference scores ($t = 2.01$, $p < .05$). Thus, a labile heart reaction to the auditory input was predictive of later smiling, but only for low reactive boys.

PAGE 220, BECAME THE MOST VOCAL AND SMILING CHILDREN IN THE SECOND YEAR: Seventeen boys (from both high and low reactive groups) were given ratings of two or three for vocalization and smiling at both fourteen and twenty-one months, while eight boys were extremely quiet and smiled rarely in the second year (these two groups make up about one-fourth of all the boys). The highly affective boys had significantly lower heart rates at four months than the subdued boys (differences of 8–10 bpm; $t = 2.36$, $p < .05$ at four months).

PAGE 220, THAN DID LOW REACTIVES WHO SMILED INFREQUENTLY: The children classified as smiling infrequently had a rating of one at both fourteen and twenty-one months; the children classified as smiling frequently had a rating of three at both ages, or a rating of two at one age and a rating of three at the other age. We also compared the highest and lowest heart rates of twenty-eight high and low reactive children (7 percent of the cohort) who were the most frequent smilers at fourteen and twenty-one months (seventeen boys and eleven girls) with an equal proportion of boys and girls who were the least frequent smilers at the two ages. One-third of the high smiling boys had low minimal heart rates at both four and twenty-one months, compared with only 10 percent of low smiling boys; there was no comparable difference for girls. Thus, more boys than girls smiled frequently and had low minimal heart rates. This coherence suggests that the central mechanisms that monitor smiling are correlated with those that monitor very low heart rates, but primarily among boys. Even though a low heart rate at four months predicted frequent smiling in the second year, smiling at four months—which was infrequent—was not associated with heart rate at any age.

PAGE 220, WAS LESS STRIKING AMONG THE GIRLS: The seven high reactive girls with consistently high heart rates at all four ages (four, nine, fourteen, and twenty-one months), however, smiled less often at twenty-one months than the seven high reactive girls with consistently low heart rates ($p < .05$ Exact Test). Further, among low reactive girls, the one-third who smiled frequently in the second year had minimal four-month heart rate values to the sentences (< 120 bpm), compared with only 5 percent of the low reactive girls who smiled infrequently (chi square $= 6.0$, $p < .05$). When we created one group of low reactive infants who were also low fear and high smiling at fourteen months and compared them with high reactive infants who had high fear and infrequent smiling, more of the former group had low four-month minimal heart rates (chi square $= 4.7$, $p < .05$) and were less likely to have a higher heart rate at twenty-one than at fourteen months (chi square $= 5.1$, $p < .05$). Thus, the profiles that combined these three qualities were more closely associated with four-month heart rate than any one quality considered alone; 72 percent of the low reactive, low fear, high smiling boys had minimal four-month heart rates under 130 bpm. Finally, we created two extreme groups. One group of thirteen was low reactive, low fear, and high smiling at fourteen months and showed a low four-month heart rate (< 115 bpm). The contrasting group of thirteen children was high reactive, high fear, and infrequent smiling at fourteen months and had a higher minimal heart rate at four months (> 130 bpm). These two groups were significantly different at twenty-one months. The former had a significantly lower minimal heart rate (105 versus 115 bpm; $t = 2.71$, $p < .05$) and vocalized more often ($t = 2.55$, $p < .01$). It will come as no surprise that the former group also had broader faces at fourteen months of age ($t = 2.5$, $p < .05$) (see chapter 6).

PAGE 220, SMILED MORE OFTEN IN THE SECOND YEAR: $t = 2.14$, $p < .05$ for smiling at fourteen months. Recall that variability is the standard deviation of the heart periods during the initial baseline.

PAGE 220, 15 PERCENT WHO SHOWED MINIMAL SMILING: $t = 2.01$, $p < .05$. When we created eight different groups based on a dichotomy of low versus high smiling at fourteen and twenty-one months and a high-stable versus a low-variable baseline heart rate at fourteen months, within low and high reactive children, only infrequent smiling made a contribution to a higher fear score in the second year. Baseline heart rate did not. Of course, reactivity at four months was the most powerful predictor of fear.

PAGE 221, THAN THOSE CHILDREN WHO SMILED INFREQUENTLY: $F = 4.14$, $p < .05$.

PAGE 221, AND A CONSISTENTLY LOW HEART RATE: The specific criteria were a minimal heart rate at four, fourteen, and twenty-one months (< 128, 115, and 110 bpm, respectively), a rating of two or three for smiling at fourteen and twenty-one months, and zero or one fear at 14 and 21 months. Not one high reactive infant met all three of these criteria. By contrast, five high reactive but not one low reactive infant met the complementary criteria of maximal heart rates at four, fourteen, and twenty-one months (> 153, 141, and 133 bpm), a rating of one for smiling, and three or more fears at fourteen and twenty-one months.

PAGES 222–23, THOSE THAT CONTRIBUTE TO REACTIVITY: The thirteen children who were high reactive, low smiling, and high heart rate had the narrowest faces (the ratio was .51 compared with ratios of .55 to .58 for the other groups).

PAGE 223, CERVICAL GANGLION TO THE FACE: P. D. Drummond and J. W. Lance, "Facial Flushing and Sweating Mediated by the Sympathetic Nervous System," *Brain* 110 (1987):793–803.

PAGE 223, PRODUCES SURFACE COOLING: R. H. Fox, R. Goldsmith, and D. J. Kidd, "Cutaneous Vasomotor Control in the Human Head, Neck, and Upper Chest," *Journal of Physiology* (London) 161 (1962):298–312; A. C. Guyton, *Textbook of Medical Physiology*, 6th ed. (Philadelphia: Saunders, 1981).

PAGE 223, VASODILATION AND SURFACE WARMING: L. B. Powell, *Human Circulatory Regulation During Physiological Stress* (New York: Oxford, 1986). The blood supply to the face derives from the external and internal carotid arteries in the form of arterial branches that serve the forehead, eyes, nose, lips, and ears. One of these branches—the frontopolar branch of the interior cerebral artery—serves the forehead; the orbital branch serves the area around the eyes.

PAGE 223, THE HANDS AND FINGERTIPS DO CONTAIN BOTH ALPHA AND BETA RECEPTORS: R. A. Cohen and J. D. Coffman, "Beta-adrenergic Vasodilator Mechanisms in the Finger," *Circulation Research* 49 (1981):1196–1201.

PAGE 223, IN OTHER SYMPATHETIC TARGETS: B. G. Wallin, "Sympathetic Nerve Activity, Underlying Electrodermal and Cardiovascular Reactions in Man," *Psychophysiology* 18 (1981):470–76.

PAGE 223, CHANGE IN EMOTIONAL STATE: K. Mizukami et al., "First Selective Attachment Begins in Early Infancy," *Infant Behavior and Development* 13 (1990):257–72.

PAGE 223, TEMPORARY STATE OF UNCERTAINTY: R. B. Zajonc, S. T. Murphy, and M. Inglehart, "Feeling and Facial Efference," *Psychological Review*, 96 (1989):395–416. These authors have reported that differences in facial temperature are correlated with an adult's self-reported hedonic state.

PAGE 223, DIFFICULT ANAGRAM PROBLEMS: N. L. Braverman, honors thesis, Radcliffe College, 1989. The cooling of the face to the anagrams problem was significant at $p < .05$.

PAGE 224, ADULTS WHO WERE WATCHING A SURGICAL FILM: B. Thyer et al., "Autonomic Correlates of the Subjective Anxiety Scale," *Journal of Behavioral Therapy and Experimental Psychiatry* 15 (1984):5–7.

PAGE 224, OF ABOUT 0.3° C: S. Svebak, O. Starfjell, and K. Dalen, "The Effect of a Threatening Context upon Motivation and Task Induced Physiological Changes," *British Journal of Psychology* 73 (1982):505–12.

PAGE 224, THE FINGER AND FOREHEAD: G. Stemmler, "The Autonomic Differentiation of Emotions Revisited," *Psychophysiology* 26 (1989):617–32; A. Hirota and H. Hirai, "The Effects of Stimulus or Response Oriented Training on Psychophysiological Responses and the Propositional Structure of Imagery, *Japanese Psychological Research* 28 (1986):186–95.

PAGE 224, THE LEFT IS TYPICALLY COOLER THAN THE RIGHT: J. Jamison, "Bilateral Finger Temperature and the Law of Initial Values," *Psychophysiology*, 24 (1987):666–69; K. M. H. Perera, M. R. M. Pinto, and R. Kay, "Surface Body Temperature Differences Between Anxious Patients and Nonanxious Controls," *Biology and Medicine: Physiology, Psychology and Psychiatry: IRCS Medical Sciences* 12 (1984):65–66.

PAGE 224, GREATER ON THE RIGHT THAN ON THE LEFT SIDE: R. J. Davidson and N. A. Fox, "Asymmetric Brain Activity Discriminates Between Positive and Negative Affective Stimuli in Human Infants," *Science*, 218 (1982):1235–37; R. J. Davidson, "Anterior Cerebral Asymmetry and the Nature of Emotion," *Brain and Cognition*, in press; R. J. Davidson et al., "Approach-Withdrawal and Cerebral Asymmetry," *Journal of Personality and Social Psychology* 58 (1990):330–41; N. A. Fox and R. J. Davidson, "Patterns of Brain Electrical Activity During Facial Signs of Emotion in Ten-Month-Old Infants," *Developmental Psychology*, 24 (1988):230–36; N. A. Fox, "If It Is Not Left, It Is Right," *American Psychologist* 46 (1991):863–72.

PAGE 224, ON THE RIGHT THAN ON THE LEFT FRONTAL AREA: R. Finman et al., "Psychophysiological Correlates of Inhibition to the Unfamiliar in Children (Abstract)," *Psychophysiology* 26 (1989):(4a, S24).

PAGE 224, GREATER ACTIVATION OF THE LEFT FRONTAL AREA: N. A. Fox, S. Calkins, and T. Marshall, "Relations Between Emotional Reactivity, Emotional Regulation, and EEG Asymmetry in Infancy" (Unpublished paper, University of Maryland, Dept. Psychology, 1993).

PAGE 224, ARTERY ON THE LEFT SIDE: R. G. Robinson, and J. T. Coyle, "The Differential Effect of Right vs. Left Hemisphere Cerebral Infarction on Catecholamines and Behavior in the Rat," *Brain Research* 188 (1980):63–78.

PAGE 224, USUAL WITHDRAWAL TO NOVELTY: M. J. Saari et al., "Neonatal Six-Hydroxydopamine Alters the Behavior of Enriched-Impoverished Rats in a Novel Test Environment," *Behavioral Neuroscience*, 104 (1990):430–37.

PAGE 224, TEN LEAST EMOTIONAL RATS: E. B. Olson and W. D. Morgan, "Rat Brain Monoamine Levels Related to Behavioral Assessment," *Life Sciences* 30 (1982): 2095–2100.

PAGE 225, OF THE LEFT STELLATE GANGLION: W. C. Randall and D. V. Priola, "Sympathetic Influences on Synchrony of Myocardial Contraction," in *Nervous Control of the Heart,* ed. W. C. Randall (Baltimore: Williams & Wilkens, 1965), pp. 214–44.

PAGE 225, "THAN DOES THE LEFT STELLATE GANGLION": M. C. Rogers et al., "Lateralization of Sympathetic Control of the Human Sinus Node," *Anesthesiology* 48 (1978):139–41; the quote is from p. 140. The right branch of the vagus nerve synapses on the heart; the left does not.

PAGE 225, SYMPATHETIC INFLUENCE ON THE HEART: E. Y. Zamrini et al., "Unilateral Cerebral Inactivation Produces Differential Left-Right Heart Rate Responses," *Neurology* 40 (1990):1408–11.

PAGE 225, GANGLIA ON THE OPPOSITE SIDE: C. B. Saper et al., "Direct Hypothalamic-Autonomic Connections," *Brain Research* 117 (1976):305–12.

PAGE 225, THAN ON THE OPPOSITE SIDE: R. Eccles and R. L. Lee, "The Influence of the Hypothalamus on the Sympathetic Innervation of the Nasal Vasculature of the Cat," *Acta Otolaryngology,* 91 (1981):127–34. The majority of autonomic nerve fibers travel ipsilaterally. Hence, greater activity in the EEG on the left side would be associated with greater vasoconstriction of the cerebral vasculature on the left and, therefore, greater cooling of the skin on the left side. See B. Gomez et al., "Presence of Alpha and Beta Adrenergic Tone in the Walls of Cerebral Blood Vessels," in *The Cerebral Vessel Wall,* ed. J. Cervos-Navarro et al. (New York: Raven, 1976), pp. 139–42.

PAGE 225, PROCESSING OF A NEUTRAL FILM: S. J. Dimond and L. Farrington, "Emotional Response to Films Shown to the Right or Left Hemisphere of the Brain Measured by Heart Rate," *Acta Psychologica* 41 (1977):255–60.

PAGE 225, WITH THE LEFT HEMISPHERE: S. J. Dimond, L. Farrington, and P. Johnson, "Differing Emotional Response from Right and Left Hemispheres," *Nature* 261 (1976): 690–92.

PAGE 225, PROCESSING BY THE LEFT HEMISPHERE: W. Wittling, "Psychophysiological Correlates of Human Brain Asymmetry," *Neuropsychologia* 28 (1990):457–70.

PAGE 226, THE EMOTIONAL OR THE NEUTRAL FILM: W. Wittling and M. Pfluger, "Neuroendocrine Hemisphere Asymmetries," *Brain and Cognition* 14 (1990):243–65.

PAGE 226, PROJECTED TO THE RIGHT HEMISPHERE: When angry and happy faces are projected simultaneously to the right or left hemisphere and accompanied by electric shock, adult women developed a conditioned skin conductance response only when the angry faces were perceived by the right hemisphere, not when they were perceived by the left hemisphere. See B. H. Johnsen and K. Hugdahl, "Right Hemisphere Reproduction of Autonomic Conditioning to Facial Emotional Expressions," *Psychophysiology* 30 (1993):274–78; K. Hugdahl and B. H. Johnsen, "Brain Asymmetry and Human Electrodermal Conditioning," *Integrative Physiological and Behavioral Science* 26 (1991): 39–44; B. H. Johnsen and K. Hugdahl, "Hemispheric Asymmetry in Conditioning to Facial Emotional Expressions," *Psychophysiology* 28 (1991):154–62.

PAGE 226, DYSPHORIC OR ANXIOUS MOOD: G. Gainotti, "Emotional Behavior and Hemispheric Side of Lesion," *Cortex* 8 (1972):41–55; R. G. Robinson and D. Szetala, "Mood Change Following Left Hemisphere Brain Injury," *Annals of Neurology* 9 (1981):447–53.

PAGE 226, "MODULATION OF THE STARTLE RESPONSE": P. J. Lang, M. M. Bradley, and B. N. Cuthbert, "Emotion, Attention, and the Startle Reflex," *Psychological Review* 97 (1990):377–95; the quote is from p. 386.

PAGE 226, STATES ASSOCIATED WITH FEAR: J. Cutting, *The Right Cerebral Hemisphere and Psychiatric Disorders* (New York: Oxford University Press, 1990); E. K. Silberman and H. Weingartner, "Hemispheric Lateralization of Functions Related to Emotion," *Brain and Cognition* 5 (1986):322–53; N. L. Etcoff, "Asymmetries in Recognition of Emotion," in *Handbook of Neuropsychology*, ed. F. Boller and J. P. Grafman (Amsterdam: Elsevier, 1989), pp. 363–82; J. B. Hellige, *Hemispheric Asymmetry* (Cambridge: Harvard University Press, 1993).

PAGE 226, TWELVE IMAGES IN ALL WERE RECORDED,

(1) *Baseline 1.* Three images were recorded while the examiner held a small toy just above the lens of the scanner in order to attract the child's attention to the lens.

(2) *Emotional photographs.* The examiner presented, one at a time, three color prints (10 × 12 in.) of three different adult men above the lens of the scanner. As each photograph was presented, the examiner said, "There it is," in order to attract the child's attention to both the photograph and the lens. The first photograph showed a man with an angry face; the second showed a fearful face; and the third showed a neutral expression. A single image was recorded one second after the photograph appeared in the child's visual field (or one second after the child looked at the photograph).

(3) *Examiner command.* The examiner then assumed a stern facial expression, put her index finger under the lens, and said in a sharp voice (simulating anger): "(The child's name), look at my finger." An image was recorded as the examiner completed the command and six and twelve seconds later, for a total of three images.

(4) *Baseline 2.* Three additional baseline images were recorded. Mean temperatures were recorded for each of four areas for each of the twelve images by a coder who had no knowledge of any of the child's prior behavior. On the few occasions when a child moved when a recording was being made, no analysis of that image was attempted. About 15 percent of the children were restless, would not keep their faces directed at the lens of the scanner, or refused the procedure completely. Hence, we obtained adequate data on 135 boys and 140 girls.

PAGE 227, AS IS TRUE FOR THE FINGERS OF THE TWO HANDS: As we noted for heart rate, each subject's maximal forehead asymmetry contained some information that was not contained in the average asymmetry value across all twelve images. The maximal asymmetry values for all children ranged from −.70 (cooler on the left) to +.60 (cooler on the right). About twice as many children had their single largest asymmetry favoring a cooler left rather than a right side (58 versus 31 percent).

We also gathered thermography data on the adolescents described in chapters 4 and 5 during a baseline period and a digit recall task when they were ten years old and during a baseline period, digit recall, and anagram problems at age thirteen. As with the two-year-olds, significantly more ten-year-olds had their largest asymmetry values favoring a cooler left rather than right forehead, and this proportion increased from ten to thirteen years. Only two children changed from a cooler left side at age ten to a cooler right side at age thirteen. Apparently, with age, the direction of asymmetry favors a cooler left side, implying a more active left hemisphere and an associated emotional state that is characterized by control of fear and anxiety. Only three children (5 percent of the group) had large changes (.20° C or more) favoring a cooler right side at both ten and thirteen years; all three were inhibited children.

The tips of the fingers, unlike the forehead, have arteriovenous anastomoses that make possible much larger changes in surface skin temperature. The anastomoses are muscular valves that, like stopcocks, can shut off blood supply to the surface in order to preserve body heat. Sara Rimm, in our laboratory, has shown that adults display much larger changes in skin temperature in the finger tips than on the forehead in response to emotional films, personal questions, and difficult cognitive tasks. Unfortunately, young children find it extremely difficult to keep the palms of both hands turned upward, without curling their fingers, while watching a film or being presented with a psychological procedure. That is why we did not measure the temperature of the fingers on the twenty-one-month-old children.

PAGE 227, REMAINING SUBJECTS SHOWED NO ASYMMETRY: $p < .05$. Cohort 1 children showed the same result.

PAGE 227, FOR A COOLER LEFT FOREHEAD: T. Chang, "Thermography and Behavior in Four-Month-Old Infants" (Honors thesis, Radcliffe College, 1993).

PAGE 227, ON ITS WAY TO THE HYPOTHALAMUS AND AMYGDALA: E. S. Kapp et al., "A Neuroanatomical Systems Analysis of Conditioned Bradycardia in the Rabbit," in *Learning and Computational Neuroscience*, ed. M. Gabriel and J. Moore (Cambridge: MIT Press, 1990), pp. 54–90.

PAGE 227, AND WITH NUMBER OF DISTRESS FEARS IN GIRLS: A child was classified as showing asymmetry if he or she met either one of two criteria, which we call *total asymmetry* and *changed asymmetry*. The simpler criterion, total asymmetry, involved the mean difference in temperature between the left and the right side of the forehead across all twelve images. If the mean left-minus-right difference was positive by .10 or more, the subject was classified as cooler on the right; if the difference was negative by .15 or greater, the subject was classified as cooler on the left. We selected a larger asymmetry value as the criterion for a cooler left side so that approximately equal proportions of children would be cooler on the right and left side (20 percent cooler on the right, 23 percent cooler on the left). Although most children retained their left or right asymmetry across all twelve images, a minority changed their side of asymmetry following the initial baseline images. Typically, these children showed an asymmetry favoring the left or right side during the baseline images, but during one or more trials on a subsequent procedure the asymmetry shifted to the side opposite to the one shown during the baseline.

In other cases, the baseline images revealed no asymmetry, but the asymmetry on a subsequent trial met the criterion for a right- or left-sided asymmetry. For these reasons we created a second index called changed asymmetry. A child was classified as displaying a changed asymmetry if he or she did not meet the criterion for total asymmetry, but the absolute difference between the mean baseline asymmetry and the largest asymmetry on a subsequent image was > .10. For example, consider a child who had a baseline asymmetry of .06 favoring a cooler left side but the largest asymmetry on a postbaseline image was .25 favoring a cooler left side. The difference between the baseline and largest asymmetry was .19. This child was classified as showing a changed asymmetry to the left. By contrast, a child who had a baseline asymmetry of .06 favoring a cooler right side and a subsequent difference of .25 favoring the right side was classified as showing a changed asymmetry to the right.

There was a second way a child could show changed asymmetry. If the direction of the largest asymmetry on any postbaseline image was opposite to that of the asymmetry during the baseline images, and the absolute difference between these two values was .10 or more, the child was classified as showing a changed asymmetry. For example, consider a child with a baseline asymmetry of .12 favoring a cooler left side, but a post-baseline diference of .09 favoring a cooler right side. This child would be classified as having a changed asymmetry favoring a cooler right side because of the difference of .21 between the cooler left side during the baseline and the subsequent asymmetry favoring a cooler right side.

For a small proportion of children—less than 5 percent—the total and changed asymmetry values were inconsistent; that is, the total asymmetry value classified the child as cooler on the left, but the changed asymmetry classified the child as cooler on the right side. Only four boys and three girls displayed this rare pattern, and these children were omitted from the analysis. The total sample with adequate data had 284 children. Fourteen percent of all children met the criteria for a cooler left side on both the total and the changed asymmetry indexes, compared with 9 percent who met both criteria for a cooler right side. There was no relation between asymmetry and reactivity at four months, but twice as many boys as girls met the dual criteria for a cooler right side (14 percent for boys versus 6 percent for girls). The proportions of boys and girls were nearly equal for a cooler left side (15 versus 14 percent). This fact suggests a clearer left side asymmetry for girls than for boys. The average correlation between the total and the changed asymmetry values was 0.3 and was similar for all reactivity groups.

PAGE 227, SMILED INFREQUENTLY WERE COOLER ON THE RIGHT SIDE: Chi square = 5.2, $p < .05$ comparing low versus high smilers. In addition, boys who had a cooler right forehead had a higher mean for the maximal heart rates at four, fourteen, and twenty-one months than boys with a cooler left side ($t = 2.30$, $p < .05$). For both boys and girls, those with a minimal four-month heart rate in the lowest quartile (< 120 bpm) were more likely to be cooler on the left side compared with those with higher values (chi square = 5.5, $p < .01$). Eighty percent of the children whose minimal four-month heart rates were equal to a less than 120 bpm were cooler on the left side, compared with 55 percent of those with minimal heart rate values higher than 120 bpm. Adults who show full smiles involving the orbicularis oculi as well as the zygomaticus major while watching films show greater EEG activity on the left side. P. Ekman, R. J. Davidson, and W. V. Friesen, "Emotional Expression and Brain Physiology" (Unpublished paper, University of Wisconsin, Madison, 1993).

PAGE 228, WERE MORE OFTEN COOLER ON THE LEFT FOREHEAD: When we combined asymmetry of forehead temperature with smiling, the children who were cooler on the right and also were infrequent smilers (about 10 percent) had higher values for the minimal four-month heart rate, compared with those who were cooler on the left side and were frequent smilers (15 percent of the sample). This result suggests that temperature asymmetry and smiling, which are correlated, reflect a state related to sympathetic reactivity (chi square = 3.9, p < .05 for the four-month heart rates). Among the children who showed all three characteristics—cooler on the left, frequent smiles, and a low heart rate at four months, who made up 7 percent of the sample, 71 percent were low reactive (only 40 percent of Cohort 2 were low reactive children), and two-thirds were low fear at fourteen months (only one-third of the sample was low fear at fourteen months). Thus, even though asymmetry, smiling, and four-month heart rate, considered alone, were only modest predictors of fear at fourteen months, a child who met all three criteria was likely to be minimally fearful. Only ten children (3 percent) had the complementary set of characteristics—cooler on the right, minimal smiling, and a high four-month heart rate. Six of these ten children were high reactive, and five were highly fearful at fourteen months. Thus, two of every three children who showed the first profile were low reactive, while two of every three who showed the latter profile were high reactive. One of the boys in the second group was the most inhibited child in both cohorts.

PAGE 228, ONLY ONE-THIRD OF THE GIRLS WITH A COOLER LEFT FOREHEAD: Chi square = 9.8, p < .001; t = 2.49, p < .01. A similar difference occurred for girls in Cohort 1. It is of interest that 21 percent of mothers of high reactive infants were also cooler on the right forehead (by .15° C or more), compared with only 10 percent of the mothers of low reactives. These mothers of high reactives also had cooler right hands (19 percent of high reactives versus 9 percent of low reactives had asymmetries as large as 1.0° C favoring a cooler right hand). In addition, children with a cooler right forehead had mothers with cooler right hands; children with a cooler left forehead had mothers with cooler left hands (chi square = 6.5, p < .01).

Finally, the occurrence of extreme asymmetry values (a difference of 0.2° C or greater) favoring a cooler left or right side was more frequent among inhibited than among uninhibited children. If a large asymmetry reflects a state of heightened sympathetic arousal, this state should be more frequent among inhibited children. More girls than boys showed extreme asymmetries (46 versus 28 percent), high heart rates, and many fears. More mothers of high than low reactive infants had large temperature differences between the finger tips on the right and left hands (19 versus 5 percent).

PAGE 228, NO MORE THAN ONE DISTRESS FEAR: The high reactive children, both boys and girls, who were highly fearful at fourteen and twenty-one months were more often cooler on the right side (total asymmetry) than those high reactives who had zero, one, or two fears in the second year (p < .05, Exact Test; 64 versus 18 percent). This relation also held for low reactive girls (19 versus 0 percent) but was absent for low reactive boys.

PAGE 228, A DISTRESSED OR A HAPPY MOOD: The boys with a cooler left forehead had broader faces than those with a cooler right forehead.

PAGE 229, IN THEIR FOUR-MONTH HEART RATES: A high and stable heart rate at fourteen months was defined by being above the mean on heart rate and below the mean for variability for the entire group. A low and variable heart rate was defined in a complementary manner. A cooler right forehead was defined as a total asymmetry score equal to or greater than +.10, while the cooler left forehead was a total asymmetry score equal to or less than −.15. The differences between the two groups were statistically significant for maximal and minimal heart rates to sentences, mobiles, and syllables at four months (t ranged from 1.85 to 2.91, $p < .05$; $t = 3.19$, $p < .01$ for difference between the two groups for lowest rate at four months). But the differences in heart rate were not significant for either the first or second baselines. Thus, these two groups differed in response to stimulus intrusions and particularly to the auditory stimuli that produced the largest cardiac decelerations. Finally, at fourteen months the children who were cooler on the left were more likely than those who were cooler on the right to display a decrease rather than an increase in heart rate to the stranger with the gas mask and to the puppets. Thirty-five percent of the children with a low and variable baseline heart rate at fourteen months had a total asymmetry score equal to a less than −.15; only 13 percent had a total asymmetry equal to or greater than +.10. Of the children with a high and stable fourteen-month baseline heart rate, 21 percent had a cooler left side and 24 percent a cooler right side (chi square = 4.6, $p < .05$). These differences were independent of the child's reactivity at four months. The total corpus of evidence suggests that the temperature asymmetry is reflecting some aspect of the child's affect state. The children with a low and variable baseline heart rate at fourteen months and a cooler left forehead at twenty-one months are likely to have lower sympathetic or higher vagal tone than the complementary group. This prediction was affirmed, for at four, fourteen, and twenty-one months the former group had significantly lower minimal heart rates—a fifteen to twenty beat difference. (The t values ranged from 3.1 to 6.0.) This is the most dramatic difference in heart rate we have found in all our analyses. Thus, the combination of a temperature asymmetry favoring a cooler left side and a low and variable heart rate at fourteen months was a better correlate of minimal heart rates at other ages than either variable alone. This means that the temperature asymmetry on the face is reflecting something important about the balance between sympathetic and parasympathetic tone. In response to the stranger at fourteen months, 50 percent of those who were cooler on the left (total asymmetry ≤ − .15) showed cardiac decelerations of at least 10 msec. (2 bpm), compared with 15 percent of those with a cooler right forehead (total asymmetry > +.10, chi square = 5.1, p < .01). By contrast, 55 percent of those who were cooler on the right accelerated to the stranger (by at least 2 bpm), compared with 36 percent of those cooler on the left. To the puppets, 66 percent of those with a cooler left side decelerated by at least 5 bpm, compared with 36 percent of those who were cooler on the right (chi square = 4.4, p < .05). Thus, there was a consistent trend for those with a cooler left side to show a parasympathetic or vagal reaction to discrepancy, rather than a sympathetic, acceleratory reaction.

Although a similar relation was found for the baseline heart rate at twenty-one months, the differences between the two groups were less striking because more children were a bit restless and less wary as the session began, compared with their behavior at fourteen months.

PAGE 233, C. P. Lange and W. James, *The Emotions* (Baltimore: Williams & Wilkins, 1885); W. James, "What Is an Emotion?" *Mind* 9 (1884):188–205.

PAGE 233, EXUBERANT AND FULL OF VITALITY: A total of twenty-one children in Cohort 2 showed a very low heart rate at four months and a cooler left forehead and frequent smiles in the second year. Fifteen children in this group were low reactive, and only five were high reactive. A total of ten children met the opposite criteria—a high heart rate, cooler right forehead, and infrequent smiling. Six of these ten were high reactive. One of these high reactive infants—a firstborn boy of middle-class parents being raised at home by an affectionate mother—was the most inhibited child in the entire cohort. During the four-month battery, he displayed a sharp drop in heart rate of eighteen beats as the first sentence was spoken, because of a surprise reaction, and two sentences later he cried in fear. To the last set of mobiles he became extremely aroused, flailing his arms and displaying a dysphoric facial expression before he began to cry. He had the highest fear scores at all three ages, and most were distress fears. This boy even cried when the radio-controlled car moved on the rug; only three children showed that distress reaction at nine months. At fourteen months, he cried when the examiner asked him to put his finger in the cup of liquid and in response to the stranger and the robot. At twenty-one months, he remained close to his mother in the risk room, refused both the electrodes and the blood pressure cuff, and cried as the clown entered. Not surprisingly, this boy has light blue eyes, an ectomorphic body build, and a narrow face. This boy is only one in over 550 children with similar longitudinal data. Most studies of children with samples of thirty to fifty subjects would not contain such an extreme case.

PAGE 235, UNUSUALLY HAPPY OR JOYFUL: In the second year 15 percent of low reactives were very vocal and smiling at fourteen and twenty-one months; only 3 percent were extremely quiet and smiled rarely. The majority showed a moderate amount of affect.

PAGE 236, LOW REACTIVE–UNINHIBITED CHILDREN: P. J. Lang et al., "Looking at Pictures: Affective, Facial, Visual, and Behavioral Reactions," _Psychophysiology_ 30 (1993):261–73.

CHAPTER EIGHT: _Implications_

PAGE 238, BECOME CIVIL YOUTH: See J. Q. Wilson, _The Moral Sense_ (New York: Oxford, 1993).

PAGE 239, AND THE MOTHER'S DISCIPLINARY STYLE: G. Kochanska, "Socialization and Temperament in the Development of Guilt and Conscience," _Child Development_ 62 (1991):1379–92.

PAGE 239, OVER WETTING THEIR BEDS: M. Kaffman and E. Elizur, "Infants Who Became Enuretics," _Monographs of the Society for Research in Child Development_ 42 (1977), no. 2.

PAGE 240, AS IF IT WERE A JOKE: J. B. Asendorpf, and G. Nunner-Winkler, "Children's Moral Motive Strength and Temperamental Inhibition Reduce Their Immoral Behavior in Real Moral Conflicts," _Child Development_ 63 (1992):1223–35.

PAGE 240, UNUSUALLY SENSITIVE TO PUNISHMENT: Two- to three-year-old girls who were unusually sensitive to objects that were broken in a laboratory were most likely to become distressed when they believed they were responsible for breaking the toy. It is likely that the small group of children who are vulnerable to anxiety over violation of standards contains many high reactive, inhibited children. G. Kochanska and A. Fuku-moto, "Sensitivity to Standard Violations and Conscience in Toddlers" (Unpublished paper, University of Iowa, Dept. of Psychology, 1993).

PAGE 240, Magnusson, *Individual Development.*

PAGE 240, VULNERABLE TO A DELINQUENT CAREER: Preadolescent sons of fathers with either a diagnosis of substance abuse (N = 78) or no psychiatric disorder at all (N = 72) were interviewed, along with the mothers of these boys. In addition, a single mid-morning saliva sample was obtained in order to assess cortisol. Cortisol levels were low in the sons who had both many features of conduct disorder and also a father who had dis-played antisocial behavior during early adolescence and was diagnosed as antisocial as an adult. See M. M. Vanyukov et al., "Antisocial Symptoms in Preadolescent Boys and in Their Parents," *Psychiatry Research* 46 (1993):9–17. By contrast, patients with obsessive-compulsive symptoms showed higher plasma cortisol levels than controls over a twenty-four-hour period. See F. Catapano et al., "Melatonin and Cortisol Secretion in Patients with Primary Obsessive-Compulsive Disorder," *Psychiatry Research* 44 (1992): 217–21.

PAGE 241, ANTISOCIAL ADULTS: I. I. Gottesman and H. H. Goldsmith, "Develop-mental Psychopathology of Antisocial Behavior," in *Threats to Optimal Development*, Minnesota Symposium on Child Psychology, ed. C. A. Nelson (Hillsdale, N.J.: Erl-baum, 1993).

PAGE 242, PANIC OR AGORAPHOBIA: About 20 percent of inhibited children were diagnosed as having a serious anxiety disorder. J. F. Rosenbaum et al., "Behavioral Inhi-bition in Childhood," *Harvard Review of Psychiatry* 1 (1993):2–16.

PAGE 242, POST-TRAUMATIC STRESS DISORDER: L. C. Terr, "Children of Chow-chilla," *Psychoanalytic Study of the Child* 34 (1979):547–623.

PAGE 242, FAR LESS FEAR: R. S. Pynoos et al., "Life Threat and Post-Traumatic Stress Disorder in School Age Children," *Archives of General Psychiatry* 44 (1987):1057–63.

PAGE 242, FOLLOWING A NEARBY EARTHQUAKE: J. M. Wood et al., "Effects of the 1989 San Francisco Earthquake on Frequency and Content of Night Terrors," *Journal of Abnormal Psychology* 101 (1992):219–24.

PAGE 242, AN EXTREMELY STRESSFUL EVENT: J. Dimsdale and J. Moss, "Plasma Cat-echolamines in Stress and Exercise," *Journal of the American Medical Association* 243 (1980):340–42.

PAGES 243–44, *Jane Austen's Letters to Her Sister, Cassandra, and Others*, ed. R. W. Chapman vol. 1 (Oxford: Clarendon, 1982). The quote is from p. 179.

PAGE 244, DISAGREED IN 15 CASES: J. E. Helzer et al., "Results of the St. Louis ECA Physician Re-examination Study of the DIS Interview," *Archives of General Psychiatry* 42 (1985):657–66. There can be disagreement even when the clinicians are observing exactly the same information. Thirty-seven professionals from four countries (China, Indonesia, Japan, and the United States) watched the same videotapes of four eight-year-old boys playing alone and in a group and then rated a variety of appropriate char-acteristics of each child that would ordinarily be involved in a diagnosis of pathology. The judges from the same country agreed among themselves, but there were large dis-agreements between professionals from different countries. The Chinese judges rated the videotapes as containing more signs of hyperactive behavior than did the American judges. E. M. Mann et al., "Cross Cultural Differences in Rating Hyperactive Disruptive Behaviors in Children," *American Journal of Psychiatry* 149 (1992):1539–42.

PAGE 245, AS HAVING ANXIETY DISORDER: Because of the poor relation, in some cases, between actual measurement of physiological activity and self-report of physiology, the patient's description of his physiological state is a poor guide to what is actually occurring in the body. The patient's description is a function of his perceptions and beliefs, which are based on more than material changes in the body. D. R. McLeod and R. Hoehn-Saric, "Perception of Physiological Changes in Normal and Pathological Anxiety," in Hoehn-Saric and McLeod, *Biology,* pp. 223–43.

PAGES 247–48, ABLE TO CONTROL THE LEVEL OF THE NOISE: Hoehn-Saric and McLeod, "Somatic Manifestations."

PAGE 249, DO WE KNOW? The work of Michael Rutter of the Maudsley Hospital in London has contributed in a major way to our understanding of childhood pathology. See especially M. Rutter, *Changing Youth in a Changing Society* (London: Nuffield Provincial Hospital Trust, 1979); M. Rutter, "Isle of Wight Revisited," *Journal of the American Academy of Child and Adolescent Psychiatry* 28 (1989):633–53; M. Rutter, C. E. Izard, and P. B. Read, *Depression in Young People* (New York: Guilford, 1986); and M. Rutter et al., "Research Report: Isle of Wight Studies," *Psychological Medicine* 6 (1976):313–32.

PAGE 249, BRIDGES OR CONFINED SPACES: W. A. Arrindell et al., "Phobic Dimensions III: Factor Analytic Approaches to the Study of Common Phobic Fears," *Advances in Behavioral Research and Therapy* 13 (1991):73–130.

PAGE 249, EQUALLY OFTEN FOR MEN AND WOMEN: M. MacDonald, *Mystical Bedlam* (Cambridge: Cambridge University Press, 1981).

PAGE 249, LESS THAN 1 PERCENT OF MEN: D. A. Regier, W. E. Narrow, and D. S. Rae, "The Epidemiology of Anxiety Disorders," *Journal of Psychiatric Research* 24, Supp. 2 (1990), pp. 3–14; M. Roth and N. Argyle, "Anxiety, Panic, and Phobic Disorders," *Journal of Psychiatric Research* 22, Supp. 1 (1988), pp. 33–54.

PAGE 250, THAN THEY ARE IN CANBERRA: J. I. Escobar, "Psychiatric Epidemiology," in *Culture, Ethnicity, and Mental Illness,* ed. A. C. Gaw (Washington, D.C.: American Psychiatric Press, 1993), pp. 43–73.

PAGE 250, WITH NO SYMPTOMS (18 PERCENT): C. G. Last et al., "Anxiety Disorders in Children and Their Families," *Archives of General Psychiatry* 48 (1991):928–34. A group of eighteen children whose mothers were diagnosed as having anxiety disorder, panic, or obsessive compulsive disorder were observed in the laboratory. Sixty-five percent of the children—age one and a half to five years—were extremely inhibited, three times the expected prevalence. K. Manassis, "Childhood Anxiety Risk Factors" (Unpublished paper, Hospital for Sick Children, Toronto, 1993).

PAGE 250, PERSIST INTO ADULTHOOD: L. G. Ost, "Blood and Injection Phobia," *Journal of Abnormal Psychology* 101 (1992):68–74.

PAGE 250, WITH THE SAME SYMPTOM: R. R. Crowe, "Panic Disorder: Genetic Considerations," *Journal of Psychiatric Research* 24, Supp. 2 (1990): 129–34; K. S. Kendler et al., "Generalized Anxiety Disorder in Women," *Archives of General Psychiatry* 49 (1992): 267–72; K. S. Kendler et al., "The Genetic Epidemiology of Phobias in Women," *Archives of General*

Psychiatry 49 (1992):273–81. Agoraphobia appears to be the most heritable, animal phobias the least heritable. The presence of panic and depression in a parent, usually a mother, places a child at greatest risk for a diagnosis of anxiety disorder; about a third of children with such a parent met the psychiatric criterion for anxiety disorder. M. M. Weissman "Depression and Anxiety Disorders in Parents and Children," *Archives of General Psychiatry* 4 (1984): 847–49.

PAGE 250, CHILDHOOD STRESS IS ALWAYS A CONTRIBUTING FACTOR: Death of a parent in early childhood or divorce in later childhood increases the risk of developing general anxiety disorder or panic in women. K. S. Kendler et al., "Childhood Parental Loss and Adult Psychopathology in Women," *Archives of General Psychiatry* 49 (1992):109–16.

PAGE 250, THAN ADULTS WITHOUT ANY OF THESE SYMPTOMS: J. S. Reznick et al., "Retrospective and Concurrent Self-Report of Behavioral Inhibition and Their Relation to Adult Mental Health," *Development and Psychopathology* 4 (1992):301–21. See also K. R. Merikangas and J. A. Angst "The Challenge of Depressive Disorders in Adolescence" (Unpublished paper, Yale University, 1993).

PAGE 251, PSYCHIATRIC CATEGORY OF ANXIETY OR PANIC DISORDER: R. G. Klein, "Questioning the Clinical Usefulness of Projective Psychological Tests for Children," *Developmental and Behavioral Pediatrics* 7 (1986):378–82.

PAGE 251, IN SOME OF THESE CHILDREN: Gottesman and Goldsmith, "Developmental Psychology." About 7 percent of boys are diagnosed as having conduct disorder, and the heritability of this diagnosis varies from 0.4 to 0.7.

PAGE 251, UNINHIBITED BOYS LIVING IN THE SAME NEIGHBORHOODS: D. P. Farrington et al., "Are There Any Successful Men from Crimonogenetic Background?" *Psychiatry* 51 (1988):116–30.

PAGE 251, PRODUCTION OF NOREPINEPHRINE: M. Galvin et al., "Low Dopamine-Beta-Hydroxylase," *Psychiatry Research* 39 (1991):1–11; G. A. Rogeness et al., "Diagnosis, Catecholamine Metabolism and Plasma Dopamine-Beta-Hydroxylase," *Journal of the American Academy of Child and Adolescent Psychiatry* 27 (1988):121–25; D. P. Farrington, "Antisocial Personality from Childhood to Adulthood," *The Psychologist* 4 (1991):389–94. It appears that levels of dopamine-beta-hydroxylase are more similar in identical than fraternal twins, suggesting that the concentrations of this compound are under heritable control. See G. Oxenstierna et al., "Concentrations of Monoamine Metabolites in the Cerebrospinal Fluid of Twins and Unrelated Individuals," *Journal of Psychiatric Research* 20 (1986):19–29.

PAGE 253, AND LOVE OF IDEAS: Female panic patients were asked to keep a diary and to write down each hour, for eight days, their thoughts and feelings. Many patients did better than chance in predicting that a panic attack would occur sometime later in the day. It is likely that the patients used a perception of enhanced visceral feedback to make the prediction. Adults with anxiety disorder or panic report a greater awareness of their heartbeat and are more accurate in detecting each beat. J. Kenardy et al., "Psychological Precursors of Panic Attacks," *British Journal of Psychiatry* 160 (1992):668–73; A. Ehlers and P. Breuer, "Increased Cardiac Awareness in Panic Disorder," *Journal of Abnormal Psychology* 101 (1992):371–82.

PAGE 253, "IT WAS BETTER NOT TO SHOW IT": M. L. Walter, *Science and Cultural Crisis* (Stanford: Stanford University Press, 1990); the quote is from p. 17.

PAGE 253, BORDERING ON THE SUBLIME: I. Kant, *Critique of Judgment* (London: J. H. Bernard, [1790] 1951), p. 116.

PAGE 254, 15 PERCENT VERSUS 1 PERCENT: Cavalli-Sforza, *Genes*.

PAGE 254, BLADDER CANCER: H. J. Lin et al., "Slow Acetylated Mutations in the Human Polymorphic N-Acetyltransferase Gene in 786 Asians, Blacks, Hispanics, and Whites," *American Journal of Human Genetics* 52 (1993):827–34.

PAGE 254, LACTOSE PRESENT IN MILK: R. McCracken, "Lactose Deficiency," *Current Anthropology* 12 (1971):479–517.

PAGE 254, METABOLISM OF THE DRUG: H. H. Zhou, R. P. Koshaki, and D. J. Silberstein, "Racial Differences in Drug Response," *New England Journal of Medicine* 320 (1989):565–70.

PAGE 254, HIGH AND LOW REACTIVE INFANTS: Population geneticists believe that the linguistic distance between two populations is correlated with their genetic distance. It is relevant to note that a strain of rhesus monkeys normally found in China is temperamentally different from a strain of rhesus normally resident in India, even when animals of the two strains are born in the same American laboratory and raised under identical conditions in a nursery. In this case the reproductive isolation of the two strains appears to have led to genetic differences with implications for behavior during the opening weeks of life. S. Suomi, telephone conversation, 1993.

PAGE 255, "MORE READILY WHEN UPSET": D. G. Freedman and N. Freedman, "Behavioral Differences Between Chinese-American and American Newborns," *Nature* 224 (1969):1227.

PAGE 255, IN THE SAME NEIGHBORHOODS: Kagan, Kearsley, and Zelazo, *Infancy*.

PAGE 255, WHEN THEIR ARMS WERE RESTRAINED: W. Caudill and H. Weinstein, "Maternal Care and Infant Behavior in Japan and America," *Psychiatry* 32 (1969):12–43; M. Lewis, "Culture and Biology: The Role of Temperament," in *Challenges to Developmental Paradigms*, ed. P. R. Zelazo and R. G. Barr (Hillsdale, N.J.: Erlbaum, 1989), pp. 203–23; M. Lewis, D. S. Ramsay, and K. Kawakami, "Affectivity and Cortisol Response Differences Between Japanese and American Infants" (Unpublished paper, Robert Ward Johnson Medical School, New Brunswick N.J., 1993). L. A. Camras et al., "Japanese and American Infants' Response to Arm Restraint," *Developmental Psychology* 28 (1992):578–83.

PAGE 255, "HIGHLY REACTIVE INFANTS WERE TO BE FOUND": G. W. Bronson, "Infants' Reactions to Unfamiliar Persons and Novel Objects," *Monograph of the Society for Research in Child Development* 37 (1972), no. 3, p. 27.

PAGE 255, AGGRESSION AND HYPERACTIVITY: J. R. Weisz et al., "Thai and American Perspectives on Over and Under Control Child Behavior Problems," *Journal of Consulting and Clinical Psychology* 56 (1988):601–9; J. R. Weisz et al., "Epidemiology of Behavioral and Emotional Problems Among Thai and American Children," *Journal of the American Academy of Child and Adolescent Psychiatry* 26 (1987):890–98.

PAGES 255–56, LIMBIC AROUSAL IN THE ASIAN PATIENTS: K. M. Lin, R. E. Poland, and I. M. Lesser, "Ethnicity and Psychopharmacology," *Culture, Medicine, and Psychiatry* 10 (1986):151–65; D. P. Ajarwal and H. W. Geodde, *Alcohol Metabolism, Alcohol Intoler-*

ance, and Alcoholism (Berlin: Springer-Verlag, 1990); K. M. Lin et al., "Pharmacokinetic and Other Related Factors Affecting Psychotropic Responses in Asians," *Psychopharmacology Bulletin* 4 (1991):427–38.

PAGE 256, "WRATH FOR THE GOSPEL TOO?" H. A. Oberman, *Luther* (York, Pa.: Image Books, 1992), p. 165; W. Bouwsma, *John Calvin* (New York: Oxford University Press, 1988).

PAGE 256, "DOUBTFUL OR OBSCURE": Bouwsma, *Calvin*, pp. 32, 37.

PAGE 256, LONG, SHARP NOSE: E. Kretschmer, *Physique and Character*, p. 248.

PAGE 257, "TRUE BRAHMAN RELEASED FROM PASSION": C. N. E. Eliot, *Hinduism and Buddhism, A Historical Sketch* (London: E. Arnold, 1921), p. 60; see also M. E. Spiro, *Buddhism and Society*, 2d ed. (Berkeley: University of California Press, 1982), for a discussion of Burmese Buddhist philosophy, and D. J. Munro, *The Concept of Man in Early China* (Stanford: Stanford University Press, 1969).

PAGE 258, "THE VALUE OF WORK AND OF JOY": P. Janet, "Fear of Action as an Essential Element in the Sentiment of Melancholia," in *Feelings and Emotions*, ed. M. L. Reymert (Worcester, Mass.: Clark University Press, 1928), pp. 297–309; the quote is from p. 309.

PAGE 259, "NEXT STAGE OF INVESTIGATION": T. H. Bullock, "Integrative Systems Research on the Brain," *Annual Review of Neuroscience* 16 (1993):1–15; the quote is from p. 14.

PAGE 260, ONE ACTION OVER ANOTHER: J. Kagan, *Unstable Ideas* (Cambridge: Harvard University Press, 1989), p. 22.

CHAPTER NINE: *Reflections*

PAGE 262, MOTOR, AUTONOMIC, CORTICAL, AND BRAIN STEM CENTERS: In a classic longitudinal study, a group of children were observed as newborns and later as preschoolers. The male newborns who cried quickly and intensely to the frustration of having a nipple withdrawn and also had rapid breathing rates were more subdued and shy with peers than those who were minimally reactive. See R. Q. Bell, G. M. Weller, and M. F. Waldrop, "Newborn and Preschooler," *Monographs of the Society for Research in Child Development* 36 (1971), no. 1 and 2.

PAGE 262, AND ITS ENVIRONMENT: Darwin believed that the embryo, not the adult form, was the more accurate guide to the animal's place in evolution.

PAGE 265, MORE GIRLS THAN BOYS ASSIGNED TO THIS CATEGORY: R. S. Benjamin, E. T. Costello, and M. Warren, "Anxiety Disorders in a Pediatric Sample," *Journal of Anxiety Disorders* 4 (1990):293–316.

PAGE 270, ALTERED THE ANIMALS' PHYSIOLOGY: S. Maccari et al., "Life Events Induced Decrease of Corticosteriod Type 1 Receptors Is Associated with Reduced Cortico-sterone Feedback and Enhanced Vulnerability to Amphetamine Self-administration," *Brain Research*, 547 (1991):7–12.

PAGE 270, THE BIOLOGY OF INHIBITED CHILDREN: A trauma or stress could lead to the induction of a gene called c-fos in the nucleus. A single avoidance trial in one-day-old chicks (a bitter taste was placed on a shiny metal object) induced this gene. As a result, other neurochemical changes might occur. S. P. Rose, "How Chicks Make Memories," *Trends in Neuroscience* 14 (1991):390–97.

PAGE 272, THE LANGUAGE AREA AT THIS TIME: R. W. Thatcher, "Cyclic Cortical Reorganization During Early Childhood," *Brain and Cognition* 20 (1992):24–50.

PAGE 276, AS A CONTINUOUS TRAIT: E. W. Labouvie, R. J. Pandina, and V. Johnson, "Developmental Trajectories of Substance Use in Adolescence," *International Journal of Behavioral Development* 14 (1991):305–28. One advantage of a categorical analysis is illustrated in a study of the relation between a person's report of her degree of perceived physiological arousal, on the one hand, and direct measures of activity in a physiological target, on the other. For example, if one correlates self reports of change in heart rate to an arithmetic test with the actual change in heart rate, the relation is low. However, a categorical analysis reveals that 37 percent of the subjects reported no heart rate change, while 63 percent reported some change. Among the larger group who said they experienced a change in heart rate, most actually showed an altered heart rate. They were inaccurate, however, in estimating how large their heart rate change actually was. C. F. Sharpley and R. K. Fleming, "Awareness of Heart Rate Activity," *Psychological Reports* 63 (1988):955–56. See also McLeod and Hoehn-Saric, "Perception," physiological changes in normal and pathological anxiety. In R. Hoehn-Saric & D. R. McLeod (Eds.), *Biology of Anxiety Disorders* (Washington, D.C.: American Psychiatric Press), pp. 223–43.

PAGES 276–77, D. Magnusson, "Individual Development: A Longitudinal Perspective," *European Journal of Personality* 6 (1992):119–38.

PAGE 277, AND IRRITABILITY DISPLAYED: Max Planck had to reject the idea of continuous energy when he posited the notion of discrete packets of energy. But this idea was necessary in order to explain why black bodies did not emit infinite energy when they were heated. Facts are healthy antidotes to favored ideas.

PAGE 278, QUALITATIVELY DIFFERENT GROUPS: Goldsmith and Campos, "Structure." Further, cardiac output and peripheral resistance in the arterial tree have been regarded as related measures that reflect a continuous index of sympathetic tone. But when adults were categorized as belonging either to a high cardiac output group or a high peripheral resistance group, following exposure to cognitive stress, the resulting data were more sensible than if one treated the average of the two measures as an overall continuous index of sympathetic tone. A. L. Kasprowicz et al., "Individual Differences in Behaviorally Evoked Cardiovascular Response," *Psychophysiology* 27 (1990):605–19.

PAGE 278, RELATIVELY INDEPENDENT VARIABLES: Bateson and D'Udine argue that the effect of genes on behavior is not additive; hence, one would expect qualitative types to be more likely than continuous differences between strains or among individuals from the same strain. P. Bateson and B. D'Udine, "Exploration in Two Inbred Strains of Mice and Their Hybrids," *Animal Behavior*, 34 (1986):1026–32. See also R. A. Hinde and A. Dennis, "Categorizing Individuals," *International Journal of Behavioral Development* 9 (1986):105–19.

PAGE 278, THESE RELATED GROUPS: A. S. Clarke, W. A. Mason, and G. P. Moberg, "Differential Behavioral and Adrenocortical Responses to Stress Among Three Macaque

Species," *American Journal of Primatology* 14 (1988):37–52; A. S. Clarke and W. A. Mason, "Differences Among Three Macaque Species in Responsiveness to an Observer," *International Journal of Primatology* 9 (1988):347–63.

PAGE 284, CAUTION TO NOVELTY: G. W. Bronson, "Infants' Reactions to Unfamiliar Persons and Objects," *Monographs of the Society for Research in Child Development* 37 (1972), no. 3.

PAGE 285, PERCEPTION OF AN INTERNAL BODY TONE: G. Aston-Jones et al., "The Brain Nucleus Locus Ceruleus," *Science* 234 (1986):734–37.

PAGE 285, BODIES DOES NOT: J. F. Bernard, M. Alden, and J. M. Besson, "The Organization of the Efferent Projections from the Pontine Parabrachial Area to the Amygdaloid Complex," *Journal of Comparative Neurology* 329 (1993):201–29.

PAGE 286, H. White, *The Content of the Form* (Baltimore: The Johns Hopkins University Press, 1987); the quote is from pp. 24–25.

PAGE 288, BITING AWAY AT MY SENSITIVE GUTS: *The Journals of Sylvia Plath*, ed. T. Hughes and F. McCullough, (New York: Ballantine Books, 1982), pp. 59, 60.

PAGE 289, W. Cannon, "The James-Lange Theory of Emotion," *American Journal of Psychology* 39 (1927):106–24; Lange and James, *Emotions.*

PAGE 289, IN GAY MEN AND STRAIGHT MEN: S. Le Vay, *The Sexual Brain* (Cambridge: MIT Press, 1993).

PAGE 290, AND MENTAL LIFE: J. R. Searle, *The Rediscovery of Mind* (Cambridge: MIT Press, 1992).

PAGE 291, FOR THEIR ILL FORTUNE: G. Zilboorg, *History of Medical Psychology* (New York: Norton, 1941).

PAGE 291, "STRONGER OR WISER": R. Monk, *Ludwig Wittgenstein* (New York: Free Press, 1990), p. 443.

PAGE 291, "HEADACHES IN THE PAST": Quoted in W. H. Sweet, I. Ervin, and V. H. Mark, "The Relationship of Violent Behavior to Focal Cerebral Disease," in *Aggressive Behavior*, ed. S. Garratini and E. Sigg (New York: Wiley, 1969), p. 350.

PAGE 292, SOME CASES OF MALE HOMOSEXUALITY: *The New York Times*, July 16, 1993.

PAGE 295, IT WOULD NOT TO GALEN: Galen believed that people, no matter what their constitution, could improve their character by selecting the proper diet and regulating their lives. He stated explicitly that humans cannot be absolved from the responsibility of their actions simply because they began life with a particular temperament.

INDEX